THE SOCIO-CULTURAL MATRIX
OF ALCOHOL AND DRUG USE

A Sourcebook of Patterns and Factors

Edited by

Brenda Forster
and
Jeffrey Colman Salloway

Interdisciplinary Studies in Alcohol Use and Abuse
Volume 4

The Edwin Mellen Press
Lewiston/Queenston/Lampeter

Library of Congress Cataloging-in-Publication Data

The Socio-cultural matrix of alcohol and drug use : a sourcebook of
   patterns and factors / edited by Brenda Forster and Jeffrey Colman
   Salloway.
      p.   cm. -- (Interdisciplinary studies in alcohol use and abuse
   ; v. 4)
   Includes bibliographical references.
   ISBN 0-88946-285-2
   1. Drug abuse--Social aspects--United States. 2. Alcoholism-
-Social aspects--United States. 3. Drug abuse--Social aspects-
-Cross-cultural studies. I. Forster, Brenda. II. Salloway,
Jeffrey C., 1941- . III. Series.
HV5825.S582   1990
362.29'12'0973--dc20
                                                               89-13794
                                                                  CIP

This is volume 4 in the continuing series
Interdisciplinary Studies in Alcohol Use and Abuse
Volume 4 ISBN 0-88946-285-2
ISAUA Series ISBN 0-88946-295-X

A CIP catalog record for this book
is available from the British Library.

The Edwin Mellen Press   The Edwin Mellen Press
        Box 450   Box 67
  Lewiston, New York   Queenston, Ontario
     USA 14092   CANADA L0S 1L0

The Edwin Mellen Press, Ltd.
Lampeter, Dyfed, Wales
UNITED KINGDOM SA48 7DY

Printed in the United States of America

Dedicated to my mentors, Howard S. Becker and Gary Albrecht, who believed in me, to Richard A. Berk, who helped me become a sociologist, and to the contributors to this book, who were willing to share their expertise.

--B. Forster

Dedicated to Peter Kong-Ming New, my mentor and colleague.

--J. C. Salloway

TABLE OF CONTENTS

APPENDIX

ACKNOWLEDGMENTS

No book this large and complex is written by individual authors without help of diverse sorts. Often, the help is historical, private, or given by those for whom footnotes and bibliographic references are insufficient and unimportant forms of thanks. These acknowledgments are meager reward to people whom I owe a great deal.

Brenda Forster, the first author of this volume, gets primary thanks for my involvement in the project. She had the insight to see the need for the book and its value to students and professionals. It was only when she had completed the tedious job of gathering chapters that she invited me to join her efforts. Mine has been the pleasure of stringing together ideas she collected laboriously and for that I thank her.

Several colleagues helped in a variety of ways. Alvin Zalinger, my professor at Boston University, gave me the social-psychological foundations to understand the problem. Shoshanna Churgin of UCLA was especially helpful in providing a systems perspective. Steven Daugherty of the University of Chicago provided me the freedom from other work pressures to write in large blocks of time. Sandra and Jonah Salloway gave liberally and lovingly of our time together in ways that only a family can give.

Most especially, I owe a debt of gratitude to Peter Kong-Ming New, my mentor and colleague, an internationally revered sociologist of medicine. It was he who taught me my craft, who nurtured my career and who left me and a multitude of his students to work on without him at the beginning of 1986. It is to him that my efforts are dedicated.

-Jeffrey Colman Salloway

I am grateful to each of my contributors whose efforts made this book a reality. I also appreciate the help of Russel Forster (my son), Sally Fagan (my typist), Carol Janis (my secretary), and Rita Kuta (my sister and word processor expert) who each worked diligently under pressure and with good cheer to ready the manuscript.

--Brenda Forster

BACKGROUND TO THE BOOK

Concern about an increasing number of persons who are using chemical substances, alcohol and illegal drugs in particular, has produced considerable research since the 1960's. The results of research tend to be published in various journals making it difficult for individuals interested in the topic to get a coherent understanding of the patterns and factors associated with drug-using behaviors. Texts on the subject tend to focus on clinical issues such as effects of major drugs, individual factors in drug use, and clinical management. Most do not present studies on sub-populations of users in order to explicate socio-cultural patterns and factors for a sociological model.

As sociologists with expertise in social-epidemiological and social-problems approaches for studying illness and deviant behavior, we felt a need to make available a sourcebook on alcohol and drug use that emphasized sub-group patterns of use and that developed a sociological model from the data. An edited book seemed the best approach. Just as there are different substance-using sub-groups in society, so there are different researchers focusing on specific sub-groups. We also wanted to include chapters which represented the substance-use situation in countries outside of the U.S. as a comparison to the U.S. experience. Finally, we felt it was important to help the reader follow the specifics of various sub-groups, yet at the same time grasp the fit of the specific information into a larger sociological model.

STRUCTURE AND FOCUS OF BOOK

The book has five major sections -- 1) U.S. Alcohol Use by Adolescents, 2) U.S. Substance Use by Adolescents, 3) U.S. Alcohol Use in Adult Populations, 4) U.S. Substance Use in Adult Populations, and 5) International Substance Use. This is a division by life cycle (adolescents and adults) and by substance category (alcohol and illegal drugs). An additional section includes information on substance use in other countries which is helpful in highlighting issues of cultural and social structural impacts developed in our model.

READER AIDS

This book is designed to be reader friendly. A general introduction is provided to help the reader understand the social context and issues surrounding substance use which form the background for the individual chapters. Each of the five sections begins with an introduction raising pertinent sub-group issues. These section introductions aid the reader in identifying common themes for the individual chapters. Each chapter also has an introduction to focus the reader on specific points for the chapter. An abstract for each chapter is available for readers who want a quick overview of core ideas. The section summaries are intended to provide a review of the concepts, issues, factors, and conclusions represented in the section. Finally, an ending summary is given to organize the information into a sociological model which can guide researchers and practitioners in future work on substance use.

Since the book is intended for a wide audience whose research skills and interests vary, data discussions are written with reader interest at fore. Chapters are written using minimal research jargon and only descriptive data for the general reader. However, data tables and statistical information in more detail are given at the end of chapters for use by researchers and advanced students who wish to pursue those complexities. Finally, to aid the reader who wishes to do additional reading, most chapters provide references which are germane to the topic.

To aid instructors who wish to use this material as a supplement to general texts, a matrix by substance, subject group, research methodologies, and sociological theory focus is provided in the Appendix. Generally, chapter titles identify materials as focusing on alcohol use, specific substances, or multi-chemicals including alcohol.

CO-AUTHOR CONTRIBUTIONS

The idea for this book was Forster's. She obtained the contributors, assembled the first draft of the manuscript, and acted as coordinator-editor for the revisions, and final production. Salloway authored the chapter introductions, aided in revisions, and contributed his marketing skills to insure publication of the book.

The major theoretical section introductions and summaries are given authorship in order of percentage of contribution to the content.

INTRODUCTION

Brenda Forster and Jeffrey Colman Salloway

HISTORICAL BACKGROUND

The topic of human substance use is an ancient one. The problem of excessive drinking of alcohol is addressed in the code of Hammurabi (2240 B.C.); there is evidence of the medicinal use of marijuana as early as 3000 B.C., and the early Egyptians (1500 B.C.) used opium to hush crying babies. However, it was not until the 1800's that concentrated and distilled forms of drugs began to be developed for marketing to the general public. While alcohol in distilled forms had long been available, it was the application of industrial manufacturing, marketing, and transport systems that caused alcohol and other kinds of drugs to be widely distributed. Not only did these newly marketed, concentrated products provide more intense effects on the user, but also public attitudes toward use of drugs began to change. On the one hand, there was an increase in legal control of substances, and on the other, an increase in acceptance of substance use in everyday life.

Before 1875, there were few legal restrictions on drugs. Marijuana, cocaine, heroin, opium, and so on, while not widely used, were not legally restricted. Many of these substances were the active ingredients in cough syrups, cold remedies, and various elixers. The "kick" in early Coca-Cola came from cocaine. However, at the turn of the century, efforts to control drug availability were initiated by the newly organizing medical profession and by a few "moral entrepreneurs" (individuals or groups who wished to "protect people against themselves"). The 1914 Harrison Narcotic Act was the forerunner of subsequent drug-control legislation in the U.S. which imposed first indirect then direct legal sanctions and controls on the possession and distribution of certain substances. Currently in the U.S., the Federal Controlled Substance Act provides the comprehensive legislative classification, control mechanisms and penalties for all substances which are considered to be prone to abuse and, therefore, in need of control. Through the 1950's, drug abusers and drug-law violators were subject to criminal penalties. Public concern about increase in use of any particular substance was followed by increased legal penalties for that substance as a deterrence and/or punishment. During the 1960's, widespread recognition of the failures of legal sanctions and of their arbitrary application led to emphasis on clinical treatment (medical, psychological, sociological) as the preferred mode for handling drug abusers. Legal penalties for distributors of illegal drugs, however, have remained high in spite of calls for decriminalization of some substances (especially marijuana) by prestigious groups such as the National Commission on Marijuana and Drug Abuse (1972) and the American Bar Association (1973).

At the same time that these legal developments were occurring, the general public as a whole became more drug oriented. According to Jones-Witters and Witters:

> We are a drug-oriented culture. We use a host
> of different drugs for a variety of purposes:
> to restore health, to reduce pain, to induce
> calmness, to increase energy, to create a
> feeling of euphoria, to induce sleep and to

2

enhance alertness. A multitude of substances are available to swallow, drink, or inhale in order to alter mood or state of consciousness. Youngsters are bombarded with many commercials exhorting them to use a chemical to solve almost any problems. The message is: Why cope with an uncomfortable problem? Try our tablet and the problems will go away. (1983:2)

This notion of a drug-oriented culture refers to the presence in popular society of several related positive beliefs about drug use and drug effects:

1. That drugs are miraculously efficacious and will take care of anything;

2. That drugs are safe and should be used freely, even for minor complaints;

3. That everyone uses drugs -- parents, doctors, workers, women, elderly, children, and so on; and

4. That some drugs are useful and even expected in social settings to help people relax and enjoy themselves (Bushry and Bromley, 1975).

Some commentators tie increased acceptance of drug use to a decline in the Protestant Ethic which stressed that individuals were entitled to enjoyment only after hard work. Today many people expect pleasure and freedom from distress as part of their ongoing lifestyle, not as a distant reward.

IMPORTANCE OF DETERMINING FACTORS IN SUBSTANCE USE

At this point in history, we are faced with a paradox. On the one hand, as we have seen, there is widespread acceptance of alcohol and drugs as a part of the everyday lives of people in Western society. On the other hand, we are beginning to recognize that abuse of alcohol and drugs are emerging as costly problems for individuals, for families, and for society as a whole.

The first approaches to the problems of alcohol and drug abuse were an extension of the Protestant Ethic itself. Alcohol abuse was seen as a sin, a failure of moral fiber. Drug use, likewise, was seen as moral lapse. These moralistic approaches then gave way to a "helping model" of adjustment, administered principally by psychologists, counselors, social workers, and drug and alcohol specialists. These professionals have been joined in the last generation by physicians who have applied a medical or disease model to alcohol and drug abuse.

The commonality among these approaches has been that they address the need for _individual adjustment and rehabilitation_. This individualized approach has been the hallmark of explanations about substance abuse and the root cause to which the problem has been attributed. However, this leaves us with some unexplained observations and unanswered questions. It is the answers to these questions which may shed further light on the causes of alcohol and drug use. Moreover, new light on causes may mean new light on interventions.

The most interesting observation is that alcohol and drug use/abuse are not randomly distributed throughout society. On the contrary, they occur in quite regular patterns. The patterns change slowly over time, and there are invariably many exceptions to the patterns, but their presence is clear. As a single example, we note that alcoholism has traditionally been very low among American Italians and Jews and very high

4

among American Irish. In the same way, we find that alcoholism is far less common in Italy than in France and very common in the Scandinavian countries (see Whitehead and Harvey, 1974, for a good review of cross-cultural differences).

These patterns cause us to ask some penetrating questions. If certain sub-groups of people are more prone to be alcohol or drug users and abusers, can it be that they have a lack of moral fiber? Or, perhaps, they have poorer psychological adjustment? Or, are they more susceptible genetically or otherwise to a "disease"? Our explanations based on individualistic theories of alcoholism and drug abuse are simply not adequate by themselves to explain these patterns.

Howard Becker suggests in his book, The Outsiders (1963) that at least one form of substance use, marijuana smoking, is a behavior which must be learned. Therefore, becoming a marijuana user, says Becker, requires that there be marijuana available in the circles in which a person socializes, that there be people present who know how to use it, that there be occasions for teaching how to use the drug, and that the prospective user be amenable and capable of learning. Thus, if there is not marijuana available in the community, or if few know how to use it, or if opportunities to share use of it are few, it may be difficult for a person to become a marijuana user.

We begin to see here that acquisition of alcohol and drug using behavior require:

1. A supply of the drug in the community,
2. A pre-existing willingness to try it,
3. A person or persons who are willing to encourage and "teach" its use, and

4. The ability of the potential user to learn use.

Thus, patterns of acquisition of alcohol-using or drug-using behavior will vary with drug availability, pre-existing attitudes toward the drug, the numbers of people who already know how to use it, and the degree of difficulty in learning use. As these vary from drug to drug and as attitudes toward drug use vary from sub-group to sub-group, we can expect that patterns of drug use by individuals will vary also.

Patterns of use now become somewhat easier to understand when placed in a socio-cultural context. Alcohol is freely available and legal for adults to use in most of the western world. Knowledge about how to use it -- what to mix and what not to mix, what to chill and what to serve warmed, and so on -- is widespread. Cost is low, compared to other drugs. And, there do not exist clear guidelines or consensus about what constitutes abuse. As a result, we expect that the pattern of use will be very widespread, and the pattern of abuse will also be widespread. And, of course, this is the case.

Alternatively, at this time, heroin is not widely distributed in all communities. Attitudes toward heroin use are generally negative. Cost of the drug is high. Knowledgeable users are a very small minority. Finally, the techniques of use and the implements necessary are difficult to acquire. As a result, heroin use, though still a serious problem, is not nearly as widespread as alcohol abuse.

Patterns of substance use then are strongly influenced by the availability of the substance, the nature of attitudes toward drug use in general and toward the particular substance in question, and the

6

nature of a sub-groups' experience with the drug. Because these factors are also patterned, use of the substance in a particular sub-group is also patterned. One might say that these patterns are a kind of socio-cultural or "epidemiological footprint." The same way that we can trace the paths of animals in the woods by their patterned footprints, and we can trace the nature and causes of an epidemic by its unique pattern of incidence, we can trace the patterns and factors of alcohol and drug use and abuse.

What we find when we trace these patterns is that some factors influencing substance use are shared in all situations and by all peoples. In addition, we find important differences appear for various sub-groups. Together the general and specific factors, once understood, can be used to adjust strategies for prevention and for treatment. The general, shared factors can help a broad approach to understanding, prevention and treatment of substance abuse, while the specific sub-group patterns can be useful for "fine tuning" and individualizing our focus.

DISCIPLINES INVOLVED IN DRUG STUDIES

Because of the complex nature of substance use and abuse, several academic and applied disciplines are involved in drug studies. The biological and pharmacological sciences study the chemical composition of drugs and their physiological effects on organisms (animals and humans). Some of these studies are done in controlled laboratory settings, others in "natural" settings with living or postmortem subjects. Both medicine and nursing in their discussion of medical and clinical management of drug abusers are concerned about handling the biochemical effects of drugs. The literature in these areas is extensive and the reader is referred to other more detailed resources for the insights that these disciplines provide. (See for example, Jones-Witters and Witters, 1983; Estes, Smith-DiJulio, and Heinemann, 1980; and Estes and Heinemann, 1977; among other good introductory materials currently available.)

Psychological research has focused on the individual to determine what personality characteristics tend to be associated with substance abusers. Early psychological studies used subjects who were receiving treatment for drug problems. These were a unique sub-sample of all substance users. These were the users who were open to admitting that they were users, that they had problems, and that they wanted to change, or they were individuals who had been forced by family members or legal agencies to undergo treatment for substance abuse. As such, they were rather unrepresentative of the user population as a whole; therefore, generalizations from these studies are suspect. Recent studies take a more social-psychological approach using general populations of drug users (not just abusers) and including measurements of social factors such as parental role models and peer pressure (not just personality and upbringing).

Sociological research has a wide range of focus, from the characteristics of substance users, to group dynamics and values which encourage and support substance use, to the larger social context of substance use. Early sociological studies tended to draw on large cross-sections of drug users and, therefore, found subjects "healthier" than the psychological studies of abusers indicated. Currently, sociological studies are helping to define various sub-categories of users and abusers. These distinctions offer a more accurate reflection of the differences in patterns of use and abuse of alcohol and drugs in different segments of society.

Research is also provided by applied disciplines such as clinical psychology, applied sociology and social work. These practitioners are usually concerned with the effectiveness of drug treatment and prevention programs.

The contributors to this book come from the sociological, psychological, and applied disciplines just mentioned. Even the most theoretically oriented are concerned about the usefulness of their findings for prevention and treatment. The research is recent (within the past 15 years) and encompasses a wide variety of sub-populations: adolescents, elderly, handicapped, women, blacks, hispanics, skid row alcoholics, professionals, and death row inmate families. This should enable the reader to get a feel for the variety of issues and approaches in drug studies today as well as to see the growing commonalities of research understandings about substance users and abusers.

WHAT IS A DRUG?

Having come this far in the discussion of drug use and its study, we must now point out that both in scientific and in everyday language, there is a disagreement over what constitutes a drug. For the general public, over-the-counter medicines, physician-prescribed medications, caffeine (in coffee, tea, cola drinks and in chocolate candies), nicotine (in cigarettes), and even alcohol are not considered

9

"drugs." Drugs for the public mean the popular, illegal substances taken by youths (marijuana, cocaine, crack, LSD and other "alphabet" drugs, heroin, various inhalants, and so on). The public's reaction to the drug-using activity of youth is

> ...overwhelmingly one of moral disgust, condemnation, and fear at the threat of social and personal chaos that drug use seems to portend....They associate drug use with moral corruption and decay. (Zinberg and Robertson, 1972)

This negative view by the public is coupled with many erroneous beliefs about the personal harm caused by popular substances used by adolescents. For example, one study found adults holding the following inaccurate beliefs about the effects of marijuana use:

- Changes user's basic personality - 90%
- Weakens user's will and self-discipline - 89%
- Leads people to commit crimes and acts of violence - 82%
- Strongly addictive - 81%   (Geiger, 1971)

Many health care professionals also share this kind of definition and reaction.

A strict scientific definition of a drug is <u>any</u> substance which when taken into the body alters it. However, a more socially conscious definition of a drug requires some not-so-subtle distinctions which have important implications for what we describe as a drug and what we do not. The most common examples are caffeine, nicotine and alcohol. In certain circumstances, we do recognize them as drugs.

Ordering coffee for a child in a restaurant raises eyebrows. Sales of cigarettes to minors are restricted. Giving alcohol to an unrelated minor is a crime in most states. Under careful scrutiny, we do recognize these substances as drugs. However, each of these is legal, widely distributed, readily available and commonly cheap. Though they are drugs, people commonly place them in a category of not-so-serious, legal substances whose use is quite tolerable in everyday life.

The other substances which we discuss in this book differ considerably. These are illegal. Once that distinction is made, a whole host of implications arise: 1) they are available only through an underground economy, 2) they are expensive compared to caffeine, nicotine and alcohol, 3) they must be used in secret among trusted partners, 4) possession or sale contains elements of danger, 5) non-users are far more common than users, and 6) public knowledge that one is a user subjects one to normative sanctions by non-users.

At this time, only two types of drugs are the subject of widespread social concern: 1) alcohol, the legal drug, and 2) a variety of illegal drugs. However, public cigarette usage is increasingly being called into question, especially since research has shown that secondary inhalation of smoke harms non-smokers. While the chapters in this book are addressed primarily to use of illegal, psychoactive, non-medicinal drugs, and of alcohol, the reader should be aware of the larger context of concern about what constitutes a drug. Often adolescent substance users point back to their adult accusers and ask why their choice of substance should be condemned and their parents' substance use ignored or accepted. Denial of the scientific definition of a drug makes it difficult for abusers of accepted drugs, such as physician-

11

prescribed tranquilizers, cigarettes, caffeine, and over-the-counter medicines, to examine their own behaviors. Finally, users and potential users often reject the counsel of their elders against "drug" use because the counsel is based on patently (to the youth) false information.

WHAT IS ABUSE?

Associated with the "what is a drug" question is the question of what constitutes abuse of a drug. For physicians, any use of a drug outside a medically prescribed context is drug abuse. Yet, questions are being asked about whether or not physicians prescribe drugs too easily, too frequently, and in too high dosages. For much of the public, any use (even experimental) of illegal substances is abuse. A drug educator in industry points out one serious problem with this view:

> I am accustomed to hearing people groan when I bring up the subject of alcoholism in connection with drug abuse. 'We came here to talk about drug abuse,' they say angrily. 'What has alcohol to do with that?' (Redfield, 1973)

There is, however, growing agreement that substance use can be described on three related continuums: 1) a continuum of frequency and dependency of use, 2) a continuum which describes the mix of drugs being used, and 3) a continuum representing various legal-illegal distinctions. In Table 1, we have a representation of the model we propose. Here the continuum of substance frequency-dependency ranges from never used, experimentation (past or current), infrequent use, moderate recreational use, frequent and dependent use,

12

TABLE 1

MODEL CONTINUUM OF SUBSTANCE USE BY BEHAVIORAL CRITERIA

Frequency of Use	No Contact	Abstinence	Experimentation	Occasional Social Use	Moderate Social/Personal Use	Frequent Social/Personal Use or Binges	Daily Routine Use
Stimulus for Use	No Use		Recreational/Controlled Use		Dependent Use	Compulsive Addictive Use	
Evaluation of Use	Non-Use		Use			Abuse*	

---

* Some tie the concept of abuse to the legality of the substance defining any use of an illegal substance as abuse. Some tie the concept to medical legitimization defining any non-prescribed use as abuse. Here we have tied the concept to behavior and functionality since legality and physician prescription are more socially problematic criteria as our discussion indicates.

and addiction. According to this model, abuse is reserved for the latter two categories where signs of physical, mental, emotional, social, economic, and/or spiritual impairment become evident. Both psychological and physical dependency are associated with abuse. Psychological dependency includes a strong desire or compulsion to use a psychoactive substance, including a craving for repetition of the pleasurable effects of the drug. Physical dependency is evidenced by an increased tolerance for the substance (larger, more frequent amounts are required to obtain the desired effects), and by withdrawal symptoms if the substance is withheld for a period of time (depression, irritability, muscle tremors, and so on).

The reader should further be aware that the definitions of what constitutes abuse or even heavy use are in flux. For example, studies of marijuana use in the 1970's used weekly smoking as criteria for heavy use/abuse. Current studies cite daily use as the standard.

At the same time, there is a continuum which describes the mix of substances used. Many alcoholics are content to sip their way through a six-pack or two every evening. They consider this behavior innocuous. They never graduate to anything more intense, and they identify anyone who drinks a "heavier" liquor as a "hard drinker." Others "graduate" from beer to liquor, use them in combination, or use these in further combination with marijuana or cocaine. In the same way that there is a continuum of frequency and of intensity of use which we have described, there is also a continuum of types of drugs used in which some people gravitate from "light" drugs to harder drugs (see Table 2). The result is that most users of "hard" drugs have

TABLE 2

CONTINUUM OF SUBSTANCE USE BY "HARDNESS"* OF DRUG

	"Hardness"		
Label	Light	Moderate	Hard
Examples	Beer, Coffee, Cola, Wine	Cigarettes, Liquor, Marijuana, Tranquilizers, Cocaine	Heroin, Crack, Narcotics PCP, Whiskey

* "Hardness" is a perception based on both the addictiveness of the drug and the degree of behavioral effect produced on intake. To a certain extent, drug laws use similar categories in defining types of controlled substances and penalties for their possession.

come to these hard drugs along the continuum of "lighter" drugs.

Finally, the legal-illegal continuum in operation relates to the formal social acceptability of a substance, including level of sanctions applied for violation of the norm (see Table 3). Some users stick to legal drugs (alcohol, caffeine, nicotine, physician-prescribed drugs, and such); others involve themselves with light penalty drugs (marijuana or under-age alcohol or cigarette use, for example); others use drugs with high legal penalties (cocaine, heroin). It is best to keep in mind that while the legal-illegal distinction is not always associated with actual physiological dangers, it does reflect public concern.

TERMINOLOGY

Because of disagreements over which terms are appropriate, the reader will find a variety of words used in this book and elsewhere. The distinctions between alcohol or drug use and abuse are occasionally difficult to make. Even the term "alcoholism" refers to a single form of alcohol abuse when, in fact, there are many forms of abuse. Drinking and driving is one example; occasional drunk episodes are another.

Some prefer the terms "substance" or "chemical" to "drug," or "dependency" to "abuse." Our approach here is not to try to make linguistic distinctions or to rely heavily on subtle shifts in concepts. Rather, we've chosen to be eclectic in the use of terms. A variety of usage is represented in the chapters that follow. In our discussions, we try to use the word "substance" to refer to use of any chemical including alcohol, nicotine, and caffeine and the word "drug" when paired with the word alcohol to refer to other

TABLE 3

CONTINUUM OF SUBSTANCE USE BY LEGALITY OF DRUG

Label		Legality*			
	Legal	Quasi-Legal	Light Penalty Illegal	Moderate Penalty Illegal**	Heavy Penalty Illegal
Examples	Alcohol, Caffeine	Over-the-Counter, Prescription (No-Doz, Valium)	Barbiturates, Tranquilizers, Amphetamines	Marijuana, LSD, PCP	Heroin, Cocaine, Morphine, Opium

---

* Legal penalties are defined by legal classification from category IV, lightest penalty, to category I, heaviest penalty. See Drug Enforcement Administration, "Drugs of Abuse," Washington, D.C.: U.S. Government Printing Office, 1977.

** Although these drugs are classified as a Schedule I along with heroin, in practice, at least at the local level, only light to moderate legal consequences are applied.

chemicals except alcohol. We also prefer the more general term "use," avoiding the judgments implied in the term "abuse."

In their discussions, not all writers separate alcohol from other drugs (substances or chemicals). However, in this book, we have grouped chapters discussing alcohol use/abuse exclusively since alcohol is a major drug which the majority of the population (adolescents and adults) use and has developed as a field and topic in its own right.

OVERVIEW OF RESEARCH ABOUT DRUG USE PATTERNS AND FACTORS

Much of the early research into substance use was concerned with questions of distribution -- how much of what substances were being used by whom. These descriptive surveys often utilized populations which were readily available to researchers (students and subjects being treated for drug-abuse-related problems). During the 1960's in the U.S., increased attention to drug use drew many researchers into studying this topic. As a result, researchers could utilize previous descriptive data and began to identify factors which were important in understanding the characteristics, motives, and social dynamics associated with substance use. More recently, there is concern about the patterns and factors associated with substance use in a variety of sub-populations -- not just adolescents, college students, and poor minorities who were previously studied. The chapters which follow reflect the most recent developments in drug studies. They build on previous work, seek to establish "causative" associations among user characteristics and social factors, and explore substance use in a variety of sub-populations, including pre-adolescents.

Researchers are currently concerned with focusing on patterns and factors for several reasons. An understanding of who is using what is useful in monitoring changes in substance use over time. That information is useful 1) to law enforcement personnel who must decide which substances need curtailing and what market needs control, 2) to legislative members who decide on regulations and penalties, 3) to treatment personnel who must be prepared for handling problem cases, and 4) to planners of prevention programs who must address appropriate audiences with current information and who want to monitor the success of their programs. Understanding what is going on and the factors causing substance use then provides a base from which prevention and treatment concerns are built.

ISSUES OF FOCUS FOR THE READER

The authors whose material follows represent a variety of disciplines (see the author descriptions on their respective chapter title pages) and utilize various methods of gathering and of presenting information. As you read the book there are several general questions you should seek to answer for yourself.

- What do the various disciplines and approaches contribute to the understanding of substance use/abuse?
- How much of what substances are being used by whom?
- What factors are associated with substance use for the various sub-populations and substance discussed?
- What problems and costs are associated with substance use/abuse?

19

- How does the experience of other countries contribute to an understanding of the effects of substance availability and of cultural factors?
- What information is still lacking that would help complete the picture?

The section introductions and conclusions are intended to help you formulate your own answers to what is known about substance use/abuse. However, you may want to go beyond the information provided in this book to answer these questions. You will find the reference section of each chapter useful for expanding your understanding of this complex, but important, subject.

OVERVIEW OF THE BOOK

Chapters 1 through 6 focus on alcohol and drug use by adolescents in the U.S. The focus on adolescent substance use is also represented in Chapters 17 and 18 which examine the drug-using behaviors of Israeli adolescents. Comparing the experience of these two cultures is useful since the one (U.S.) provides a context in which substance use is widely accepted and practiced throughout the society and the other (Israel) generally has a negative attitude toward drug use, including alcohol. Adolescents using drugs in these two societies are doing so in response to different social messages about what is appropriate behavior.

Chapters 7 through 16 examine substance-using behavior of various U.S. sub-populations. It is important in reading these chapters to determine not only what the patterns of substance use are in these groups whose drug-taking behavior is not typically discussed, but also one should determine what special needs and motivations, if any, are associated with

20

substance use by these groups. In addition, one should try to understand the commonalities of factors which are shared across groups.

Chapters 17 through 21 present a sample of concerns about drug use from societies outside the U.S. -- Israel, Australia and the Netherlands. While there are some unique aspects of substance use in the international scene (including a generally lower rate of drug use than the U.S.), the discussion by these authors has relevance to issues in the U.S. Sargent's discussion (Chapter 17) points to the role of governments in stimulating use of some substances (alcohol, in particular). This concern with the wider social context in stimulating use of certain substances is shared by the authors of Chapters 4 and 18. Governments gain revenue from the sale of alcohol and cigarettes and, thus, have a vested interest in those substances being available. This is a consideration that is usually foreign to most people concerned with substance use. Comparison of Oriental Jews' and adolescents' substance-use patterns in and outside the U.S. highlights the effects of social structures and sub-cultures. Finally, van de Wijngaart's portrayal of heroin use in the Netherlands should alert the reader to the international traffic and control problems which impact on the availability of heroin in the U.S., the concern of Wiebel in Chapter 15.

Pay particular attention to Chapters 5, 11 and 18 which seek to develop comprehensive models for understanding the relationships of the many factors which other studies have shown to be associated with substance use. Each chapter is preceded by an introduction to help you focus on the new issues and tie together the previous ideas. At the end of each section, we provide a summary of the main ideas in the section.

REFERENCES

American Bar Association. 1973. Report to the House Of Delegates Section of Individual Rights and Responsibilities. Chicago: American Bar Association.

Becker, H. S. 1963. Outsiders: Studies in the Sociology of Deviance. New York: The Free Press.

Bushry, B. C. and Bromley, D. G. 1975. Sources of non-medicinal drug use: A test of the drug-oriented society explanation. Journal of Health and Social Behavior 1:50-62.

Drug Enforcement Administration. 1977. Drugs of Abuse. Washington, D.C.: U.S. Government Printing Office.

Dusek, D. and Girdano, D. A. 1980. Drugs: A Factual Account (3rd ed.). Reading, Mass.: Addison Wesley.

Estes, N. J. and Heinemann, M. E. 1977. Alcoholism: Development, Consequences, and Interventions. St. Louis: C. V. Mosby Co.

Estes, N. J., Smith-DiJulio, K., and Heinemann, M. E. 1980. Nursing Diagnosis of the Alcoholic Person. St. Louis: C. V. Mosby Co.

Geiger, L. H. 1971. Age, reported marijuana use, and belief in some assumed negative effects of the drug. Paper presented at the meeting of the 26th Annual Conference of the American Association for Public Opinion Research, Pasadena, CA.

Goode, E. 1970. The Marijuana Smokers. New York: Basic Books.

Jones-Witters, P. and Witters, W. L. 1983. Drugs and Society: A Biological Perspective. Monterey, Ca: Wadsworth Health Sciences.

Peyrot, M. 1984. Cycles of social problem development: The cast of drug abuse. Sociological Quarterly 25:83-96.

22

Ray, O. S. 1972. <u>Drugs, Society and Human Behavior</u>.
St. Louis: C. V. Mosby Co.

Reasons, C. 1974. The politics of drugs: An inquiry
in the sociology of social problems. <u>Sociological
Quarterly</u> 15:318-404.

Redfield, J. T. 1973. Drugs in the work place --
substituting sense for sensationalism. <u>American
Journal of Public Health</u> 63:1064-1070.

Shafer, R. P. (Chair). 1972. <u>Marijuana: A Signal of
Misunderstanding</u>. New York: Signet.

Whitehead, P. C. and Harvey, C. 1974. Explaining
alcoholism: An empirical test and reformulation.
<u>Journal of Health and Social Behavior</u>. 15:57-64.

Zinberg, N. E. and Robertson, J. A. 1972. <u>Drugs and
the Public</u>. New York: Simon and Schuster.

SECTION 1
U.S. ALCOHOL USE BY ADOLESCENTS

INTRODUCTION

As we discussed in the preceding introduction, use of alcohol and drugs is not a random phenomenon. There are widespread patterns of use (and abuse) of these substances. It is the discovery of these "epidemiological footprints" or socio-cultural patterns which can provide us with insights into the origins of these behaviors, the potential for prevention and the structure of treatment.

In examining alcohol use, we find that drinking behavior most often begins during pre-adolescence or adolescence. Moreover, it occurs most often in the social context of the peer group. It is also at this time that the community begins to be aware of adolescent alcohol use and to indicate levels of concern.

Thus, we see immediately two important patterns: 1) initial use of alcohol around early adolescence and 2) a concerned response on the part of the community to use of alcohol. The general assumption on the part of the community, however, is that it is drinking in specific contexts (for example, extremely under-aged children or in association with driving) that is a problem, not drinking in general.

This begins to raise interesting questions with regard to patterns of alcohol use and abuse. For example, is there a difference in early drinking patterns between urban or suburban youth and rural youth? Are there differences between males and females, between blacks and whites? And more important still, do we find that there are other factors which are associated with either higher or lower rates of drinking? If we can discern such patterns, we will have a great insight into the origins of problem drinking behavior.

INTRODUCTION TO CHAPTER 1

In the first chapter, Wylie et al. examine the factors associated with drinking among adolescents in a small town and a rural setting. Their approach is to search for predictor variables which are associated statistically with age at first drink, frequency, and amount of drinking. Using this method, they find a pattern or "footprint." This finding has three implications for use:

1. It alerts us to the socio-cultural pattern of drinking;
2. It helps us to predict who in the small town or rural area is most at risk of becoming a problem drinker; and
3. It immediately sets us thinking about means of intervention and prevention.

A key consideration then is the patterning of early behavior and what implications this patterning might have for the growth of problems associated with the behavior.

Later, in Chapter 5, Forster demonstrates the prevalence of drinking and drug use in an even younger population and provides us a test of several explanatory theories. At that point, Forster also begins to demonstrate some hypotheses about the development of behavior problems associated with alcohol and drug use.

CHAPTER 1

ADOLESCENT ALCOHOL USE IN A SMALL TOWN AND RURAL SETTING

Mary Lou Wylie, Stephen Gibbons, Lennis Echterling, and Joan MacAllister French

ABSTRACT

In this chapter, we analyze the results of a survey which we administered to 650 students in grades 7-12 (12-18 year olds) of a small city and the surrounding county in a mid-Atlantic state during May, 1983.

The factors we used to predict alcohol use included the student's gender, religion, socioeconomic status, involvement in extracurricular and social activities, and grade in school. The variables we predicted were the age at first drink, frequency of drinking, and amount of drinking. We were particularly interested in predicting problem drinkers, who are those students high in both frequency and amount.

We found the gender, grade, time spent in social activities, and mother's occupational level were consistently significant predictors. Males tend to drink earlier, more frequently, and in greater amounts than females. As students progress through school, they are more likely to have had their first drink, drink more often, and drink a greater amount each time they drink. The amount of

---

MARY LOU WYLIE is Associate Professor of Sociology at James Madison University; STEPHEN GIBBONS is Assistant Professor of Sociology at Western Oregon State College, Momenth, Oregon; LENNIS ECHTERLING is Assistant Professor of Psychology at James Madison University; JOAN MACALLISTER FRENCH is Prevention Specialist at Pear Street Center in Harrisonburg, Virginia.

problem drinking. Religious involvement and receipt of welfare predicted age at first drink.

We discuss the implications of these findings, emphasizing the prevention of problem drinking behavior.

INTRODUCTION

In recent years, there has been renewed concern and interest in problems associated with alcohol and drug abuse. Anti-drunk driving organizations such as Mothers (or Many) Against Drunk Driving (MADD) have formed and have grown in power. The passage in many states of strict new laws regulating alcohol and driving under the influence also exemplifies this concern and interest. Many of these organizations and laws are specifically concerned with teenage drinking. Several states have raised the legal drinking age, and the U.S. Congress has passed a bill which will make a percentage of highway funds contingent upon states making 21 the minimum drinking age.

This renewed interest and concern has also stimulated a steady flow of research on alcohol and its effects on teenagers. The research, for example, documents the increasing consumption of alcohol among teenagers (Johnston, Bachman, and O'Malley, 1982). It has also found some association between alcohol use and the use of other, usually illicit, drugs (see Kandel, Treiman, Faust, and Single, 1976; and Single, Kandel, and Faust, 1974). But almost all of this work has focused on urban or suburban youth, although some researchers have looked at national samples of adolescents. Researchers have given very little attention specifically to rural adolescent alcohol use. The research which has been done among rural residents in general tends to indicate a lower level of alcohol use and abuse than is prevalent among urban populations. However, the data are adequate to demonstrate that the problem is not strictly urban and that the trend is toward increased use of alcohol among rural youth (Hampe, 1976).

This chapter assesses the quantity and frequency of alcohol use among a sample of rural junior and senior high school students and examines some of the factors associated with such use. We also discuss the implications of our findings and make some suggestions for prevention programs.

FACTORS ASSOCIATED WITH ALCOHOL USE

Researchers consistently have found several factors to be related to alcohol and drug use by young people. These factors include gender, age, grade in school, religiosity, socioeconomic status, and involvement in extracurricular activities (Johnston, Bachman, and O'Malley, 1982; Fischer, 1975-76; and Wechsler and Thum, 1973).

Exactly how these factors affect the use and abuse of alcohol is the subject of some disagreement, but relationships between these factors and alcohol use are frequently, though not consistently, found. For example, it is usually found that males tend to be heavier drinkers than females and that they start drinking at an earlier age. Second, older adolescents tend to drink alcohol more frequently, and, when they do drink, they drink more. Third (and related to the second point), students in the upper grade levels tend to drink more, and drink more often, than students in grade levels 7-9 (11 to 13 year olds). Fourth, those adolescents who are more religious are more likely to abstain from alcohol consumption. Fifth, those students from lower socioeconomic status groups are more likely to abuse alcohol, although alcohol abuse is not found exclusively in these groups. Finally, students involved in extracurricular activities are less likely to drink alcohol, and, when they do drink, they tend to consume less. In sum, older males in higher grades, who are not very religious or involved in extracurricular activities and who come from lower socioeconomic backgrounds are more likely to drink alcohol, and to drink in excess.

METHOD

In May, 1983, we gave a Student Alcohol Survey to 650 students attending grades 7-12 in the school systems of both a small city and the surrounding county. The city has a population of about 25,000 and the surrounding county has about 53,000. They are located in a mid-Atlantic state. The nearest metropolitan area is over one hundred miles away, and mountain ranges on both the east and the west contribute to the area's sense of isolation.

Survey Instrument

Our questionnaire was a modified version of the Student Alcohol Inventory developed by the staff of the CASPAR Alcohol Education Program in Somerville, Massachusetts. The questionnaire contained questions on demographic data, students' activities, attitudes about the use of alcohol, factual knowledge about alcohol, students' own alcohol use, and their parents' use of alcohol. A local substance-abuse agency administered the questionnaire as part of an alcohol education program in the public schools.

Sample

Students in required classes, such as Health and Physical Education, American History, and U.S. Government completed the questionnaires. Although a strict random sample was not possible because of limits imposed by the school principals, these classes contained a broad representation of each grade level. The final sample at each grade level was 5-10% of the students.

Measurement

We included a number of variables in this study: gender, age, grade in school, level of parents' education, parents' occupations, receipt of welfare, frequency of attending religious services, time spent working, time spent studying, time spent playing video games, time spent in social activities, time spent in extracurricular activities, number of extracurricular activities, age at first drink, frequency of drinking during the past twelve months, and amount usually drunk.

We also added each person's frequency of drinking and amount usually drunk to construct a problem drinking score.

DATA ANALYSIS

After we obtained frequency distributions of the data, we performed other statistical analyses to explore the relationships among the variables and to determine how well the variables could predict drinking behavior.

Patterns

Fifty-five percent of the respondents were female

and 45% were male. The range of the respondents' ages was 12 to 20, with an average of 16 years.

A majority of the students' parents had a high school education or less. Most of the fathers had a blue-collar occupation, while the mothers were evenly divided among homemaking, blue-collar, and white-collar occupations. Seven percent of the families received welfare of some kind.

In examining how students spent their time, we found that 80% spent five hours or less each week studying. Almost half of the students were not employed, and most of those who were employed worked ten hours or less each week. Nearly half of the students attended religious services every week, and only 16% never attended services. In general, students were very involved in extracurricular activities. Twenty-one percent of the respondents were not involved in extracurricular activities, 22% were involved in one, 36% were involved in two or three, and 20% were involved in four or more activities. Half of the students spent less than five hours a week in social activities, while 28% spent 6-10 hours a week, and 21% spent 11 hours or more a week.

Of the students who indicated that they had drunk alcohol, 32% had their first drink of alcohol on their own by the age of ten, 9% at age eleven, 16% at age twelve, 13% at age thirteen, 11% at age fourteen, 11% at age fifteen, 5% at age sixteen, and 1% each at ages seventeen and eighteen. During the past twelve months, 12% of the subjects had not drunk anything alcohol, 12% had drunk once, 25% had drunk three or four times, 13% had drunk about once a month, 17% had drunk two or three times a month, 10% had drunk weekly, 10% had drunk two or three times a week, and less than 1% had

31

drunk daily. When they drank, 37% usually had one drink or less, 28% had two or three drinks, 15% had four or five drinks, and 19% had six or more drinks.

Variable Relationships

After we learned the characteristics of the sample, we then turned to an investigation of the relationship between these variables and drinking behavior. We initially examined age at first drink. We found that grade level, age, being male, lack of extracurricular activities, infrequent attendance at religious services, and family receipt of welfare were related to age at first drink. We expected that grade level in school and age would be strongly related to the age at first drink. Of course, younger respondents who have drunk an alcoholic beverage would report a lower age at first drink. We found sex to be a significant predictor of age at first drink. For example, a large proportion of males, 46%, had had their first drink by the age of ten, while only 21% of females had had a drink by this time. Though males started drinking at an earlier age than females, females were "catching up" quickly. By the age of fourteen, 82% of the males and 80% of the females had had their first drink. Fifty percent of the subjects whose families were receiving welfare had had their first drink by the age of ten, compared to 30% of the rest of the sample. By the age of thirteen, the figures had increased to 96% and 67%, respectively. In short, males who are not involved in either extracurricular activities or religious services and whose families receive welfare were most likely to being drinking at an early age.

We next turned to an analysis of frequency of drinking. We found that grade level and time spent in social activities were positively related to how often the students drank. Girls drank less frequently than boys. Grade in school was the most powerful predictor of frequency of drinking. The vast majority (86%) of seventh graders, for example, drank no more often than three or four times in the past year, while 30% of the twelfth graders drank at least weekly. Sex of the student was again significant. For instance, 56% of the females drank fewer than four times during the past year, and 59% of the males drank at least once a month. Thus, socially active males in higher grades were more likely to drink often.

The third factor we examined was the amount of alcohol students usually drank. We found that grade in school, amount of time spent in social activities, and mother's occupational level were positively related to amount of alcohol usually drunk, while being female and the amount of time spent studying were negatively related. Grade in school had great explanatory power. As an illustration of this explanatory power, 76% of the seventh graders reported one drink as their usual amount. Only 20% of the seniors usually had one drink, and 19% had six or more drinks. The majority of females (62%) usually had only one or two drinks, while most of the males (59%) had three or more drinks.

Finally, we analyzed problem drinking. Significant predictors of problem drinking were grade level, amount of time spent in social activities, and mother's occupational level, while the amount of time spent studying and being female were negatively related. Again, grade level was the most powerful predictor. For example, 90% of seventh graders could be categorized as light drinkers, but by the twelfth grade, only 39% were light drinkers and 13% were heavy drinkers. We also found sex differences again. Forty-three percent of the males and 63% of the females were light drinkers, 46% of the males and 31% of the females were moderate drinkers, and 11% of the males and 6% of the females were heavy drinkers. Therefore, socially active males in higher grades, who studied little, and whose mothers had higher-level occupations, not only drank more alcohol but also were more likely to be problem drinkers.

DISCUSSION

The findings of the present study indicate that the prevalence of alcohol use in a small mid-Atlantic city and county is quite high. Only 17% of the respondents indicated that they had never drunk alcohol. This is very similar to findings from other rural studies (Napier, Carter, and Pratt, 1981; Hampe, 1976), but lower than recent national figures which indicate that 93% of the students had used alcohol (Johnston et al., 1982). For a discussion of use of alcohol among a younger, upper-middle class suburban population, see the article by Forster in Section 1 of this book. It seems that rural youth may be "catching up" to their urban peers in their drinking, but have not quite caught them. The data also indicate that these respondents begin drinking at a very early age -- 57% had had their first drink by the age of twelve. Again, this is comparable to findings from other studies of rural students.

Not all of the factors discussed in the introductory section were important in predicting age at first drink, frequency and amount of drinking, and problem drinking. Both gender and grade level, however, were significant predictors for all four dependent variables. Males do tend to drink earlier, more frequently, and in greater amounts. Also, as young people progress through school, they are more likely to have had their first drink, will drink more often, and when they do drink, will drink more.

Time spent in social activities predicted all but age at first drink. It seems that for the sampled students, time spent going to parties and dances, going on dates, and going out with friends does not affect when these youth start to drink. However, these social activities do affect how often and how much they drink, and whether or not they are problem drinkers.

The failure of religiosity to be a consistent predictor was somewhat puzzling, although it was a predictor for age at first drink. The studied community has a relatively high population of Baptists, Mennonites, and Church of the Brethren members. All of these denominations have an official church policy of abstinence. Therefore, we suspected that frequency of attending religious services would be a significant negative predictor of frequency and amount of drinking. Since it was not, we are left with the conclusion that either religiosity is not an important factor in predicting alcohol use, or that we did not adequately tap "religiosity" with the question asked. Perhaps focusing on the importance of religion to a person's life might provide more information than merely how often he or she attends services.

The failure of socioeconomic status measures was also somewhat of a puzzle. Although receipt of welfare was significant in predicting age at first drink, it did not predict any other drinking behavior.

Apparently, receiving government assistance has no effect on these students' drinking habits other than when they start drinking. The only other indicator of social status which was significant in predicting both amount usually drunk and problem drinking was mother's occupational level. It could be that students whose mother's work in higher level occupations have more money to spend on alcohol. Thus, when these students drink, they drink more. It is also possible that sons and daughters of working mothers may have less supervision, which may contribute to a drinking problem.

Obviously, this work is only exploratory and descriptive, filling a need for information on rural youth's drinking patterns. But the results have potentially practical applications. First, the young age at which these students began drinking indicates that junior high schools may be a more important socializing environment than high schools -- a majority of the students had had their first drink well before high school. Consequently, the trend toward beginning prevention programs in the lower grades should continue.

Second, males are a higher risk for problem drinking. The fact that they begin drinking earlier, drink more, and drink more often suggests that alcohol plays an important part in the socialization process of young males. We believe that any prevention program must address the question of whether young people, particularly males, see alcohol as a rite of passage into adulthood. If so, then prevention programs will have to present alternative ways of achieving adult status.

Finally, youthful drinking is definitely not only an urban problem. Although our sampled group did not have the same drinking patterns as some of their urban peers, there were enough who fell into the "heavy drinker" category on the problem drinking index to cause concern (13% of the seniors fell into this category). It has been shown elsewhere that alcohol use is highly associated with the use of illicit drugs (Potvin and Lee, 1980; Kandel et al., 1976; Single et al., 1974) and that moderate and heavy users of alcohol are much more likely to use other drugs than light users of alcohol (Wechsler, 1976). Therefore, educating students in rural and small-town areas on the effects and nature of alcohol and on the responsible use of this drug may go far in curtailing other forms of substance abuse at a later age. We need prevention programs for students in rural and small-town areas; however, in designing these programs, we must take into account the unique needs and values of these areas.

REFERENCES

Fischler, M. L. 1976. Drug usage in rural, small town New England. Journal of Altered States of Consciousness 2:171-183.

Hampe, G. D. 1976, August. Adolescent drinking in two rural areas of Mississippi; 1964 and 1975. Paper presented at the meeting of the Rural Sociological Society, New York, NY.

Johnston, L. D., Bachman, J. G., and O'Malley, P. M. 1981. Highlights from Student Drug Use in America, 1975-1981. Rockville, MD: National Institute on Drug Abuse.

Johnston, L. D., Bachman, J. G., and O'Malley, P. M. 1982. Student Drug Use, Attitudes and Beliefs: National Trends, 1975-1982. Rockville, MD: National Institute on Drug Abuse.

Kandel, D. B., Treiman, D., Faust, R., and Single, E. 1976. Adolescent involvement in legal and illegal drug use: A multiple classification analysis. Social Forces 55:438-458.

Napier, T. L., Carter, T. J., and Pratt, M. C. 1981. Correlates of alcohol and marijuana use among rural high school students. Rural Sociology 46:319-332.

Potvin, R. H. and Lee, C. 1980. Multistage path models of adolescent alcohol use: Age variations. Journal of Studies on Alcohol 41:531-542.

Single, E., Kandel, D., and Faust, R. 1974. Patterns of multiple drug use in high school. Journal of Health and Social Behavior. 15:344-357.

Wechsler, H. 1976. Alcohol intoxication and drug use among teenagers. Journal of Studies on Alcohol 37:1672-1677.

Wechsler, H. and Thum, D. 1973. Teenage drinking, drug use, and social correlates. Quarterly Journal of Studies on Alcohol 34:1220-1227.

Post-adolescent use of alcohol is widespread in the United States. This pattern of widespread use implies that drinking behavior and attitudes associated with it have been acquired by most young people as they make the transition from high school into adult life. It is also at this time that the "community" may begin to take notice of the effect of alcohol on young people. Typically, the unit of the "community" which becomes concerned is an organization such as a college which assumes some responsibility for the well-being of its students.

This raises a number of interesting questions about the pattern of alcohol use and abuse. The first thing we must learn is: Does the pattern of alcohol use change as people make the transition from adolescence to adulthood? If it does, then we must ask further: What are the variables which are associated with development of heavy or light patterns of drinking? This, in turn prompts us to ask: How should we measure levels of drinking? By frequency? By amount? By alcohol content of the drinks?

If we can discriminate between heavy and light drinking, are there social forces which facilitate or prevent heavy drinking? Are there systems of attitudes, group memberships, or cultural norms which operate to affect drinking behavior? If we find that there are, then we begin to become aware that the "problem" of drinking is not simply one of individual behavior or misbehavior but is embedded in a socio-cultural context. If that is our conclusion, then our solutions in the forms of prevention and treatment will have to be embedded in a socio-cultural context as well.

A simple test which we might apply to this entire issue is that of change in pattern over time. We might expect that alcohol-consuming behavior would change with age. This is a matter of development or maturation. But we also know that a community's culture changes over time. If this is the case, do we then find that alcohol-using behavior changes for an entire community over time? If that is the case, we have an important piece of evidence that drinking is embedded in the culture of the community and needs to be addressed in that context.

CHAPTER 2
THE DRINKING BEHAVIOR OF COLLEGE STUDENTS

Joyce Miller Iutcovich and Susan M. Vaughn

ABSTRACT

The purpose of this chapter is to establish the pattern of drinking behavior among college students in a localized region of Northwestern Pennsylvania. Data from two studies -- one in 1977 and one in 1982 -- are analyzed. Although the survey instruments for these studies were different, results indicate that, on similar dimensions of drinking behavior, there were few discernible differences between the drinking

----
JOYCE MILLER IUTCOVICH is Assistant Professor of Sociology at Villa Marie College and President of Keystone University Research Corporation in Erie, Pennsylvania; SUSAN M. VAUGHN is Assistant Researcher at Keystone University Research Corporation.

behaviors of the students in the 1977 study and those in the 1982 study.

The 1982 study also measured and analyzed the normative structures of college students in regard to drinking behavior, to determine whether this factor plays a significant role in the use and abuse of alcohol among students. A regression analysis indicates that normative structures of students are indeed significantly related to drinking, although this factor in and of itself could not explain the greatest portion of variation in drinking behaviors. The importance and implications of these findings are discussed.

INTRODUCTION

The abuse of alcohol among college students and the problems resulting from such behavior has been a concern of educators, parents, and the general public for many years. There is concern over student drunkenness, violent behavior, vandalism, and personal injury. A large number of students get "smashed" quite often and consider it socially accepted behavior. Moreover, this behavior is not only acceptable, but it is encouraged. On most college campuses, according to national surveys, between 70% and 95% of the college students drink to some extent (Ingalls, 1983; Engs, 1977; Kraft, 1976). This is not to say that most college students are alcoholics, but some clearly have a drinking problem. In a national survey of college students, Hanson and Engs (1984) found an increase in the proportion of heavy drinkers -- from 11.6% in 1974 to 17.2% in 1982. Thus, the problem is that many college students use alcohol quite extensively, and they do not recognize the possible consequences and implications of their drinking.

Today, many college students have already acquired their habits and attitudes toward drinking during their teenage years. Indeed, the prevalence of teenage

41

drinking and alcohol abuse is on the rise. However, it is also felt that the college surroundings may accentuate the learned behavior or may encourage new behavior to be acquired regarding alcohol consumption.

As a result of the widespread use and abuse of alcohol among teens and college students, many programs have been initiated to help students understand and deal with alcohol more responsibly. Not all of these programs have been very successful. The literature suggests that alcohol education programs have been ineffective in reaching their goals of reduced alcohol consumption (Kinder, Pape, and Walfish, 1980). Developing programs to prevent alcohol abuse on college campuses requires a great deal of planning, and an essential first step of this process is data collection. Effective ameliorative programs must be able to draw on accurate data regarding the prevalence and extent of alcohol consumption among college students. It is also important to delineate some of the key factors that may contribute to the consumption of alcohol and its abuse.

The purpose of this chapter is to report the results of two surveys of students -- one in 1977 and one in 1982 -- from several colleges and universities in Northwestern Pennsylvania. Comparison of these two surveys establishes the pattern of drinking behavior of the students within these colleges. Moreover, the 1982 survey examines the normative structures of these students and determines if these structures are important factors in accounting for the amount of alcohol consumption among college students.

THEORETICAL FRAMEWORK

This study measures a number of variables which can

42

be used to describe the prevalence and extent of alcohol abuse among college students. The first set of variables pertain to the background characteristics of the student: age, sex, marital status, religious preference, and type of living accommodation. These background variables will be used to determine if there are any significant differences in drinking behavior within certain sub-groups of college students.

Secondly, and most importantly, there are a set of variables used to measure drinking behavior and its effects. Indeed, there is a long-standing controversy regarding what factor or factors should be considered when measuring drinking behavior. Drinking behavior has traditionally been measured in terms of the amount of alcohol that one consumes over a specific period of time (that is, quantity and frequency). According to the quantity-frequency criterion, then, a person who drinks X number of drinks in Y number of days would ideally be classified as a certain "type" of drinker -- for example, light, moderate, or heavy. The 1977 study measured drinking behavior in this fashion.

In the past two decades, however, professionals have become cognizant of the fact that several variables must be measured to acquire an accurate understanding of a person's drinking behavior -- these variables must be measured as well as quantity of alcohol consumed and frequency of drinking episodes.

One such scale developed and used in the 1982 survey is the Adolescent Alcohol Involvement Scale (AAIS). Mayer and Filstead (1979) originally developed this scale and identified 12 other factors, in addition to the quantity-frequency criterion, that describe an adolescent's drinking behavior. These variables, which were previously verified as indicators of alcohol abuse among adolescents, measure adolescents' drinking behavior in terms of the extent to which drinking interferes with psychological functioning and/or social relations and/or family living. Consequently, when, where, why, how, what, and with whom one drinks, in addition to how much and how often one drinks, are all questions of equal importance in understanding drinking behavior.

Finally, the normative structures of college students with regard to drinking behavior are measured and analyzed to determine whether this factor is a significant predictor of alcohol use and abuse among college students.

Normative structures are beliefs individuals have regarding what is appropriate and inappropriate behavior. As children, we learn norms (through our parents, our families, our peers, and the church) and carry them with us into adulthood. Norms provide individuals with rules and regulations which are used as guidelines to decide how to behave in particular situations.

Normative structures, as they pertain to the consumption of alcoholic beverages, have been identified as proscriptive, prescriptive, and nonscriptive (Mizruchi and Perrucci, 1962). Proscriptive norms are those which negatively sanction the consumption of alcoholic beverages, prescriptive norms positively sanction the consumption of alcoholic beverages, and nonscriptive norms neither prohibit drinking nor provide adequate guidelines for acceptable drinking behavior. Thus, students with proscriptive norms are those who believe that one should not drink; students with prescriptive norms are those who believe that drinking is acceptable, but only in certain situations, and within certain limits; and students with nonscriptive norms are those who really don't know how they feel about drinking -- whether it is acceptable or not.

The relationship between the normative structures of college students and patterns of drinking behavior was only tested in the 1983 study. It was hypothesized that students who had nonscriptive normative structures were more likely to misuse alcohol; students who had prescriptive normative structures were more likely to drink alcohol, but have no alcohol-related behavior problems; and students who had proscriptive normative structures were more likely to drink very little or be abstainers.

METHOD

Both studies reported here were conducted in a county in Northwestern Pennsylvania. Each study administered a structured questionnaire to a sample of students from the area colleges. The first study, in the spring of 1977, surveyed students from four area colleges. One college was state-related and co-educational; the other three were church-related (Catholic) -- two of which were co-educational and the third was a woman's college. The sample was stratified according to class standing; that is, freshman, sophomore, junior, and senior. Faculty members were secured to administer the questionnaires to a "captive audience"; that is, students within their classrooms.

The second study, in the fall of 1982, surveyed students from the same four colleges plus one other area college -- a state-related, co-educational institution. There were a total of 547 students

45

surveyed in 1982; at all of the colleges the questionnaire was administered to classes of students by members of the faculty or by the researcher. The classes were chosen in such a way that there would be a good cross-section of freshman, sophomores, juniors, and seniors.

The questionnaires administered in 1977 and 1982 were not the same, although they were similar in their intent. In 1977 the questionnaire included items on age; sex; academic standing; religious preference; type of living accommodation; the amount, frequency, and type of alcohol consumption; characteristics of the drinking situation; perceptions of how much others drink; age of first drink; types of influence on student's drinking; reasons for drinking or not, and the effects of drinking. In 1982 the questionnaire included the following items: age; sex; marital status; academic standing; religious preference; type of living accommodation; normative structure; the amount, frequency, and type of alcohol consumption; age of first drink; time of last drink; effects of drinking; source of drinks; drinking situation; perception of howmuch they and others drink, and reasons for not drinking.

RESULTS
Background Characteristics
The first task in reporting the results of the two surveys will be to present the background characteristics of those sampled. Table 2.1, page 55, summarizes the data on this. Both samples, the one in 1977 and the one in 1982, were very similar in their characteristics. Slightly less than two-thirds of the students were female and over one-third were male. The

46

over-abundance of females in the sample can be attributed to the fact that one of the institutions was a woman's college. Also, as to be expected on college campuses, the greatest percentage of the students were under 21 years of age: 65% (1977) and 69% (1982). In Pennsylvania 21 is the legal age of drinking. Therefore, both these samples consisted of a high percentage of students who were legally not allowed to drink. The academic standing of the students represented what would typically be found within a college population -- the largest percentage of students were freshmen (around 30-35%) and there was a slightly smaller percentage in each of the remaining levels. Close to two-thirds of the students sampled were Catholic, and approximately one-fourth were Protestant. The high percentage of Catholics, again, is due to the nature of the colleges from which the students were sampled -- three of the five colleges were affiliated with the Catholic church. Finally, approximately half of the students lived in a dorm on campus. For the remaining students, one-forth lived with parents or relatives, and one-fourth lived in a room/apartment/house off campus. In 1977 and in 1982, only 2% of the students (respectively) lived in some other type of accommodation.

Drinking Behavior

The variables used to characterize the drinking behavior of the students in 1977 and in 1982 were not always comparable. However, the data presented in Table 2.2, page 56, takes variables that were similar in their intent and summarizes the results from both years.

47

In 1977 the students were asked if they drank alcoholic beverages; 92% of the students indicated they did. In 1982 the students were asked how often they drank (that is, never, once or twice a year...every day); only 5% of the students in 1982 indicated they "never drank." Therefore, over 90% of the students, for both survey years, said they drank alcoholic beverages. This is within the range reported in other studies of college students, but it is on the upper end of the continuum. In the 1977 survey, 21% of the students were assessed as heavy drinkers, whereas in 1982 only 16% were considered heavy drinkers. The differences between these two figures, however, may be a reflection of the different measurements of "heavy drinking" used in the two years. (See note at the bottom of Table 2.2, page 56, for an explanation of the differences.) This percentage of students (for both years) who were "heavy drinkers" is comparable to figures other studies have reported over the past decade. The percentage of "heavy drinkers" reported in other studies has ranged between 11% and 18%.

The alcoholic beverages the students were drinking in 1982 were considerably different from what they were drinking in 1977. The choice of alcohol in 1977 was beer -- 61% of the students preferred it. In comparison, in 1982 the highest percentage of students (74%) chose to drink liquor -- although two-thirds of those students were most often drinking mixed drinks. What is most surprising from these data is the switch from beer to liquor as the preferred alcoholic beverage among college students. This cannot be easily explained. Alvin Ferro, President of Paddington Corporation which manufactures J & B (one of the leading liquor brands in 1980) has recognized the popularity that liquors and cordials have gained on college campuses. He speculates that college students are consuming such products because they are "compatible with pot -- and pot is as much a competitor for us as other types of liquor" (Business Week 1981:115).

Both in 1977 and 1982 the greatest percentage of the students (95% and 96%, respectively) started drinking alcoholic beverages before they entered college. There are some differences, however, with regard to how early the students started to drink. For example, in 1982 the students started drinking at much earlier ages -- 10% of the students started before the age of 10 (only 2% in 1977 did). For both years, however, the greatest percentage of students started drinking between the ages of 15-18.

When asked why they took their first drink, nearly two-thirds of the students who were surveyed in 1977 indicated they were subject to peer group pressure -- "friends encouraged me." Indeed, in 1982, most students indicated they took their first drink "out of curiosity" or because "parents/relatives offered it to me." Some of the differences in reasons identified in 1977 and in 1982 may be due to the way the questions were worded. However, it does appear that students in the 1982 survey were not as likely to identify "peer group pressures" as an element in their decision process.

In 1977 students indicated that they frequently or occasionally drink in a variety of places -- apartments, houses, bars, and so on. The dorm was the place students would least likely drink -- although 35% of the students said they did drink there. Most students drink in small groups with friends of their own age. The 1982 survey showed that most drinking is done at night.

Overall there does not appear to be any drastic differences in the drinking behavior of college students from 1977 to 1982 -- except for the change from beer in 1977 to liquor in 1982. Otherwise, it is evident that students still drink and that most students drink moderately, although there is an alarming portion of young people who are "heavy drinkers." Finally, most drinking is done within friendship circles.

Effects of Drinking

Most of the students that were surveyed both years do not feel that the consumption of alcohol has had any profound effect on their lives. (Table 2.3, page 58, presents the responses of the students for the different questions asked about "effects" in 1977 and 1982.) Indeed, in 1982 67% of the students said there has been no effect. For those students who did indicate that drinking alcohol has had some effect on their lives, the greatest percentage (8%) said drinking has interfered with their school work, gotten them into trouble at home (7%), and resulted in accident/injury, arrest or punishment at school (7%). When asked what the greatest effect is that they have felt from drinking alcohol, the greatest percentage of students (23%) said a "loose/easy feeling." However, an almost equal percentage reported becoming ill (21%) and several students (22%) reported that they were drinking so heavily that, the next day, they couldn't recall what had happened. Also, 87% of the students in 1982 indicated they felt they had no drinking problems at all or that they could control and set limits on their drinking. And 95% of the students felt that others would view them as a normal drinker for their age. In 1977, 63% of the students said they seldom or never worried about the long-range consequences of drinking and 84% said they seldom or never worried about becoming dependent on alcohol. Also in 1977, the students were asked if the consumption of alcohol has frequently or occasionally had certain specified effects. A large percentage of students (24%) said it caused conflict with their friends. On the other end of the continuum, very few students (0.5%) indicated they lost a job because of alcohol consumption. This is to be expected since very few of these students in 1977 would have had any job from which they could be fired.

Overall, these data indicate that the students, both in 1977 and 1982, do not appear to be bothered by their drinking and do not perceive any negative effect from it. This is probably to be expected, though, since the greatest percentage of the students are only "moderate" drinkers.

Normative Structures and Drinking Behavior

In 1982 the students were asked to indicate the norms they hold with regard to the consumption of alcohol. The greatest percentage of students (85.9%) indicated holding prescriptive normative structures. In other words, they believe that drinking is acceptable, but only in certain situations and within certain limits. Very few of the students (2.4%) identified with a proscriptive normative structure (the prohibition of drinking). The remaining students indicated holding a nonscriptive normative structure (5.1%) or did not choose any of the three patterns

51

identified (6.1%). (See Table 2.4, page 60, for this data.)

The question of interest, though, is to what extent do these normative structures influence the actual drinking behavior of students? The results of the analysis of the data are presented in Table 2.5, page 61. The AAIS score (indicator of the quantity-frequency of drinking as well as the social and psychological effects of drinking) was used as the dependent variable. This score can be used to identify students as abstainers, those who barely drink, those who drink but have no alcohol-related problems, those who misuse alcohol, and alcoholic-like drinkers.

The normative structure variable along with the other background variables were used as the independent variables in a regression analysis to determine their significance in explaining the variation in alcohol use and misuse (AAIS score). By far, the most significant factor in the analysis was the proscriptive normative structure. Students who held proscriptive norms were most likely to have a low AAIS score. Students holding prescriptive and nonscriptive norms were more likely to have higher AAIS scores, although the strength of the relationship was not as great for these students as it was for those holding proscriptive norms. The students holding the nonscriptive norms, however, were the students most likely to have the highest AAIS scores; that is, they were alcohol abusers.

In terms of the other independent variables, sex differences were also significant. Males were likely to be misusers of alcohol rather than females.

The remaining independent variables, although they may have slightly improved the ability to predict the AAIS score, overall were not significant predictors.

52

Furthermore, all the independent variables taken together could explain no more than 17% of the variation in the AAIS scores among our sample of college students. Thus, although many of the factors are significantly related to the use and abuse of alcohol, it would appear from this analysis that there are other independent variables that need to be identified and included in this regression model. In other words, knowing a student's normative structure and some background characteristics does not give us enough information to accurately predict one's use or abuse of alcohol.

CONCLUSION

The findings from both surveys, one in 1977 and one in 1982, indicate that the greatest majority of students drink -- in fact, over 90%. Most students are moderate drinkers. However, a sizable percentage (between 16% and 22%) could be classified as "heavy drinkers." There were few discernible differences between the drinking behaviors of the students surveyed in 1977 and 1982; the most significant change was with regard to the preference for liquor rather than beer in 1982.

The normative structures of students did not prove to be significantly related to their drinking behavior. However, this variable and the other independent variables could not explain the greatest portion of the variation in drinking behaviors. An implication of this finding is that alcohol use and abuse is a socio-cultural phenomenon. Therefore, the norms that young people learn about drinking are important; those without norms to use as guidelines were, indeed, more likely to abuse alcohol. Thus, if young people are provided with specific guidelines for drinking alcohol (and in today's society the earlier the better, since drinking begins at younger and younger ages), whether these guidelines proscribe or prescribe drinking, these young people will carry these norms with them into adulthood. If the norms taught young people remain resistant to change, as adults these young people will not be as likely as those who were not provided with specific guidelines to misuse alcohol.

REFERENCES

Engs, R. C. 1977. Drinking patterns and drinking problems of college students. Journal of Studies on Alcohol 38:2144-2154.

Hanson, D. and Engs, R. 1984. College students' drinking attitudes: 1970-1982. Psychological Reports 54:300-302.

Ingalls, Z. 1983. Although drinking is widespread, student abuse of alcohol is not rising, new study finds. Chronicle of Higher Education 29(5):9.

Kinder, B., Pape, N., and Walfish, S. 1980. Drug and Alcohol education programs: A review of outcome studies. International Journal of the Addictions 15:1035-1054.

Kraft, D. P. 1976. College students and alcohol: The 50 & 12 Project. In DHEW Public Health Service, Alcohol, Drug Abuse, and Mental Health Administration. Alcohol Health and Research World 10-14.

Larsen, D. E. and Abu-Laban, B. 1968. Norm qualities and deviant drinking behavior. Social Problems 15:441-450.

_____. Liquor's thirst for a younger market. 1981, April 20. Business Week 10:17.

Mayer, J. and Filstead, W. J. 1979. The adolescent alcohol involvement scale. Journal of Studies on Alcohol 40:291-299.

Mizruchi, E. and Perrucci, R. 1962. Norm qualities and differential effects of deviant behavior: An exploratory analysis. American Sociological Review 27:391-399.

TABLE 2.1

BACKGROUND CHARACTERISTICS OF
STUDENTS IN 1977 AND 1982 SURVEYS

	Percentages	
Characteristics of Students	1977	1982
Sex:		
Males	39%	38%
Females*	61%	62%
Age:**		
under 21	65%	69%
over 21	35%	31%
Marital Status:		
Single	—	92%
Other	—	8%
Academic Standing:		
Freshman	30%	35%
Sophomore	25%	31%
Junior	26%	15%
Senior	18%	17%
Graduate	—	2%
Religious Preference:		
Protestant	24%	25%
Catholic	64%	63%
Jewish	1%	1%
None	8%	6%
Other	3%	5%
Living Accommodation:		
Dorm on campus	50%	46%
Parents or relatives	23%	24%
Room/apartment/house off campus	25%	26%
Fraternity/Sorority House	1%	0.5%
Other	1%	3.5%

----

* The overabundance of females can be accounted for because one of the colleges is all female.

** The age of 21 was used as a cut-off point since in Pennsylvania the legal drinking age is 21.

— Data not available.

TABLE 2.2

DRINKING BEHAVIOR OF THE STUDENTS
IN 1977 AND 1982

DRINKING BEHAVIOR	Percentages 1977	1982
(percentages based on total sample size)		
Drinkers	92%	95%
Non-Drinkers	8%	5%
Heavy Drinkers*	21%	16%
(percentages based on those who indicated they do drink)		
TYPES OF DRINKS		
Wine	12%	4%
Beer	61%	22%
Liquor	27%	—
Mixed Drinks	—	48%
Straight Liquor	—	26%
AGE OF FIRST DRINK		
After entering college	5%	4%
Before entering college	95%	96%
Before age 10	2%	10%
Between 10-13	10%	19%
Between 14-15	30%	27%
Between 15-18	53%	40%
REASONS FOR FIRST DRINK		
Peer group pressure	65%	—
Adult influence	34%	—
Other	1%	—
Parents/relatives offered	17%	32%
Curiosity	—	31%
Friends encouragement	—	16%
To feel more like adult	—	3%
To get high or drunk	—	18%

* Heavy drinking was measured differently in 1977 and 1982. In 1977 anyone who reported averaging 11 or more drinks per week was considered a "heavy drinker." In 1982, two measurements were used. First, anyone who reported that drinking "until high or drunk" was considered a "heavy drinker." Secondly, anyone scoring over 41 on the AAIS was a "misuser of alcohol." On both measurements, 16% of the students fell into the "heavy drinker/alcohol abusers" categories.

TABLE 2.2 (continued)

DRINKING BEHAVIOR	Percentages 1977	1982
DRINKING SITUATION		
Places where frequently/occasionally drink		
Own home/apartment	56%	—
Friend's house/apartment	69%	—
Dorm	35%	—
Night clubs/bars	67%	—
Restaurants	42%	—
Other	68%	—
With whom drink		
Parents or relatives only	—	2%
Brothers or sisters only	—	1%
Friends own age	—	56%
Older friends	—	34%
Alone	—	7%
Family only	6%	—
Small groups	70%	—
Large groups	24%	—
Time of Drinking		
Nighttime	—	82%
Other	—	18%

TABLE 2.3

EFFECTS OF ALCOHOL CONSUMPTION

EFFECT	Percentages	
	1977	1982
Greatest effect on life		
None/no effect	—	67%
Has interfered with talking to someone	—	6%
Has prevented from having a good time	—	3%
Has interfered with school work	—	8%
Have lost friends because of drinking	—	1%
Has gotten into trouble at home	—	7%
Was in a fight/destroyed property	—	2%
Has resulted in accident/injury, arrest or punishment at school	—	7%
Drinking has frequently or occasionally had this effect		
Interfered with class attendance	8%	—
Interfered with study	5%	—
Caused conflicts with friends	24%	—
Caused missed appointments	2%	—
Caused job loss	5%	—
Caused accident/injury	2%	—
Caused monetary hardship	7%	—
Perceptions of own drinking		
No problem at all	—	27%
I can control it and set limits on myself .	—	60%
I can control myself, but my friends easily influence me	—	7%
I often feel bad about my drinking	—	2%
I need help to control myself	—	0.5%
I have had professional help to control my drinking	—	0.5%
Perceptions of others regarding own drinking		
Can't say or a normal drinker for my age ..	—	95%
When I drink I neglect my family/friends ..	—	0%
My family/friends advise me to control or cut down	—	4%
My family/friends advise me to get help ...	—	0.5%
My family/friends have already gone for help	—	0.5%

TABLE 2.3 (continued)

EFFECT	Percentages	
	1977	1982
Worried about long-range consequences		
Frequently	8%	—
Ocassionally	29%	—
Seldom	26%	—
Never	37%	—
Worried about becoming dependent on alcohol		
Frequently	3%	—
Occasionally	13%	—
Seldom	17%	—
Never	67%	—
Greatest effect from alcohol consumption		
Loose/easy feeling	—	23%
Moderately high	—	13%
Drunk	—	10%
Became ill	—	21%
Passed out	—	11%
Didn't remember what happened the next day	—	22%

TABLE 2.4

NORMATIVE STRUCTURES OF STUDENTS IN 1982

Normative Structure	Percentages
Proscriptive	2.4%
Prescriptive	85.9%
Nonscriptive	5.1%
Other	6.6%

TABLE 2.5

RESULTS OF DUMMY VARIABLE REGRESSION ANALYSIS WITH ALCOHOL ABUSE SCORE AS DEPENDENT VARIABLE

Multiple R	0.41195
R Square	0.16970
Adj. R. Square	0.14079
Stand. Error	9.12227

Analysis of Variance of		Sum of Squares	Mean Squares	F
Regression	18.	8793.27972	488.51554	5.87046
Residual	517.	43022.58409	83.21583	

VARIABLES IN THE EQUATION

VARIABLE	B	BETA	STD ERROR B	F
Proscriptive Norms	2.20373	0.26149	3.65026	33.742
Prescriptive Norms	2.709076	0.09396	1.60759	2.840
Nonscriptive Norms	5.378346	0.12172	2.33108	5.323
Male	2.845679	0.14026	0.85242	11.144
Freshman	8.831660	0.42812	2.81890	9.816
Sophomore	7.279477	0.34118	2.80713	6.725
Junior	8.461420	0.31133	2.87874	8.639
Senior	7.059528	0.26838	2.86602	6.067
Protestant	1.605282	0.06998	1.80188	0.794
Catholic	2.350962	0.11540	1.68075	1.957
Jewish	0.633144	0.00480	5.62246	0.013
No Religion	0.607055	0.01441	2.29088	0.070
Dorm	2.798796	0.14176	2.24333	1.557
House	1.127249	0.03422	2.47891	0.207
Parents	2.815949	0.12211	2.28767	1.515
Dorm Off Campus	4.939114	0.08703	4.07773	1.467
Apartment Off Campus	5.289123	0.19461	2.37829	4.946
Frat./Sorority House	6.465595	0.04009	6.83483	0.895

INTRODUCTION TO CHAPTER 3

We have now seen that drinking behavior in a community changes over time. This implies that culture and definitions of drinking change. The culture at Time One is different than the culture at Time Two. Different cultures imply differences in behavior. Our next logical inference then is that different cultural groups may display different patterns of drinking at any single time as well as over time.

In the next chapter, Hanson and Engs raise the cultural question with regard to this country's largest minority -- American blacks. They raise the issue of cultural change over time by examining the origins of black drinking behavior in Africa, its evolution through the slave experience, and the period of migration from South to North. More important, they examine a sub-group of blacks -- college students. We have already considered white college students in some detail. Thus, we can compare black students and their white counterparts in terms of their drinking patterns. Comparing these findings to those of the two chapters which precede this is quite instructive.

CHAPTER 3
BLACK COLLEGE STUDENTS' DRINKING PATTERNS

David J. Hanson and Ruth C. Engs

ABSTRACT

In this chapter, we review the background of black drinking in the United States in general and examine drinking among black college students in particular. We have concluded that, at least today, a lower percentage of black collegians drink than do their white counterparts and that those black students who drink tend to do so less frequently, less heavily, and with fewer negative consequences than white students. We suggest implications for alcohol education, but stress that black college students are not a high-risk group in comparison to others.

BACKGROUND

Twenty years ago it was observed (Maddox and Borinski, 1964) that very little was known about the drinking behavior of blacks in general and of black collegians in particular. The same remains true even today. Blacks are the largest racial or ethnic minority in the United States, yet much more is known about the drinking behavior of smaller groups such as Jews, Italian-American, and Irish-Americans. Even the

DAVID J. HANSON is Professor and Chair of the Department of Sociology at the State University of New York's College of Arts and Sciences at Potsdam; RUTH C. ENGS is Associate Professor of Health and Safety Education at Indiana University, Bloomington and a nurse.

drinking practices of many small preliterate societies in remote parts of the world have been carefully described and documented. This stands in marked contrast to our knowledge about blacks.

It does appear that blacks in North America have drinking patterns somewhat different from the dominant white culture because of their different history. In Africa, beer drinking in religious rituals and ceremonies was common, but, like many other groups, it was done in a controlled situation and caused few, if any, alcohol-abuse problems. The early slave traders from Europe bartered rum and whiskey in exchange for black men and women in the slave trade. Upon arriving in the new world, liquor was used for a different purpose. In the United States, it was often distributed generously to slaves on holidays and as a reward for hard work and obedience. It was also used for religious celebrations and the norm was to drink quickly until drunkenness occurred (Davis, 1974; Harper, 1976, 1980).

Because alcohol was fairly readily available, it was not uncommon for slaves to drink heavily on weekends. This drinking pattern was encouraged by many slave owners as a means of pacifying their charges in an effort to keep them from escaping or causing problems. This pattern of heavy drinking on weekends is still practiced by many present-day blacks in North America.

After the Nat Turner revolt of 1830 in the United States, slave owners in many of the states realized the potential danger of mass drunkenness and its possibility of stimulating insurrection. As a result of white hysteria following this riot, a number of states enacted laws placing tighter controls on Negroes. In 1831, South Carolina passed a law prohibiting any free Negro from owning or operating a still. This legal action started a trend in the South until the Civil War. However, the prohibition regarding stills was left intact for Negroes in many southern states even after the Civil War, thus causing a lively black market in illegal liquor to flourish in that region.

Slaves and other Negroes who moved to the northern part of the United States and to Canada, where alcohol was freely available, still tended to drink in the pattern of heavy weekend or celebration drinking. The migration to the northern industrial cities caused further social upheaval. The majority of migrants were forced into slum ghettos because of discrimination, low economic status, and lack of marketable skills. For many, family structure and relationships were disrupted when black men initially had to leave wives and children behind to find work and housing in northern cities. It is thought that this stress caused some individuals to drink heavily as a means to cope with the stressful changes in their lives.

During the past century, there have been mixed signals from the dominant white culture about drinking among blacks. Some individuals felt that blacks became violent and destructive after using alcohol while others felt that drinking caused pacification. These attitudes and the religious backgrounds of most blacks, which frowned upon drinking, have led to a sense of ambivalence about consuming alcoholic beverages which still exists today in the black community.

Some research with both adult and college-age drinkers has indicated that blacks have a higher rate of problem drinking than do whites (Cahalan, 1970; Maddox and Williams, 1968; Haberman and Sheinberg, 1967; Zax et al., 1964). To the extent that drinking is used as a means to cope with anxiety, we might expect higher levels of drinking among blacks, who presumably experience greater anxiety than do whites (Higgins et al., 1977). Drinking alcoholic beverages is a learned behavior and an important source of such learning tends to be in the home. Some writers (Moynihan, 1965) have argued that the black family is disorganized or even pathological. While this view has been challenged (Hill, 1971), it suggests that drinking among blacks might be relatively uncontrolled and excessive in response to stress and turmoil. These observations, however, might be more relevant to lower status than to higher status blacks.

Religious affiliation also has a strong impact on drinking. In particular, the highest percentage of drinkers is found among Jews, a lower percentage is found among Catholics, and the lowest percentage is found among Protestants. Among Protestants, the lowest percentage tends to be found among Baptists, Methodists, and other fundamentalist groups. Since a large percentage of blacks affiliate with Baptist and other fundamentalist churches, we would expect to find a low percentage of blacks drinking. However, those individuals who drink but belong to churches that prohibit or strongly discourage drinking are much more likely to experience problems when they do drink (Hanson, 1972). Thus, we would expect a higher percentage of those blacks who do drink to experience

difficulties   as   a   result   of   their   religious
backgrounds.

COLLEGIATE PATTERNS OF DRINKING

In their classic study of drinking among 15,747
students at 27 colleges and universities during the
period 1949-1951, Straus and Bacon (1953) found the
incidence of drinking among black males to be among the
lowest of any ethnic group in the United States, but
higher than that of white males. However, the
percentage of black female drinkers was much lower than
that of any other ethnic group as well as lower than
that of white females. The percentage of black males
who had ever been intoxicated was in what could be
called the mid-range (that is, neither high nor low in
relation to the other groups). Unfortunately,
intoxication among females was not reported.

In the early 1960's, a study of black male students
was conducted (Maddox and Borinski, 1964) at a small,
Protestant, church-related, co-educational, black
college in the deep South. Ninety percent of the
students reported some current drinking compared to 81%
of black males reported by Straus and Bacon and 75% of
white students. However, the black collegians studied
by Maddox and Borinski tended to be light drinkers who
consumed alcohol infrequently and in small amounts.

The frequency of intoxication reported by these
college males compared favorably with all males
reported by Straus and Bacon. Of those students who
drank, 21% had never been "tight" compared to 20% of
those studied by Straus and Bacon. ("Tight" refers to
definite unsteadiness or loss of control, aggressive
behavior, and slight nausea.) The percentage (38%) who
had ever been drunk, which refers to intoxication

short of passing out, was identical to that reported by Straus and Bacon. Similarly, 64% reported no drinking-related social complications (such as failure to meet social or academic obligations, loss of friends or damage to friendships, accidents or injury, or formal punishment or discipline), which is almost identical to the 66% reported by Straus and Bacon. However, 57% reported one or more "warning signs" of drinking (blackouts or temporary amnesia, drunkenness while alone, drinking before or instead of breakfast, or aggressive behavior when drinking) compared to only one-third of Straus and Bacon's sample.

At about the same time, Maddox and Allen (1961) compared interview data on alcohol use from 24 white and 24 black college students and reported that 21 of the whites (87.5%) and 19 of the blacks (79.2%) were current drinkers.

In 1963, all males who entered as freshmen at a state-supported black college in North Carolina were studied by Maddox and Williams (1968), who found 76% of the students to be drinkers. This proportion is almost identical to that found among collegians in general by Straus and Bacon, whose respondents included generally older second, third, and fourth year students. Since the proportion of students who drink increased with age and year in college during this time period, it would appear that the proportion of drinkers among these freshmen was relatively high (Maddox and Williams, 1968). Additionally, a very high (25%) proportion of heavy drinkers was found. This sample of freshmen had about twice the proportion of heavy drinkers reported by Straus and Bacon among male freshmen in general.

The black freshmen compared favorably to Straus and Bacon's sample in terms of consequences of drinking. Fifty-six percent of the freshmen had never been drunk (compared to 38% for Straus and Bacon) and 84% had never passed out while drinking (compared to 66% for Straus and Bacon). Only 20% had experienced any of Straus and Bacon's social complications (versus 34%) and only 26% (versus 34%) reported at least one warning sign. However, since heavy drinking and social complications increased with years in college, freshmen would be expected to have lower percentages. The researchers concluded that "given the precocious drinking behavior of the freshmen, one may predict less favorable comparisons in each succeeding year in college" (Maddox and Williams, 1968: 124). Additionally, they exhibited a very high degree of preoccupation with alcohol, a characteristic which is frequently associated with alcoholism.

In the early 1970's, Strimbu and Sims (1974) analyzed the current and planned future use of alcohol among 1,955 black and 18,254 white college students. Of all ethnic groups studied (white, black, Indian, Oriental, and other), blacks had the lowest use score other than Orientals. Black students were also less likely than whites to report that they expected to drink in the future.

More recently, Engs (1977) studied 1,128 students at 13 colleges and universities throughout the United States and found that approximately 84% of white and 60% of black middle-class college students drank once a year or more and about three times as many whites as blacks appeared to be heavy drinkers. Further analysis indicated that only 5% of the black males were heavy drinkers compared to 22% of the white males. The percentage of heavy drinkers among female students of either race was about 5%.

Wechsler and McFadden (1979) analyzed the drinking behaviors of over 7,000 college students in New England and found an equal percentage (3.3%) of white males and females to be abstainers, while a lower proportion (1.5%) of black males and a much higher proportion of black females (12.3%) were non-drinkers. However, 30.0% of white males were frequent heavy drinkers, while only 16.2% of the black males were. Similarly, 11.3% of white females were frequent heavy drinkers while only 3.7% of black women were. Kaplan (1979) also found heavy drinking to be more common among white male college students.

Humphrey and his colleagues (Humphrey et al., 1983) studied 1,044 students at two universities in the southeastern United States. They found that whites were significantly more likely to drink to intoxication than were blacks and that men were significantly more likely to become intoxicated than were women.

In 1982, Engs and Hanson (1984) completed the first study of drinking behaviors of students at colleges in every state in the U.S. Their sample of 6,115 was drawn from 81 colleges and approximated the proportion, as indicated by the Yearbook of Higher Education (1982), of students attending four-year institutions of higher learning in terms of institutional size, support (public or private), community size, and racial composition of student body. Subsequent analysis revealed that while 85.4% of the white students drank at least once a year, only 58.2% of the black students did (see Table 3.1, page 76). Of students who drank, 26.1% of the blacks drank infrequently while only 9.2% of the whites were infrequent drinkers. On the other

70

hand, 26.4% of the white students who drank were heavy drinkers while only 7.3% of the black students fell into that category (see Table 3.2, page 77).

Since the white college students tended to be much heavier drinkers than were the blacks, it is not surprising that whites tended to experience more difficulties as a result of their drinking (see Table 3.3, page 78). Students were asked to report the following occurrences:

- had a hangover
- gotten nauseated and vomited from drinking
- driven a car <u>after</u> having several drinks
- drinking <u>while</u> driving a car
- come to class after having several drinks
- "cut a class" after having several drinks
- missed a class because of a hangover
- arrested for DWI (driving while intoxicated)
- been criticized by a date because of drinking
- gotten into trouble with the law because of drinking
- lost a job because of drinking
- gotten a lower grade because of drinking
- gotten into trouble with the school administration because of behavior resulting from drinking too much
- gotten into a fight after drinking
- thought might be having a problem with drinking
- damaged property, pulled a false fire alarm, or other such behavior after drinking.

71

In every case except one, a much higher proportion of whites had experienced the behavior. The only exception was that more blacks than whites reported having lost a job because of drinking (1.5% compared to 0.8%).

In summary, research suggests that, at least today, a lower percentage of black collegians drink and that those who drink tend to do so less frequently, less heavily, and with fewer negative consequences than white students.

IMPLICATIONS

Black college students come from a variety of social, educational, and geographic backgrounds, and alcohol education should take into account these differences. It would appear that carefully tailored and targeted efforts would have the greater chance for success.

In the face of evidence that much alcohol and drug education is ineffective (Hanson, 1982), it is important to take special efforts to enhance the chances of achieving success. Any preventative education undertaken should be tailored so as to be as effective as possible among black collegians.

Alcohol education should also employ themes and symbols relevant to black culture. Specific effort should be made for these materials or methods to enhance students' self-concepts.

Alcohol education targeted for black females should stress their "independence and aggressiveness," their possible victimization from alcohol-related assaults, child-care concerns, and physiological matters of potential concern (pregnancy, fetal alcohol syndrome, and so on). These concerns may sometimes differ in type and degree from those of many white women (Harper, 1979).

However, the major implication of this chapter is that black collegians are not a high-risk group in comparison to others. Thus, some alcohol-education funds could be allocated to other purposes for which the need might be greater.

REFERENCES

Cahalan, D. 1970. Problem Drinkers. San Francisco: Jossey-Bass.

Davis, F. 1974. Alcoholism among American Blacks. Addictions 3(2):8-16.

Engs, R. 1977. Drinking patterns and problems of college students. Journal of Studies on Alcohol 38(11):2144-2156.

Haberman, P. and Sheinberg, J. 1967. Implicative drinking reported in a household survey: A corroborative note on sub-group differences. Quarterly Journal of Studies on Alcohol 28(4):538-543.

Hanson, D. 1972. Alcohol Norms and Deviant Drinking Behavior. Unpublished Ph.D. dissertation, Syracuse University.

Hanson, D. 1982. The effectiveness of alcohol and drug education. Journal of Alcohol and Drugs 13:151-165.

Hanson, D. and Engs, R. 1984. College students' drinking attitudes: 1970-1982. Psychological Reports 54:300-302.

Harper, F. (Ed.) 1976. Alcohol Abuse and Black America. Alexandria, VA: Douglass Publishers.

Harper, F. 1979. Alcoholism Treatment and Black Americans. Rockville, MD: National Institute on Alcohol Abuse and Alcoholism.

Harper, F. 1980. Research and treatment with Black alcoholics. *Alcohol Health and Research World* 4(4):15-21.

Higgins, P., Albrecht, G., and Albrecht, M. 1977. Black-white adolescent drinking: The myth and the reality. *Social Problems* 25(2):215-224.

Hill, R. 1971. *The Strengths of Black Families*. New York: Emerson Hall.

Humphrey, J., Stephens, V., and Allen, D. 1983. Race, sex, marijuana use, and alcohol intoxication in college students. *Journal of Studies on Alcohol* 44(4):733-738.

Kaplan, M. 1979. Patterns of alcoholic beverage use among college students. *Journal of Alcohol and Drug Education* 24(2):26-40.

Maddox, G. and Allen, B. 1961. A comparative study of social definitions of alcohol and its use among selected male Negro and White undergraduates. *Quarterly Journal of Studies on Alcohol* 22(3):418-427.

Maddox, G. and Borinski, E. 1964. Drinking behavior of Negro collegians. *Quarterly Journal of Studies on Alcohol* 25(4):651-668.

Maddox, G. and Williams, J. 1968. Drinking behavior of Negro collegians. *Quarterly Journal of Studies on Alcohol* 29(1):117-129.

Marquis Academic Media. 1982. *Yearbook of Higher Education*. Chicago: Author.

Moynihan, D. 1965. *The Negro Family: The Case for National Action*. Washington, DC: U.S. Department of Labor.

National Institute on Alcohol Abuse and Alcoholism. *Alcohol and Blacks: Alcohol Topics in Brief*. Rockville, MD.

Straus, R. and Bacon, S. 1953. *Drinking in College*. New Haven: Yale University Press.

Strimbu, A. and Sims, O. 1974. A university system drug profile. *International Journal of the Addictions* 9(4):569-583.

Wechsler, H. and McFadden, M. 1979. Drinking among college students in New England. *Journal of Studies on Alcohol* 40(11):969-996.

Zax, M., Gardner, E., and Hart, W. 1964. Public intoxication in Rochester: A survey of individuals charged driving in 1961. <u>Quarterly Journal of Studies on Alcohol</u> 25(4):669-678.

APPENDIX

TABLE 3.1

QUANTITY-FREQUENCY CATEGORIES BY
RACE FOR TOTAL SAMPLE IN PERCENT

Quantity-Frequency Category* Percentages					
Race	Abstainer	Infrequent Drinker	Light Drinker	Moderate Drinker	Moderate Heavy Drinker	Heavy Drinker
White	14.6%	7.6%	11.3%	19.0%	25.2%	22.3%
Black	41.8%	13.8%	11.7%	17.4%	10.9%	4.4%

$$x^2 = 458.4, \underline{df} = 5, \underline{p} = <.0001$$

---

* The quantity-frequency category for each subject was calculated from the beverage (beer, wine, or distilled spirits) most frequently used and the amount consumed on typical occasions. This placed the drinker into the category of ABSTAINER, drinking less than once a year or not at all; INFREQUENT DRINKER, drinking more than once a year but less than once a month; LIGHT DRINKER, drinking at least once a month but not more than 1 to 3 drinks at any one sitting; MODERATE DRINKER, drinking at least once a month with no more than 3 to 4 drinks or at least once a week with no more than 1 to 2 drinks at any one sitting; MODERATE HEAVY DRINKER, drinking 3 to 4 drinks at least once a week or drinking 5 or more drinks at least once a month; HEAVY DRINKER, drinking 6 or more at any one sitting more than once a week.

76

TABLE 3.2

QUANTITY-FREQUENCY CATEGORIES BY
RACE FOR DRINKERS IN PERCENT

Quantity-Frequency Category Percentages

Race	Infrequent Drinker	Light Drinker	Moderate Drinker	Moderate Heavy Drinker	Heavy Drinker
White	9.2%	13.2%	21.9%	29.2%	26.4%
Black	26.1%	18.8%	29.7%	18.2%	7.3%

$x^2 = 143.3$, $\underline{df} = 4$, $\underline{p} = <.001$

TABLE 3.3

PERCENTAGE OF STUDENTS WHO HAVE
EXHIBITED SELECTED BEHAVIORS

Behavior	Race Percentages	
	White	Black
Had a hangover	82.3%	58.1%
Gotten nauseated and vomited from drinking	76.9%	49.5%
Driven a car _after_ having several drinks	73.2%	39.8%
Driven a car when you know you have had too much to drink	60.1%	20.3%
Had a drink _while_ driving a car	59.8%	32.4%
Came to class after having several drinks	19.3%	12.0%
"Cut a class" after having several drinks	17.2%	10.1%
Missed a class because of a hangover	32.8%	12.4%
Arrested for driving while intoxicated	2.5%	2.1%
Criticized by a date because of drinking	21.2%	16.3%
Had trouble with the law because of drinking	11.4%	3.1%
Lost a job because of drinking	0.8%	1.5%
Got a lower grade because of drinking too much	10.0%	4.8%
Gotten into trouble with the school administration because of behavior resulting from drinking too much	5.0%	3.5%
Gotten into a fight after drinking	23.3%	11.3%
Thought might have a problem with drinking	18.3%	6.2%
Damaged property, pulled false fire alarm, or other such behavior after drinking	22.2%	6.7%

78

SUMMARY: U.S. ALCOHOL USE BY ADOLESCENTS

What we have learned thus far is that alcohol use begins at an early age. If we generalize from Wylie et al. (Chapter 1), we find that it is already present among adolescents in a small town, that it is more common among males than among females, and that it is more common among those who are less well-integrated into such institutions as family and church.

Looking at a slightly older population (Iutcovich and Vaughn, Chapter 2), we learn that drinking patterns have changed over time. Further, we find that alcohol use increases for individuals as they age. As earlier, those who are better integrated into other social institutions drink less.

It is when we consider the work of Hanson and Engs (Chapter 3) that we get special insights into some of our primary concerns. Drinking has a different meaning among black college students and, in fact, for blacks generally, than it does for comparable white populations. Rates of drinking are lower for blacks than they are for a comparable white population as well.

Our conclusions then are that drinking behavior is, in part, a feature of the life cycle, that it differs by sexes, and that it is different from one sub-culture to another. These are findings which will assume importance later in the sections which follow.

SECTION 2
U.S. SUBSTANCE USE BY ADOLESCENTS

INTRODUCTION

In Section 1 we examined use of alcohol by adolescents, college students, and black college students. In the course of the discussion, we paid particular attention to the existence of patterns of use and found that, indeed, there were specific factors which were associated with use or non-use of alcohol.

In particular, we found that use of alcohol changed over time in a single community, that it changed through the life cycle, and that it was different from one subcultural group to another.

From these initial findings we are led to speculate about some of the causes of drinking behavior. We find that, by and large, it is accepted behavior which is normatively prescribed by peer groups and not strongly sanctioned by adults. It seems to already be present in some populations by adolescence. Further, we note that legal sanctions are by and large minimal, despite the fact that there are, indeed, laws regulating use of alcohol by these age groups.

Of importance is the fact that alcohol is legally or semi-legally available in this society. Further, it is plentiful, being found in most homes, and legally purchasable in liquor stores and drinking establishments in most communities.

Having considered use of alcohol, we may now turn our attention to the early patterns of use of illegal drugs in addition to alcohol. Drugs are not nearly as plentiful as alcohol and are subject to severe legal sanction. Will we find similar patterns of use to those seen in alcohol or will they be different? Having been alerted to the widespread use of alcohol by adolescents (Chapter 1, Wylie et al.), we are led to wonder just how early drug use enters as well. Next we must consider what factors predict this early drug use. From there we can ask whether there is a progression of drug use as people move towards adulthood.

INTRODUCTION TO CHAPTER 4

Even as Wylie et al. (Chapter 1) alert us to the early use of alcohol in rural adolescent populations, Forster takes us in search of the earliest use of both alcohol and illegal drugs. In contrast to Wylie et al., Forster studies a well-to-do suburban community. Beginning with fifth and sixth-graders, the researcher finds surprising rates of use and patterns of use.

Of particular value is her review of major theories of drug and alcohol use. She identifies these as:
1. Pathological;
2. Alienation;
3. Subcultural; and
4. Normative.

With an empirical data base, she then goes on to test each of these theories of drug use. By doing this, Forster provides us some surprising insights into how widespread the use of alcohol and drugs is at very early ages.

There are a number of things that we gain from this chapter. First, Forster provides a good example of the interplay between theory and research. Her theory is a guide for the data which she will collect and further directs her data analysis.

Second, having identified several competing theories of early drinking and drug use, she gathers data which test how well each theory predicts her findings. Thus, she is able to reject one theory as an explanation for these results. She then finds that her study sample can be sub-divided: one type of theory seems to work well for one group and another type of theory seems to work better for another group. Finally, having identified the pattern of use, she is able to speculate about the causes of drug and alcohol use and to suggest means to prevention.

CHAPTER 4

MIDDLE-CLASS PRE-TEEN DRUG USE: PATTERNS AND FACTORS

Brenda Forster

ABSTRACT

The purpose of this chapter is to determine the patterns and factors of illegal drug use by a suburban, middle-class population of 752 ten and eleven year olds.

Seventy-two percent of fifth graders had already used alcoholic beverages -- wine

---

BRENDA FORSTER is Professor of Sociology at Elmhurst College and a nurse.

introduced in family settings. About a fourth of ten year olds were involved with beer, hard liquor, and cigarettes. Four percent were using marijuana. These early used drugs were also the three most popular drugs used by teens and adults. Early drug users had parents who were reported to use alcohol frequently, were willing to disobey their parents, and had enough money to purchase drugs. A smaller portion of this early drug-using group of ten year olds had older siblings who used drugs. And a minority were experiencing family, school, and emotional troubles.

These affluent youth reported that they tried drugs to find out what they were like, rather than because of peer pressure or rebellion against parents. They continued using a drug in social settings because of positive physiological effects and the drugs' availability and acceptability. Suggestions are made for prevention programs based on these findings.

INTRODUCTION

The events of the 1960's gave impetus to concern about use of drugs by youth in the U.S. Early studies used college students (18 to 21 year olds) who were readily accessible to researchers and who were the main initiators of drug use in the 1960's. Later some studies focused on high school students (14 to 17 year olds) as use of drugs spread to younger students (for example, Blum et al., 1970). The study reported here is unique in having affluent, suburban, upper-middle-class youth in fifth and sixth grades (10 and 11 year olds). The full study reported elsewhere (see Forster, 1984; Richards, Berk, and Forster, 1979, and Forster, 1977) included fifth graders through high school, but my focus in this discussion will be on the elementary school data.

We gained access to this population because a concerned parent group in the community wanted to know the extent of drug use among their children and the factors associated with drug use so they could take action. The community did have a drug education program at the junior high level (12 and 13 year olds). At the same time, we had a slightly different focus for our activities. Besides being able to study a population to which research access is usually denied, we were interested in determining which of the many predicative factors given in previous studies of drug use were most important when analyzed together. That is, previous drug studies had been either descriptive (how many students are using what drugs) or had tested one theoretical or casual idea rather than several to guide the questions and interpretation.

THEORIES ABOUT DRUG USE

There were four main theories explaining drug use which the various studies had used previously. Some studies used a Pathological view which instructs one to look for 1) disturbed psychological states among drug users (poor self-image, hostility, alienation), 2) social isolation (non-participation in normal school, family and community activities), 3) a history of family disorganization or stress (broken homes, working mothers, inadequate and/or intermittent family income, family conflicts, improper family socialization repre-

----
I acknowledge with gratitude the help of Dr. Richard Berk and Pamela Richards in preparing the study and analyzing the data on which this article is based. The study was funded by the Youth Commission of the suburb in which the study was done.

sented by poor rule enforcement, and lack of home responsibilities), 4) a strong tendency to use drugs to escape life and its problems, and 5) chronic, heavy, multi-drug involvement. The cause of drug use in the Pathological view is seen as stemming from improperly socialized, psychologically disturbed individuals and/or disorganized, disturbed social environments.

The Alienation view became prevalent during the 1960's to explain how "decent" middle-class youth could be using drugs previously associated with lower-class minorities. In this model, estrangement from self, others, social institutions, and accepted values is characteristic of drug users. Users show 1) a deeper, more serious sense of powerlessness (feeling that they are not taken seriously, that nothing they do makes any difference, and that they are ordered about and hassled by everyone), 2) dissatisfaction with themselves (feeling that no one likes them and not liking their own sex), and 3) general discontent (bored, worried about the future, and angry at parents and school authorities). In addition to subjective measures of attitudes, there may also be objective indicators such as social isolation from family, lack of school and community involvement, and rejection of usually valued educational and/or career goals. It is also to be expected that alienated drug users would hold unconventional attitudes toward use of drugs. The emphasis of this Alienation perspective is on the individual's lack of conventional values and goals as the source for non-conforming behavior.

The Subcultural model posits the existence of a drug culture distinct from the general non-using adolescent culture. This sub-group is comprised of interacting peers whose activities center on drug use and whose values regarding drug-using behavior are not shared by their non-using peers. Involvement in a drug subculture is shown by 1) reduced conventional involvements in the family, school, and community, 2) attitudes which accept and value use of drugs, and 3) association primarily with other drug users.

Finally, a few researchers viewed drug use as Normative. According to this idea, youth view drugs as a normal part of adult social and recreational activities. This view focuses on the presence of positive customers, values, sanctions, and role models surrounding the use of drugs. Persons see significant others (peers and family members) using drugs and accept it as expected behavior, particularly when the behavior is widespread. In addition, they are exposed to positive evaluations and justifications for use of drugs which provide a reinforcement for the behavior.

To summarize, together the four theories indicated that we had to measure the following factors in order to find out which factors were the most important:

Pathological View
    Disturbed Psychological States
    Social Isolation
    Family Disorganization
    Family Stress
    Drug Use to Escape Life's Problems
    Chronic, Heavy, Multi-Drug Involvement
Alienation View
    Sense of Powerlessness
    Self-Dissatisfaction
    General Discontent
Subcultural View
    Reduced Family, School and Community In-
      volvements

Attitudes Accepting and Valuing Drugs

Association with a Small Group of Drug Users

Normative View

Parental Drug Use and Acceptance of Drug Use for Social Occasions

Peer Drug Use in Social and Relaxation Settings

Which of these models is most accurate is important not only for testing theories but also for guiding the design of prevention and education programs to change youth drug-using behaviors. We hoped our study would shed light on the development of drug use, and, therefore, investigated pre-teens' contact with drugs in order to discover the earliest causes of drug use.

Our questions is what are the patterns and predictors (causes) of pre-teen drug use, and what does that information suggest for prevention?

METHOD

Because of the sensitive and controversial, as well as illegal nature of the questions we asked, we took elaborate precautions to preserve anonymity and confidentiality (see Forster, 1977). We also spent considerable preparatory time in meetings with community adults, officials, and students to explain our purpose and role. In spite of these measures, we were almost prevented from carrying out the study when a lawyer parent threatened an injunction against us. While any researcher has to assure the cooperation of the group to be studied, affluent communities pose special difficulties and indeed often refuse research.

We designed three equivalent forms of our questionnaire since the study spanned 8 grade levels

87

(one for 5th and 6th grade, and one for 7th and 8th grade, one for high school). While the high school questionnaire, with some 293 variables, was the most complex, we made sure that the core questions on drug experimentation (ever tried the drug) and use (using the drug within the previous 6 months of school) were contained in all the questionnaires. The questionnaires were self-administered during a regular class period by 752 elementary students, 842 junior high students, and 1,240 high schoolers. This was 90% of the students enrolled in the school system the spring of 1975.

The drugs investigated were alcohol, cigarettes, marijuana, inhalants, psychedelics, "uppers," "downers," cocaine, heroin, and narcotics (see Table 4.1, page 97).

DRUG-USING PATTERNS

In any analysis of social phenomena, one must first assess the prevalence of the behavior. The patterns give one a sense of what is going on and are necessary in order to judge both the applicability of the findings and the extent of general versus limited casual circumstances.[1]

Originally, we had believed that going back as far as fifth grade (10 year olds) would allow us to pinpoint the beginnings of drug use. We found that this belief was naive. Among fifth and sixth graders, 3/4 had had previous experience with wine and more than 1/3 had taken wine in the previous six months. Another

----
[1] While my focus in this discussion is on the youngest students, Table 4.2, page 98, presents the summary data for the three groups of students. This information helps to put the drug using behavior of the pre-teens into its fuller social context.

question allowed us to determine that most of these students had wine in a family context -- holidays, family meals or a family party. However, almost 1/4 had taken hard liquor by this age, almost 10% in the previous six months. About 1/4 were already sampling cigarettes ("to find out what it was like" another question told us), and a small percentage were experimenting with marijuana. As the findings show, these three drugs -- alcohol, marijuana and cigarettes -- continued to be the most popularly used drugs across the grades. High school seniors in this population indicated that 83% of them were using alcohol, 53% were using marijuana, and 34% were using cigarettes.

The next most popular grouping of drugs was psychedelics, "uppers," and "downers." But their use began later in high school and fewer students used them (10-17%). Cocaine and other narcotics had been tried by fewer than 1% of these affluent elementary schoolers. (Since the time of this study, use of cocaine has increased slightly while use of marijuana has decreased a bit.) Inhalants and heroin were not being used by this age group or by older teens.

One interesting finding was that females' experimentation and use of these drugs, including the most popular drugs, lagged substantially behind that of males until the ninth grade freshman group. Then the girls use patterns were more similar to that of junior males. This probably reflects the introduction to drug use by male boyfriends. Girls tend to begin dating as freshmen in high school and often date males a year or two older. In this younger age group, girls' drug use is substantially less than same-aged boys.

Older students told us that they use drugs (alcohol and marijuana primarily) in social settings -- parties and small gatherings of friends -- where others are using the same drugs and where it is considered appropriate (Table 4.3, page 99). These 10 year olds are included in alcohol use at parental and sibling parties and try cigarettes and marijuana in small gatherings of friends. Initially, these youth use drugs (especially the popular alcohol, cigarettes, and marijuana) out of curiosity, "to find out what it is like"; later, a drug is continued for its rewarding effects, "to relax." Few of the students believed that they used drugs because of peer pressure, "to be liked," or "because it's cool." Nor did they view their drug use as a means of acting out against parents or authorities (see Table 4.4, page 100).

In summary, almost 3/4 of these affluent pre-teens have had experience with alcohol (wine) in family settings. A fourth were using hard liquor, a fourth cigarettes, and 4% marijuana. A drug is commonly tried, according to these youths, "to find out what it is like" not because of peer pressure, and continued for its rewarding physical effects in social and recreational settings where its use is accepted.

FACTORS ASSOCIATED WITH USE OF DRUGS

Now that we have a sense of the patterns and context of drug use, we need to investigate the factors which are most closely associated with drug experimentation and use by these pre-teens. This information will help us understand the stimulus of drug use and thereby imply possible preventions (see Table 4.5, page 101).

The various measures of respondent background, family rules and rule enforcement, respondent school and career goals, and activity involvement were not very useful as drug use predictors. Only disobeying parents and amount of weekly spending money were important for the younger students. Both of these factors make sense. To use drugs illegally at this age, a child has to be willing to disobey his or her parents. And purchasing drugs costs money which a child must have to actually obtain the drug. Of less importance was having an older sibling (important for use of drugs other than alcohol), disliking school, and more frequently missing school. Poor school work is important only for youths who use the least popular, most serious drugs. Most of the traditional measures of social pathology were not important -- working mother, broken home, family rules and conflicts, and extracurricular involvements.

The variables measuring parental, sibling, and friend drug use were consistently the best predictors. Parental drug using behavior had a strong effect on pre-teens. Parents' use of alcohol was the most important predictor of youth alcohol use. And the more frequently alcohol was reported to be used by parents, the more likely the child was to use alcohol. The use of alcohol by parents also had a positive effect on youth use of other drugs, but the relationship was not as strong as it was with child alcohol use. Second in importance was the influence of siblings. Siblings' use was the primary influence for pre-teens' use of drugs other than alcohol and of secondary influence on alcohol use. Finally, friends' use of drugs was of least importance (and quite a bit less important) and was drug specific (if the respondent had friends who used alcohol he/she was more likely to use alcohol, with friends who use marijuana, the respondent was more likely to use marijuana, and so on). While the other analyses indicate that parental influence decreased over the grades and peer influence increased, in the younger age groups parental influence is still most important. This finding is also consistent with the belief that parents have less impact on their children as they move toward adulthood while peers move to the fore.[2]

The variables measuring respondents' sense of alienation, powerlessness, low self-esteem, and hostility toward authorities were of lowest importance. Given the young age of these respondents, this finding is not really surprising. At this age very few students are actually regularly using any drugs. Mostly they are just beginning to try drugs experimentally. However, we can be aware of the patterns even though they are weak. Youth who try using hard liquor and cigarettes tend to feel angry. There are some associations of drug use with "feeling no one listens," "being unliked," and "feeling ordered around." At the same time and perhaps surprisingly, "feeling happy to be alive" is the most important and consistent psychological predictor of drug use. These variables did not survive the simultaneous test. That the psychological variables were not shown to be

---

[2]   This study drew upon research by Krandel (1975:912) who acted as a consultant to our questionnaire construction. Her data based on high school students shows the impact of peers over parents. Our data adds to hers by demonstrating the strong impact of parents on younger students' drug-using behaviors.

strong factors in drug use of pre-teens may indicate that, in my data at least, psychological difficulties are associated with drug use for some children, but that most are responding more strongly to role models (parents and peers) and to social expectations.

In summary, the analyses highlighted several factors which were important in explaining the drug use of these middle-class pre-teens. Of primary importance was parents' role-model influence especially for use of alcohol and cigarettes. Older siblings provided both a model and access to use of marijuana. These early drug users were willing to disobey their parents, had enough spending money to purchase drugs, and felt happy to be alive. A minority (fewer than 10%) of these early drug users disliked and missed school, got poor grades, and felt unliked, ordered around, and not listened to. Youth who try cigarettes and hard liquor tended to feel more angry than non-users.

The data from this study indicates that most of these ten year olds experimented with drugs (especially alcohol, marijuana, and cigarettes) when exposed to drug use by role models and when given opportunity to find out what the drug is like. Then they continued to use a drug to enjoy its physiological and social effects. These findings fit the Normative model. A minority (fewer than 10% of drug users) did show some signs of psychological and social (school) problems. These students tended to use the harder, less popular drugs as well. Their behavior better fits the Alienation or Pathological models.

PREVENTION CONCLUSIONS

In this section, I am going to go beyond the findings of the study in order to discuss some prevention applications which might be drawn from the data. Keep in mind, however, that this data is taken from a suburban, middle-class, well-educated, white group of pre-teens. While our usage findings parallel other national studies of the same time period, we can not be absolutely certain that the factors are similar.

My data suggests that there may be at least two groups using drugs -- one group which has no serious social or psychological disturbances who seek sensation and social fit (the "normals") and another group (10% or fewer of the students in my sample) who do have some social and emotional disturbances (the "troubled"). It is the "troubled" who I would expect to be more likely to become addicted to drugs and to act out in other ways against society. They are more likely to need counseling help. They are also likely to be among the youngest users of the popular drugs as well as the main users of the less popular drugs. They have more school problems.

The "normals" mostly use the popular drugs. The progression or spread of drug use, as my data depicts it, is that most of these children are introduced to wine at home at very young ages. At ten years of age, a fourth of the youth (those who believe their parents use alcohol fairly often along with some youth who have older siblings using drugs) are experimenting with the most popular teen and adult drugs -- alcohol (beer and hard liquor), marijuana, and cigarettes. These early users serve as role models for their friends who see no untoward effects of use of these drugs and who, as they

94

enter high school, mix in social settings where these drugs are accepted and used.

Drug-education programs as they are normally done -- using scare tactics to emphasize the awful consequences of drug use by showing "horror" cases -- are not a deterrent to "normal" pre-teen drug use. In my study, while all students were required to take the school drug-education course in junior high (12-13 year olds), only half of them mentioned it as a source of drug knowledge. Other questions indicated that many of those who did list the drug program found it to be misleading and stimulated a need to turn for guidance to their friends who were using the drugs without appearing to experience the dire consequences the drug program warned about. Other of my information indicated that "normals" avoided those drugs they believed were more harmful and hard to get. As I indicated, once they reached high school and began dating, girls were highly influenced by their older male dates.

It seems to me that for the "normal" group, prevention programs must begin earlier than fifth grade (10 year olds) and must involve parents who introduce their young children to the social acceptability of drug use. Youth need help in recognizing and resisting the subtle effects of peer pressure. Apparently, youth either are not aware of the influence of their friends or are not willing to admit even to themselves that they are so influenced. Youthful desires to try new experiences, "to find out what it is like," and to seek sensation need to be recognized and channels other than use of drugs need to be available. Cohen (1971) has useful suggestions for alternatives to the main effects that drugs produce. Drug education programs should help youth evaluate the positive reasons for drug use (social, recreation, good effects, experimentation, and so on) and then work on alternatives to meet those goals. Value clarification techniques and assertive, "no-saying," training could help pre-teens formulate and follow more healthful, less abusive behavior for themselves.

REFERENCES

Blum, R. H. et al. 1970. Drugs II: College and High School Students and Drugs. San Francisco: Jossey Bass.

Cohen, A. Y. 1971. The journey beyond trips: Alternative to drugs. Journal of Psychedelic Drugs 3:16-21.

Forster, B. 1977. Middle Class Adolescent Drug Use: Deviance or Normative Learning? Ann Arbor: University Microfilms.

Forster, B. 1984. Upper middle class adolescent drug use: Patterns and factors. Advances in Alcohol and Substance Use 4:27-36.

Richards, P., Berk, R., and Forster, B. 1979. Crime as Play. Cambridge, MA: Ballinger Press.

TABLE 4.1

VARIABLE SETS USED FOR TESTING DRUG USE EXPLANATORY MODELS

PUSH
(Social Structural Background)

General Demographic
Education/Career Goals
Family Involvement/Conflict
School Involvement
Community Involvement
Financial/Work Independence

PULL
(Role Model/Subcultural
Associations)

Parental Drug Use
Sibling Drug Use
Peer Drug Use

PSYCH
(Subjective Attitudes)

Alienation/Hostility
Drug-Use Beliefs

DEVIANCE
(Behavioral Output)

Drug Experimentation, Use

Alcohol
Marijuana
Cigarettes
Inhalants
Psychedelics
Uppers
Downers
Cocaine
Heroin
Narcotics

TABLE 4.2

PERCENTAGE USE AND EXPERIMENTATION OF DRUGS AND AVERAGE NUMBER OF TIMES THE DRUG WAS USED IN 6 MONTHS BY STUDENTS

DRUGS*	Ever Used			Used in Previous 6 Months				
	5th & 6th Graders** (752) %	7th & 8th Graders (842) %	High Schoolers (1,240) %	5th & 6th Graders (752) %	7th & 8th Graders (842) %	MEAN USE	High Schoolers (1,240) %	MEAN USE
Wine	73	—	—	37	—	—	—	—
Alcohol	23	57	85	9	56	6.00	83	21.20
Cigarettes	27	55	—	21	30	—	34	—
Marijuana	4	19	58	3	19	3.90	53	20.96
Psychedelics	—	2	20	—	5	0.18	17	0.98
Uppers	—	—	19	—	—	—	16	1.90
Downers	—	—	14	—	—	—	10	0.62
Cocaine	—	—	10	—	—	—	9	0.41
Narcotics	—	2	9	—	2	0.09	5	0.35
Pills	—	5	—	—	5	0.18	—	—
Other	1	—	—	1	—	—	—	—

* Since there was almost no use of heroin and inhalants, they are not reported here.

** The respective age groupings are 10-11 year olds (5th and 6th grade), 12-13 year olds (7th and 8th grade), and 14-17 year olds (high school).

TABLE 4.3

WHERE DRUGS ARE USED
BY HIGH SCHOOLERS WHO USE THEM

Situation	Drugs Percentages	
	Alcohol	Other Drugs
Parties and dances	66%	41%
Small gatherings of friends	56%	40%
Concerts and movies	34%	35%
Alone with the opposite sex	30%	20%
Religious occasions	22%	0%
On dates	21%	15%
When there's nothing else to do	19%	21%
Before sleeping	4%	5%
Studying	2%	3%
Before sports	2%	3%

TABLE 4.4

WHY CIGARETTES ARE USED
BY STUDENTS WHO HAVE USED THEM

| Reason | Percentages | |
	5th & 6th Graders	7th & 8th Graders
To find out what it's like	58%	33%
To relax	14%	40%
Fr ause it's "cool"	16%	15%
To feel good	12%	13%
To feel older	13%	10%
To be liked	10%	13%
To get away with it	7%	6%
To annoy parents	3%	3%
To feel friendly	2%	8%
To annoy teachers	1%	2%

NOTE FOR TABLE 4.5

In order to test the predictive usefulness of the many independent variables we measured, three statistical measures were used from regression analysis -- 1) the proportion of variance explained (R^2) as a test of the "best set" of variables, 2) the raw regression coefficient (b) as a measure of the importance of each independent variable, and 3) the part correlation squared to show the unique contribution of each variable. Tests of significance were not used since the data base was a population, not a sample. The PUSH, PULL, and PSYCH variable groupings were first tested independently for each data set and each drug for both trial and use. Then the best of the predictors of the 3 sub-groupings were tested simultaneously. Because of the extensive nature of this data, only the final table for Fifth and Sixth grade (10 and 11 year olds) is given here.

TABLE 4.5

FIFTH AND SIXTH GRADE STUDENTS: MAJOR VARIABLES RELATED TO DRUG USE

	A	B	C	D	E	F	G	H	I	J	K	L	M	N
Tried wine or beer*	.14	.39				.149** (.027)***					.098 (.064)			.067 (.021)
Use wine or beer	.17	.12	.077 (.011)					.112 (.015)			.129 (.083)			
Tried hard liquor	.21	.03		.030 (.013)				.085 (.011)			.106 (.059)		.091 (.012)	
Use hard liquor	.18	-.01		.031 (.011)							.051 (.032)		.115 (.044)	
Tried marijuana	.55	-.03		.029 (.010)					.123 (.017)	.566 (.226)			.062 (.016)	
Use marijuana	.36	-.00					.255 (.026)	.113 (.041)	.112 (.025)				.060 (.041)	

* Experimentation and use responses: "No" = 0; "Yes" = 1
** Regression coefficient
*** Unique variance explained

KEY A = R Squared value; B = Intercept; C = Disobeys parents; D = Amount of weekly spending money; E = Average of school work; F = Father's use of alcohol; G = Parents' use of marijuana; H = Siblings' use of alcohol; I = Siblings' use of marijuana; J = Siblings' use of drugs; K = Friends' use of alcohol; L = Friends' use of cigarettes; M = Friends' use of marijuana; N = Feels no one listens.

TABLE 4.5 (continued)

	A	B	C	D	E	F	G	H	I	J	K	L	M	N
Tried cigarettes	.20	-.00	.102 (.022)						.157 (.012)		.058 (.015)	.135 (.058)		
Use cigarettes	.30	-.03	.097 (.024)						.158 (.015)			.165 (.136)		
Tried other drugs	.58	.00					.218 (.020)			.425 (.440)				
Use other drugs					-.014 (.013)		.180 (.040)			.115 (.090)		-.012 (.090)	.042 (.011)	-.01 (.010)

*   Experimentation and use responses: "No" = 0;   "Yes" = 1
**   Regression coefficient
***   Unique variance explained

KEY   A = R Squared value; B = Intercept; C = Disobeys parents; D = Amount of weekly spending money; E = Average of school work; F = Father's use of alcohol; G = Parents' use of marijuana; H = Siblings' use of alcohol; I = Siblings' use of marijuana; J = Siblings' use of drugs; K = Friends' use of alcohol; L = Friends' use of cigarettes; M = Friends' use of marijuana; N = Feels no one listens.

INTRODUCTION TO CHAPTER 5

Forster has alerted us to the remarkably early age at which drinking and drug use is initiated in a middle-income suburb. In the next chapter, Coombs and Fawzy take us another step along the life cycle. They review the literature on use of alcohol and drugs among adolescents and alert us particularly to the increase in simultaneous drug use. They delineate for us not only the frequency of use as reported in the literature but the physical and social effects of simultaneous use as well.

Having identified and specified the problem, Coombs and Fawzy next attempt to assess the pattern of drug and alcohol use in a non-random survey of adolescents. They use an epidemiological approach to their research, breaking their sample into users and abstainers. They then asked whether a long list of potentially related factors such as broken homes, familial substance abuse, peer use, and so on is associated with drug use or abstaining. In this way, they provide a test of a number of implicit theories of drug and alcohol use; for example, use is related to family disruption, use is related to peer use, and so on.

Their conclusions are enlightening. Dealing with an age group somewhat older than Forster's (Chapter 4), their findings both support that work as well as that of Wylie et al. (Chapter 1) and of Iutcovich and Vaughn (Chapter 2). Coombs and Fawzy then take us a few steps further into the lives of the adolescents.

Their results are, on the one hand, encouraging. We find that the development of patterns of use are consistent from small towns and rural areas (Wylie et al.) to the cities of California and from pre-teens

(Forster) through to college (Iutcovich and Vaughn). On the other hand, Coombs and Fawzy paint a picture of danger in multiple drug use that is frightening.

Beginning with the pattern they find and the associated factors, they give us some direction in seeking prevention.

CHAPTER 5

ADOLESCENT DRUG USE: PATTERNS AND PROBLEMS OF USERS AND ABSTAINERS

Robert H. Coombs and Fawzy I. Fawzy

ABSTRACT

This chapter analyzes the social and familial factors related to alcohol and drug use among teenagers. The research involves an analysis of interviews with teenage subjects (half of whom use drugs and half of whom abstain) and with their parents.

Results fail to support popular explanations of juvenile substance use. Users are not more likely to come from broken homes or to belong to families that are economically disadvantaged.

ROBERT H. COOMBS is Professor of Biobehavioral Sciences at the UCLA School of Medicine and Director, Office of Education, UCLA Neuropsychiatric Institute; FAWZY I. FAWZY is Associate Professor of Psychiatry in the UCLA School of Medicine, Chief Consultation-Liaison Psychiatry Service, UCLA Neuropsychiatric Institute and a physician.

This research was funded by a grant from a California Department of Alcohol and Drug programs, No. A-003-2, R. H. Coombs and F. I. Fawzy, Principal Investigators.

The quality of youth-parent relationships and the relative influence of the peer network differentiate between comparison groups. Consumption of alcohol is more common among parents of substance users, and a higher proportion of users' sibling have previous substance-use experience.

Youth who refrain from drugs and alcohol perform better in school and have higher educational goals. They attend religious services more frequently and are more likely to be affiliated with a club or an established organization, but are less likely than substance users to be employed. Adolescent users are more often involved in anti-social activities such as fighting, stealing, and vandalizing property; and they are more inclined to feel that their behavior is not in line with what others expect of them.

THE PROBLEM

Heavy drinking has traditionally been recognized as primarily an adult problem. In the 1970's, however, it has also become a serious one among teenagers and even pre-teens. So pervasive is adolescent drinking that some claim it has reached epidemic proportions (see Hastens, 1976 and Smart, 1976). Numerous studies have consistently shown that during the 1960's and early 1970's, the vast majority of youth (about 90% of the boys and an almost equal percentage of girls) had experience with alcohol before leaving high school (see Wechsler and Thum, 1973 and Johnson et al., 1971). During this period, the typical teenager drank sporadically or occasionally, with one-fourth to one-third drinking at least once a week, and 5% drinking daily (see Schuckit et al., 1977; Alcohol Task Force, University of Massachusetts, 1975; Lee et al., 1975; Brunswick and Tarica, 1974; National Institute on

Alcohol Abuse and Alcoholism, 1974; Globetti, 1970; and Riester and Zucker, 1968).

A Massachusetts survey of students between 1965 and 1974 (see Demone and Wechsler, 1974) found that the percentage of high school youth who had been drunk sometime before leaving high school increased from 61% to 74% among boys and 59% to 69% among girls. Getting drunk, having inter-personal difficulties, and minimizing school performance go hand in hand. A national survey of 13,000 youth conducted by the Research Triangle Institute for the National Institute on Alcohol Abuse and Alcoholism (Rachal et al., 1975) found that 28% reported themselves as drunk at least four times in the year surveyed or said that their drinking had got them in trouble with peers or superiors at least twice during that year. This survey found that less than 18% of the nation's 17 year olds have never taken a drink. Only 38% of the 13 year olds said they were teetotalers. Close to half of all students surveyed said they had been drunk during the previous year.

Furthermore, the alcohol-using trend appears to have been increasing in recent years. A comparative study of over 22,000 upper classmen in San Mateo, California, high schools revealed a pronounced increase in drinking patterns during the past decade -- from 77% of the boys and 71% of the girls who reported some drinking in 1968 to 91% of both sexes in 1977. Moreover, the percentage who drank weekly increased sharply during this period -- 40% of the boys and 32% of the girls (Blackford, 1977). And while the ten-year summary results from this annual survey sponsored by the National Institute on Drug Abuse indicate that some drugs seem to be "peaking out" in use among youth (amphetamines, barbiturates, LSD), increases in the use of alcohol were larger in 1977 than in any year since 1971. Prior to the publication of these final summary results in 1977, it has been assumed that a leveling off also had begun for alcohol use (Blackford, 1977).

However, the most recent data indicate that, among both high school and junior high school youth, earlier and heavier drinking are prevalent. For example, not only has the average age of first drinking declined from 14 in the 1940's and 1950's to 12 in the 1970's (Demone and Wechsler, 1974); but, also it is estimated that over 31% of high school youth misuse alcohol (Rachal et al., 1980). In fact, in its 1978 report to Congress, the National Institute on Alcohol Abuse and Alcoholism stated that 3.3 million teenagers, or about 19% of the adolescent population, are problem drinkers or are using alcohol for destructive purposes (Noble, 1978).

Intoxication and its consequences are rapidly increasing among youthful drinkers. According to a recent national survey (Johnston et al., 1979), 32% of drinking high school seniors reveal that "most or all of their friends get drunk at least once a week" (1979:75) Fewer seniors now disapprove of weekend "binge" drinking (five or more drinks once or twice a weekend) than in 1977. More than 8,000 teens die in alcohol-related automobile accidents annually, while over 40,000 youth are disfigured (Crippins and Eppinga, 1980).

It is not surprising then that a recent report (December 1980) by the U.S. Surgeon General lists alcohol and drug abuse as major factors contributing to a sharp increase in death rates among adolescents and young adults: "Alcohol-related accidents are the

108

leading cause of death for those 15 to 24 years of age...Sixty percent of all alcohol-related highway traffic fatalities are in this are group" (Richmond, 1980).

In Los Angeles County alone, Alcoholics Anonymous reportedly has 25 groups exclusively for teenagers (Teen-Anon), and 75 other chapters have some teenaged members. For adolescents afflicted with alcoholism, the lifetime impact can be profound (Cockerham, 1975; Globetti, 1972; Sterne and Pittman, 1972; Swanson et al., 1971; Widseth and Mayer, 1971; Riester and Zucker, 1968; Blacker et al., 1965; Wattenberg and Moir, 1956). Studies indicate that teenage alcoholism is increasing and that the physical and psychosocial consequences of alcohol use include blackouts, amnesia, malnutrition, accidental injuries, failure to accomplish school-related and work-related tasks, disruption of inter-personal relationships, and depression (Smart, 1976).

Drinking problems are compounded by the fact that youthful consumption is often combined with other forms of substance abuse (Schuckit et al., 1977; Hamburg et al., 1975; Singh and Haddy, 1973; Weitman et al., 1972; Dodson et al., 1971). In the past, this pattern existed primarily among teenagers who drank heavily; but now it is reportedly popular at teen parties to have punch bowls full of wine, vodka, and assortments of "downers." When combined together in this way, these drugs can intensify the effects of each other; that is, alcohol (given a value of 2) plus barbiturates (given a 2) does not necessary equal 4; it can compound to 6, 8, 10, or more. This potentiation principle is clearly exemplified by the Karen Quinlan case, widely popularized in the mass media in which potentiated drugs produced coma. Yet, despite such tragic happenings, evidence indicates an increase in poly-drug use among teenagers.

As surveys of youth in drug treatment programs reveal, alcohol is almost always one of the abused substances (Farley et al., 1979). Other drugs, such as PCP, a popular hallucinogenic substance nicknamed "super pot," are often mixed with alcohol. PCP has been implicated in thousands of injuries and deaths. In 1977, the Drug Abuse Warning Network (DAWN) reported that among the system's 662 participating hospital emergency rooms, PCP was the second most frequently mentioned substance cited in 4,000 cases. In 1978, this figure rose to 5,753 (Newmeyer, 1980).

An unprecedented rise in drowning deaths off Los Angeles County beaches was linked to alcohol and other drugs, particularly PCP, which reportedly promotes an unusual but pleasant sensation from the water but also causes disorientation. Compounding the problem of PCP-abuse prevention is that the substance has at least 30 analogs. And in spite of its unpredictable, sometimes lethal properties, PCP continues to increase in popularity, particularly in urban areas. Hundreds of deaths by drowning, self-inflicted wounds, and homicides by intoxicated users have been, and continue to be, reported. Admissions to psychiatric hospitals also are common. In one recent study at a major urban hospital, over 25% of recently admitted "acute schizophrenics" were later found to be suffering from PCP-induced psychotic reactions (Peterson, 1980).

Marijuana, youth's drug of choice after alcohol and often used with it, is now regularly used by 19% of 12 to 17 year olds. The recent spread of marijuana into non-metropolitan areas indicates that this drug, rather than peaking out, has been discovered by even more adolescents (Miller and Cissin, 1980).

Prescription medications are also abused by some youth. Ironically, the fourth most frequently mentioned drug involved in youths' emergency hospital admissions (reported to the DAWN system) is the "controlled" substance diazepam (Valium) (Schnoll, 1979). Barbiturates, also ostensibly "controlled," were implicated in 25,000 hospital visits and 5,000 deaths in 1976 alone (Beschner and Friedman, 1979). "Implicated" often means combined with alcohol; that is, the synergistic effect commonly results in a medical emergency -- overdose, prolonged coma, or death.

In addition to increasing consumption of alcohol, the use of inhalants and solvents is reportedly rising among 12 to 13 year olds, as is the incidence of "sudden sniffing deaths" (SSD) (Cohen, 1979). Substances as easily obtained as nail polish remover can, when inhaled rapidly from a paper bag, cause a sudden, sometimes fatal, drop in blood pressure. Some inhalants, such as amyl nitrite, are sold legally in paraphernalia shops under the name "popper."

Regarding criminal justice involvement, drug-related offenses within the juvenile population account for millions of dollars annually. The cost of incarcerating one youth is between $8,000 and $12,000 yearly, and the rate of recidivism is over 70% (Sorrentino, 1979). Even though the "Baby Boom" has long since ended, Federal Bureau of Investigation data clearly show that the rates of crimes committed by youths are higher than ever and that juvenile delinquency and substance abuse are positively linked (Leukefeld and Clayton, 1979).

However, many youths who enter drug treatment programs are not "street people"; they have, nevertheless, come to the attention of the criminal justice system via the commission of substance-involved crimes, such as theft and drug trafficking. In short, growing numbers of "normal" adolescents are experiencing severe social, not to mention medical and psychological, consequences of substance abuse.

Adolescence is a critical period of life during which development tasks must be accomplished before youth move into adult roles. Youth must establish independence from parents, achieve a coherent and functional philosophy of life, and develop the self-confidence and social skills necessary for competing successfully in mate selection and the work world. Unfortunately, as we have indicated, alcohol and other substances adversely affect healthy development during the crucial period of adolescence.

As our society becomes increasingly drug oriented, with substance use establishing itself as the "in thing" among teens and adults alike, youth have little difficulty obtaining alcohol and other drugs. Subject to age restrictions, which have been lowered recently in some states, alcohol can be sold legally in most areas; and the refrigerator, liquor cabinet, and medicine chest at home usually can be counted on for a ready supply of alcoholic beverages and prescription drugs. As Miller and Cissin have noted in analyzing their national survey data for 1979, increased opportunities further the potential for increases in substance use.

METHODS

Research subjects for our study consist of 262 California youths, ages 13 through 17, and their parents. For comparison purposes, more than half of the teens are classified as substance users (N=145, 55%), and the others as abstainers (N=117, 45%). Operationally defined, a "user" is one who, during the month preceding the interview, drank alcoholic beverages or used illegal drugs, prescription drugs obtained illegally, or other substances for the expressed purpose of altering mood, affect, or state of consciousness. By contrast, an "abstainer" is one who did not use any of these substances during the same time period.

Every effort was made to match the user and abstainer comparison groups on three control variables -- age, sex, and ethnicity. The two groups were also very similar in several measures of socioeconomic status.

Our research approach has been to utilize ethnographic research procedures by studying high-risk youth in their natural environments -- on the streets and in their own homes. Communities near Los Angeles were selected because drug availability and social reinforcement for drug use are reportedly high, and economically depressed minorities reside there in large numbers. High-risk youth who "hang out" on the street were contacted, mainly at Boys' Clubs (one-third of whose members are girls).

Because the study population is not a probability sample, generalizations from this data should be made with caution. Unlike opinion pools, for example, subjects were not randomly drawn from a population whose social parameters are known. Unfortunately, there are no convenient lists of substance users or abstainers from which to derive probability samples. But a comparison of our study population with demographic characteristics of those in the same locality revealed them not to be appreciably different.

Alcohol and marijuana are by far the most popular substances consumed by these youthful subjects. Almost all of the adolescent users (99%) have tried alcohol in the form of beer, wine, hard liquor, or a combination of these.

During the month preceding the interview, 94% of those classified as users had had an alcoholic drink. Among those remaining, most had consumed alcohol in the recent past. Only two youths said that they have always been non-drinkers. Nearly half (48%) have used marijuana or hashish, and four out of ten (39%) do so regularly. Some youngsters have experimented with other substances, such as PCP (12%), amphetamines (10%), cocaine (9%), paint (8%), and barbiturates (7%), but only a few use these substances regularly (Coombs, Fawzy, and Gerber, 1984).

It is important to note that "users" and "abstainers," as classified in this study, are not polar opposites with regard to the use of substances. To some extent, the dichotomized classification of our comparison design draws a line between youth whose substance use actually ranges on a continuum. (The criterion for dividing subjects into comparison groups was whether or not they had used alcohol or other drugs during the month preceding the initial interview.) Less than half of the non-users (48%) report a lifetime record of having abstained from the consumption of alcohol. Not only have the majority (52%) had a drink at some time during the past, but over half of these

53%) have consumed alcoholic beverages as recently as six months ago.

Eighty-four percent of the abstainer group, compared with 35% of the users, have never used other drugs. Of those "abstainers" who have, all but two (15%) have quit. (These two are classified with the abstainer group because they had not used substances during the month preceding the interview.) Of the 17 abstainers who have quit, six (35%) used drugs as recently as within the past six months.

FAMILY FACTORS
Familial and Economic Deprivation

Broken homes and economic hardship, the usual explanation for juvenile problems, were not found to be significantly related to substance use among these youth. In this subject population, substance users are no more likely than abstainers to come from broken homes than from intact families, neither are their parents of lower socioeconomic status.

Family Sentiment

Almost all measures of family sentiment differentiate significantly between comparison groups, suggesting that adolescent abstainers have a more positive, satisfying, and encouraging relationship with parents than do youth who use substances. Three-fourths of the abstainers, compared to half of the users, feel quite close to their father. A similar, though less pronounced, difference exists in the mother-child relationship. Youth who are not involved with substances respect their parents to a larger degree and have a greater desire to emulate them as adults.

Adolescent abstainers also rely more on their parents for advice and guidance than do substance users.

Youth who abstain from alcohol and other drugs, as compared to those who do not, generally receive more favorable feedback from family members. They receive more praise and encouragement, experience more conversational sharing regarding problems and future plans, and feel more trust and caring.

Family Power and Decision Making

Characteristically, most youth come from homes in which the father makes the major decisions either independently or jointly with the mother, though the latter tends to be more common among parents of abstainers. On the other hand, independent decisions on major issues by mothers are more common in homes in which youngsters use substances. Both parents appear to share in the duties of disciplining these youth.

Adolescents who use substances tend to see their parents as less strict than do non-using youth, especially in regard to mother's discipline. One-fourth (28%) of the users as compared to 12% of the abstainers report their mothers to be more permissive than average. However, perceived lenience is not characteristic of the majority. Nearly 80% of all youth rate the discipline of parents between "average" and "extremely strict."

Parents of abstainers are generally more firm in establishing conduct rules for their adolescent children. While most parents have rules restricting cigarette smoking and the use of drugs, proportionately more of the non-users' parents have rules governing school homework, dating, television viewing, and drinking alcohol. Yet parents of abstainers are not more punitive in response to disobedience.

Substance Use by Parents and Siblings

Adolescents who use drugs and alcohol report a higher degree of substance use among family members than do their non-using peers (Fawzy, Coombs, and Gerber, 1984). For example, significant differences are found in regard to parental drinking habits. Not only do more of the users' fathers and mothers drink hard liquor, beer, and wine, but they tend to imbibe more often as well. These differences are confirmed by the accounts of parental subjects.

Cigarette smoking by mothers differentiates between adolescent comparison groups. According to youth reports, mothers of drug users are much more likely to smoke than mothers of abstainers, and they also smoke more heavily. A similar difference is observed in regard to consumption of coffee. Nearly three-quarters (72%) of users' parents drink one or more cups of coffee each day, while only half (50%) of the parents of abstainers consume this amount.

Use of prescription medications and over-the-counter drugs for non-medical reasons is not a common practice among parents, and no differences were found between comparison groups. However, the same cannot be said in regard to the use of certain illegal substances. A significantly great proportion of users' fathers (14% as compared to 4% of abstainers' fathers) have smoked marijuana or hashish. While parental use of other illegal drugs is not widespread, most of those with prior experience are parents of substances users.

117

Even more striking is the relationship between adolescent and sibling substance use. Over half (53%) of the users are aware that their brothers and sisters have used marijuana or hashish, while only 30% of the non-using youth say the same. Likewise, a much greater number of users versus abstainers report sibling use of LSD, PCP, amphetamines, barbiturates, qualudes, and cocaine. With respect to sibling use of other substances, the differences between comparison groups are not significant, but the proportion of users is greater in every case.

SOCIAL FACTORS
Peers

Being accepted and liked by friends is almost universally important to adolescents regardless of whether or not they use substances. Youths who abstain from substances, as compared to users, do not spend less time with their friends, and neither group is more likely than the other to share with friends their personal problems or discuss educational and vocational plans. By these criteria, drug users are no more peer oriented than non-using youth.

Friend selection is what distinguishes between comparison groups. Generally speaking, youth who use substances are much more likely to have close friends who also use, whereas non-using youth feel closer to peers who abstain from substance use.

Peers Versus Family

Though popularity and peer acceptance are important during adolescence, maintaining a positive relationship with parents is generally regarded by youths as even more important. The majority feel closer to their families than to peers, and most say that they would turn to one or both parents in the time of serious trouble. Yet in assessing the competing influences of family and peers, substance users as compared to abstainers seem to be more influenced by their friends. Youth who use substance tend to feel more comfortable with friends than with family members, they may regard peers as more understanding than parents, and they are considerably less likely to value parental ideas or to be bothered by parental disapproval.

The extent of differential parent influence among users and abstainers is most evident in specific situations, such as when a parent strongly objects to a youngster's choice of friends. In such cases, substance users are much less likely to comply with the parent's wishes. Twice as many users (39%) as non-users (16%) say they would disregard parental objections by continuing to see their friends and to do so openly.

School

Almost all of the educational measures utilized in this research indicate that performance and behavior in school are related to whether or not youth use substances. Adolescent abstainers tend to spend a greater number of hours each week on homework, and they earn higher grades than do substance users. According to their own reports, seven out of ten abstainers average A or B grades, while only four out of ten users do the same. On the other hand, more of the users received unsatisfactory marks on their most recent grade card.

Absenteeism is more common among users than abstainers, and the latter are much less prone to cut classes. Youth classified as "users" also see less importance or future relevance in what they are learning and report more frequent boredom with classroom activities. Dropping out of school has been seriously considered by 30% of the users and 20% of the abstainers.

The majority (86%) of parents want their children to pursue formal education beyond high school, yet they differ by comparison group in the degree of education desired. In general, parents of users want their offspring to at least attend, if not graduate from, college; whereas, the abstainers' parents want their youth to finish college and, perhaps, move on to graduate school. The youths' own aspirations toward educational goals differ along similar lines. Over half of the abstainers, compared to 29% of the users, expect to graduate from college, and one-fourth (23%) of the former, contrasted with 9% of the latter, expect to do graduate work.

Voluntary Organizations

Youth in the study population report a wide range of social interests, and involvement in these activities does not appear to distinguish between comparison groups. While fewer users than abstainers are affiliated with clubs or established organizations, the former may be more "fun oriented" in general. Adolescent substance users place greater importance on "having a good time" than do those who abstain, and they may favor less structured kinds of activities for recreation and enjoyment.

Most youths have a high regard for religion in their lives, though youth who do not use drugs or alcohol generally attribute greater importance to religion than do substance users. Adolescent abstainers go to their church or synagogue significantly more often as well. Over two-thirds (68%) of non-users attend religious services at least two or three times each month, while less than 40% of the substance users attend as often. Conversely, 43% of the users (compared to 16% of abstainers) go to church or synagogue no more than two or three times a year.

EMPLOYMENT

Interestingly, youths who use substances are more likely to be employed (52%) than are the abstainers (30%), but the comparison groups do not differ in regard to the type of work performed. Most of the youths work in part-time jobs or seek out odd jobs on a regular basis, though some work in family business establishments. Of those who are employed, all but four report an average or high level of job satisfaction.

ADJUSTMENT AND WELL-BEING
Antisocial Behaviors

Antisocial behaviors are more common among youths who use substance than those who do not. All but one of the 19 measures of antisocial behaviors utilized in this study demonstrate the contrast.

During the three-month period preceding the initial interview, 28 youths were involved in serious fighting; 20 of these youngsters are users. Even more pronounced differences exist with regard to group fighting (22 of

24 participants are users). Injuring someone seriously enough to require bandages or medical care was reported by seven users and one abstainer. Threatening others in order to gain a personal goal is reported by ten users and four abstainers. Only three youths, all users, struck an instructor or employer.

Altercations at home, though not common, also are more typical of substance users than abstainers. During the three month report period, five adolescents, all users, struck their fathers; four youths (10%; one of whom was an abstainer) struck their mothers. An artifact of the subject classification system, this latter finding is as expected.

Stealing is also more typical of users than abstainers. Of the 27 adolescents involved in shoplifting during the three month period, 22 are drug users. Similarly, petty theft is more characteristic of users; 22 of 34 youths so involved use substances. Only six youngsters, five of whom are users, stole more valuable items. All three who stole automobiles use substances.

Property violations such as trespassing and vandalism are also more typical of users. Eighteen of 20 youths who have recently damaged school property use substances. Arson is the only antisocial measure that does not distinguish between comparison groups. Only two subjects admit to setting someone else's property on fire; one is a user and the other an abstainer.

Physical Health and Emotional Well-Being
No pronounced differences in health exist between comparison groups. Youth who use substances tend to feign illness more often in order to avoid unpleasantries, but overall youth report feeling quite

well. Eighty percent of the users and 82% of the abstainers say that they are in good or excellent physical health.

Adolescent abstainers tend to have a greater measure of emotional well-being. Youth who do not use drugs or alcohol tend to feel happier, and they may feel a higher level of self-satisfaction. While the majority of youths are content with themselves, slightly more of the users are aware of things about themselves that they would like to change. Adolescent users may be more inclined to feel as if they are not living up to personal beliefs and values; and they are significantly more likely to feel that their behavior is not in line with expectations. Three times as many users (22%) as non-users (7%) feel this way often.

CONCLUSION

These findings make clear for this group of youth that drug use goes hand in hand with poor school performance and antisocial behaviors. They also indicate that, for prevention and intervention programs to be effective, the focus must be on the family and school. If youth are to avoid drugs and stay out of trouble with the law, they need to be happy at home and to do well at school.

Teenagers who abstain from the use of substances typically have parents who, though firm, treat them affectionately and share family power by involving them in decisions. These parents typically abstain from the use of substances and provide a religious ideology for such practice.

Youthful drug users, by contrast, tend to have more strained relationship with their parents and look to their youthful peers for support and personal acceptance. Their parents are more likely to use drugs and provide a negative inter-personal environment for them at home.

This seems to suggest that parent training should be the first line of defense against adolescent drug abuse (primary prevention) and that family therapy may be the best intervention for youngsters already engaged in drug abuse and related behaviors (secondary prevention) (Coombs et al., 1984).

REFERENCES

Alcohol Task Force, University of Massachusetts. 1975. Alcohol Task Force: Report of activities, findings and recommendations. Amherst: University of Massachusetts.

Beschner, G. M. and Friedman, A. S. (eds.). 1979. Youth Drug Abuse: Problems, Issues, and Treatment. Lexington, MA: D.C. Heath and Company

Blacker, E., Demone, H. W., and Freeman, H. W. 1965. Drinking behavior of delinquent boys. Quarterly Journal of Studies on Alcohol 26:223-237.

Blackford, L. 1977. Summary Report -- Survey of Student Drug Use. San Mateo County, CA: Department of Public Health and Welfare.

Brunswick, A. F. and Tarica, C. 1974. Drinking and health: A study of urban black adolescents. Addictive Diseases 1:21-42.

Cockerham, W. D. 1975. Drinking patterns of institutionalized and non-institutionalized Wyoming youth. Journal of Studies on Alcohol 36:993-995.

Cohen, S. 1979. Inhalants and solvents. In George M. Beschner and Alfred S. Friedman (eds.), Youth Drug Abuse: Problems, Issues, and Treatment (pp. 285-314). Lexington, MA: D. C. Heath and Company.

Coombs, R. H. (ed.). 1975. Junkies and Straights: The Camarillo Experience. Lexington, MA: Lexington Books, D. C. Heath and Company.

Coombs, R. H., Fawzy, F. I., and Gerber, B. E. 1984. Patterns of substance use among children and youths: A longitudinal study. Substance and Alcohol Action/Misuse 5:59-67.

Coombs, R. H., Santana, W. A. and Fawzy, F. I. 1984. Parent training to prevent adolescent drug use: An educational model. Journal of Drug Issues 14:393-402.

Crippins, D. and Eppinga, A. 1980. Alcohol Awareness Television Program for Young People: A Proposal. Unpublished manuscript. Los Angeles, CA.

Demone, H. W., Jr. and Wechsler, H. 1974. The non-use and abuse of alcohol by the male adolescent. In M. E. Chafetz (ed.), Proceedings of the Second Annual Alcoholism Conference of the National Institute on Alcohol Abuse and Alcoholism. Washington, D.C.

Dodson, W. E., Alexander, D. F., Wright, P. F., and Wunderlich, R. A. 1971. Patterns of multiple drug abuse among adolescents referred by a juvenile court. Pediatrics 47:1033-1036.

Farley, E. C., Santo, Y., and Speck, D. W. 1979. Multiple drug-abuse patterns of youths in treatment. In George M. Beschner and Alfred S. Friedman (eds.), Youth Drug Abuse: Problems, Issues, and Treatment (pp. 149-168). Lexington, MA: D.C. Heath and Company.

Feldman, H. 1973. Street status and drug users. Society 10:32-38.

Globetti, G. 1970. The drinking patterns of Negro and White high school students in two Mississippi communities. Journal of Negro Education 39:60-69.

Globetti, G. 1972. Problem and non-problem drinking among high school students in abstinence communities. International Journal of the Addictions 7:511-523.

Hamburg, B. A., Kraemer, N. C., and Jahnke, W. 1975. A hierarchy of drug use in adolescence: Behavioral and attitudinal correlates of substantial drug use. American Journal of Psychiatry 132:1155-1163.

Hastens, J. 1976. Teenage Alcoholism. New York: Hawthorne.

Hughes, P., Crawford, G., Barker, N., Schumann, S., and Jaffe, J. 1981. The social structure of a heroin coping community. American Journal of Psychiatry 128:551-558.

Johnson, K. D., Donnelly, J., Scheble, R., Wine, R., and Weitman, M. 1971. Survey of adolescent drug use. I: Sex and grade distribution. American Journal of Public Health 61:2418-2432.

Johnston, L. D., Bachman, J. G., and O'Malley, P. M. 1979. 1979 Highlights -- Drugs and the Nation's High School Students: Five Year National Trends. Rockville, MD: National Institute on Drug Abuse.

Lee, E. E., Eishman, R., and Shimmel, G. M. 1975. Emerging Trends of Alcohol Use and Abuse Among Teenagers. Paper presented at the national Council on Alcoholism National Meeting. Milwaukee, WI.

Leukefeld, C. G. and Clayton, R. R. 1979. Drug abuse and delinquency: A study of youths in treatment. In George M. Beschner and Alfred S. Friedman (eds.), Youth Drug Abuse: Problems, Issues, and Treatment (pp. 213-227). Lexington, MA: D.C. Heath and Company.

Miller, J. and Cissin, I. A. 1980. Highlights from the National Survey on Drug Abuse: 1979. Rockville, MD: National Institute on Drug Abuse.

National Institute on Alcohol Abuse and Alcoholism. 1974. Subject Area Bibliography on Sociocultural Aspects of Alcohol Use and Alcoholism: Part B: Teenage Drinking (Subject Area Bibliography 1-B-4). Rockville, MD: National Clearinghouse for Alcohol Information.

Newmeyer, J. R. 1980. The epidemiology of PCP use in the late 1970's. Journal of Psychedelic Drugs 12: 3-4.

Noble, E. P. (ed.). 1978. Alcohol and Health (Third) Special Report to the United States Congress). Rockville, MD: National Institute on Alcohol Abuse and Alcoholism.

Petersen, R. C. 1980. Phencyclidine: A NIDA perspective. Journal of Psychedelic Drugs 12:3-4.

Preble, E. and Casey, J. J., Jr. 1967. Taking care of business: The heroin user's life on the streets. International Journal of the Addictions 4(1):1-24.

Prendergast, T. J., Jr. 1974. Correlates of drinking and drunkenness among high school students. Quarterly Journal of Studies on Alcohol 35:232-242.

Prendergast, T. J., Jr. 1974. Family characteristics associated with marijuana use among adolescents. The International Journal of the Addictions 9(6):827-839.

Rachal, J. V., Guess, L. C., Hubbard, R. L., Maisto, S. A., Cavanaugh, E. R., Waddell, R., and Benrud, C. H. 1980. Adolescent Drinking Behavior. Triangle Park, NC: Research Triangle Institute.

Rachal, J. V., Williams, J. R., Brehm, M. L., Cavanaugh, B., Moore, R. P., and Eckerman, W. C. 1975. A National Study of Adolescent Drinking Behavior, Attitudes, and Correlates (Publication #PB-246 002/OWS).

Richmond, J. 1980. Health United States: 1980. (Cited in ADAMHA News, Volume III, No. 1, January 9, 1981.) Rockville, MD: Alcohol, Drug Abuse, and Mental Health Administration.

Riester, A. E. and Zucker, R. A. 1968. Adolescent social structure and drinking behavior. Personnel and Guidance Journal 47(4):304-313.

Schnoll, S. H. 1979. Pharmacological aspects of youth drug abuse. In George M. Beschner and Alfred S. Friedman (eds.), Youth Drug Abuse: Problems, Issues, and Treatment (pp. 255-276). Lexington, MA: D. C. Heath and Company.

Schuckit, M. A., Morrisey, E. R. and Lewis, N. J. 1977. Adolescent problem drinkers. In Frank A. Seixas (ed.), Currents in Alcoholism 2. New York: Grune and Stratton.

Singh, R. N. and Haddy, L. E. 1973. Alcohol consumption and the students' use of hallucinogenic drugs. West Virginia Medical Journal 59:88-90.

Smart, R. G. 1976. The New Drinkers: Teenage Use and Abuse of Alcohol. (Addiction Research Foundation Program Rep. Ser. No. 4). Tyrant, Canada: Addiction Research Foundation of Ontario.

Sorrentino, A. 1979. How to Organize the Neighborhood for Delinquency Prevention. New York: Human Science Press.

Sterne, M. W. and Pittman, D. J. 1972. _Drinking_ _Patterns_ _in_ _the_ _Ghetto_. St. Louis: Washington University Social Science Institute.

Swanson, D. W., Bratrude, A. P., and Brown, E. M. 1971. Alcohol abuse in a population of Indian children. _Diseases of the Nervous System_ 32:835-842.

Wattenberg, W. W. and Moir, J. B. 1956. A study of teenagers arrested for drunkenness. _Quarterly_ _Journal of Studies on Alcohol_ 17:426-442.

Wechsler, H. and Thum, D. 1973. Teenage drinking, drug use and social correlates. _Quarterly_ _Journal_ _of_ _Studies_ _on_ _Alcohol_ 34:1220-1227.

Weitman, M., Scheble, R., Johnson, K., and Abbey, H. 1972. Survey of adolescent drug use: III. Correlations among use of drugs. _American Journal_ _of Public Health_ 62:166-170.

Widseth, J. C. and Mayer, J. 1971. Drinking behavior and attitudes toward alcohol in delinquent girls. _International_ _Journal_ _of_ _the Addictions_ 6(3):454-461.

Yancy, W. S., Nader, P. R., and Burham, K. L. 1972. Drug use and attitudes of high school students. _Pediatrics_ 50:730-745.

INTRODUCTION TO CHAPTER 6

What we have seen thus far is the emergence of patterns of alcohol and drug use at early stages of the life cycle. We have taken special note of the differences in these patterns by sub-culture. In the next chapter, Clark, Salloway, and Daugherty ask a further question: What are the substance-use patterns of a population which begins as a relatively homogeneous group? They examine alcohol and drug use behavior among medical students, a very homogeneous group in terms of social class, age, and education. In addition, medical students are all under similar stress. The differences in alcohol and drug use behavior in such a group may offer some insights into individual decisions to use these substances.

The authors suggest that early patterns of drug using behavior tend to "crystallize" or "harden," that is, to become an enduring feature of the behavior system. It will be interesting to compare their findings with those of Winick in Chapter 14 when he discusses substance use by older physicians and nurses.

One of the unique features of Clark, Salloway, and Daugherty's work is that the study is longitudinal. They have followed this group of medical students for four years. The data, therefore, gives a sense of the development and change that takes place in substance use, rather than a simple cross-sectional analysis, taken at one point in time.

CHAPTER 6
SUBSTANCE USE BY MEDICAL STUDENTS

David C. Clark, Jeffrey Colman Salloway,
and Steven R. Daugherty

ABSTRACT

The authors examine the problems
encountered when one generalizes from national
survey research data on alcohol and drug use
patterns to the alcohol and drug use behavior
of young adults in a delimited, relatively
homogeneous population. The authors go on to
report preliminary data from a longitudinal
study of alcohol and drug use by one class of
medical students, describing: 1) a method for
quantifying community norms for alcohol use, 2)
a method for assessing the global drug
involvement of individual students, 3) the
relationships between excessive drinking and
alcohol abuse and between high drug involvement
and drug abuse, and 3) psycho-social
characteristics associated with greater alcohol
and drug use.

INTRODUCTION

National survey research has shown the degree to
which alcohol and drug use patterns crystallize during
the high school and college years and has documented a
number of socio-demographic forces which shape these
patterns. These findings may not, however, generalize

DAVID C. CLARK is Assistant Professor of Psychiatry and Psychology
at Rush Medical College; JEFFREY COLMAN SALLOWAY is Director of
the Center for Health Promotion and Research at the University of
New Hampshire; STEVEN R. DAUGHERTY is Instructor of Psychology and
Social Sciences at Rush Medical College.

to smaller, more homogeneous groups. Socio-demographic forces are less useful when we begin to look for patterns in more limited samples, as for example among medical students.

Groups of medical professionals undergo a socialization process and have extra exposure to drugs. These may contribute to their patterns of drug and alcohol use. Such factors as a good grounding in pharmacology, the ability to self-prescribe, and the stresses associated with medical education, training, and practice cannot be overlooked as elements altering drug-using behavior. At least they add complexity to efforts to understand substance abuse patterns among medical professionals. At most, they may alter those patterns beyond recognition.

How does one differentiate the forces leading to substance-use behavior in a homogeneous population, especially when that population is under stress? We answer this larger question by breaking it down into smaller ones. What is the range of differences in this substance-using behavior? What factors identify those in the population who drink or use drugs more or less than their colleagues? What characteristics identify those who become dependent on alcohol or drugs?

We have sought systematic answers to these questions by examining data from a longitudinal study of a medical school class. The study began on the first day of medical school (orientation day) and continued to a point half-way through the fourth and final year. An inter-disciplinary research team attempted to identify normative patterns of alcohol and drug use, to define psychosocial characteristics correlated with heavier substance abuse or change in use patterns, and to identify students at greater risk for alcohol and drug impairment.

PROBLEMS IN APPLYING SURVEY RESEARCH FINDINGS

Several methodological concerns guided the planning and design of the project. These pertain to three major stumbling blocks which researchers encounter when they try to apply national survey data on alcohol and drug abuse patterns to specific work settings or professional groups.

First, every community or sub-group has norms for drinking and drug use. These specific community norms can be expected to vary from national or even regional norms. Defining such community norms is not simply a matter of averaging indices of drug-taking quantity or frequency. The idea of "norms" in a social-psychological sense suggests a shared notion as to what is acceptable or unacceptable behavior within the community. To understand behavior, it is necessary to identify the norms of the specific community.

Second, the forces shaping substance use patterns in a large heterogeneous population (such as national samples) are not necessarily the same forces that explain differences in smaller, more homogeneous populations (for example, the student population at a single medical school). Such small, rather isolated groups develop norms of their own which may be different from larger populations.

Third, survey studies rarely specify the differences between moderate and heavy substance users on the one hand, and those with problems or impairment related to alcohol or drugs on the other hand. Therefore, many profiles of users may actually be profiles of the larger population of moderate-to-heavy substance users (some of whom may never exhibit impairment). Another problem is that such research doesn't consider instances of substance abuse or dependence among low quantity or intermittent substance users. We can discuss potential solutions to each of these problems.

Community Norms

Individuals in the population attach labels to levels of drug and alcohol use. These are value labels which reflect the norms of the community. The extent to which these norms modify behavior are a measure of the degree to which the community is a reference group for individual behavior. In discussing drug and alcohol use, we must first specify this normative context. Harburg et al. (1980) proposed a method for quantifying alcohol consumption as a basis for establishing "community norms" of alcohol intake based on respondents' subjective evaluation of drinking behavior. It is this norm-based method which has been used here.

Norms can also be defined for drug use patterns. Clark et al. (in press) proposed a method for scaling "drug involvement" on a continuum based on the subjects' responses to questions about which drugs they have ever used in their lifetime. This method asks respondents about their drug use and then analyzes the data to produce a single dimension which we may call "drug involvement."

Clark proposes that we classify individuals along this dimension of drug involvement, rather than by the substance they use (for example, cocaine users) or even by the frequency of use. This provides a clear,

133

unambiguous measure of drug involvement which
facilitates determining those characteristics
associated with greater or lesser degrees of "drug
involvement."

Thus, methods do exist for defining community norms
for alcohol and drug use in bounded populations. The
normative classification schemes allow us to compare
and rank order subjects on a quantity/frequency
continuum, but also capitalize on the community's own
social definition of what constitutes discrete levels
of alcohol or drug involvement.

Heterogeneous and Homogeneous Subject Populations

Most of the available data on characteristics of
youthful drinkers and drug users come from national or
regional surveys of high school or college students,
where sociodemographic diversity is substantial. Such
studies provide a string of variables to relate to
substance use patterns. There is, however, implicit
bias operating in these surveys. Large-scale
population surveys tend to discover sociodemographic
differences among subgroups, while smaller population
studies of closed or strictly bounded groups are more
likely to reveal differences based on inter-personal
factors or personality style. This is true because
smaller bounded groups tend to be more socially
homogeneous. Thus, one would expect that when we
examine a bounded and relatively homogeneous class of
medical students, for example, person-specific
variables (such as character organization and interpersonal functioning) will emerge as the most
significant correlates of individual differences in
drinking or drug use, rather than the oft-cited
sociodemographic factors documented by survey research.

Non-Correspondence of Heavier Users and Problem Users

Identifying the "problem drinkers" or "problem drug-users" in a research population can be risky for several reasons. The distinction between heavy drinkers and problem drinkers, for example, is one that is made by the investigator. Thus, if problem drinkers represent a minority of the heavy drinkers in a sample, characteristics of all heavy drinkers may be erroneously attributed to problem drinkers. In addition, many alcoholics (or drug users) cycle between heavy use and abstinence. Analyses that are based solely on current patterns of use may then link problem users with other users or even non-users.

To deal with this problem, it is essential to identify psychosocial variables associated with drinking or drug use level for an entire sample rather than focusing on differences between problem drinkers or drug users and all other users. Only in this way can an investigator contrast (for example) heavy-drinking characteristics with problem-drinking characteristics.

STUDENT PHYSICIAN ALCOHOL AND DRUG-USE PATTERNS

A number of recent studies have concluded that the prevalence of alcoholism among U.S. physicians is similar to that in the adult population of comparable socioeconomic status (between 7% to 10%) (McCue, 1982; Bissell and Jones, 1976). But, drug addiction is estimated to be 30 to 100 times more common among physicians than among the general population: physicians take more tranquilizers, sedatives, and stimulants than well-matched controls, and self-medication with drugs or alcohol is the cause of one-third of the total time physicians spend as hospital in-patients (Vaillant et al., 1970-1972; Modlin and Montes, 1964). Thus, the forces shaping drug use patterns and drug abuse/dependence may be more apparent in a student physician population than most other young adult populations. Clearly important preventive implications follow from documentation of characteristics associated with drug abuse or dependence within a medical school population.

A freshman medical school class is a newly constituted group that remains relatively self-contained over a four-year period. Students begin medical school knowing few, if any, of their classmates. However, common work loads, close proximity, little time away from school, and the shared evolution of a physician identity all contribute to the development of an elaborate social network. Despite the frequency of classmate contact, students are free to choose or avoid social activity with any of their classmates. Thus, a medical school class provides a unique natural laboratory in which the relationships among individual drinking and drug use patterns, social affiliation, and person-specific factors (that is, family history, personality, mood, and academic ability) can be studied.

SUBJECTS AND METHODS
Subjects

Subjects were 116 first-year medical students (96% of the freshman class) at a mid-western medical college who gave their informed consent to participate in a comprehensive four-year longitudinal study of adaptation to medical school. Respondents completed questionnaires in one sitting during school orientation prior to starting the first year and again at six-month intervals through their first three years of medical school. Two-thirds of the subjects were males, and 12% were married. The mean age for all student subjects was 23.9 years (Standard deviation = 4.4). The confidentiality and anonymity of each student participant were protected by means of an elaborate coding scheme.

Drinking Behavior Assessment

Three questionnaire items adapted from Harburg et al. (1980) and Cahalan et al. (1969) were used to elicit the frequency of drinking occasions, the quantity of alcohol consumed per occasion, and a self-descriptive rating of drinking habits (abstaining, very light, light, moderate, heavy, or very heavy) for the prior six-month period. The first two items were presented for beer, wine, and liquor separately. Using Harburg's protocol for converting item responses to ounces of pure ethanol per week (Ozgoren et al., 1978), an "ethanol oz/wk" score was calculated for each subject to represent his/her average weekly beer, wine, liquor, and total alcohol consumption. The ethanol oz/wk index may be converted to an approximate average number of drinks per day by multiplying by 2/7 (that is 0.5 oz ethanol is approximately one drink, or one bottle of beer, or one glass of wine). In this way, quantitative alcohol-use rates (ethanol oz/wk) and self-label ratings of alcohol use (abstaining to very heavy) were used to characterize each student's drinking pattern over the six months preceding each questionnaire assessment. The reliability and validity of similar self-reporting ratings of alcohol use have been reported elsewhere and were generally found to be good (Hesselbrock et al., 1983; Fine et al., 1978; McCrady et al., 1978; Guze et al., 1963).

Drug-Use Behavior Assessments

At the first time point (the first day of medical school), students were asked whether they had ever (even once) used substances in the following twelve categories: coffee, cigarettes, beer, wine, liquor, marijuana, cocaine, amphetamine-like stimulants, barbiturates or other sedatives/hypnotics, Valium or other tranquilizers, hallucinogens, narcotics, or any other illicit drugs. Prescribed and non-prescribed drug use were documentated and examined separately, so that excessive use of prescribed drugs for ambiguous reasons could be recoded as illicit use. Questionnaire items adapted from Cahalan et al. (1969) were employed at the initial and all subsequent assessments to elicit ratings of the frequency of substance use for all twelve drug categories during the prior six-month period. The reliability and validity of similar self-report ratings of drug use have been reported elsewhere and were generally found to be good (O'Malley et al., 1983; Stacy et al., 1985; Lord, 1980; Single et al., 1975).

Procedure

Students were administered the questionnaire containing the drinking and drug use items at pre-announced and maximally convenient times. Questionnaires were completed by members of the class on the first day of medical school (N=116), in spring of the first year (N=106), in fall (N=82) of the second year, and winter (N=82) of the third year. There were a variety of reasons why subjects were lost to individual follow-up assessments: 1) inconvenient timing of the assessment, 2) out-of-town travel or clerkship rotations, 3) study pressures, and 4) loss of interest in the study.

Constructing Community Norms of Alcohol Use

The total ethanol oz/wk scores by each self-label (light, moderate, heavy) at each assessment were examined separately for men and women. Frequency plots of the ethanol oz/wk scores for each self-label category suggested that subjects' alcohol consumption within each self-label category differed enormously. A simple mean would not provide an adequate summary statistic in this situation because means are intended to describe the central tendency of normal distributions. Therefore, the median alcohol intake scores for each self-label distribution by sex was employed as the measure of central tendency.

Since the method for establishing normative categories needs to be clearly understood, a single example will prove helpful. When all the male students who described themselves as "light" drinkers on the first day of school (N=29) were examined, the median ethanol oz/wk score for the subgroup was 2.41. To define a normative range of alcohol intake for light male drinkers at that assessment, the investigators selected "cut points" that encompassed 25% of the subgroup on either side of the median (cut points = 1.74 and 3.62 ethanol oz/wk). Thus, only 50% of the male drinkers who described themselves as "light" drinkers were classified as "normatively light"; the rest were classified as lighter or heavier drinkers.

Constructing Norms of Drug Use

Individual subjects were assigned a score for "drug involvement" based on their lifetime drug use or their drug use while attending medical school. Descriptions of similar models have been reported (Bock and Aitken, 1981; Lord, 1980; Samejema, 1973; Bock and Lieberman, 1970). This method permits us 1) to test that "drug involvement" is a single phenomenon as opposed to two or more dimensions, 2) to determine how well each item discriminates between individuals on the basis of their drug involvement, and 3) to test how well the model describes actual drug use.

Characterizing Differences by Alcohol or Drug Norm Categories

The relationship between low-, medium-, or high-level substance use during the school year and each psychosocial variable assessed serially over time was examined using the repeated measures multi-variate analysis of variance (O'Brien and Kaiser, 1985). This model allows for serial dependence of observations and permits an analysis of differential change over time within the three sub-groups.

RESULTS

Alcohol-Use Norms

The normative ranges of alcohol consumption for the index medical school class on the first day of school, the end of the first and second basic science years, and the middle of the third year (clinical clerkships) appear separately for male and female students in Table 6.1, page 154. While the normative ranges defined for each sex tended to remain relatively stable over the three-year period (the smaller number of females made

140

the female range definitions more skittish), the upper boundary of light drinking for males dropped by two drinks per week (about 1.0 ethanol oz/wk) over the second and third years. Thus, men in the upper end of the "light" range during the first year of school tended to be reclassified as "moderate" drinkers during subsequent years by class consensus, which was more consistent with the stable female normative classification.

The threshold separating acceptable (very light, light, and moderate) from excessive (heavy) drinking ranged from 7.27 to 10.22 ethanol oz/wk (between 2 and 3 drinks per day) for men, and from 2.94 to 8.03 ethanol oz/wk (from 1 to more than 2 drinks per day) for women.

Psychosocial Characteristics of Moderate/Heavy Drinkers

We compared abstaining/very light drinkers (N=43), light drinkers (N=36), and moderate/heavy drinkers (N=27) on psychosocial variables representing the following domains: 1) sociodemographic, 2) parental psychiatric history, 3) mood, 4) personality, 5) academic performance, and 6) inter-personal. the variables entered into this analysis were assessed on the first day of school and again at the end of the first year. These repeated assessments were related to three drinking levels using a repeated measures multi-variate analysis of variance (O'Brien and Kaiser, 1985).

Eight variables exhibited a significant overall relationship with drinking level: emotional toughness; academic confidence; and, to a lesser extent, competitiveness; emotional expressiveness; size of social network; absolute number (not proportion) of females in the network; proportion of relatives in the network; and concern with evaluation by others. Examination of the associated pair-wise contrasts revealed that these main effects were all largely due to the high-level drinking group, inasmuch as contrasts between that group and each of the other two were significant. In general, then, students in the high-level drinking group consumed more alcohol per week, and evidenced more emotional toughness, higher academic confidence, more competitiveness, less emotional expressiveness, larger social networks with a larger number (not proportion) of females and with a smaller proportion of relatives cited therein, and less concern about evaluation by others.

The most important observation concerning drinking level as a moderator of change concerned alcohol-use rates. The analysis shows that high-level drinkers increased their drinking over time, whereas the other two groups reduced their drinking.

None of the following variables, assessed at a single point in time, demonstrated a significant relationship with drinking level: sex, age, marital status, religion, political philosophy, political involvement, family history of alcoholism or depression, academic rank, and class sociometric ratings based on popularity, attributes of best physician, and best medical knowledge.

Relationship Between Moderate/Heavy Drinking and Alcohol Abuse

Nine students (seven males, two females) reported

drinking excessively by class standards for at least one six-month period during the first two-and-a-half years of medical school. Four of these drank excessively on a consistent basis (all males).

Six of the nine excessive drinkers (67%) had met Research Diagnostic Criteria (RDC) (Spitzer et al., 1978) for alcoholism before beginning medical school, as compared to a 30% class history of alcoholism. Five of the nine excessive drinkers (56%) met RDC criteria for a current episode of alcoholism on the first day of medical school, compared to a 12% class point-prevalence rate. Three of the nine excessive drinkers (33%) had meet RDC criteria for drug abuse before beginning medical school, as compared to a 16% class history of drug abuse. The excessive drinkers were not more likely to exhibit a family history of alcoholism, a family history of drug abuse, a family history of depression, or academic difficulties in medical school when compared to the rest of the class.

The four chronically excessive drinkers all reported a history of both alcoholism and drug abuse, and three of the four met criteria for a current episode of alcoholism when assessed on the first day of medical school.

The excessive drinkers were not well characterized by the already described psychosocial profile of moderate/heavy drinkers, nor were they well characterized by any other single profile. Thus, the excessive drinkers distinguished themselves from other moderate/heavy drinkers only because they were more likely to report a history of both alcohol and drug abuse and were more likely to be in a current episode of alcohol abuse, when compared to their classmates on the first day of medical school.

Drug-Use Classification

We employed latent trait analysis to analyze data on drugs ever used, as reported on the first day of medical school, and to test the likelihood that responses could be explained by their relationship to a single underlying dimension of "drug involvement." We found a single dimension of drug involvement. The resulting model of drug involvement is summarized in Table 6.2, page 155. Use of cigarettes, coffee, and "other" drugs were relatively poor discriminating items for our single dimension; the remaining nine items discriminated well. The latter nine items defined a nine-step model of drug involvement for the medical students. Although we refer to "steps" of drug involvement for convenience, we emphasize that, in fact, the item-response model has defined a <u>continuum</u> of "drug involvement," and our steps simply represent arbitrary milestones on that continuum.

The drug-involvement model makes the explicit assumption of a drug-use hierarchy. Individuals at each step have used the drug at that step and all those of lower-ranked steps, but none of those defining higher steps. In fact, the responses of 79 students (68%) fulfilled this assumption perfectly. Sixty-two percent of the exceptions were limited to students classified at the highest levels of drug involvement who reached that level despite never having used the drug defining a single subsidiary step.

In the second phase of analysis, we next tested the predictive validity of the original nine-step model (Table 6.2, page 155) longitudinally by examining the responses of students from the original sample who participated in the initial assessment and no less than two subsequent ones (N=99 or 85% of the original respondents). The drugs actually used during medical school by each of the 99 students, summed over the second, third, and fourth assessment periods, were noted without reference to the information collected at the first-time point. Students' cumulative school-year use was classified according to the highest-ranking drug used during the eighteen-month interval. As a result, we would compare drug involvement status estimated at first-day school orientation (as already described) with actual substance use during the first eighteen months of medical school.

In this way, we tested whether drug-use behavior during the school year conformed to the assumption of a drug-use hierarchy and whether changes in use level conformed to the model by progressing no more than one step at a time. Note that this test of the hierarchical assumption differs from that in the first phase of analysis. Now we are testing whether drug use is cumulative in the sense that the step-defining drug and all those of lower-ranked steps are simultaneously being used. With respect to the "cumulative" hierarchical assumption of the model, the school year responses of all but 26 students (26%) conformed perfectly. Seven of the 26 exceptions were due to students who used wine or liquor, but not both; six more exceptions were due to students who failed to use one drug defining a single subsidiary step. Examination of the remainder suggests that students at

145

the sedative level were using alcohol and marijuana, but not necessarily cocaine or stimulants, during the follow-up interval; and that students at the narcotics level tended to use all subsidiary-level drugs except for hallucinogens.

A small minority of students (N=11 or 11%) began to use a drug characterizing a higher level of drug involvement than their baseline position. One began to use beer, two began to use marijuana, two began to use cocaine, one began to use stimulants, and one began to use sedatives, all advancing a single step beyond their baseline level. Two students began to use sedatives and two others began to use narcotics, advancing two, three, five, and six steps and without using the drugs defining intervening steps, in violation of the model prediction. The two students who used narcotics out of sequence both reported "occasional" use during a single (the same) six-month period.

Thirty-two students (32%) remained at their baseline level of drug involvement over the follow-up interval. These subjects did not use any drugs characterizing a higher level of involvement, and they tended to use every one of the drugs defining their baseline model position (that is, the step-defining drug and all those previous steps) over the follow-up interval.

The remaining 56 students (57%) "regressed" from their baseline model position, using drugs that characterized a lower level of drug involvement over the follow-up interval. Most of the 56 (N=43 or 77%) had not used the drugs that defined their baseline level for six months or more at baseline assessment, so that the "regression" was from a lifetime high-water mark that typically did not characterize their actual drug-use level for the months immediately preceding the first day of medical school.

Thus, the overwhelming tendency was to maintain the original cumulative pattern. The changes that did occur tended to follow the steps defined by the model; most changes (34/67 or 51%) involved a single step up or down the scale. Students initially classified at high levels of drug involvement were more likely to change their classification, usually downward, and to change more than one step.

Psychosocial Characteristics of Drug-Involved Students

The index of drug involvement correlated significantly with the following psychosocial variables over time: 1) less emotional expressivity as measured by The Personal Attributes Questionnaire (Spence et al., 1974), 2) less capacity for pleasurable experiences as measured by the Fawcett-Clark Pleasure Scale (Fawcett et al., 1983), 3) less social empathy as measured by the Interpersonal Reactivity Index (Davis, 1983), more satisfaction with social relationships as assessed by the Salloway Social Networks Inventory (Salloway and Dillon, 1972), and 5) poorer performance in medical school classes and the National Board Part I examination. There was also a non-statistically significant tendency for drug-involvement scores to correlate with severity of depression as measured by the Beck Depression Inventory (Beck and Beamesderfer, 1974). Thus, drug involvement appears to be associated with less inclination to become emotionally involved with one's social contacts, with more satisfaction with that kind of social network, and with a worse academic record in medical school.

Relationship Between Drug Involvement and Drug Abuse

Twenty-three students reported using substances defining high-level drug involvement during the first eighteen months of medical school; that is, use of sedatives, hypnotics or tranquilizers, hallucinogens, or narcotics.

Eight of the 23 more drug-involved students (35%) had met Research Diagnostic Criteria for drug abuse or dependence before beginning medical school, as compared to a 16% class history of drug abuse/dependence. The more drug-involved students were not more likely to exhibit a current episode of drug abuse/dependence or alcoholism on the first day of medical school; a history of alcoholism, a family history of drug abuse, alcoholism, or depression; or academic difficulties when compared to the rest of the class.

There was considerable overlap between the excessive drinkers and the more drug-involved students in the class. Four of the nine excessive drinkers (and three of the four chronically excessive drinkers) were ranked among the most drug-involved students in the class.

DISCUSSION

Our preliminary data illustrate the viability of our approach to studying alcohol and drug-use patterns in a sample of medical students. On the first day of medical school, students described drinking patterns for the previous six months that were shaped by idiosyncratic reference groups and by the relative absence of any academic performance pressures. By the end of the first year, overall alcohol consumption declined and students were converging on a normative definition of light and moderate drinking in the

148

medical school setting. Students became very reliable and objective in their classification of their own alcohol-consumption rate relative to their peers. While the general decline in alcohol consumption can easily be attributed to academic work demands, the development of normative standards is clearly a product of social experience. Over time, students developed a better awareness of the range of their classmates' drinking behavior and a better grasp of the evaluation standards employed by their classmates.

Moderate and heavy drinkers described themselves as emotionally invulnerable, competitive, confident, not much concerned with the opinion of others, and emotionally unexpressive. Yet these same qualities did not characterize well those who met diagnostic criteria for alcohol abuse during school. Alcohol-abusing students distinguished themselves with a more frequent history of alcohol and/or drug abuse prior to medical school, and a higher level of drug involvement, when compared to their classmates.

Student drug-use histories and school-year drug-use patterns could be well characterized on a dimension of drug involvement. More drug involvement was associated with less emotional expressivity, less pleasure capacity, less social empathy, more satisfaction with social relationships, and poorer academic performance. Self-description as less emotionally involved with friends was a characteristic shared by moderate-heavy drinkers and the more drug-involved students. Drug-abusing medical students distinguished themselves with a more frequent history of drug and/or alcohol abuse prior to medical school, and a greater likelihood of excessive drinking, when compared to their classmates.

More than half of the excessive drinkers, but only a third of the most drug-involved students, met diagnostic criteria for substance abuse. The substance abusing students were generally not well characterized by the psychosocial profiles of excessive alcohol or drug users. Substance abusers share, however, a high likelihood of a history of alcohol or drug abuse (often both) prior to beginning medical school. Over the first three years of medical school, we find no clear-cut association between excessive drinking and academic performance; but high levels of drug involvement were associated with lower grade point averages over the first two years of medical school, and lower scores on National Boards Part I.

As the class under study progresses into internships and residency training, it will become possible to assess the impact of substance-use patterns during medical school on subsequent career performance. We would like to learn whether the excessive drinkers and more drug-involved students persist in their substance-use patterns through their residency years, whether students with no prior history of excessive alcohol or drug use begin excessive use during their residency years, and what is the precise impact of excessive substance use on a resident's clinical performance. These questions, important for optimizing patient care and planning prevention/ intervention programs, can only be addressed in the context of a longitudinal study.

REFERENCES

Beck, A. T. and Beamesderfer, A. 1974. The Depression Inventory. Modern Problems in Pharmacopsychiatry 7:151-169.

Bissell, L. and Jones, R. 1976. The alcoholic physician: A survey. American Journal of Psychiatry 133:1142-1146.

Bock, R. D. and Aitken, M. 1981. Marginal maximum likelihood estimation of item parameters: An application of the EM algorithm. Psychometrika 46:443-459.

Bock, R. D. and Lieberman, M. 1970. Fitting a response model for N dichotomously scored items. Psychometrika 35:179-197.

Cahalan, D., Cissin, I. H., and Crossley, H. M. 1969. American Drinking Practices. New Brunswick, NJ: Rutgers Center of Alcoholic Studies.

Clark, D. C., Gibbons, R. D., Daugherty, S. R., and Silverman, C. M. In Press. Model for quantifying the drug involvement of medical students. International Journal of Addiction.

Davis, M. H. 1983. Measuring individual differences in empathy: Evidence for a multi-dimensional approach.Journal of Personality and Social Psychology 44:13-126.

Fawcett, J., Clark, D. C., Scheftner, W. A., and Gibbons, R. D. 1983. Assessing anhedonia in psychiatric patients: The Pleasure Scale. Archives of General Psychiatry 40:79-88.

Fine, E. W., Steer, R. A., and Scoles, P. E. 1978. Relationship between blood alcohol concentration and self-reporting drinking behavior. Journal of Studies on Alcoholism 39:466-472.

Guze, S. B., Tuason, V. B., Stewart, M. A., and Picken, G. 1963. The drinking history: A comparison of reports by subjects and their relatives. Quarterly Journal of Studies on Alcoholism 24:249-260.

Harburg, E., Ozgoren, F., Hawthorne, Y. M., and Schork, M. A. 1980. Community norms of alcohol usage and blood pressure. Tecumseh, MI. American Journal of Public Health 70:813-820.

Hesselbrock, M., Babor, T. F., Hesselbrock, V. et al. 1983. "Never believe an alcoholic?" On the validity of self-report measures of alcoholic dependence and related constructs. International Journal of Addictions 18:593-609.

Lord, F. M. 1980. Applications of Item Response Theory to Practical Testing Problems. Hillsdale, NJ: Erlbaum.

McCrady, B. S., Paoline, T. J., and Longabaugh, R. 1978. Correspondence between reports of problem drinkers and spouses on drinking behavior and impairment. Journal of Studies on Alcoholism 39:1252-1257.

McCue, J. 1982. The effects of stress on physicians and their medical practice. New England Journal of Medicine 306:458-463.

Modlin, H. C. and Montes, A. 1964. Narcotics addiction in physicians. American Journal of Psychiatry 121:358-365.

O'Brien, R. G. and Kaiser, M. K. 1985. MANOVA method of analyzing repeated measures designs: An extensive primer. Psychological Bulletin 97:316-333.

O'Malley, P. M., Bachman, J. G., and Johnston, L. D. 1983. Reliability and consistency in self-reports of drug use. International Journal of Addictions 18:805-824.

Ozgoren, F., Schork, M. A., and Harburg, E. 1978. Measures of alcohol usage and ethanol oz/wk and categories of use N-1672. Report No. 7, Tecumseh Family Health Project. Program for Urban Health Research. Ann Arbor: University of Michigan.

Salloway, J. C. and Dillon, P. B. 1972. A comparison of family networks in health care utilization. Journal of Comparative Family Studies 4:1-11.

Samejema, F. 1973. A comment on Birinbaum's three-parameter logistic model in the latent trait theory. Psychometrika 39:221-233.

Single, E., Kandel, D., and Johnson, B. D. 1975. The validity and reliability of drug use responses in a large scale longitudinal survey. Journal of Drug Issues 5:426-443.

Spence, J. T., Helmreich, R. L., and Stapp, J. 1974. The Personality Attributes Questionnaire: A measure of sex-role stereotypes and masculinity-femininity. JSAS Catalog of Selected Documents in Psychology 4:43.

Spitzer, R. L., Endicott, J., and Robins, E. 1978. Research Diagnostic Criteria: Rationale and reliability. Archives of General Psychiatry 35: 773-782.

Stacy, A. W., Widaman, K. F., Hays R., and DiMatteo, N. W. 1985. Validity of self-reports of alcohol and other drug use: A multi-trait/multi-method assessment. Journal of Personality and Social Psychology 49:219-232.

Vaillant, G. E., Bright, J. R., and McArthur, C. 1970. Physicians' use of mood-altering drugs. A 20-year follow up report. New England Journal of Medicine 282:365-370.

Vaillant, G. E., Sobowale, N. C., and McArthur, C. 1972. Some psychological vulnerabilities of physicians. New England Journal of Medicine 287:372-375.

TABLE 6.1
MALE NORMATIVE RANGES (ETHANOL OUNCES PER WEEK)

	First Day	End 1st Year	End 2nd Year	Middle 3rd Year
Never	.00-.04	.00-.03	.00-.14	.00-.12
Very light	.04-1.51	.03-1.44	.14-1.71	.12-1.22
Light	1.51-3.92	1.44-4.30	1.71-2.70	1.22-2.94
Moderate	3.92-9.87	4.30-7.99	2.71-10.22	2.94-7.27
Heavy	9.87 and up	7.99 and up	10.22 and up	7.27 and up

FEMALE NORMATIVE RANGES (ETHANOL OUNCES PER WEEK)

	First Day	End 1st Year	End 2nd Year	Middle 3rd Year
Never	.00-.19	.00-.14	.00-.10	.00-.10
Very light	.19-1.18	.14-1.12	.10-1.18	.10-1.34
Light	1.18-2.72	1.12-1.60	1.18-2.66	1.35-4.08
Moderate	2.72-2.94	1.60-8.03	2.66-5.63	4.08-4.13
Heavy	2.94 and up	8.03 and up	5.63 and up	4.13 and up

TABLE 6.2

MODEL PARAMETERS FOR DRUG-USE ITEMS

(Step)	Substance	Ever Used		Model Parameters		Students at Each Step	
		N	%	Discriminability	Commonality	N	%
0	None	—	—	—	—	—	—
1	Liquor	108	93	.74	− 1.42	7	6
1	Wine	108	93	.82	− 1.41	7	6
2	Beer	103	89	.88	− 1.13	20	17
3	Marijuana	84	72	.94	− 0.57	32	28
4	Cocaine	32	28	.86	0.58	7	6
5	Stimulants	29	25	.73	0.62	10	9
6	Sedatives Hypnotics	25	22	.69	0.77	11	9
7	Tranquilizers Hallucinogens	22	19	.84	0.86	12	10
8	Narcotics	15	13	.80	1.12	15	13
X	Cigarettes	68	59	.46	− 0.21		
X	Coffee	102	88	.36	− 1.16		
X	Other Drugs	6	5	.26	1.56	116	100

155

SUMMARY: U.S. SUBSTANCE USE BY ADOLESCENTS

In Section 1, we looked at alcohol use by adolescents in the U.S. Here in Section 2, we have taken a first look at drug use in the U.S. As in the previous section, we have adopted a life-cycle perspective and paid special attention to very early patterns of drug use and the way that they change through young adulthood.

One of the reasons that this is an effective approach is that patterns of use by the very young gives us a sense of the cultural context of drug use in the same way that we derived a sense of the cultural context of alcohol use. If very young people have access to illegal drugs and, in fact, are using them, then we must assume a de facto permissive culture.

Also important in our approach to this topic is the assumption that experiences with alcohol or with other drugs early in the life cycle will have implications for long-term use of these substances.

In Chapter 4, Forster looks at patterns of early use of drugs among adolescents in an affluent, suburban community. Breaking her study into the discovery of patterns and the factors associated with these patterns, she finds first that use of alcohol, marijuana and cigarettes begins before 5th grade (10 year olds) for a sizeable minority of students and is quite widespread by the senior year of high school (83% for alcohol, 53% for marijuana, and 34% for cigarettes). Even "uppers" and "downers" are being used by 10-17% of high school students.

In an examination of factors associated with drug use, Forster finds that role modeling by parents and older siblings plays an important part in the initiation of the behavior in early life. By high school, peer influences seem to be associated with both experimentation and continuing use. For a minority, there is an association of drug use with alienation from school and community and psychological problems. Forster concludes by suggesting the need for very early drug education as a program of prevention.

In the next chapter, Coombs and Fawzy describe the use of alcohol and drugs by older adolescents, especially in the Los Angeles area. The authors point out that these young people are very often multiple drug users. In addition, they use different drugs simultaneously, leading to compounded levels of risks.

Like Forster, Coombs and Fawzy move from an epidemiological consideration to the analysis of associated factors. By and large, their findings support the work of Forster. They find that both quality of family relationships and role modeling within the family are important predictors of substance use by youth. Also important is the use of substances by peers, indicating a normative component. Again, they find that for some users use of substances is associated with social and psychological pathology.

Clark, Salloway, and Daugherty examine drug and alcohol use in a population which is older still, medical students. In the course of their discussion, they identify the problems of applying national norms to a specific sub-group of the population. They point out that drug use among physicians is substantially higher than for the population as a whole. Some of the reasons have to do with availability, different norms surrounding drug use, and high levels of stress. Given these special circumstances, patterns of use in this population are likely to be different from the general population. They also point out that this is a rather homogeneous group. Thus, the socio-cultural patterns which distinguish between substance users and non-users are less likely to discriminate here. Instead, individual and interpersonal influences are more likely to be the key discriminators.

The pattern of drinking over time which they find is in keeping with the findings of Iutcovich and Vaughn (Chapter 2). The norms for the group change over time. In addition, within their sample they find that there is a specific sub-group of heavy drinkers which is responsible for much of their statistical findings. These drinkers are competitive, confident, emotionally tough, and have large social networks of friends (as opposed to family). Moreover, these heavy drinkers increase their drinking over time.

Drug use among some of these medical students is on a progressive continuum. This abusing sub-group begins using drugs low on the continuum (for example, alcohol and marijuana) and continues in step-like progression to sedatives and then narcotics. About 8% of these medical students use hard drugs. Moreover, there is substantial overlap between those who are heavy drinkers and those who are using drugs. It should be noted, however, that the majority of medical students use minimal problematic drugs and do not increase their usage over time. As with Forster's data, we see about 10% of this sub-group having abuse problems.

What we learn from this section is that in the U.S. there is a strong undercurrent of drug usage present in the society. Moreover, this undercurrent begins to affect behavior at a very early age. While there is acceptance of specific substances as being permissible for social use, a substantial minority extend that acceptability to more dangerous drugs and to excessive use of acceptable drugs. By the end of high school, substance usage of the most popular and available drugs -- alcohol, marijuana, caffeine, and nicotine (cigarettes) -- is pervasive. But, about 10% of the sub-groups studied show indications of serious and problematic drug involvement. The major factors associated with drug use at an early age seem to be curiosity, availability, acceptability, and pleasurable drug effects.

We also learn that role models and peer groups are potent forces in fostering this behavior. For most, role modeling and peer influences encourage "casual" use of popular substances. For a smaller group, however, this substance-using behavior is associated with social or psychological pathologies. These pathologies seem to include high levels of perceived stress, a "macho" image, and weakened familial ties which are replaced by a supportive peer sub-group which abuses substances. Implicit in several of these chapters is the sense that this early substance-using behavior "hardens" as people enter early maturity. What remains to be seen in the next section is the extent to which these behaviors then become a form of pathology on their own.

SECTION 3
U.S. ALCOHOL USE IN ADULT POPULATIONS

INTRODUCTION

In the two sections which precede this one, U.S. Alcohol Use by Adolescents and U.S. Substance Abuse by Adolescents, we examined the use of alcohol and drugs in essentially youthful populations. The issue which confronted us there was the initiation of these behaviors: Why do they begin? To answer this question, we looked at different patterns of alcohol and drug use and tried to make generalizations about the acquisition of the behavior.

In this next section, we begin to consider the use of alcohol in adult populations. Later, in Section 4, we will consider substance use in adult populations.

Our earlier conclusions about youthful alcohol use virtually determine the nature of our inquiry into alcohol use in adult populations. We have concluded that alcohol is the legally available drug, that use of alcohol begins at a remarkably early age in this society, and that its use through adolescence is not necessarily associated with pathology -- in fact, it is rather normative.

Thus, for adult populations, drinking is not a new behavior, nor is it a negatively sanctioned behavior under most circumstances. We find ourselves asking the same questions which guided our inquiry earlier: What are the patterns of adult alcohol use? Under what conditions is use problematic? What guide do these patterns give us toward prevention of alcohol abuse for adults?

A central issue which will confront us during the next section is that of alcohol use as a situational adaptation. We have seen in Sections 1 and 2 that alcohol is readily available and that the behavior of using it is widespread. Now we are led to ask: Are there situations in which people increase their alcohol-using behavior dramatically as an adaptation to the situations in which they find themselves?

To answer this question, we consider drinking behavior among impaired and non-impaired elderly (Butler et al.), among the residents of skid row (Fagan), among the families of death-row inmates (Smykla), and as a concomitant of acculturation and marital satisfaction in a Mexican-American population (Markides and Krause).

INTRODUCTION TO CHAPTER 7

The reasons that people begin drinking and the reasons for which drinking either continues or becomes problematic are very different issues. We have dealt extensively with the initiation of drinking behaviors in Section 1. Here, Butler, Schuller-Friedman, and Shichor raise for us some important questions about the continuing use of alcohol and other drugs among adults.

They begin their research report with the appropriate question: What are the patterns of use? Implicit within this question are several hypotheses: Does drinking behavior change with age? Certainly we saw this in the transition from adolescence to college (compare Wylie et al., Chapter 1, to Iutcovich and Vaughn, Chapter 2). If there is evidence of further change with aging, is it because of the loss of meaningful activity as people get old? Is it to anesthetize against the ailments associated with aging?

Factors associated with increased alcohol use is a topic which has been dealt with extensively in other studies (Wood, 1982 and especially Counte et al., 1982). Previous studies, however, have typically dealt with one variable at a time: age differences, sex differences, differences in disability, and so on. In this chapter, Butler, Schuller-Friedman, and Shichor bring these three sets of variables together in a single analysis that is very informative and somewhat surprising for its results.

Two related issues arise in their analysis which bear close scrutiny for our purposes. First, this adult sample distinguishes between "drugs" and "medications" which often includes legal, over-the-counter drugs. They perceive them as different categories. Thus, though we might define them as "drug users" in the sense that they consume chemical substances frequently, they do not define themselves as drug users.

Secondly, Coombs and Fawzy (Chapter 5) have alerted us to the potentiating effects of alcohol and drugs. Thus, these people are at special risk for these interactive effects. However, as people age, their tolerance for drugs often diminishes. Here we have a triple-threat situation: people 1) who tend to be compromised in their ability to handle drugs, 2) are mixing alcohol and other drugs which may have potentiating effects, and 3) do not see themselves as taking drugs. This is a potentially dangerous situation and one that is difficult to alter.

CHAPTER 7

ALCOHOL AND DRUG USE AMONG IMPAIRED AND NON-IMPAIRED ELDERLY PERSONS

Edgar W. Butler, Susan Schuller-Friedman, and David Shichor

ABSTRACT

The research reported in this chapter examines several key questions about the drug use of the elderly by utilizing data from a general community sample of older people in a southern California medium-sized city. We have examined the extent of drugs used by the elderly, including how many and what types of drugs are used. Focus also is on drug-use differences by impaired as opposed to non-impaired older persons.

The non-impaired at all ages are more likely than the impaired to drink alcoholic beverages. However, except for the frail elderly (80 years of age and over), the impaired who drink do so more than the non-impaired who drink. The use of illegal drugs is relatively minor among these older people. The use of legal drugs, however, is extensive, especially for tranquilizers and barbiturates. For all ages examined, the use of drugs, legal and illegal, is nearly the same or greater by the non-impaired as opposed to the impaired. Many of these older persons

EDGAR W. BUTLER is currently Principal Investigator of a National Institute on Aging grant and Chair of the Department of Sociology, University of California, Riverside. SUSAN SCHULLER-FRIEDMAN is Assistant Professor and Director of Research and Grants at the College of Osteopathic Medicine of the Pacific. DAVID SHICHOR is Professor in the Department of Criminal Justice, California State University, San Bernadino.

also are consuming alcohol in combination with a variety of drugs.

One of the reasons often reported for greater drug use by older persons is that they are more likely than younger persons to have both physical and mental disorders. In contrast to this belief, this research shows consistently that the non-impaired are greater users of alcohol and drugs than are the impaired. However, the extent of drug use by this elderly population can be considered extensive and a matter of great concern.

INTRODUCTION

Currently there are few studies examining drug use among the elderly (Petersen, 1975; Glantz, 1983). Much of the research reported so far relies upon institutionalized populations, people living in hospitals, or in a variety of community care facilities. These studies have used a variety of research techniques ranging from gathering anecdotal data to using physicians and/or hospital records. For the most part, previous research has used non-representative samples rather than representative community samples (Glantz et al., 1983).

The literature has focused primarily on the following questions: 1) the extent of drug use by the elderly (How many and what types of drugs are taken?), 2) the patterns of this use (Who takes many

----

This investigation was supported by Public Health Service Research Grant No. AG-00320 from the National Institutes of Health, National Institute of Aging, Edgar W. Butler, Principal Investigator; Public Health Service Research Grant No. MN-08667 from the National Institute of Mental Health, Department of Health, Education and Welfare, Edgar W. Butler, Principal Investigator; and National Institute of Education Grant No. NIE-G-74-0095, Edgar W. Butler, Principal Investigator. David M. Petersen read an earlier draft and made valuable suggestions. The expressions reported herein are those of the authors and do not necessarily represent those of the reviewers or granting agencies.

drugs for what reasons or under what conditions, and
who takes few drugs or none?), 3) the extent of drug
misuse and abuse among the elderly (What types of
problems occur with various types of drugs, and what is
the frequency of each problem?), and 4) the causes of
this misuse and abuse (What factors precipitate or
exacerbate these problems?) (Petersen et al., 1979:19)
Yet, as Petersen and his colleagues noted, most of
these issues remain unresolved and the research so far
has raised more questions than it has settled.[1]

The research reported in this paper examines
several of these key questions about the drug use of
the elderly by utilizing data from a general community
sample of older people in a southern California medium-
sized city. Thus, this research avoids at least some
of the limitations of previous studies. We delineate
the extent of drug use by the elderly, including how
many and what types of drugs are used. We also examine
who does and who does not take drugs, and the extent of
legal use and illegal drug use among the elderly.

RESEARCH METHODOLOGY

Our basic research model, from which this chapter
is derived, posits that there are a number of
environmental, individual, and family characteristics,
which, when mediated by several different intervening
factors, lead to differential adjustment outcomes,
including alcohol and drug use. To test this
hypothesis, a survey, conducted in 1963, consisting of
a ten-percent sample of the households in a southern
California city, stratified geographically and socio-

---

[1] No attempt is made in this chapter to relate our findings to
the myriad "theories" of drug abuse. Our review of them suggests
that all of them are deficient (Lettieri, Sayers, and Pearson,
1980).

economically, served as a baseline from which a follow-up survey was conducted in 1977.[2] The 1977 follow-up survey included extensive questions about alcohol and drug use. In addition, the 1977 questionnaire included personal and demographic data, family attitudes toward the individual, physical health, medical and behavioral history, school and family background data.

The original 1963 sample included 8,556 individuals, with 1,218 being between 36 and 45 years old, 919 being between 46 and 55, 587 between 56 and 65, and 666 being 66 years of age or older. Thus, the original 1963 household study included data on 3,390 persons who were 36 years of age and older, of which 2,724 were between the ages of 36 and 65 years, while 666 were 66 years of age or older. These two age categories were not considered as separate sub-samples in the original 1963 study, but we treat them as distinct sub-samples here to facilitate comparisons with the two 1977 follow-up sub-samples described below.

Since the 1963 sub-samples were representative of the community, age distributions were skewed toward the more youthful end of the age ranges under study. Thus, while 44.7% of the young elderly sub-sample was between the ages of 36 and 45 years, only 21.6% of this sub-sample was between the ages of 56 and 65 years. The distribution of the older age sub-sample, "frail

----

[2] For a more detailed discussion of the 1963 baseline sample selection see Mercer (1973). For a discussion of the overall project, see Butler and Friedman (1984). The sample was also followed up in 1984.

elderly," was even more skewed with 65.3% in the more youthful end (age 65-75 years) of the two age ranges in the older sample. This distribution reflects different population proportional declines due to the increased mortality risks associated with increasing age.

The sample selection procedures for the 1977 follow-up study produced two sub-samples: 1) those aged 36 to 65 years in 1963, and 2) those aged 66 years and over in 1963. All persons 66 years of age and over in 1963, whether impaired (N=341) or non-impaired (N=325), were selected for one follow-up sub-sample (N=666). For those aged 36-65 years, all impaired persons (physically, intellectually, or with multiple impairments) were included in the second follow-up sub-sample (N=489). In addition, for each of six five-year age categories, a matching proportion (N=483) of non-impaired persons within each five-year age category was randomly selected (by computer) to be included in the second follow-up sub-sample. Thus, from the 1963 community study sample of 3,390 persons age 36 years and over (50 years of age and over in 1977), the total follow-up sub-sample figures were: age 36 to 65 years (50 to 79 in 1977), 972 subjects, and age 66 years and over (80 and over in 1977), 666 subjects (for a total follow-up sample of 1,638).

For the ages 36 to 65 in 1963, we located 93.6% (including the deceased) and interviewed 72.8% (excluding the deceased) in 1977. For those 66 years and over in 1963, we located 88.3% (including the deceased) and interviewed 71.6% (excluding the deceased) in 1977. Both the 1963 and 1977 sub-samples included a somewhat higher proportion of females than males (52.8% and 58.3% respectively). The ethnic distribution of both sub-samples included primarily anglos (89.6% and 91.4% respectively), with chicanos (approximately 5%) forming the second largest ethnic category in both sub-samples. These percentages parallel the ethnic distribution of this city in 1963 for these age categories.

Both sub-samples were composed primarily of married persons. However, the proportion of marrieds in the youngest sub-sample was much higher than in the older sub-sample (86.2% and 55.9% respectively). This is primarily a reflection of the increased risk of widowhood accompanying old age. Thus, the widowed formed the second largest proportional grouping (37.4%) in the older age sub-sample, while divorced and separated persons proportionally formed the second largest marital status category (5.4%) in the youngest age sub-sample. An overwhelming proportion (93.6% and 89.4% respectively) of both sub-samples were either heads of household or spouses of heads of household.

The younger age sub-sample was almost evenly distributed among the three educational attainment levels (30.8% had completed 0 to 11 years of school, 32.2% had completed 12 years, and 37% had completed 13 or more years. The older age sub-sample differed markedly, with fully 60.2% in the lowest educational attainment category. Again, this is primarily a reflection of cohort differences in average educational attainment levels. The socioeconomic status of both sub-samples was primarily in the middle range, 49.7% and 44.4% respectively, with the second most predominant socioeconomic status category being at the lowest end of the range (this was particularly the case for the eldest age sample, of which 36.6% were in the lowest socioeconomic status category). The religious composition of both sub-samples was primarily Protestant (71.6% and 77.5% respectively), with Catholics forming the second largest religious grouping.

As a result of extensive analyses comparing the sub-sample interviewed for the 1977 follow-up study, we know that they differ in several significant sociodemographic ways from the 1963 sample. Some of these sociodemographic differences are inevitable accompaniments of longitudinal research among the middle-aged and aged. For these age categories in particular, aging is associated with increased mortality. Since mortality is also differentially distributed among various sociodemographic population characteristics, it is to be expected that those socio-demographic segments of the population which are less at risk, even with advancing age, will increasingly form greater proportions of the population in question. Distribution differences in this sub-sample also are a reflection of the follow-up sampling procedure over-representing impaired persons in the sub-sample selection. Also not to be ignored is the combined effect of impairment and mortality since the impaired have a higher risk of mortality.

Thus, for cross-sectional and longitudinal analyses, differential longevity patterns resulted in both of these follow-up sub-samples, especially the older age sub-sample, being a distinct population of survivors. In particular for the younger aged sub-sample analysis, results may have been influenced by the proportion of impaired persons in the sample; therefore, in analyses not directly exploring impairment per se, caution should be exercised in generalizing to other aged populations.

In all of the analyses presented in the findings section, the age categories of 50 to 64 years (middle-aged), 65 to 79 years (young elderly), and 80 years and over (frail elderly) are used. To our knowledge this is the first time such a refined age breakdown has been used to examine variation in drug use among older people. The ages referred to in our analyses are as of the 1977 follow-up interview.

IMPAIRMENT STATUS

"Impairments" in this paper are defined using a criterion of functioning at the bottom sixteen percent (one standard deviation below average) for adult persons along three dimensions of impairment: 1) physical, 2) intellectual, and 3) both physical and intellectual impairments. "Physical" includes persons with impaired functioning in at least one of the following: walking, seeing, hearing, talking, feeding, dressing, sleeping, and being epileptic. "Intellectual" impairment includes persons who experienced at least two of the following situations in their school careers: 1) below age grade norm, 2) trouble learning, 3) special education classes, 4) same grade twice, and 5) school or learning problems. For analytic purposes, four categories of impairments are specified: 1) physical, 2) intellectual, 3) multiple, including both impairment categories, and 4) the non-impaired.

In our previous analyses of the 1963 baseline data, we found that persons 50 years of age and over had higher rates of impairment than people in younger age categories (Petersen, 1983).

Table 7.1, page 183, shows that exactly half of those between the ages of 50 and 64 were non-impaired. Of course, this was the basis for our follow-up sample design for these age categories -- that is, including all of the impaired and an equal-sized sample of the non-impaired. At the older age categories (young elderly and frail elderly), the follow-up sample design included all of the population, both impaired and non-impaired. Differences in impairment status by age in these sub-samples are partially a result of sub-sample selection procedures.

FINDINGS
Alcohol

Alcohol use was analyzed by impairment status and by age. As shown in Tables 7.2, 7.3, and 7.4, pages 184, 185, and 186 respectively, there is a clear and significant[3] trend for alcohol use to be negatively related to age: 61.6% of those 50 to 64 years, 53.5% of the 65 to 79 year olds, and 28.8% of those 80 years and over reported that they drink alcoholic beverages. To determine if the negative relationship between age and alcohol use was due to the different sex distributions by age in the sample populations, we further analyzed the data controlling for sex. Our analysis shows that the relationship between age and alcohol use is significant for both females and males; however, the

----
[3] Whenever the term "significant" is used in this paper it means statistically significant differences exist.

reduction by age in alcoholic consumption for males and females is different because at all three of the age categories a greater proportion of males than females drink (on the order of 13% to 20%).

In all age categories studied, more of the non-impaired than the impaired drink alcoholic beverages, but the difference between the non-impaired and impaired is largest and significant in the middle-aged (50 to 64 years) category -- 70.9% versus 52.1%. Alcohol use for the young elderly (65 to 79 years of age) was considerably lower and the difference between the non-impaired and impaired was less -- 42.3% versus 34.5% -- but was still statistically significant. The trend for alcohol use by the frail elderly (80 years of age and over) was similar, but the difference between the non-impaired and impaired was smaller and not statistically significant.

Among the different impairment categories, the pattern of alcohol use is not clear-cut since consumption varies by age. In the middle-age years, the most substantial use is by the physically impaired, with the multiple impaired being least likely to drink. Yet, an exact opposite pattern occurs for the young elderly with the multiple impaired being most likely to be drinkers and the physically impaired being least likely to drink. Among the frail elderly (80 years and over), the physically and multiply impaired were about equally likely to consume alcohol.

There is a difference in whether a person drinks or not, how much he or she drinks, and the pattern of drinking (Dunham, 1981). We categorized the quantity of drinking as slight, moderate, or heavy as reported by the respondent. Our analyses show quite clearly that there is a negative relationship between age and quantity of alcoholic beverages drunk. However, for quantity of use by impairment status, the results reveal a somewhat different pattern. Among the middle-aged, the non-impaired drink heavier quantities than do the impaired; however, for the young elderly, the percent of heavier drinkers by impairment status is about equal. Finally, among the frail elderly, the impaired are significantly more likely to be heavier drinkers than the non-impaired.

Of those who drink, the frequency of drinking varies in an opposite direction to use and quantity. That is, frail elderly drinkers drink more frequently than middle-aged or young elderly who drink. Similarly, except for the frail elderly, the impaired who drank were much more frequent drinkers than the non-impaired who drank. Thus, both age and impairment are positively related to frequency of alcohol consumption (Smart and Liban, 1981).

The survey questionnaire also included a question on whether or not alcohol use had ever caused the person any "trouble" with relatives, at work, and so on. Only a very few of these older people reported any trouble because of alcohol use. The differences between the impaired and non-impaired were small, except for the frail elderly in which 8.6% of the impaired reported trouble, whereas none of the non-impaired reported trouble because of their alcohol use.

Drug Use

At all age levels examined in this research, drug use is extensive (National Commission, 1973: 58ff). As shown in Tables 7.5, 7.6, and 7.7, pages 187, 188,

173

and 189 respectively, for almost every drug and at all age levels, drug use is greater for the non-impaired than for the impaired. Females at all ages were more likely to be drug users than were males. Drug use by females is similar for all three age categories examined in this research; for males there are some minor differences, with frail elderly males being slightly less likely to use drugs than are frail elderly females.

According to these self-reports, the use of illegal drugs is not widespread among these middle-aged and older-aged respondents. In contrast to alcohol use, narcotics use does not vary with age but remains virtually the same (about 11%). No one in this sample reported the use of hallucinogens, and the use of marijuana is virtually non-existent. Thus, such legal drugs as tranquilizers and barbiturates account for most of the drug use by this middle-aged and elderly population. For the middle-aged and young elderly, the most extensively used drugs are tranquilizers, 39.3% and 63.7% respectively. For the frail elderly, the use of tranquilizers (19.7%) and barbiturates (18.1%) is about equal; however, there is a significant difference between the frail elderly and the others in tranquilizer use. The slight use of amphetamines is negatively related to age.

For all ages examined, and almost every impairment, the use of drugs, legal and illegal, is nearly the same or is greater for the non-impaired as opposed to the impaired (Guttman, 1978). While there is, in general, a negative relationship between age and drug use, attributable primarily to fewer males, age is only a somewhat useful predictor of drug use. Once a person begins using a drug, that use continues for an extended period. Thus, older persons who indicated that they had ever used drugs were quite likely to indicate that they were continuing to do so. This continued use suggests that a drug dependency develops, both for illegal and legal drugs.

While age is a somewhat useful predictor of drug use, major sex differences were found in the number of drugs used and the length of drug use. Females take significantly more drugs than males and are more likely to continue using drugs for an extended period (Hale et al., 1979; Guttman, 1978). Generally the trend is for more of the non-impaired to be drug users than the impaired. The difference in using drugs, by impairment status, however, varies by age. For the middle-aged, the non-impaired were only slightly more likely than the impaired to be drug users. For the young elderly, the non-impaired were substantially more likely to be drug users than the impaired (+17%), while for the frail elderly, the non-impaired were even more likely than the impaired to be drug users (+20%).

Within impairment categories, both the older physically and intellectually impaired were less likely than the middle-aged physically impaired to use drugs. For those who had multiple impairments, the older were less likely than the middle-aged multiply impaired to use drugs, but the differences are not very large.

By drug categories, only barbiturates and tranquilizers had enough users so that an analysis could be carried out. For those who used barbiturates, no differences exist in frequency of use by age; for tranquilizers, the frail elderly had lower levels of use than those in the middle-ages. Only a very small percentage of drug users reported getting into any kind of "trouble" because of drug use.

Multiple Use of Alcohol and Drugs

Of special concern is the extent of alcohol and drug use in combination and use of multiple drugs (Eisdorfer and Basen, 1979; for a contrasting view, see Inciardi et al., 1978). As Table 7.8, page 190, shows, 22.3% of these older people do not drink alcohol or use drugs. A slightly greater percentage do not drink alcohol but do use drugs. Also, there are alcohol drinkers who do not use drugs (16.3%). Finally, over one-third of these people both drink alcohol and use drugs, many of them in combination.

For those who consume alcohol and use drugs, the main combination is alcohol and "other drugs" (those not elsewhere classified). However, there is substantial alcohol consumption in combination with the use of tranquilizers. In addition, about half of those who consume alcohol also ingest at least two or more different drugs; for example, tranquilizers and some other drug. A similar multiple drug-ingestion pattern is exhibited by those who do not drink alcoholic beverages.

The general impression one gains form this data is that there is a substantial portion of this middle-aged, young elderly, and frail elderly population that is consuming alcohol in combination with a variety of drugs, and that some drug users who do not consume alcoholic beverages use a variety of drugs in combination (Raffoul et al., 1981).

DISCUSSION AND CONCLUSIONS

Overall, with the exception of the frail elderly, alcohol use by middle-aged and young elderly is widespread. The use of alcohol differs by age. These age differences may be a result of cohort differences or differential mortality rather than individual decline in the use of alcohol. Which of these alternatives offers the best explanation, of course, can be determined only by longitudinal data on individual consumption patterns; while this investigation was part of a large longitudinal study, the original 1963 baseline survey did not include alcohol or drug-use questions. In addition, for those who drink alcoholic beverages, age is negatively related to quantity of alcohol consumed. Again, whether this should be attributed to individual decline in use, to cohort differences, or differential mortality cannot be ascertained by us. With regard to age and frequency of alcohol use, for those who drink, an almost opposite relationship exists, with frequency increasing by age category.

The non-impaired at all ages are more likely than the impaired to drink, although there is some variation regarding quantity by impairment status. However, except for the frail elderly, the impaired who drink do so more frequently than the non-impaired who drink. At all age categories, more males than females drink, although within age categories fewer of both males and females drink at the older ages. Some variation exists in drinking behavior among impairment categories, but the findings are mixed.

The use of legal drugs by the middle-aged, young elderly, and frail elderly is extensive. Among the middle-aged, the primary drug used is tranquilizers, while the frail elderly equally use tranquilizers and barbiturates. Amphetamine use is relatively minor at all of these ages.

For all ages examined and for almost every impairment category, the use of drugs, legal and illegal, is nearly the same or is greater by the non-impaired than the impaired. Age is only a slight predictor of drug use, perhaps because once individuals begin using a drug, they apparently continue to use it. This continued use suggests that a drug dependency can develop for legal as well as illegal drugs. In contrast to alcohol consumption, females ingest more drugs than males and are more likely to continue using them for an extended period. Few people reported getting into any kind of "trouble" because of drug use.

This research also demonstrated that many of these people are consuming alcohol in combination with a variety of drugs. Ignorance is not bliss when both drugs and alcohol are used simultaneously by the same person. In certain combinations, they are deadly. According to some reports, over one million elderly people each year are hospitalized because of drug reactions, drug and alcohol, or drug and food interaction. Similarly, some elderly people in our sample are taking multiple drugs, some over-the-counter and some prescription, without any notion of their possible lethal interaction. Some of these drugs in combination with each other or with alcohol may result in what appears to be senility, but what in fact is an adverse drug reaction (Williamson and Chopin, 1980).

One of the reasons often reported for greater drug use by older persons is that they are more likely to have both physical and mental disorders than are younger people (Lofholm, 1978). Yet our research shows consistently, for both alcohol consumption and drug use, impaired persons in all three age categories are less likely to be alcohol and drug consumers than are the non-impaired. Despite being more likely to have chronic conditions, many of these older impaired people do not rely on drugs for long-term management and symptomatic control, objectives generally abscribed to drug therapy. This research calls into question the idea that drug use is a necessary concomitant of being impaired. Apparently, drug use is related to factors in addition to health status since the impaired are less likely to use drugs than are the non-impaired. In fact, the use of drugs may be causing greater suffering than would their non-use.

Three caveats are in order regarding these analyses. First, it is possible that not all respondents were fully aware of the nature of the prescription drugs they were using. Some prescriptions and over-the-counter drugs may have included specific drugs we inquired about but the respondent may not have been aware of them. Second, the middle-aged and older population may view drugs in a substantially different manner than do young people.[4] When queried regarding drug-use patterns, older respondents in our sample tended not to view prescription drugs (amphetamines, tranquilizers, and barbiturates) as being "drugs." "Drugs" to them are marijuana, hallucinogens, opium, and so on. -- They would not and do not use them. Thus, especially for the older generation, careful evaluation of the wording of questions and inquiries

----
[4]   In another phase of this research, drug use among young adults was analyzed. At the time of the re-interview, the young adult respondents were 20 to 26 years of age. Their drug use was substantially less than the drug use by these middle-aged and older respondents. Younger people, however, had a greater level of alcoholic beverage consumption (Kawaguchi and Butler, 1981).

about the use of various individual substances must be made before one can have much faith in the reported use of "drugs." Third, since our measures of impairments were of 1963 status, our findings indicating greater drug use among the non-impaired than the impaired may have reflected higher drug use among the non-impaired who recently experienced the onset of chronic illness and disability.

If it is accepted that not all respondents are aware of the drugs that they are taking via prescription and over-the-counter, these reports of drug use and drug misuse must be considered as underestimating the total drug ingestion by these people. If this is so, the extent of drug use by these middle-aged, young elderly, and frail elderly is extremely large, suggesting a great extent of drug dependency, albeit perhaps of legal as opposed to illegal drugs. If this drug ingestion is coupled with alcoholic consumption, the use of drugs by this elderly population can be considered extensive and a matter of great concern (Warheit et al., 1976).

REFERENCES

Butler, E. W. and Schuller-Friedman, S. 1984. Longitudinal studies of impaired competence in the community: A description of the Riverside Community Research Project (1963 to 1979). In S. A. Mednick, M. Harway, and K. M. Finello (eds.), Handbook of Longitudinal Research, Vol. Two (pp. 182-196). New York: Praeger.

Dunham, R. G. 1981. Aging and changing patterns of alcohol use. Journal of Psychoactive Drugs 13:143-151.

Eisdorfer, C. and Basen, M. M. 1979. Drug misuse by the elderly. In R. L. DuPont, A. Goldstein, and J. O'Dennell (eds.), Handbook on Drug Abuse (pp. 171-178). Rockville, MD: National Institute on Drug Abuse.

Glantz, M. D. 1983. Drugs and the elderly adult: An overview. In M. D. Glantz, D. M. Petersen, and F. J. Whittington (eds.), Drugs and the Elderly Adult. Rockville, MD: National Institute on Drug Use.

Glantz, M. D., Petersen, D. M., and Whittington, F. J. (eds.). 1983. Drugs and the Elderly Adult. Rockville, MD: National Institute on Drug Use.

Guttman, D. 1978. Patterns of legal drug use by older Americans. Addictive Diseases 3:337-356.

Hale, W. E., Marks, R. G., and Stewart, R. B. 1979. Drug use in a geriatric population. Journal of the American Geriatrics Society 27:374-377.

Inciardi, J. A., McBride, D. C., Russe, B. R., and Wells, K. S. 1978. Acute drug reactions among the aged: A research note. Addictive Diseases 3:383-388.

Kawaguchi, R. and Butler, E. W. 1981. Impairments and community adjustment of young adults: Alcohol use, drug use, and arrest. Addictive Diseases 4:127-148.

Lettieri, D. J., Sayers, M., and Pearson, H. W. (eds.). 1980. Theories on Drug Abuse. Washington, DC: National Institute on Drug Abuse.

Lofholm, P. 1978. Self-medication by the elderly. In R. C. Kayne, (ed.), Drugs and the Elderly (pp. 8-28). Los Angeles: University of Southern California Press.

Mercer, J. R. 1973. Labeling the Retarded. Berkeley: University of California Press.

National Commission on Marijuana and Drug Abuse. 1973. Drug Use in Americans: Problem in Perspective. Washington, DC: U.S. Government Publishing Office.

Petersen, D. M. and Thoms, C. W. 1975. Acute drug reactions among the elderly. Journal of Gerontology 30:552-556.

Petersen, D. M., Whittington, F. J., and Beer, E. T. 1979. Drug use and misuse among the elderly. Journal of Drug Issues 9:5-26.

Petersen, D. M. 1983. Epidemiology of drug use. In M. D. Glantz, D. M. Petersen, and F. J. Whittington (eds.), Drugs and the Elderly Adult. Rockville, MD: National Institute on Drug Use.

Raffoul, P. R., Cooper, J. K., and Love, D. W. 1981. Drug misuse in older people. The Gerontologist 21: 146-150.

Smart, R. G. and Liban, C. B. 1981. Predictors of problem drinking among elderly, middle-aged and youthful drinkers. Journal of Psychoactive Drugs 13:153-163.

Warheit, G. J., Arey, S. A., Swanson, E. 1976. Patterns of drug use: An epidemiologic overview. Journal of Drug Issues 6:223-237.

Williamson, J. and Chopin, J. M. 1980. Adverse reactions to prescribed drugs in the elderly: A multi-centre investigation. Age and Aging 9:73-80.

TABLE 7.1
IMPAIRMENT STATUS BY AGE

Impairment Status	AGE PERCENTAGES		
	Middle-Aged (50-64)	Young Elderly (65-79)	Frail Elderly (80 and over)
Non-Impaired	50.0%	51.5%	62.4%
Physically Impaired	9.4%	5.8%	7.1%
Intellectually Impaired	37.4%	35.8%	22.7%
Multiple Impaired	3.1%	6.8%	7.8%
TOTALS	99.9%* (N = 286)	99.9%* (N = 293)	100.0% (N = 141)

---

* Rounding error.

183

TABLE 7.2

ALCOHOL USE, QUANTITY, FREQUENCY, AND TROUBLE BY IMPAIRMENT STATUS: AGES 50 TO 64

| | Impaired Status Percentages | | | | | |
	Phys. (N=27)	Intel. (N-104)	Mult. (N=9)	Impaired Subtotal (N=140)	Non-Imp. (N-141)	Total (N=281)
ALCOHOL						
Use*	63.0%	51.0%	33.3%	52.1%	70.9%	61.6%
Quantity-Moderate Or More	19.4%	13.2%	33.3%	16.4%	26.0%	21.4%
Frequency-At Least Weekly	56.3%	49.1%	33.3%	39.6%	30.0%	31.4%
Trouble	0.0%	5.8%	0.0%	5.3%	6.2%	5.3%

---

* Statistically significant between impaired and non-impaired, ever used.

TABLE 7.3

ALCOHOL USE, QUANTITY, FREQUENCY,
AND TROUBLE BY IMPAIRMENT STATUS:
AGES 65 to 79

	Impaired Status Percentages					
	Phys. (N=15)	Intel. (N=104)	Mult. (N=40)	Impaired Subtotal (N=139)	Non-Imp. (N=149)	Total (N=188)
ALCOHOL						
Use*	26.7%	34.6%	60.0%	34.5%	42.3%	53.5%
Quantity-Moderate Or More	0.0%	22.2%	12.5%	18.8%	18.6%	18.7%
Frequency-At Least Weekly	50.0%	63.9%	75.0%	64.6%	31.4%	35.8%
Trouble	0.0%	2.8%	0.0%	2.1%	0.0%	0.8%

---

* Statistically significant between impaired and non-impaired, ever used.

TABLE 7.4

ALCOHOL USE, QUANTITY, FREQUENCY,
AND TROUBLE BY IMPAIRMENT STATUS:
AGES 80 AND OVER

	Impaired Status Percentages					
	Phys. (N=12)	Intel. (N=32)	Mult. (N=11)	Impaired Subtotal (N=55)	Non-Imp. (N=86)	Total (N=141)
ALCOHOL						
Use*	33.3%	18.8%	27.3%	28.8%	32.1%	28.8%
Quantity- Moderate Or More	25.0%	0.0%	33.3%	15.4%	7.4%	10.0%
Frequency- At Least Weekly	75.0%	50.9%	33.3%	53.8%	55.5%	55.0%
Trouble	25.0%	0.0%	0.0%	8.6%	0.0%	0.7%

---

* Statistically significant between impaired and non-impaired, ever used.

186

TABLE 7.5

ALCOHOL USE, TYPE, AND TROUBLE
BY IMPAIRMENT STATUS:
AGES 50 TO 64

| | Impaired Status Percentages | | | | | |
	Phys. (N=27)	Intel. (N=104)	Mult. (N=9)	Impaired Subtotal (N=140)	Non-Imp. (N=141)	Total (N=281)
ALCOHOL						
Use*	73.9%	55.6%	44.4%	58.1%	71.1%	64.7%
Barbiturates	23.1%	9.8%	11.1%	12.4%	18.7%	15.6%
Tranquilizers**	55.6%	34.0%	33.3%	30.9%	40.4%	39.3%
Amphetamines	11.1%	1.9%	0.0%	3.6%	7.1%	5.3%
Marijuana	3.7%	1.0%	0.0%	1.4%	0.7%	1.1%
Hallucinogens	0.0%	0.0%	0.0%	0.0%	0.0%	0.0%
Narcotics	8.3%	8.8%	0.0%	8.1%	15.1%	11.7%
Trouble	0.0%	0.0%	0.0%	0.0%	1.4%	0.8%

----

*   Ever used.

**   Statistically significant.

TABLE 7.6

ALCOHOL USE, TYPE, AND TROUBLE
BY IMPAIRMENT STATUS:
AGES 65 TO 79

| | Impaired Status Percentages | | | | | |
	Phys. (N=15)	Intel. (N=100)	Mult. (N=19)	Impaired Subtotal (N=134)	Non-Imp. (N=144)	Total (N=278)
ALCOHOL						
Use*	64.3%	53.8%	72.2%	57.7%	72.4%	65.4%
Barbiturates	40.0%	8.0%	15.8%	12.7%	18.1%	4.5%
Tranquilizers**	53.3%	25.3%	36.8%	29.9%	42.1%	63.7%
Amphetamines	0.0%	2.0%	5.3%	2.2%	4.1%	3.2%
Marijuana	6.7%	0.0%	5.0%	1.4%	0.0%	0.7%
Hallucinogens	0.0%	0.0%	0.0%	0.0%	0.0%	0.0%
Narcotics	26.7%	7.8%	26.3%	12.5%	11.0%	11.7%
Trouble	0.0%	0.0%	0.0%	0.0%	1.2%	0.7%

---

* Ever used.

** Statistically significant.

188

TABLE 7.7

ALCOHOL USE, TYPE, AND TROUBLE
BY IMPAIRMENT STATUS:
AGES 80 AND OVER

	Impaired Status Percentages					
	Phys. (N=12)	Intel. (N=32)	Mult. (N=11)	Impaired Subtotal (N=55)	Non-Imp. (N=86)	Total (N=141)
ALCOHOL						
Use*	44.4%	48.3%	50.0%	47.9%	66.7%	59.5%
Barbiturates	25.0%	15.6%	10.6%	16.7%	21.7%	19.7%
Tranquilizers**	8.3%	9.4%	10.0%	9.2%	23.8%	18.1%
Amphetamines	9.1%	0.0%	0.0%	1.9%	3.6%	2.9%
Marijuana	0.0%	0.0%	0.0%	0.0%	0.0%	0.0%
Hallucinogens	0.0%	0.0%	0.0%	0.0%	0.0%	0.0%
Narcotics	8.3%	13.3%	0.0%	9.2%	12.2%	11.2%
Trouble	0.0%	0.0%	0.0%	0.0%	0.0%	0.0%

---

* Ever used.

** Statistically significant.

189

TABLE 7.8

ALCOHOL AND DRUG USE IN COMBINATION*

	Number	Percent
Non-Alcohol and Non-Drug Users	136	22.3
Alcohol Users but Non-Drug Users	99	16.3
Non-Alcohol but Drug Users	157	25.8
Alcohol and Drug Users	217	35.6
	609	100.0

---

*   Unknowns excluded.

190

INTRODUCTION TO CHAPTER 8

In the preceding chapter, Butler et al. alert us to the pattern of alcohol use as people age. We next ask: What proportion of those people become alcoholics and what happens to them? There is a popular image of the alcoholic as a down-and-out skid row bum. In this chapter, Fagan tells us that perhaps only 25% of alcoholics become residents of skid row. Moreover, he provides us substantial insights into what skid row is and what life on it is like.

In the course of the discussion, Fagan provides several vital classifications. He classifies the different types of alcoholics on skid row and the different types of treatment programs that exist for these people. His descriptions are vivid and ethnographic in quality, offering us insights that are not available to the casual observer.

From a conceptualization of the patterns of life on skid row, he is then able to define the problem of treatment as one of the re-entry into "normal" society as opposed to "cure for alcoholism." This is an important insight which provides some understanding of why treatment programs most often fail.

CHAPTER 8
SKID ROW ALCOHOLISM

Ronald W. Fagan

ABSTRACT

While skid row alcoholics constitutes only
20 to 30% of the alcoholic population, their
unique problems have generated very divergent
strategies for control and rehabilitation.
Most contemporary authors focus on skid row as
a human condition emphasizing the social and
economic characteristics of skid row
residents. The problems of skid row alcoholics
are not primarily alcoholism but are at their
root social problems. Therefore,
rehabilitation strategies must address the skid
row alcoholic's social- ization needs.
The traditional approach to the problems of
skid row alcoholics and public inebriates has
been based on the criminal-legal mode of social
control; that is, they are repeatedly arrested
for public drunkenness. In response to the
criticisms of this model, many states have
decriminalized public drunkenness and adopted a
medical or medical-legal model of social
control and rehabilitation with emphasis on
detoxification programs and provisions for a
continuum of care. Another social control and
rehabilitation approach is the skid row rescue
mission and its emphasis on spiritual
conversion. Finally, a rehabilitation strategy
for skid row alcoholics based on a social
reentry model of treatment is presented.

RONALD W. FAGAN is Professor of Sociology at Seaver College,
Pepperdine University.

INTRODUCTION*

When many people today think about what kinds of people are alcoholics, they typically think of the skid row alcoholic. The image of a shabbily dressed, elderly, male sitting in a doorway, clutching a cheap bottle of fortified wine in a brown paper bag, comes readily to mind. Yet research shows that this type of alcoholic constitutes about 25% of the alcoholic population.

We can divide the alcoholic population into the following major categories: 1) the upper- and middle-class white-collar alcoholic (20-25% of all alcoholics), 2) the lower-middle- and upper-lower-class blue-collar alcoholic (40-50% of all alcoholics), and 3) the inner-city alcoholic and the skid row alcoholic (20-30% of all alcoholics) (Kissin, 1977:18-21; Cahalan et al., 1969). (We will discuss the differences between inner-city and skid-row alcoholic populations in the next section.) Royce (1981:114) estimates that only 30% of the skid row residents are alcoholics.

The term "skid row" has been used in three interrelated ways. The traditional view is that skid

---

* Portions of this chapter are based on Fagan, R. 1987. Skid row rescue missions: A religious approach to alcoholism. Journal of Religion and Health 26:153-171; Fagan, R. 1986. Ministering in the hinterland: A survey of rescue mission directors. Journal of Pastoral Counseling 11:79-87; Fagan, R. 1986. Modern rescue missions: A survey of the international union of gospel missions. Journal of Drug Issues 16:495-509; Fagan, R. and Mauss, A. 1986. Social margin and social re-entry: An evaluation of a rehabilitation program for skid row alcoholics. Journal of Studies on Alcohol 47:413-425.

row is a place; that is, skid row is a residential district in the city typically located near the central business district. It is a district that consists of a mixture of commercial and residential enterprises including cubicle and inexpensive restaurants and liquor stores, day-labor agencies, industrial and commercial businesses that require unskilled or low-skilled labor, and, in some cases, public and private social service agencies (Bogue, 1963:1).

But, the dispersal of traditional skid row areas caused by, among other factors, negative public attitudes and urban renewal (Lee, 1978) led to a focusing of attention on two additional ways to describe skid row. The two perspectives commonly share the conception that skid row is not just a residential area but is more correctly seen as a human condition. One perspective within this tradition focuses on the social and economic characteristics of skid row residents. Blumberg, Shipley, and Barsky (1978:154) describe the skid row person as 1) poor, 2) living outside the context of "normal" family relationships, 3) living in extremely low cost (rental) housing, 4) having a high probability of coming to the attention of the police, 5) being more vulnerable to victimization than other destitute people, 6) having a superficial style of social relations, and 7) having not only a low status but a relatively high probability of moving to the lowest level of esteem. This perspective also notes the similarities between skid row residents and other individuals in the city. Feldman et al. compared skid row alcoholics and inner-city alcoholics in terms of social, psychological, and medical pathology and found that the only significant difference was in their ethnicity. Bahr and Caplow (1974) compared a sample of skid row (Bowery) men with a sample from an ethnically poor district of Brooklyn and found they were very similar. "Many of the supposed characteristics of skid row life are merely attributes of poverty and aging" (1974:312).

The final perspective stresses the uniqueness of the skid-row lifestyle. For example, Wallace (1965:96-97) defines skid row as "...an isolated and deviant subcultural community expressing the features of a distinct and recognizable way of life." One feature of the skid row lifestyle which is often stressed is the "bottle-gang" where drinking takes place in a group context (Wilmont, 1978). Whatever perspective is adopted, most all commentators agree that of the alcoholic population, the skid row alcoholic is the most difficult to treat and has the worst prognosis for true rehabilitation.

Wiseman (1970:9) describes the daily life of skid row alcoholic regulars in this way:

> The alcoholic ambles through the day, alone a great deal of the time, sleeping in a cheap hotel, drinking in a tavern if he can afford it, or with a bottle-gang if he is short on funds. He eats in a "greasy spoon" restaurant, watches television in the lobby of his hotel (if he is lucky enough to have one), and goes to bed. If he is without a bed for the night, he goes to a reading room to keep warm or drops in on a mission for soup and salvation. Then he "carries the banner" (walks around all night).

Wilmont (1978) identifies three types of skid row drinking (within what Hobfoll et al. (1980) calls the "homeless unemployed" alcoholic[1]). "Functional drinkers" drink to a level that does not impair functioning. The level of functional intoxication varies from one culture to another (see McAndrew and Edgerton (1969) and their concept of "drunken comportment"). He found that while drinking is not officially allowed in most skid row hotels and missions, drinking is tolerated if it does not result in disruptive or offensive behavior to the staff or other residents. The second type, "pathological drinker," drinks to alleviate stress or pain. Such drinking is uncontrolled, in that the drinker uses alcohol to get himself unconscious. Finally, the "competitive subcultural drinkers" drink in a group setting, a setting where the objective is to drink until he becomes more intoxicated than his peers but still manages to maintain control and uphold the rules of the group. For men who lack traditional status, the "bottle-gang" provides him with an alternative status group, one with more opportunities than traditional institutional arrangements. For the "functional" and "competitive subcultural" drinkers, traditional rehabilitation programs may not be attractive because they do not provide for their status needs. "A

----

[1] Hobfoll et al. (1980) identify four groups on Anchorage's skid row: 1) highly mobile workers, 2) working residents, 3) semi-employed residents, and 4) the homeless unemployed. While the classification is useful, it may be biased due to the unique characteristics of the Anchorage population including the high concentration of Indians and the highly transient nature of the population.

treatment program which recognizes the importance of taking risks, developing status, and feeling competent can offer the skid row alcoholic essential prerequisites for rebuilding a new identity" (Wilmont, 1978:109). A fourth type of skid row alcoholic, "mission stiffs," are those minority of men (and women) who become dependent upon missions for their regular care.

It can be said that the problems of the skid row alcoholic are not primarily alcoholism, but are at their root social problems (Cook, 1975). The skid row alcoholic has developed a set of skills or lifestyle that has significance for him and enables him to survive on the edge (Hobfoll et al., 1980).

Archard (1979:184) notes:

Homeless alcoholics are not socially isolated, as is commonly supposed, but have constructed a web of relationships that are socially meaningful to them....Nevertheless, it would be incorrect to claim that alcoholics find skid row attractive; they are frequently critical of life on the row, of other men they encounter there, and in particular of the institutions and personnel that attempt to alter their status. Rather, in the absence of any acceptable alternatives, alcoholics are drawn to the social organization of life on the row -- a life that provides them with a set of survival strategies of their own making.

Skid row alcoholics need to be differentiated from other types of alcoholics; moreover, they need different types of rehabilitation. The skid row alcoholic needs different and generally more intensive types of treatment than most other groups in the alcoholic population. He needs what Armor et al. (1976) call an "alternative total social milieu" or what Spradley (1970:18) calls "rites of passage" out of their skid row subculture and environment into a new identity which is reinforced outside their familiar skid row subculture.

REHABILITATION AND SOCIAL CONTROL OF THE SKID ROW ALCOHOLIC

Historically, there have been a number of different rehabilitation strategies used with skid row alcoholics. The most distinctive have been "drunk tanks" and jail terms under the criminal-legal model, the detoxification programs under the medical-legal model, the rescue mission approach under the religious model, and rehabilitation programs under the re-entry model.

Criminal-Legal Model of Social Control

For over 350 years, the traditional approach to the problems of the skid row alcoholic and public inebriate has been based on the criminal-legal model of social control. Under this model, inebriation is seen as caused by a voluntary incapacitation or unwillingness of the public inebriate to assume acceptable roles and responsibilities. Public intoxication laws fit into the category of laws (including vagrancy and disorderly conduct) designed to regulate behavior that is defined as morally or esthetically offensive or harmful. The police exercise broad discretion in application of these laws. To the public inebriate, the use of the criminal-legal model meant that many of them served long court sentences on the "installment plan" consisting of endless 30-day, 60-day, and 90-day sentences. This is often referred to as the "revolving door" syndrome (Pittman and Gordon, 1958).

The legal processing of public inebriates has come under increasing criticism for a number of years for the following reasons: 1) criminal sanctions did not appear to be deterring drunkenness nor preventing recidivism (Nimmer, 1971; Pittman and Gordon, 1958); 2) the use of criminal sanctions against public drunkenness were seen as improper attempts at regulating public morals (in particular, so-called "victimless" crimes), especially when they were increasingly being used as "peacekeeping" devices (along with other status-based statutes like vagrancy) to deal with public (but especially downtown business owners') complaints (Wilson, 1972; Grad et al., 1971; Morris and Hawkins, 1970; Spradley, 1970; Kadish, 1967; Bittner, 1967); 3) dealing with public inebriation as a crime places a very heavy (and often unwanted) burden on the criminal justice system, including serious compromises with the legal concepts of due process and representation that accompanied the "assembly line" nature of the adjudication of public drunkenness cases (Pastor, 1978; Room, 1972; Nimmer, 1971; Kittrie, 1971; Grad et al., 1971; Parker, 1968; Kadish, 1967); and 4) with the increasing recognition of alcoholism as a disease by many significant agencies and individuals, criminal penalties were seen as not an appropriate response to the problems of public inebriation. These criticisms reinforced the claims of what Kurtz and Regier (1975) call the "alcohologists" for a medical, disease or illness definition of alcoholism (Conrad and Schneider, 1980; Twaddle, 1973; Kittrie, 1971).[2] Also significant were a number of judicial decisions (Powell v. Texas, 392 U.S. 514, 549-552 (1968); Driver v. Hinant, 356 F. 2d 761 (1966); Easter v. District of Columbia, 361 F. 2d 50 (1966); Robinson v. California, 370 U.S. 660 (1962)) that separated out homeless derelicts and provided some guidelines for their legal processing.[3]

In response to these pressures, in 1971 the National Conference of Commissioners on Uniform State Laws formulated and adopted the model legislation entitled: The Uniform Alcoholism and Intoxication Act. Section I states:

It is the policy of this State that alcoholics and intoxicated persons may not be subjected to criminal prosecution because of their consumption of alcoholic beverages but rather should be afforded a continuum of treatment in order that they may lead normal lives as productive members of society.

----

[2] But the disease concept had to be extended to the skid row alcoholic. The skid row alcoholic was often not seen as blameless as the disease model required. Kurtz and Regier (1975) argue that the model was extended to skid row alcoholics because the skid row alcoholic was used as a symbol of the threat of the disease to generate public support for the treatment of all alcoholics.

[3] But Room (1976) points out that many of the pressures for change within the judicial system came from local judges as they tried to deal first-hand with public inebriates by either refusing to convict them or by providing alternative processing or sentencing.

Approximately two-thirds of the states in the Union have adopted the basic tenets of the Act. The Uniform Act defines alcoholism as a disease, decriminalizes public drunkenness, establishes public detoxification centers as an alternative to criminal processing for public drunkenness, provides for a "continuum of care"; that is, detoxification will ideally lead to referral to other treatment facilities, and emphasizes the voluntary nature of the public inebriate's participation.

But the Uniform Act did not adopt a purely medical definition of alcoholism, rather elements of the legal model were retained, especially the potential need for involuntary commitments to detoxification and other treatment centers. Section 126 of the Act provides that persons who appear to be "incapacitated" by inebriation may be taken into custody by force for as long as 48 hours, either for their own protection or for that of others. Moreover, many states still rely on the police to intercept and transport public inebriates to the detoxification facilities (Aaronson et al., 1977).

Medical Model of Social Control

In America the concept of detoxification began as a change in police arrest procedures rather than as a formal alternative to criminal processing (Room, 1976). The detoxification concept is modeled to some extent on the "sobering-up stations" that have operated in several Eastern European countries since the 1950's (Annis, 1979). The first detoxification center opened in St. Louis, Missouri in 1966, funded by the Justice Department as a demonstration center. Detoxification centers have numerous goals including removing of the

201

criminal label from the public inebriate, providing some humane and medically supervised treatment, reducing dependence upon the criminal justice system (especially the police), and, probably most important, providing initiation of referrals to longer-term rehabilitation programs.

In a review of over 4,000 person admitted to 17 NIAAA-funded public inebriate programs (PIP), Ferguson and Kirk (1979) found that the typical admission was very similar to those persons arrested repeatedly for public inebriation: white, male, divorced or separated, long-term heavy drinker, older (average age 42 years), unemployed (if employed, a laborer with average yearly income of $4,103), and previous treatment experience. The majority of the admissions were either self-referred or referred by other treatment programs. Police referrals accounted for only 5% of the admissions (Fagan and Mauss (1978) report similar findings). Other studies report that the detoxification centers are attracting a much broader population (especially more socially stable individuals, both male and female) than previously processed by the criminal justice system (Annis, 1979; Schuckit and Morrisey, 1976). This fact led Diesenhaus (1982) to conclude that "the major proportion of detoxification admissions would appear to be from...the socially disrupted inner-city alcoholic and the blue-collar alcoholic" (as compared to what Kissin (1977) calls the skid row alcoholic).

In terms of detoxification programs realizing their treatment and referral goals, the results are somewhat mixed but tend to be rather pessimistic. The 17 NIAAA-funded public inebriate programs found that after 180 days of treatment, there were decreases in number of days drinking, amount of alcohol consumed, and in impairment from alcohol. In addition, the percentage abstinent in the preceding 30 days rose from 8% to 46% and percentage working rose from 21% to 43% (Ferguson and Kirk, 1979).

In a study done in Seattle, Washington (in response to the decriminalization of the public drunkenness offense), we found that recidivism rates (to the new detoxification facility as compared to previous arrests) quadrupled (Fagan and Mauss, 1978). It appears that the revolving door may have been replaced by a faster spinning door. In fact, there is some evidence that the use of more humane detoxification centers may actually facilitate the perpetuation of the skid row lifestyle rather than deter or rehabilitate it.

Religious Model of Social Control

One institution that is almost synonymous with skid row and the skid row population is the rescue or gospel mission. Urban rescue missions have been an American institution for over a century. Most commentators identify Jerry McAuley's Water Street Mission established in 1872 in New York as the first religious institution open "...every night of the year specifically for outcasts of society" (Bonner, 1967:11). There were certainly relief efforts for the disaffiliated and homeless before 1872, but they tended to focus primarily on impoverished and homeless women and children, especially seamen's families (for example, in 1852, the Five Points House of Industry was established) (Bahr, 1973). As skid row areas began to grow and develop in the major metropolitan areas, rescue missions began to cater increasingly to the needs of the disaffiliated, homeless man.

In terms of numbers (as well as factors such as political power and social vitality), the skid row population reached its zenith during the late 1920's and early 1930's with the Great Depression. The rescue missions developed during the period of time when the so-called social gospel movement arose. This was a period of time when some people within the Protestant movement became increasingly concerned about the adequacy of traditional explanations for the social, psychological, and economic problems associated with urbanization and industrialization (that is, problems such as crime and suicide rates, factory conditions, inadequate urban housing, changing family patterns, and alcoholism). Liberal Protestants were also concerned about the problems associated with increased immigration of Irish, Italian, and Eastern European people to the United States including their associated religious practices and lifestyles (Johnstone, 1983). The so-called social gospel movement arose out of this context.

Adherents of the social gospel "...repudiated an individual conception of moral and social ills in favor of an interpretation of such phenomena as resulting from social, political, and economic realities over which the individual had little or no control" (Hunter, 1983:28). Therefore, true adherents to the social-gospel perspective believed that reform was to be found in changing the social structure of society. These people only represented a minority of church leaders. As a reaction to what many church leaders felt was an overemphasis on social conditions to the exclusion of the spiritual dimensions, a number of individuals proposed a more balanced approach based on both the physical and spiritual needs of the population. One of the best examples of this approach is the development of the Salvation Army out of British Wesleyanism (Clark, 1948). These "rescue missions," while addressing social needs, saw their primary goal as "rescuing" people from their sins by spiritual conversion. This emphasis is still the predominate theme in missions today.

The International Union of Gospel Missions (IUGM) was organized during this period on September 17, 1913 in New York City. Thirty mission superintendents were charter members. The IUGM is divided into twelve districts each having a constitution, by-laws (in harmony with the IUGM's standards), and an elected president. The organization is governed by a Board of Trustees which is composed of the president, first vice-president, secretary-treasurer, and the presidents of the twelve districts. The board meets twice annually. There are two types of membership -- individual and mission. Included in the latter category are "non-member missions" whose executives are members. There are about 213 member missions in the United States and twelve foreign member missions. There are about 745 individual members (Fagan, 1987, 1986a, 1986b).

The motto of the IUGM is: "Seeking the least, the last, and the lost." A pamphlet put out by the IUGM entitled: "What Is a Gospel Rescue Mission?" defines it as:

An arm of the church given to a soul-saving ministry among rejected and neglected peoples everywhere....It is a gospel orientated agency dedicated to helping those people the church does not reach. Although it may be called upon to aid an individual's domestic or material

205

needs, this is over shadowed by the paramount task of preaching the Gospel of the Lord Jesus Christ to all who will hear.

Wallace (1968) identifies three types of skid row missions. "Conservative institutional missions" are the most professional and bureaucratic type of mission. They are often sponsored by a denomination, association, or group of churches. They typically offer the full range of services, "soap, sleep, soup, and salvation." The "ballyhoo institutional mission" often omits some of the services offered by the conservative institutional missions. They typically are run by the founder and owner. They solicit support from individuals and churches using mail, newspaper, and radio solicitations. "Wildcat missions" typically offer no more than soup and salvation. They are the smallest of the mission types. They are typically the most conservative of the missions reflecting the personality and lifestyle characteristics of their founder and director. They usually rely totally on individual, private contributions and avoid any state or federal funds. Wiseman (1970) identifies another type of mission that utilizes "work therapy" for skid row alcoholics. The best example of this type is the Salvation Army's Harbor Light Centers. Also separate from the above types are the assistance and rehabilitation programs of Catholic and some Episcopal churches as well as some more independent missions that provide assistance, but most do not require attendance at religious services or religious instruction. As the above discussion indicates, one cannot speak of rescue missions as a single type.

In a similar vein, one cannot talk about skid row individuals as a single type. Wallace (1965), after reviewing the many definitions of skid row, discovered five concepts that describe the person on skid row: place of residence, amount of residential mobility, degree of participation in skid row institutions, strength of family ties, and extent of poverty. Bahr (1970) notes that what the characteristics have in common is "... detachment from society characterized by the absence or attenuation of the affiliative bonds that link settled persons to a network of interconnected social structures" (pp. 41-42) or, what he calls "disaffiliation."

Rooney (1980) identifies four major groups of people who use the rescue missions: unemployed workers, pensioners, alcoholic spree drinkers, and mission stiffs. Contrary to the public stereotype, a large percentage of skid row residents work regularly. Missions are used until work becomes available again. Some pensioners utilize the missions to supplement their disability pension or welfare benefits. It is estimated that only about one-third of the skid row inhabitants are problem drinkers or alcoholics (Bahr, 1973). But even the alcoholics on skid row curtail or even stop their drinking for periods of time. The missions are used often as a last resort when other more attractive resources are not readily available.

Skid row is changing. With the recovery of the late 1930's and World War II, the skid row population began to decline dramatically. Accompanying this decline was a change in the types of persons on skid row. Skid row began to change from an employment pool (as it was at its peak) to an "old age rest home" (Wallace, 1965) to what some have characterized as an "open asylum" inhabited increasingly by the mentally ill (as a result of the deinstitutionalization movement of mental hospitals) and the more or less permanently poor and dispossessed. Only within recent years are we seeing an increase in the skid row population brought about by economic recession and disputation of traditional blue-collar employment. While the traditional skid row population remains, their ranks are being joined by dispossessed families as well as various immigrant groups. As one mission director expressed it:

> Several years ago the responsibility of the mission was to provide religious services, food, clothing, and skills to the typical ... alcoholic, 'wino,' and drifter. Today the mission must be able to change from this single purpose role to a versatile facility caring for a larger number of people and an array of problems that are as diversified as the people.

Partially in response to the generally low rates of conversion and rehabilitation and increased support and funds for other needy groups, many of the missions are developing new outreach programs.

Therefore, many missions have responded to the changing population characteristics and disbursement of skid row by developing new programs. Some missions have continued to serve the traditional skid row population while developing these new programs. Other missions have essentially abandoned skid row individuals in favor of groups that are more amenable to public and private financial support and rehabilitation. Some missions have relocated outside skid row. Some of these relocations have been motivated by a desire to follow skid row type of individuals where they have relocated in other areas of the city. This disbursement was brought about by negative public attitudes about skid row and increased economic competition for urban property (urban renewal and gentrification). Some of the relocations have been motivated by a desire to serve other populations. Some of the relocations have been forced upon the missions by increased competition for urban land, needed building renovations, and safety requirements. Some missions have dropped "mission" from the title of their organization ostensibly to broaden their appeal.

We found that the typical mission director is male, white, 45 years of age or older, a college graduate with some religious training, Baptist, politically conservative, religiously conservative, evangelical, and has a modest income. Feeling a sense of being "called" to a "mission" neglected by other rehabilitation agencies and the traditional church, despite reputed low rates of conversion and the hostilities of many of the people they service, they express high rates of vocational commitment. While acknowledging the physical needs of the people they serve, they feel that the only true solution to the social problems that affect the skid row resident is a spiritual one involving a conversion experience. Consistent with this belief, the missions typically require religious instructions or attendance at a religious service to receive material benefits (Fagan, 1986a).

Our research showed that missions still rely almost exclusively on private, individual contributions. But some of the larger missions are utilizing other funding sources including state, federal, and private, nonreligious funds. Most missions continue to offer the traditional "soap, sleep, soup, and salvation" (shelter, meals, clothing, and religious instruction), but they are also offering medical care, psychological counseling, vocational training, benefits counseling, and alcoholism treatment. The missions continue to have spiritual conversion as their primary goal. Most of the missions continue to require religious instruction to receive services including alcoholism rehabilitation.

Those missions with alcoholism treatment programs use primarily psychological counseling, but many programs do use vocational training and Alcoholics Anonymous. Most of the programs are staffed by professionally trained people, but the emphasis remains on spiritual conversion and religious instruction. Most of the mission directors feel they are successful, despite few of the missions utilizing formal evaluation techniques. Finally, the missions are serving new populations, sometimes at the expense of their traditional populations (Fagan, 1986b).

Social science commentators have generally been critical of the skid row rescue missions (Rooney, 1980; McSheehy, 1979; Bahr, 1973; Blumberg et al., 1973; Wiseman, 1970; Wallace, 1965). Most of the commentators assert that the typical skid rower resents the missions' approach. They especially resent the required religious service used by most missions in order for persons to receive benefits. As one skid row resident notes: "I'll tell you why most of us go there. Because we're desperate. We need a roof over our heads" (Wiseman, 1970:187). All, except the "mission stiffs," use the missions as a last resort when other resources have been exploited. The skid rower's negative attitudes are reflected in the jargon they use to refer to the missions (sermons are "earbeatings," religious service participation is "singing for your supper," one who feigns a profession of faith to receive food and shelter is a "cold-weather Christian," a mission regular is a "mission stiff," a conversion is a "nosedive," and a convert who joins the mission staff is a "curb-stone canary"). Bahr (1973:138) notes that, while all skid row residents do not speak negatively about the missions, most skid rowers resent the "... strings attached to charity which demands the facade of penitence, interest in religion, and repudiation of the values of home-lessness...." Blumberg et al. (1973) compare the missions to colonial missionaries in underdeveloped countries. They both use material goods such as food and shelter to attract potential converts. But, in turn, both groups have the problem of how to convert "... rice Christians into actively committed believers" (p. 87).

Some commentators characterize the relationship between the mission and the skid rower as an "exchange" (Bahr, 1973) or a "symbolic relationship" (Mauss, 1982). The men see themselves as providing the mission director's and staff's career opportunities and the basis of the mission's appeals for funds. The men, in turn, accept what the missions give at the lowest possible cost to themselves in order to meet their immediate and desperate needs for food and shelter. In skid row terms, the men see the directors as conning the public, and they feel justified in conning the mission directors in turn (Blumberg et al., 1973:90).

While some authors characterize this relationship as mutual exploitation, other authors feel that the

skid rower is more exploited. For example, McSheehy
says:

> Skid row missionaries....who lack qual-
> ifications and expertise, prove incapable of
> understanding skid row beyond the simple-minded
> diagnosis, sin, and the offering of the
> prescription to embrace Christ. Perhaps, the
> most significant consequence of the
> missionaries' efforts for 'salvation' on skid
> row is their own attainment of income, status,
> and power (1979:33).

Rooney says that the transactions between the missions
and the skid row residents are not an equal exchange;
he defines it as "... a superior-inferior relationship
due to the invidious implications of failure and
unworthiness" (1980:909). He compares the missions to
Goffman's (1959) "total institutions" because of the
degrading and humiliating aspects of the service and
the call for repentance. "The gospel service thereby
serves as a degradation ceremony through which members
of the congregation are shorn of membership in the self-
supporting working class and are newly defined as
belonging to a lower stratum of thoroughly inadequate
persons" (pp. 911-912).

One mission leader defended their approach in this
way: "If you are not religious, you may look upon the
hour-and-a-half service as a performance in which you
must sing for your supper. In fact, though, you are
required to do no more than sit in a pew and expose
yourself to the mission's ministrations (Bendiner,
1961:23-24 as quoted in Bahr, 1973:133). Mauss feels
that Rooney (1980) "... exaggerate(s) greatly the
perniciousness of the hapless mission leaders and
preachers, while underestimating both the resource-

fulness and guile of many skid row denizens" (1982:898). The mission's use of religious services is consistent with their view of the etiology of (and solutions to) social problems.

Some of the criticisms may be misguided because many commentators fail, first of all, to distinguish between the various types of rescue missions discussed in the introduction. The focus of our study was on those missions that require attendance at a religious service. Most of the criticisms have been directed at missions that use "work therapy." These programs have added dimensions (especially the very low wages paid to the people who work in their salvage program) that warrant separate analysis.

Many commentators appear to be blaming the rescue missions for the general failure to rehabilitate skid row alcoholics and clean up skid row. It is true that the missions have been on skid row over a century, and they are almost synonymous with skid row, but the low conversion or rehabilitation rates by the missions have their parallels in other rehabilitative efforts on skid row. Some commentators appear to be exaggerating the impact of the missions on the typical skid rower. For example, while Rooney compares the missions to "total institution" and describes the mission service "... as a degradation ceremony," he also states that only about one-third of skid rowers attended a religious service at a mission during the course of a year. While for a minority of skid rowers the missions may have a negative effect, the majority are not significantly influenced by the missions. There are other agencies on skid row which have a greater impact on the typical skid rower, especially the police. It is an exaggeration to view the typical skid rower "... as the

213

pitiful pawn of pernicious preachers." Habitual skid row residents have acquired a set of socialized values and attitudes, a wide range of survival skills, and a relationship network that allows them to survive in a world which has significance for them. The mission's emphasis on conversion is consistent with the approach used by Alcoholics Anonymous and other programs influenced by AA. The mission's emphasis on abstinence is shared by almost all other rehabilitative efforts on skid row.

We also need to compare the missions to other religious organizations, especially traditional churches. Mauss notes that: "Churches in general constantly have to contend with sanctimoniousness, bureaucratic expediency, and unintentional misanthrophy on the part of the clergy, as well as with cynicism, occasional hostility, and frequent opportunism on the parts of many who attend religious services" (1982:803). As discussed earlier, most churches are not very successful in converting individuals not already familiar with Christianity. Many commentators have objected to the mission's use of religion as "bait." But it should be remembered that the missions are using a technique that is consistent with their theology and history. In addition, because they rely almost exclusively on private donations, they have limited resources. The religious requirement is a vehicle by which the missions feel they can screen individuals who might be most responsive to their message and rehabilitative approach.

Finally, to understand contemporary missions properly, we must focus on their supporters. This perspective is best summed up by one mission director who said: "As long as a mission remains in contact with

214

its supporters and can give evidence of the effective outreach to those who support or would support such work, it can be effective." The missions actively seek our support from individuals, associations, and churches.

You as a person, and your church as a Christian Community can pray for your local Gospel-Rescue mission and those charged with its operation....You can, with full assurance of being appreciated, participate in its programs and services...contribute of your money, to its financial needs...become acquainted with the staff and share constructively its problems and burdens (Mission statement to supporters).

The missions have traditionally resisted city, county, state, and federal funds primarily because they do not like the restrictions that often accompany such funds. Private supporters receive information about the missions from newsletters published by the missions, guest participation at the services, and the mission staff making presentations at church functions.

Goffman talks about a working consensus between the principal actors and the audience. While the actors project a definition of the situation, so too does the audience project a definition of the situation by their response to the actor.

Together the participants contribute to a single overall definition of the situation which involves not so much a real agreement as to what exists but rather a real agreement as to whose claim concerning what issues will be temporarily honored (1959:29).

There are three primary constituencies involved with the missions: individuals who attend the mission services, the mission staff, and the Christian supporters. While the missions may be ineffective in terms of their official goals, they do appear to be meeting the needs of the three constituencies. The individuals who attend the services, while having to sit through a service and listen to some "earbeating," do receive some of the basic necessities they need for survival (food and, in some cases, extended benefits). The mission leaders and staff have employment, a place to minister to individuals with spiritual needs, and a rehabilitation strategy which is different from many other programs generally available to skid row alcoholics. For uptown, suburban, Christian supporters, the missions provide an outreach function. The missions allow them to minister to a "needy" population within a relatively safe, non-threatening environment.

Skid rowers will probably always need the resources provided by the missions. For various reasons, individuals will continue to be attracted to the missions as an occupation and area of service. The most tenuous link is the outside Christian supporters. As we have discussed above, some people will continue to support the missions because their participation in the service gives them a direct outreach vehicle. A larger group of supporters and a group whose support is more tenuous are those individuals who do not participate directly in the services or the mission but give financial support. Their contact with the missions is usually limited to newsletters published by the missions. In our limited analysis of the newsletters, they often contained stories of individuals who are not true skid rowers; rather, they tended to be individuals whose presence on skid row was owing to some crisis event. Other newsletters contained stories of individuals whose lives were "improved" by the missions, but whether they were truly rehabilitated remains to be seen. None of the newsletters we evaluated contained any data that indicated an overall success rate. The only data that was reported were total numbers of people served. It would appear that the supporters do not demand more than this type of information.

The biggest problems facing skid row rescue missions in the future will be the changing nature and, in many instances, relocation of skid row. Some missions will not survive, others will re-focus their programs, others will move where the skid row population moves, and others will become more secular and professional and align themselves with the general alcohol rehabilitation movement. But, as missions become secular, they begin to operate within a different organizational matrix with different goals, restraints, and constituencies. The most direct way missions might become more secular is soliciting secular financial support (United Way funds, for example). In seeking such support, different criteria of their effectiveness may be applied. In addition, they run the risk of alienating their Christian support system. While most missions will continue to offer their brand of "soap, sleep, soup, and salvation," only the future can determine exactly how these services will be offered (Fagan, 1987).

Re-entry Model of Social Control and Integration

Most programs for skid row alcoholics continue to focus treatment solely on the client's obtaining control over his alcohol consumption. They assume that once the client is able to achieve control over his alcohol consumption (usually defined as abstinence), social rehabilitation will be the natural consequence. As a result of having participated in a treatment program (usually an in-house program), the skid row alcoholic is expected to give up drinking; avoid old drinking buddies and establish new non-drinking friends; find a steady job despite often having few, if any, skills, a sporadic job history, and few references; return to any existing family or relatives and assume "appropriate" roles; find a suitable place to live outside the skid row environment; settle any legal claims and secure any entitled benefits; develop a positive self-concept; and patiently work and wait for acceptance, integration, and the "good life."

Wiseman in describing the process of "making the loop" whereby skid row alcoholics go from agency to agency sums up the most common outcome of rehabilitative efforts on skid row:

> The skid row man leaves any station on the loop cleaned up, sobered up, dried out, physically built up, psychologically investigated and "purged," perhaps spiritually renewed, and some-times even occupationally placed. However, de-spite the hopeful pronouncements of the sta-tions and the rather elaborate programs to im-plement them, most skid row alcoholics even-tually return to skid row, to heavy drinking, and then back onto the loop, regardless of which was the last station visited (1970:218).

Rehabilitation for the skid row alcoholic needs to involve more than traditional in-house treatment strategies, for many of these individuals have never achieved basic psychological and social integration (Pattison, 1979:152). Research has documented the advantage of aftercare especially for the disengaged, skid row, alcoholic (Diesenhaus, 1982:229; Griffith et al., 1977; Costello, 1975a; 1975b; Blumberg et al., 1973). While results are not unanimous (see Armor et al., 1976; Dubourg, 1969; Levinson and Sereny, 1969, for studies reporting aftercare as not more effective), most studies indicate that aftercare is as effective (Stein et al., 1975; Edwards et al., 1974; Pokorny et al., 1973; Gallant et al., 1970) or more effective (Chuapel et al., 1978; Vannicelli, 1978; Griffith et al., 1977; Harris and Walter, 1976; Costello, 1975a; Azrin, 1976; Hunt and Azrin, 1973; Pittman and Tate, 1969; Simpson and Webber, 1971) than in-patient treatment where no aftercare is provided.

An example of a successful rehabilitation program for skid row alcoholics is the Lighthouse Christian Center's Re-Entry Program (Fagan and Mauss, 1986). A unique component of the treatment program was the use of small teams of volunteer sponsors who assisted the skid row alcoholic in the recovery process. Using a number of outcome measures, the program obtained approximately a 50% abstinence rate at follow up. In addition, there were gains in employment and monthly income. The program also influenced family contact, development of new friendship groups, and Alcoholics Anonymous attendance, factors that, in turn, significantly influenced the recovery process.

SUMMARY AND CONCLUSION

Patterns of alcoholism among skid row populations demonstrate a complexity not revealed in the typical stereotype. The complexity is an interaction between individual types or patterns and the social milieu of the skid row environment which includes the attitudes and roles of legal, social welfare, religious, and other agencies. About 1/4 of all alcoholics are of the skid row variety. Skid row alcoholics, however, comprise only about 1/3 of the skid row population. There are four types among skid row alcoholics -- 1) functional drinkers, 2) competitive drinkers, 3) pathological drinkers, and 4) "mission stiffs." Each type varies on situations, reasons, amounts, and frequency of drinking. But for all groups, two main factors need to be identified and dealt with -- 1) their social lifestyles which include homelessness, unemployment, and limited social networks among "normative" groups (relatives, spouses, children) and 2) their status needs which are fulfilled by belonging to "bottle gangs." These complex factors have not always been recognized in treatment programs.

The criminal-legal model applied to the skid row alcoholic blames them for their choice of behavior and uses the police lockups for control of public drunkenness. The medical-legal model views alcoholism as a disease in need of treatment through medically supervised detoxification (a model which is more effective with working-class and middle-class alcoholics). The religious model attributes alcoholism to sin and seeks to convert skid row alcoholics through the mission system which also provides basic food and shelter needs in conjunction with "preaching the word." More effective is the re-entry model which provides rites of passage, an alternative social milieu, and long-term support-group follow up in order to address the complex social factors associated with a skid row alcoholic lifestyle.

With an increase in homelessness, the population of skid row is expanding to members of groups not previously found there (for example, out-of-work blue collar working class). These homeless groups are likely to show increased alcohol use with subsequent rise in alcoholism. In the future, the skid row alcoholic group will, therefore, likely vary further from the stereotypical view.

As we have discussed, the traditional image of the homeless has been of a middle-aged or elderly, skid row alcoholic male living on the streets. As long as this was the image, relief efforts were spotty, usually coming from the private sector (rescue missions, for example) or government welfare and relief payments. Recently the "derelict" has been joined by other types of homeless persons -- the mentally ill, recently displaced blue collar families, single women, young people, and minorities. Some of these types of people have always been among the homeless, while others are relative newcomers.

The increase in the complexity and numbers of homeless are due to a number of factors including the recent downturns in the economy, cutbacks in federally funded public assistance programs, conversion of low-income inner-city housing units, and deinstitutionalization of the mentally ill. With few exceptions relief efforts have been targeted on the symptoms of the problem -- food and shelter -- rather than the root causes. An emphasis on simply food and shelter may actually contribute to the problem by making it easier for people who lack motivation and resources to live on the dole indefinitely. For example, many states have removed public inebriates from the criminal justice system and created more humane health-oriented detoxification centers. Research shows that in some states this has resulted in an increase in the public inebriate's use of such assistance because the alcoholic knows he is likely to land in a more pleasant detoxification center than be arrested and put in a jail cell. Moreover, research shows that a principal failing of such programs is that rather than being the beginnings of a continuum of assistance as they were intended, such assistance very infrequently resulted in a referral to a rehabilitation or vocational program, either because the alcoholic was not interested in such a referral or such referrals were not available.

While there is much debate about the causes of alcoholism and about the success of the various treatment approaches, the ultimate goal of most rehabilitation programs is to return their clients to the desired community. Our research has shown that rehabilitation programs for skid row problem drinkers can be effective if they address the total life-health including employment, family and friend contact, and support group follow-up.

REFERENCES

Aaronson, D. E., Dienes, T. C., and Musheno, M. C. 1977. The impact of decriminalization on the policing of public inebriates: A summary of methods and findings. Paper presented at the Alcoholism and Drug Abuse Institutes Summer Conference.

Annis, H. M. 1979. The detoxification alternative to
the handling of public inebriates: The Ontario
experience. Journal of Studies on Alcohol 40:196-
219.

Archard, P. 1979. Vagrancy: A literature approach.
In T. Cook (ed.), Vagrancy: Some New Perspectives.
London: Academic.

Armor, D. J., Polich, J., and Stanbul, H. B. 1976.
Alcohol and Treatment, Final Report Prepared for
the Department of Health, Education and Welfare.
Santa Monica, CA: The Rand Corporation.

Azrin, H. M. 1976. Improvements in the community-
reinforcement approach to alcoholism. Behavior
Research and Therapy 14:339-348.

Bahr, H. 1970. Disaffiliated Man: Essays and Bio-
graphy on Skid Row, Vagrancy, and Outsiders.
Toronto: University of Toronto Press.

Bahr, H. 1973. Skid Row: An Introduction to Disaffiliation. New York: Oxford University Press.

Bahr, H. and Caplow, T. 1974. Old Men Drunk and Sober.
NY: New York University Press.

Bendiner, E. 1961. The Bowery Man. New York: Nelson.

Bittner, E. 1967. The police on skid row: A study of
peace keeping. American Sociological Review 32:
699-715.

Blumberg, L., Shandler, I., and Shepley, T. 1973. Skid
Row and its Alternatives. Philadelphia: Temple
University Press.

Blumberg, L., Shipley, T., and Moor, J. 1971. The
skid row man and the skid row status community:
With perspectives on their future. Quarterly
Journal of Studies on Alcohol 32:909-941.

Blumberg, L., Shipley, T., and Barsky, S. 1978.
Liquor and Poverty: Skid Row as a Human Condition.
New Brunswick, NJ: Rutgers Center for Alcohol
Studies.

Bogue, D. 1963. Skid Row in American Cities.
Chicago: Community and Family Center of Chicago.

Bonner, A. 1967. Jerry McAuley and His Mission.
Neptune, NJ: Loizeaux Brothers.

Cahalan, D., Kissin, I. H., and Crossley, H. M. 1969.
American Drinking Practices: A National Survey of
Behavior and Attitudes (Monograph No. 6). New
Brunswick, NJ: Rutgers Center of Alcohol Studies.

Chuapel, M., Hymes, H., and Delmastro, D. 1978. Out-patient aftercare as a factor in treatment outcome: A pilot study. Journal of Studies on Alcohol 39: 540-544.

Clark, S. 1948. Church and Sect in Canada. Toronto: University of Toronto Press.

Conrad, P. and Schneider, J. 1980. Deviance and Medicalization. St. Louis: C. V. Mosby.

Cook, T. 1975. Vagrant Alcoholics. London: Rootledge and Kegan Paul.

Costello, R. M. 1975a. Alcoholism treatment and evaluation, I: In search of methods. International Journal of Addiction 10:251-275.

Costello, R. M. 1975b. Alcoholism treatment and evaluation, II: Collation of two years' follow up studies. International Journal of Addiction 10: 857-868.

Dalton, M. S., Chegiridden, M. J., and Duncan, D. 1972. Wisteria house: Results of transition of alcoholics from treatment unit to community house. International Journal of Social Psychiatry 18:213-216.

Diesenhaus, H. 1982. Current trends in treatment programming for problem drinkers and alcoholics. In U.S. Department of Health and Human Services, Prevention, Intervention and Treatment: Concerns and Models (Alcohol and Health Monograph #3). Rockville, MD: National Institute on Alcohol Abuse and Alcoholism.

Dubourg, G. O. 1969. Aftercare for alcoholics: A follow up study. British Journal of Addiction 64:155-163.

Edwards, G., Kyle, E., and Nicholls, P. 1974. Alcoholics admitted to four hospitals in England. Quarterly Journal of Studies on Alcohol 35:499-522.

Fagan, R. 1986b. Modern rescue missions: A survey of the International Union of Gospel Missions. Journal of Drug Issues 16:495-509.

Fagan, R. 1986a. Ministering in the hinterland: A survey of rescue mission directors. Journal of Pastoral Counseling 11:79-87.

Fagan, R. 1987. Skid row missions: A religious approach to alcoholism. Journal of Religion and Health 26:153-171.

Fagan, R. and Mauss, A. 1986. Social margin and social re-entry: An evaluation of a rehabilitation program for skid row alcoholics. Journal of Studies on Alcohol 47:413-425.

Fagan, R. and Mauss, A. L. 1978. Padding the revolving door: An initial assessment of the uniform alcoholism and intoxication treatment act in practice. Social Problems 26:2.

Feldman, D. J., Pattison, E. M., Sobell, L. C., Graham, T., and Sobell, M.B. 1975. Out-Patient alcohol detoxification: Initial findings on 546 patients. American Journal of Psychiatry 132:407-412.

Ferguson, L. and Kirk, J. 1979. Statistical Report: NIAAA-Funded Treatment Programs. Rockville, MD: National Institute on Alcohol Abuse and Alcoholism.

Gallant, D. M., Bishop, M. P., Stoy, B., Faulkner, M. A., and Paternostro, L. 1969. The value of a "first contact" group intake session in an alcoholism out-patient clinic: Statistical confirmation. Psychosomatics 7:349-352.

Gallant, D. M., Rich, A., Bey, E., and Terranova, I. 1970. Group psychotherapy with married couples: A successful technique in New Orleans alcoholism clinic patients. Journal of the Louisiana State Medical Society 122:41-44.

Gallant, D. M. 1976. Evaluation of Compulsory Treatment of the Alcoholic Municipal Court Offender. Washington, DC: U.S. Government Printing Office.

Gallant, D. M., Faulkner, M., Stoy, B., Bishop, M. P., and Langdon, D. 1968. Enforced clinic treatment of paroled criminal alcoholics. Quarterly Journal of Studies of Alcohol 29:77-83.

Gallant, D. M., Bishop, M. P., Mouledoux, A., Faulkner, M., Brisulara, A., and Swanson, W. 1973. The revolving door alcoholic: An impasse in the treatment of the chronic alcoholic. Arch General Psychiatry 28:633-635.

Goffman, I. 1959. The Presentation of Self in Everyday Life. NY: Doubleday.

Grad, F. P., Goldberg, A. L., and Shipiro, B. A. 1971. Alcoholism and the Law. Dobbs Ferry, NY: Oceana Publications.

Griffith, E., Orford, J., Egert, S., Guthrie, S., Hawkin, A., Hensman, C., Mitcheson, M., Oppenheimer, E., and Taylor, C. 1977. Alcoholism: A controlled trial of "treatment" and "advice." Journal of Studies on Alcohol 38:1004-1031.

Harris, R. N. and Walter, J. 1976. Outcome Reliability and Validity Issues of Alcoholism Follow Up. Paper presented at the meetings of the Alcohol and Drug Problems Association of North America, New Orleans.

Hobfoll, S. E., Kelso, D., and Peterson, W. J. 1980. The Anchorage skid row. Journal of Studies on Alcohol 41:94-99.

Hunt, G. M. and Azrin, H. M. 1973. A community reinforcement approach to alcoholism. Behavior Research and Therapy 11:91-104.

Hunter, J. 1983. American Evangelicalism. New Brunswick, NJ: Rutgers University Press.

Johnstone, R. 1983. Religion in Society. 2nd Edition. Englewood Cliffs, NJ: Prentice-Hall.

Kadish, S. H. 1967. The crisis of over-criminalization. The Annals of the American Academy of Political and Social Science 374:157-170.

Kissin, B., Platz, A., and Su, W. H. 1970. Social and psychological factors in the treatment of chronic alcoholism. Journal of Psychiatric Research 8:13-27.

Kissin, B., Platz, A., and Su, W. H. 1971. Selective factors in treatment choice and outcome in alcoholics. In Recent Advances in Studies of Alcoholism. Washington, DC: U.S. Government Printing Office.

Kissin, B. 1977. Comments on alcoholism: A controlled trial of "treatment" and "advice." Journal of Studies on Alcohol 38:1804-1805.

Kittrie, Nicholas, N. 1971. The Right to be Different. Baltimore, MD: John Hopkins Press.

Kurtz, N. R. and Regier, M. 1975. Uniform alcoholism and intoxication treatment act: The compromising process of social policy formation. Journal of Alcohol Studies 36:1421-1441.

Lee, B. 1978. The Disappearance of Skid Row, Some Ecological Evidence. Paper presented at the American Sociological Association annual meeting, San Francisco.

Levinson, T. and Sereny, G. 1969. An experimental evaluation of "insight therapy" for the chronic alcoholic. Canadian Psychiatric Association Journal 14:143-146.

Mauss, A. L. 1975. Social Problems as Social Movements. Philadelphia: J. B. Lippincott.

Mauss, A. 1982. Salvation and survival on skid row: A comment on Rooney. Social Forces 60:894-904.

McAndrew, C. and Edgerton, R. B. 1969. Drunken Comportment. Chicago: Aldine.

McSheehy, W. 1979. Skid Row. Cambridge, MA: Schenkman.

Morris, N. and Hawkins, G. 1970. The Honest Politician's Guide to Crime Control. Chicago: University of Chicago Press.

Nimmer, R. T. 1971. Two Million Unnecessary Arrests. Chicago: American Bar Foundation.

Parker, H. 1968. The Limits of Criminal Sanctions. Stanford, CA: Stanford University Press.

Pastor, P. A. 1978. Mobilization of public drunkenness control: A comparison of legal and medical approaches. Social Problems 25:373-384.

Pattison, E. M. 1979. The selection of treatment modalities for the alcoholic patient. In J. J. Mendelson and N. K. Mello (eds.), The Diagnosis and Treatment of Alcoholism. NY: McGraw-Hill.

Pattison, E. M. 1976. A conceptual approach to alcoholism treatment goals. Addictive Behavior 1:177-192.

Pattison, E. M. 1979. The Diagnosis and Treatment of Alcoholism. NY: McGraw-Hill.

Pattison, E. M., Coe, B., and Doer, H. O. 1973. Population variation among alcoholism treatment facilities. International Journal of Addiction. 8:199-229.

Pattison, E. M., Sobell, M. D., and Sobell, L. C. 1977. Emerging Concepts of Alcohol Dependence. NY: Springer.

Pittman, D. J., and Gordon, C. W. 1958. Criminal careers of the chronic police case inebriate. Quarterly Journal of Studies on Alcohol 19:255-268.

Pittman, D. M. and Tate, R. L. 1969. A comparison of two treatment programs for alcoholics. Quarterly Journal of Studies on Alcoholism 30:888-899.

Pokorny, A. D., Miller, B. A., Kansas, T., and Valle, J. 1973. Effectiveness of extended aftercare in the treatment of alcoholism. Quarterly Journal of Studies on Alcohol 34:435-443.

Pokorny, A. D., Miller, B. A., and Cleveland, S. E. 1968. Response to treatment of alcoholism: A follow up study. Quarterly Journal of Studies on Alcohol 29:364-381.

Room, R. 1972. Drinking and disease: Comment on the alcohologist's addiction. Quarterly Journal of Studies on Alcohol 33:1049-1059.

Room, R. 1976. Comment on the uniform alcoholism and intoxication treatment act. Journal of Studies on Alcohol 37:113-144.

Rooney, J. 1980. Organizational success through program failure: Skid row rescue missions. Social Forces 58:904-924.

Royce, J. 1981. Alcohol Problems and Alcoholism. NY: Free Press.

Schuckit, M. A. and Morrisey, E. R. 1976. Alcoholism in women. In M. Greenblatt and M. A. Schuckit (eds.), Alcohol Problems in Women and Children. NY: Grune and Stratton.

Simpson, W. S. and Webber, P. W. 1971. A field program in the treatment of alcoholism. Hospital and Community Psychiatry 22:170-173.

Spradley, J. P. 1970. You Owe Yourself a Drunk. Boston: Little, Brown and Co.

Stein, L. I., Newton, J. R., and Bowman, R. S. 1975. Duration of hospitalization for alcoholism. Archives of General Psychiatry 32:247-252.

Sterne, M. W. and Pittman, D. J. 1974. The concept of motivation: A source of institutional and professional blockage in the treatment of alcoholics. Quarterly Journal of Studies on Alcohol 35:196-209.

Twaddle, A. C. 1973. Illness and Deviance. Social Science and Medicine 7:751-762.

Vannicelli, M. 1978. Impact of aftercare in the treatment of alcoholics: A cross-legged panel analysis. Journal of Studies on Alcohol 39: 1875-1886.

Wallace, S. E. 1965. Skid Row as a Way of Life. Totowa, NJ: Bedminster Press.

Wallace, S. E. 1969. The road to skid row. Social Problems 16:92-105.

Wilmont, R. 1978. The skid row imperative: An analysis of status and identity on skid row. Journal of Drug Issues 8:97-111.

Wilson, J. Q. 1972. Varieties of Police Behavior The Management of Law and Order in Eight Communities. NY: Atheneum.

Wiseman, J. P. 1970. Stations of the Lost: The Treatment of Skid Row Alcoholics. Englewood Cliffs, NJ: Prentice-Hall.

INTRODUCTION TO CHAPTER 9

In this chapter Smykla's respondents are the families of death-row inmates. Smykla asks: Does the stress of this situation drive these people to drink? Is this a situational adaptation to an awesome stressor?

His data is the respondents' self-reports. Throughout his discussion there is tension between the author's sympathetic view of his respondents' situation and his realistic appraisal that this behavior may be a part of their subculture.

The self-reports are clear in their answer to our questions. For them, alcohol is bottled anesthesia. Moreover, in several cases Smykla permits us to hear how they have slowly healed from the pain which alcohol has temporarily dulled for them. But what happens to those for whom pain is never dulled?

CHAPTER 9
ALCOHOL USE IN DEATH-ROW INMATE FAMILIES

John Ortiz Smykla

ABSTRACT

The focus of this chapter is on the description of alcohol use associated with the experience of death row inmate families. Interviews were conducted with forty relatives who had been facing the threat of legal

----

JOHN ORTIZ SMYKLA is Associate Professor of Criminal Justice at the University of Alabama.

executions of a family member from six months to seven years.

The nature of alcohol use in death-row inmate families is both situational and distorted. Situational in the sense that it is used as an escape from the objective reality of the threat of execution of a family member, and distorted in the sense that it alters a family's behavior in ways it otherwise might not be. The situational and distorted nature of alcohol use is further shaped by three social-psychological factors identified in the interviews: 1) self-accusation, 2) social isolation, and 3) powerlessness.

Ending the family's suffering to this absolute and irrevocable method of crime control means nothing short of the abolition of capital punishment itself. In the interim, the professional community must draw attention to family members' suffering, all of whom have such low socioeconomic status that they are unable to cope effectively without help. Families can be helped to find alternative means of coping with this stress.

INTRODUCTION

Have criminologists lost their moral compasses? Are we so overwhelmed by technological changes in the world that we've become too numb to recognize good and evil in crime control strategies in proper proportion? Is the good or evil done to persons on death row without balance? Do we recognize that the consequences of capital punishment are not just confined to the individuals who have been condemned to die but reverberate to include persons in what Turnbull (1978) describes as an ever-widening circle of tragedy? The circle begins with the victim and offender and ends up including families, judges, jurors, prison officers, wardens, witnesses to the execution, governors, pardon board

231

members, attorneys, and on and on. Innocent bystanders are drawn into the execution scenario because of an event, over which they had no control or direct responsibility. They suffer a stigma that criminologists have ignored, what Camus (1959) describes as "a misery that punishes beyond the bounds of all justice." By focusing on the alcoholic drinking of relatives of persons on death row, I hope to show that moral judgments of criminologists do matter. In particular, the moral judgments implicit in commonplace reports about crime fly in the face of real issues of good and evil.

METHODOLOGY

In the summer and fall of 1983, I traveled through five southern and mid-western states meeting and interviewing relatives of Alabama's death-row inmates. My purpose was to understand what impact the death sentence of a relative has on the family. I began my research by writing the women and men on Alabama's death row. I explained to them who I was and who I was not ("I was not a reporter"), what I wanted to do, how I would do it, my opinion of capital punishment, and what I could give them in return. I asked for their participation by sending me the names, addresses, and telephone numbers of persons in their families who they thought willing to be interviewed. Forty-three out of sixty-five death-row inmates responded, identifying almost 250 relatives. Because time and funds were limited, I designed a trend study to vary the length of time families had been facing the threat of legal execution. Included in the interviews were forty family members of eight death-row inmates who had been on death row from six months to seven years. These included four mothers, one father, four brothers, eight sisters, one wife, one daughter, two grandmothers, two grandfathers, four aunts, three uncles, eight cousins, one sister-in-law, and one girlfriend. Whether they were describing their anger and isolation, their problems at home or on the job, the impact of the sentence on their physical or emotional health, families that faced the death sentence the longest experienced no meaningful reduction in suffering compared to families that faced the threat of legal execution for shorter periods of time. This is prolonged suffering, and it appeared in every relative I interviewed. Accompanying it were alternations or distortions in behavior patterns such as over-activity without a sense of loss, acquisition of medical illnesses, alterations in social relationships, furious hostility toward the justice system, conduct that resembled schizophrenic behaviors, behavior that was detrimental to their social and economic well-being, and depression. Only one distorted grief reaction, namely, alcohol use, is reported on here.

The reader should bear in mind several precautions in this analysis. First, I do not claim it is true for all families of death-row inmates. What I think I know about alcohol use in death-row inmate families appears to me as regularly reoccurring themes among the families I interviewed. Second, I wish to avoid the notion that a death sentence causes distorted alcoholic drinking in the family. The problem is multi-dimensional in these hidden victims of crime. They have a low socioeconomic status; they are unable to do anything about the problem over which they had no control, and they bear no direct responsibility for the crime itself. Finally, I regard the humanistic or phenomenological observation and unstructured interview approach used in this research as complementary to, rather than in conflict with, other methods of inquiry that proceed from different perspectives.

TOWARD A GENERAL THEORY OF ALCOHOL USE IN DEATH-ROW INMATE FAMILIES

One of the most distorted behaviors experienced by relatives of death-row inmates is the alteration of social relationships and loss of patterns of social interactions that occur in the first four to six months following the death sentence. During these months families exile themselves in their own homes to avoid contact with the outside world. Unlike families in other situations resulting from loss or from separation with the threat of loss, families of death-row inmates rarely know each other. No organization exists to join them together to help each other with information, mutual support, and emotional release. In the current climate of public support for executions and the prevailing political image of death-row inmates as subhuman, it is difficult, if not impossible, for the families to find outsiders sympathetic to their suffering. They must bear the added burden that their relatives' deaths are actively desired by others, a desire ranging from general expressions of approval for capital punishment to very explicit calls for the execution of particular inmates (Radelet, Vandiver, Berardo, 1983).

While a comprehensive understanding of the impact of capital punishment on death-row inmate families has yet to be developed, some preliminary observations can be made. Beginning in the first four to six months following a relative's death sentence, prolonged and distorted grief reactions surface and continue to persist in varying degrees and form for as long as the person on death row remains alive. Discussion of these prolonged and distorted grief reactions can be found elsewhere (Smykla, in press). The attempt here is to focus on the prolonged and distorted effects of alcohol use in the relatives of death-row inmates.

To gauge a relative's experience with alcohol use and its connection with the death sentence of a family member, each interview sought to discover a person's experience with alcohol prior to and following the death sentence, the conditions under which persons now drink, what they drink, and whether they combine alcohol with other drugs. As experienced by relatives themselves, alcohol use prior to the death sentence of a family member was never as prolonged over any event in their lives as it has been over the death sentence of a relative. On prior occasions whether alcohol use was a reaction to death, divorce, low income status, unemployment, or family problems, it did not manifest itself as clearly, predictably, or with as much suffering as it did over a relative's death sentence and time spent waiting to die. For occasions other than capital punishment, families succeeded in pulling through the crisis because they believed they exercised some control over the way the crisis affected their lives. However, that is not the case with capital punishment. Because they believed they had no control over the crime or the punishment meted out by the court, feelings of hopelessness, futility, and meaningless in life are met with an obsession for alcohol use. Drinking was expected to lessen the pain and suffering, but most discovered it intensified their feelings. The mother of a man on death row for seven

235

years told me that during the first three to four months following her son's death sentence, she started drinking too much and never left the house. That continued for three years. "I'd put a little coke in it and I'd drink all day. I always fixed the meals, but drinking kept my mind from thinking too much, or else it would intensify my feelings and make me drink more." In the fourth year, the condemned men's parents adopted the death-row inmate's five-year-old daughter. They told me the adoption was a central force in changing the prolonged and distorted use of alcohol in the death-row inmate's mother. Drinking may not be an everyday reaction for her now, but it's frequent and predictable enough that her husband told me it happens after a letter arrives from their son, after lengthy conversation about him, pending an appeals decision, or at the news of an execution elsewhere.

Prolonged and distorted alcohol use was observed in other families as well. One sister of a person two years on death row told me that before her brother was sentenced to die, she barely used alcohol. But after the sentence and during his first two months on death row, she would buy beer at the expense of food for the family. "I didn't care. I didn't have any worries for two months. I'd lie for it. It was real bad. I couldn't face the fact that my brother was on death row. I couldn't get started in the mornings. I'd stay in my room alone. My children would call me, and I'd wish I didn't have children. There was nothing I could do to help him." Recognizing she was the only parent her children had and with the help of her church, she managed to change her alcohol use and says she only drinks now when she hears of an execution or something happens in her brother's appeal. Her sister, however, still reacts with prolonged alcohol use after two years time. "I'm still up until two or three in the morning. I'll go to Jiffy-Mart and buy beer. That will make me sleep. In the afternoon, I'll have a couple of shots and a couple cans of beer. Before all this happened, I only drank occasionally. But now I can't wait 'til the kids go to bed in order to drink. When Texas executed that guy, I drank a six-pack."

Two more examples demonstrate the prolonged and distorted nature of alcohol use in relatives of death-row inmates. The sister of a man on death row for one year told me she drank more after her brother's sentence than ever before. "When I started drinking, I drank, and I drank more than a couple. I'd go home for lunch and have whiskey and coke. After work I'd have five more. It put it all out of my mind for awhile." For her, prolonged alcohol use changed nine months after the sentence when she became pregnant; second, when she realized the neglect and sometimes abuse she was giving her four-year-old daughter when she drank; and, third, when she become more active in the church.

And finally, the interview with the woman who had recently experienced four months of isolation and alcohol abuse following her father's death sentence: "I started drinking a lot after this happened. I drank real heavy and stopped exercising. I'd go to the bars each night. I'd drink, and I wouldn't talk with anyone. I'd get so drunk I couldn't walk. Someone would have to take me home. Then it got to the point I didn't like the crowds, so I'd buy a bottle, bring it home and get drunk. This went on for four months. I was taking amphetamines in the morning to get going and depressants at night. I about killed myself with the alcohol and pills. I put so much on my mind I almost drove myself crazy. I used it all to escape, to get drunk, so I wouldn't have to think about nothing but having a good time. Then one day I looked at myself and realized I was losing it. I had let myself go. I had to take care of my grandfather and my brother. I'm not drinking like that anymore."

Despite the wide variation in the external facts of alcohol use in death-row inmate families, an outline of broadly shared features emerged with disturbing clarity. This outline is shaped around three social-psychological dimensions drawn from the interviews: self-accusation, social isolation, and powerlessness.

Self-accusation literally shatters the self-esteem of relatives of death-row inmates. Despite the surface ability of some to maintain a confident exterior, the situation for most is usually to the contrary. Relatives are typically overflowing with guilt and self-hatred. Prolonged use of alcohol magnifies the bitter self-accusation. For example, after three years of prolonged and distorted alcohol use in reaction to a son's death sentence, one mother expressed the guilt feelings that many felt when she said, "It's all my fault. If I had done things differently, this might not have happened. I go over my whole damned life. It's all my fault. Everything that happened is my fault." For relatives who were facing the threat of legal execution even longer, these distorted guilt feelings continued even though they insisted they no longer mixed guilt with prolonged alcohol use. In most cases, bitter self-accusation was accompanied by distorted behavioral patterns such as over-activity without a sense of loss, a lack of self-assertion particularly in conversation with someone new when one might admit the person on death row is a relative but doesn't, and a neglect of self-interest.

Social isolation in the first four to six months following the death sentence is routinely accompanied by distorted alcohol use and thereafter to a lesser extent among death-row inmate families. At six months following her son's death sentence, the mother of one particularly poor country family expressed it perfectly when she said, "We just moved here when this happened. The neighbors were calling the landlord threatening to move if he didn't evict us. They wouldn't allow their children to play with my kids. I knew we couldn't go any where else. All we could do was stay here. I didn't have a car. We lived too far from town. We couldn't go any place. I'd drink. That'd occupy my mind. It'd calm me down when I got real nervous. I'd just drink a couple of cans of beer."

The loneliness, the self-imposed isolation surfaced even in crowd situations. In spite of the social lubricant of alcohol which quite often makes one lively and outgoing, relatives of death-row inmates remain withdrawn and quiet. Recall, for example, the interview quoted earlier in this chapter when the daughter of a man seven months on death row admitted using alcohol a lot after her dad was condemned to die. She still remained apart from others. "I drank real heavy and stopped exercising. I'd go to the bars each night. I'd get so drunk I couldn't walk. Someone would have to take me home. I wouldn't talk with anyone. Then it got to the point I didn't' like the crowds so I'd buy a bottle, bring it home and get drunk. This went on for four months."

It was generally the case that relatives of death row inmates feel totally unique, different from all others. The social facts of public support for executions and the knowledge that their relatives' deaths are actively desired by others are experiences unique to death-row inmate families. This life situation accentuates and contributes to prolonged and distorted alcohol use as relatives of death-row inmates experience loneliness, isolation, and exile into their own homes. The sister of a man twenty months on death row, who has been progressively drinking more since the sentence and who now drinks a couple of shots of whiskey in the afternoon and a couple of cans of beer a day to avoid people and the stigma, told me, "I visit my old friends less now. They ask too many questions. I'm alone. It's like nobody cares or is concerned. Others enjoy life, and we go through this alone."

Powerlessness and feelings of hopelessness and helplessness in conjunction with alcohol use further complicates life for death-row inmates families. Starting in the first four to six months, relatives become depressed, drinking large quantities of a depressant drug. Feelings of powerlessness because of the inability to influence the death sentence, death-row conditions, appeals, and the public outcry for more executions reflect the emptiness caused by the separation with the threat of death and by the image of death row as the living death (Johnson, 1981). In trying to fill this emptiness, many pursue alcohol use and obsessions with other things such as compulsive working, religion, and moving.

Feelings of powerlessness were expressed by death-row inmate relatives. After seven months, the first four of which involved heavy alcohol use, a daughter said, "What can you do? There's nothing you can do except accept it, write, and visit when you can. I don't know what to do. I have to live with the thought that he wants to kill himself. After drinking real heavy for four months, I've started going out again, meeting people. It took me four months to accept he's there. Now I will just be here if he needs something." In others, however, powerlessness is prolonged. After seven years, the first three of which involved heavy alcohol use, one mother told me, "It's hopeless in the fact there's nothing we can do about it. You have to live with it."

PREVENTION

Is there nothing we, the professional community, can do about the unnatural use of alcohol in relatives of death-row inmates? Are we so anesthetized and do we uncritically accept legislatively mandated crime control policies, whatever their empirical effectiveness, that we fail to consider what might be called "the morality of deterrence" (Andenaes, 1970). It is morally compelling to take into account moral acceptability in weighing the deterrent argument of a penalty and in deciding whether to authorize it by law or, having authorized it, whether to use it. Such moral considerations take us well beyond capital punishment. They apply to all modes of punishment adopted for any crime.

We are now confronted with the knowledge that alcohol use in relatives of death-row inmates is prolonged and distorts their behavior. It is morally arguable that as innocent victims they have as much right to be free from the unnatural impact of alcohol as the rest of us. As professionals we face two choices. First, we can push to abolish capital punishment and thereby end the tragic suffering that it brings because "death is different." Or, we can admit that the death penalty punishes innocent relatives of death-row inmates through their prolonged and distorted alcohol use and begin immediately to help millions of low-socioeconomic-status relatives cope with a constellation of health and social problems caused in response to the state's effort to control crime.

REFERENCES

Andenaes, J. 1970. The morality of deterrence. University of Chicago Law Review 37:649-664.

Camus, A. 1959. Reflections on the Guillotine. Michigan City, IN: Fridtjof-Karla Publications.

Johnson, R. 1981. Condemned to Die. NY: Elseview.

Radelet, M. L., Vandiver, M., and Berardo, F. M. 1983. Families, prisons, and men with death sentences. Journal of Family Issues 4:593-612.

Smykla, J. (in press). Study of the impact of capital punishment on death row inmate families. USA Today Magazine.

Turnbull, C. 1978. Death by decree: An anthropological approach to capital punishment. Natural History 87:51-67.

INTRODUCTION TO CHAPTER 10

Smykla's discussion of the drinking behavior of families of death-row inmates in the preceding chapter leaves us with a view of alcohol use as a response to an onerous situation. Smykla offers us a sense that, for at least some of his respondents, eventually the pain of the situation heals, at least enough for the alcohol abuse to cease. For his study, the situation is highly specific.

In this next chapter, Markides and Krause examine a Mexican-American population and the patterns of alcohol use associated with a long-term stressor: marital dissatisfaction. Here, the problem of analysis is far more complex. The authors are studying a single subculture. However, they alert us to two important variables in drinking behavior: 1) drinking is sex-role specific; that is, the norms for male drinking and female drinking are very different and 2) since Mexican-Americans are acculturating, the normative patterns regarding drinking vary from generation to generation.

If this is the case, and we wish to analyze the degree to which drinking is a situational adaptation to marital dissatisfaction, we must first understand 1) the pattern associated with male drinking, 2) the pattern associated with female drinking, and 3) the effect of acculturation on each of these sex-role specific patterns. Only then can we ask what the impact of marital satisfaction or dissatisfaction is on drinking behavior.

Markides and Krause provide a sophisticated analysis to answer the question. They are careful in their attribution of causality, and they are cautious in generalizing. They add to our knowledge not only

243

that marital satisfaction is negatively related to drinking behavior for young men, but that young women who are similarly dissatisfied become depressed. From this we learn that drinking is not only culturally prescribed, but it is specific to sex-roles as well. Here then is a dual effect: 1) drinking behavior is normatively defined for each sex and 2) over-use of alcohol is a response to a specific situation.

CHAPTER 10
ALCOHOL CONSUMPTION IN THREE GENERATIONS OF MEXICAN-AMERICANS: THE INFLUENCE OF MARITAL SATISFACTION, SEX-ROLE ORIENTATION, AND ACCULTURATION

Kyriakos S. Markides and Neal Krause

ABSTRACT

This chapter investigates the influence of marital satisfaction, sex-role orientation, and acculturation on patterns of alcohol consumption among Mexican-Americans. The data come from a three-generation study of Mexican-Americans residing in the San Antonio, Texas area.
The authors find wide differences in alcohol consumption by gender and by generation. Older people and women drink considerably less and do so less frequently than younger people and men. In addition, middle-aged and younger men exhibit higher

----
KYRIAKOS S. MARKIDES is Professor of Preventive Medicine and Community Health at the University of Texas Medical Branch, Galveston; NEAL KRAUSE is Associate Professor, School of Public Health, the University of Michigan.

levels of heavy drinking than the general population. Marital satisfaction is (other things being equal) strongly associated with drinking among younger men but only weakly associated among younger women as well as in both sexes in the other two generations. Further analysis suggests that younger women express their marital distress through higher levels of depression, while younger men are more likely to resort to alcohol; however, males also become depressed.

Sex-role orientation has no influence on the drinking behavior of men, while it has some influence on the drinking of younger women. As expected, younger women with modern sex-role orientations drink more frequently than women with more traditional orientations.

Finally, acculturation has a negative effect on the drinking levels of middle-aged men suggesting that acculturative stress, which is more likely to be present in the middle-generation, may lead to increased use of alcohol. Older men are relatively unacculturated and younger men quite acculturated, so that acculturative stress may be less of an issue in these groups. In addition, acculturation is positively associated with drinking among younger women. Acculturated younger women are more likely to violate traditional norms sanctioning drinking among Mexican-American women.

INTRODUCTION

In recent years, there has been an increase in the drinking behavior of Hispanics, America's second and most rapidly growing minority population. In general, Hispanics (most of whom are Mexican-Americans) have been found at the extreme ends of the distribution of alcohol consumption: there is a higher proportion of abstainers among women and a higher percentage of heavy drinkers among men (Gilbert and Cervantes, 1986).

Differences in alcohol consumption between men and women among Mexican-Americans appear to be wider than among other ethnic groups (Maril and Zavaleta, 1979; Paine, 1978).

In the above research, there has been special focus on the influence of acculturation on drinking levels. It has been suggested, for example, that the stresses accompanying acculturation may lead to heavy drinking. Thus, those not yet fully acculturated may resort to more extreme drinking as a way to relieve acculturative stress (Neff, Hoppe and Perea, 1987; Alcocer, 1982; Gomberg, 1982; Graves, 1967; Madsen, 1964).

As with other ethnic groups, less is known about the drinking behavior of Mexican-American women than Mexican-American men. It has been suggested that traditional cultural norms permit Mexican-American men to consume large quantities of alcohol, while women are expected to abstain from alcohol.

The few studies of Mexican-American drinking patterns have been primarily descriptive. Little effort has been made to specify factors (other than basic demographic ones) that predict drinking behavior and few studies have attempted to examine the simultaneous influence of multiple factors (Gilbert and Cervantes, 1986). In this chapter, we examine predictors of drinking patterns in a three-generation sample of Mexican-American men and women. Thus, in addition to gender, generation or stage in the life cycle is an important component of our study. We give primary focus to marital problems as a key predictor of high alcohol consumption, particularly among men. We hypothesize that marital satisfaction will be a stronger predictor of levels of drinking among men than among women. It has been found that, in general, men are more likely to resort to drinking to deal with life's stresses, including marital problems. High levels of drinking may thus be a good indicator of psychological distress for men, while for women, on the other hand, depression may be a more appropriate measure of how they express their distress (Dohrenwend and Dohrenwend, 1976). Thus, we would expect marital problems to be associated with high levels of drinking among men and high levels of depression among women.

Another variable of interest in our analysis is sex-role orientation. We would expect women with more traditional sex-role orientations to drink less than women with more modern orientations. Based on the literature cited earlier, traditional sex-role orientations would be associated with higher levels of drinking among Mexican-American men. We also expect a similar situation with regard to acculturation; other things being equal, less acculturated men will drink more, while less acculturated women will drink less.

We conduct our analyses separately for men and women, and by generation. Although previous investigators have noted large differences in amounts of alcohol consumed by generation (for example, Meyers et al., 1981), few have investigated the influence of marital problems, sex-role orientations, and acculturation on drinking patterns in different generations or at different stages of the life cycle.

METHODS
The Sample

The data employed are based on interviews with 1,125 Mexican-Americans during 1981 and 1982 in the San Antonio area. Older Mexican-Americans (aged 65 to 80) with three-generationally linked families within a fifty mile radius of San Antonio were selected using multi-stage area probability sampling procedures (Markides et al., 1983). Information on their children and married or previously married adult (18 years and above) grandchildren was subsequently obtained. Three-generation lineages, including the older person, a middle-aged child, and a grandchild were selected randomly, yielding a sample of 1,125, 375 in each generation. Of these, approximately two-thirds were women, owing to a large extent to women's greater longevity in the older generation, and their tendency to marry and bear children at younger ages than did the men. The mean age of the older generation was 74; it was 49 for the middle and 26 for the younger generation.

Since we place major focus on the influence of marital satisfaction on alcohol consumption, we restrict our analysis to currently married persons with a spouse present. This yielded a total of 761 persons, 181 in the older, 293 in the middle, and 287 in the younger generation.

Measures

Our measures of alcohol consumption were based on two questions: 1) "During the past two months, how often have you drunk wine, beer, or drinks containing alcohol?" (coded 1 to 6, from never to once a day or more); and, 2) "When you drink wine, beer, or drinks containing alcohol, about how many glasses do you usually have in one day?" (The exact number was coded up to seven or more glasses.) We analyze these two measures separately and also by combing them to form a frequency-by-volume measure. In addition, we created a dichotomous variable capturing high levels of drinking by assigning a value of one to persons consuming 6 or more drinks on a given day and zero to all others.

Marital problems were measured with a ten-item scale that assesses marital satisfaction (Gilford and Bengtson, 1979). Respondents were read a list of "some things husbands and wives may do when they are together" and asked how often each took place with their spouse. Items were scored 1 to 5 ("hardly ever" to "very often" or "all the time"). Negatively phrased items were reversed and scores on all items were summed to yield a total marital satisfaction score that may range from 10 (low) to 50 (high). Using the present data, the scale demonstrated an alpha reliability coefficient of .80.

A second key independent variable employed in our analysis is traditional sex-role orientation. We employ a scale consisting of seven items covering male dominance (or female submissiveness) in decision-making, attitudes toward sharing housework by husbands and wives, beliefs about whether women should be actively interested in politics, and beliefs about whether women should be able to continue their education after marriage. Responses to each item ranged from strongly agree to strongly disagree (scored 1 to 5). The total scale score may range from 5 to 35 with high scores denoting a more traditional sex-role orientation. The scale demonstrated an overall alpha reliability of .63. (See Markides and Vernon, 1984, for more information on the scale.)

Past research has suggested that acculturation might be an important correlate of alcohol consumption among Mexican-Americans. The literature has suggested that an important indicator of acculturation is language use (Cuellar et al., 1980). We developed a scale utilizing four items relating to language of television programs watched, language of radio programs listened to, language used with one's spouse, and language used with friends (each item coded 1 for Spanish only, 2 for mostly Spanish, 3 for Spanish and English about equally, 4 for mostly English, and 5 for only English). The four were, summed to yield a total possible score ranging from 5 (only Spanish) to 25 (only English). The scale had an alpha reliability of .74.

We also included a dichotomous variable capturing whether a person's current marriage was his or her second (or later) marriage (coded 1) or whether it was his or her first (coded 0). This variable has been found to predict psychological distress in the general population (for example, Warheit et al., 1976), and we felt it should be included as a predictor of drinking behavior particularly since it might be related to marital satisfaction.

We employ three sociodemographic variables as controls: age (measured in actual years of age), education (years of school completed), and income (monthly household income, ranging from $0 to $199 to $2,000 and over, coded 1 to 11).

Analysis

We employ multiple regression analysis to examine potential correlates of drinking behavior separately by generation and by sex. The analysis involving the variable high drinking (6 or more drinks on a given day) was not performed with all women or with older generation men because there were too few high drinkers in these groups for meaningful analysis. In fact, in the case of older women, only the analysis involving frequency of drinking in the past two months was performed because the other variables were too skewed toward the lower end of the distribution. Number of drinks consumed and the frequency by volume measure were also skewed for all subjects, and thus we employed a logarithmic transformation of these variables in our analyses.

Before we present the regression analyses, we present and discuss data on frequency and level of alcohol consumption by generation and by sex.

PATTERNS OF DRINKING BY GENERATION AND SEX

Table 10.1, page 262, presents data on frequency of alcohol consumption during the two months prior to the interview, the average number of drinks consumed on a given day by those who said they drank at least a few times a month, and percent of all respondents who consumed an average of six or more drinks on a given day. Women and older people appear to drink considerably less frequently and consume lower quantities of alcohol than men and middle-aged or younger people. For example, the percentage of abstainers ranges from 7% among younger men to 80.3% among older women. Middle-aged and younger men are considerably more frequent drinkers than the other groups. Of those who drank at least a few times a month, middle-aged men consumed the highest number of drinks on a usual day (3.7%), and older women the least (1.9%). Finally, none of the older women and negligible percentages of older men and middle-aged and younger women had six or more drinks a day when they drank. However, 22.4% of middle-aged and 22.4% of

251

younger men reported drinking six or more drinks a day when they drank.

The data indicate somewhat greater abstinence from alcohol consumption among older Mexican-American women than among older women in the general population. The consumption patterns of middle-aged and younger Mexican-American women are quite similar to patterns for women in the general population (Munch et al., 1981; Klatsky et al., 1977).

Similar trends were observed for older Mexican-American men. However, there are significantly fewer abstainers and significantly more heavy drinkers among middle-aged and younger Mexican-American men (Clark and Midanik, 1982). These, in fact, are the only groups in our study for which alcohol consumption appears to be a problem. Further analysis will reveal factors associated with the drinking behavior of these two as well as the other groups.

Determinants of Drinking Behavior Among Men

Potential determinants of the four alcohol variables described earlier were examined through regression analysis. Table 10.2, page 263, presents the results for men by generation. The variable capturing high drinking was not analyzed for older men since there were too few high drinkers in this group.

Table 10.2, page 263, shows that only the two socioeconomic variables are significant predictors of drinking behavior among older men, but they have opposite effects: income is positively related to both the number of drinks consumed and the frequency-by-volume measure while education exhibits a negative association with these variables. It appears that among older Mexican-American men, who drink quite

252

moderately and who are generally quite poor, the ability to buy alcohol is a significant factor predicting their consumption. Why more educated older men, (other things being equal), on the other hand, drink less is not evident at this stage of the analysis, although it may be related to greater knowledge of the hazards of alcohol to one's health.

None of the other independent variables proved to be significant correlates of drinking behavior. Age, marital satisfaction, and traditional sex-role orientation exhibited effects in the hypothesized direction, but these were not statistically significant. It must be noted, however, that the relatively small number of cases makes the detection of significant associations difficult.

The analysis involving middle-generation men reveals more significant associations. Income is again positively associated with frequency of drinking, number of drinks, and the combined frequency by volume measure. As with older men, income appears to be a resource enabling middle-aged Mexican-American men to consume more alcohol and to do so more frequently. Education is not significantly related to these variables, but it is significantly and negatively related to high drinking suggesting, again, the possible influence of greater knowledge of the negative effects of extreme levels of drinking on one's health. Acculturation, as measured by the language scale, is negatively and significantly related to three of the four alcohol variables as hypothesized: more acculturated middle-aged Mexican-Americans drink less and do so less frequently than less acculturated or more traditional men in the same age group. The association with the fourth variable, high drinking, is not significant although it is in the same, negative, direction.

As expected, age is negatively associated with three of the alcohol variables. None of the other variables proved to be significant. Marital satisfaction is consistently related to less drinking as hypothesized, but the associations do not reach significance. On the other hand, opposite to what was predicated, traditional sex-role orientation exhibits consistent negative associations with drinking, but none of the associations are statistically significant.

The results for younger men show that the only significant predictor of drinking behavior is marital satisfaction, which is negatively and quite strongly related to all four alcohol variables. These effects are also significantly higher than the effects of marital satisfaction in the other two generations. Younger men with marital problems engage in considerably more drinking. While it is likely that marital problems are driving these men to alcohol, part of this association may result from a possible negative effect of high levels of drinking on one's marriage. What is notable, however, is that this association is so strong and that it is considerably stronger than what is observed with middle-aged and older men.

None of the remaining independent variables appears to be important. A trend is observed with education which is negatively and consistently associated with all alcohol variables, but none of the associations reaches statistical significance. No trends are observed in the effects of the remainder of the variables.

Determinants of Drinking Behavior Among Women

Table 10.3, page 264, presents the results of the regression analysis among women. As mentioned previously, only frequency of drinking was analyzed for women. The only significant predictor of this variable is income which is consistent with what was found among older men. The strong positive effect of income suggests the importance of financial resources enabling older Mexican-American women to purchase alcoholic beverages. As expected, age and sex-role orientation are negatively related to frequency of drinking, but these effects do not reach statistical significance.

Among middle-aged women, second (or later) marriage appears to be a strong and consistent predictor of higher levels of drinking. It is quite possible that previous marital dissolution may have led to use of alcohol as a way to relieve stress or that previous drinking behavior may have contributed to marital dissolution and that these levels of drinking have persisted into their second marriage. However, the drinking levels reported by these women do not appear to be excessive.

The only other variable that is significantly associated with drinking behavior among middle-aged Mexican-American women is age: an expected negative association is observed with two of the three alcohol variables.

Among younger women, acculturation, as measured by the language scale, is consistently and significantly associated with more drinking. This is consistent with our hypothesis and is opposite to what was found with middle-aged men. More acculturated younger women are less traditional and, therefore, more likely to violate traditional norms sanctioning alcohol consumption among

Mexican-American women. This gains partial support from the negative associations between traditional sex-role orientations and the three alcohol variables among younger women. However, only in the case of frequency of consumption does the association reach statistical significance.

Finally, marital satisfaction is negatively related to drinking, although the association is only statistically significant in the case of frequency of alcohol consumption. Even this latter association is modest, however, and is considerably lower than what was observed among younger men.

DISCUSSION

We have shown that the reported frequency and levels of alcohol consumption among Mexican-Americans in San Antonio are quite comparable to those of the general population among middle-aged and younger women and among older men. Older Mexican-American women report less drinking, while middle-aged and younger men report more drinking than comparable groups in the general population.

We also hypothesized that drinking patterns might be differently related to a number of predictor variables in men and women and in different generations. In general, our hypotheses regarding these effects are supported by the data. For example, less acculturated middle-aged men appear to consume more alcohol, giving support to the notion that acculturative stress may lead them to resort to alcohol (Alcocer, 1982; Graves, 1967). Older men are not similarly affected, suggesting, perhaps, that acculturative stress is not an issue in the older generation. In fact, on this measure, older men, as a

256

group, are not acculturated at all. Younger men are also not affected, suggesting that they may be sufficiently acculturated so that acculturative stress may not be an issue. Among younger women, acculturation has a positive effect on drinking, as hypothesized. Since drinking among Mexican-American women is quite moderate, it is not a good indicator of distress. Thus, acculturative stress would not necessarily lead to greater drinking. On the other hand, greater acculturation into the larger society, which is more tolerant of drinking among women, should be correlated with greater drinking among women as our data on younger women show (Maril and Zavaleta, 1979). Why this is not also observed among middle-aged women is not clear. In fact, the effects for middle-aged women are in the opposite direction (negative), but they are not significant.

Another interesting finding is that middle-aged women who are currently in their second (or later) marriage drink more than other women. We suggested earlier that this may indicate that previous marital dissolution may have contributed to increased drinking which has persisted into the later marriage. This is not observed among younger women, possibly because of restricted variation on this variable. Only around 7% of younger women were in their second or later marriage. The absence of the effect among middle-aged men, on the other hand, is curious. However, it is among middle-aged women where traditional cultural norms related to marriage and family may have prohibited drinking; thus, some of these controls may have been relaxed after the breakup of the marriage which permitted these women to consume more alcohol and to continue to do so at higher rates than women who are married only once.

As we had hypothesized, marital satisfaction was very strongly related to drinking among younger men. The relationships were non-significant but also in the expected direction among middle-aged men. It should also be acknowledged that the direction of causality between marital satisfaction and drinking may very well work the other way. Thus, it is possible that high levels of drinking among men may cause marital problems. If this is true, the weak association between marital satisfaction and drinking among middle-aged men may reflect greater tolerance of their drinking by their wives, who are more traditional than the wives of the younger men.

We also predicted that the negative association between marital satisfaction and drinking would be stronger among men than among women (as shown in our findings for the third generation) because men are more likely to relieve their distress through alcohol. Women, on the other hand, are more likely to express their distress through higher levels of depression. If this hypothesis has any merit, then marital satisfaction should have stronger effects on depression among women than among men. We examined this by regressing the Center for Epidemiologic Studies Depression Scale (Radloff, 1977) on the seven predictors employed in the analysis of drinking behavior separately for men and women. Among younger people, marital satisfaction has significant negative effects of similar magnitude on both men and women. In the middle generation, the effects were also negative for both men and women but were not statistically significant. In the older generation, we observe a significant negative effect among women and a weak and insignificant effect among men. Based on this evidence, we conclude that, at least among younger people, marital problems lead to depression among women but not to greater alcohol consumption. Men, however, are more likely to turn to alcohol in the face of marital problems but also become depressed.

In sum, we have observed interesting findings regarding the drinking behavior of Mexican-Americans. These findings also suggest that the drinking behavior of Mexican-Americans is a complex issue. Much of this complexity is related to the differential effect of such key factors as acculturation and marital satisfaction in the different sex and generation groups. Finally, we have found evidence, supported by previous literature, that considerable amounts of excessive drinking exist among middle-aged and younger Mexican-American men.

REFERENCES

Alcocer, A. M. 1982. Alcohol use and abuse among the Hispanic American population. In National Institute on Alcohol Abuse and Alcoholism. Alcohol and Health (Monograph No. 4, Special Population Issues). Rockville, MD: Department of Health and Human Services.

Clark, W. B. and Midanic, L. 1982. Alcohol use and alcohol problems in U.S. adults. In National Institute on Alcohol Abuse and Alcoholism, Alcohol Consumption and Related Problems. Alcohol and Health (Monograph No. 1). Washington, DC: U.S. Government Printing Office.

Cuellar, I., Harris, L. C., and Jasso, R. 1980. An acculturation scale for Mexican-American normal and clinical populations. Hispanic Journal of Behavioral Science 2:199-287.

Dohrenwend, B. and Dohrenwend, B. S. 1976. Sex differences in psychiatric disorders. American Journal of Sociology 81:1447-1459.

Gilbert, M. J. and Cervantes, R. C. 1986. Patterns and practices of alcohol use among Mexican-Americans: A comprehensive review. Hispanic Journal of Behavioral Sciences 8:1-60.

Gilford, R. and Bengtson, V. L. 1979. Measuring marital satisfaction in three generations: Positive and negative dimensions. Journal of Marriage and the Family 41:387-398.

Gomberg, E. L. 1982. Special populations. In E. L. Gomberg, H. R. White, and J. A. Carpenter (eds.), Alcohol, Science, and Society Revisited. Ann Arbor: University of Michigan Press.

Graves, T. D. 1967. Acculturation, access, and alcohol in a tri-ethnic community. American Anthropologist 69:306-321.

Klatsky, A. L., Friedman, G. D., Siegelaub, A. B., and Gerard, M. J. 1977. Alcohol consumption among White, Black, or Oriental men and women: Kaiser-Permanent multi-phasic health examination data. American Journal of Epidemiology 105:311-323.

Madsen, W. 1964. The alcoholic agringado. American Anthropologist 66:355-361.

Maril, R. L., and Zavaleta, A. N. 1979. Drinking patterns of low-income Mexican-American women. Journal of Studies on Alcohol 40:480-484.

Markides, K. S., Hoppe, S. K., Martin, H. W., and Timbers, D. M. 1983. Sample representativeness in a three-generations study of Mexican-Americans. Journal of Marriage and the Family 45:911-916.

Markides, K. S. and Vernon, S. W. 1984. Aging, sex-role orientation, and adjustment: A three-genera-tions study of Mexican-Americans. Journal of Gerontology 39:586-591.

Meyers, A. R., Goldman, E., Hingson, R., and Scotch, N. 1981. Evidence for cohort or generational differences in the drinking behavior of older adults. International Journal of Aging and Human Development 14:31-43.

Munch, N., Lloyd, N., Malin, H., Coakley, J., and Kaelber, C. 1981. How Americans say they drink: Preliminary data from two recent national surveys. In M. Galanter (Ed.), Currents in Alcoholism: Volume III, Recent Advances in Research (pp. 233-251). NY: Grune and Stratton.

Neff, J. A., Hoppe, S. K., and Perea, P. 1987. Acculturation and alcohol use: Drinking patterns among Anglo and Mexican-American male drinkers. Hispanic Journal of Behavior Sciences 9:151-181.

Paine, H. J. 1978. Attitudes and patterns of alcohol use among Mexican-Americans: Implications for service delivery. Journal of Studies on Alcohol 39:894-902.

Radloff, L. 1977. The CES-D scale: A self-report scale for research in the general population. Applied Psychological Measurement 7:459-464.

Warheit, G., Holzer, C., Bell, R., and Arey, S. 1976. Sex, marital status, and mental health: A reappraisal. Social Forces 55:459-470.

TABLE 10.1

PERCENT OF FREQUENCY OF DRINKING CATEGORIES
IN PAST TWO MONTHS, AVERAGE NUMBER OF
DRINKS ON A GIVEN DAY BY THOSE WHO DRANK
AT LEAST A FEW TIMES A MONTH, AND PERCENT
OF ALL RESPONDENTS WHO CONSUMED SIX OR
MORE DRINKS ON A USUAL DAY, BY
GENERATION AND SEX

	Older Generation		Middle Generation		Younger Generation	
	Male (N=105)	Female (N=269)	Male (N-125)	Female (N=245)	Male (N=143)	Female (N=231)
Frequency of alcohol consumption in past two months (percent)						
Several times a week or more frequently	12.4	2.2	31.2	4.5	25.2	1.3
Once a week to a few times a month	21.0	3.0	44.4	22.8	41.3	24.2
Once a month or less frequently	39.0	14.5	24.0	34.3	26.6	40.3
Never	27.7	80.3	10.4	38.4	7.0	34.2
Average number of drinks by those who drank at least a few times a month	2.6	1.9	3.7	3.0	2.9	3.1
Percent of all respondents who drank an average of six or more drinks on a given day	1.9	0.0	22.4	3.3	22.4	3.0

TABLE 10.2

RESULTS OF MULTIPLE REGRESSION ANALYSIS
BY GENERATION: MEN

Independent Variables	Older Generation (N=81)			Middle Generation (N=110)				Younger Generation (N=119)			
	Freq. of Drinking	No. of Drinks	Freq. x Volume	Freq. of Drinking	No. of Drinks	Freq. x Volume	High Drkg.	Freq. of Drinking	No. of Drinks	Freq. x Volume	High Drkg.
Marital Satisfaction	0.005# (-0.018)	-0.039 (-0.048)	-0.033 (-0.004)	-0.095 (-0.027)	-0.098 (-0.006)	-0.099 (-0.011)	-0.160 (-0.012)	-0.449* (-0.116)	-0.411* (-0.029)	-0.422* (-0.052)	-0.284 (-0.002)
Sex-Role Orientation	0.173 (-0.075)	0.058 (-0.004)	0.098 (0.014)	-0.142 (-0.061)	-0.122 (-0.115)	-.0149 (-0.024)	-0.144 (-0.016)	-0.071 (-0.029)	-0.043 (-0.048)	-0.054 (-0.010)	0.073 (0.010)
2nd Marriage (or higher)	-0.013 (-0.049)	0.024 (0.016)	0.016 (0.019)	0.019 (0.090)	0.030 (0.031)	0.043 (0.078)	-0.013 (-0.017)	-0.049 (-0.259)	-0.112 (-0.157)	-0.119 (-0.279)	-0.085 (-0.140)
Language Scale	0.094 (0.041)	0.068 (0.005)	0.075 (0.011)	-0.352* (-0.192)	-0.251* (-0.030)	-0.312* (-0.065)	-0.157 (-0.023)	0.017 (0.009)	0.068 (0.009)	0.071 (0.016)	-0.038 (-0.006)
Age	-0.086 (-0.030)	-0.140 (-0.009)	-0.125 (-0.014)	-0.187* (-0.461)	-0.288* (-0.016)	-0.260* (-0.025)	-0.079 (-0.005)	0.104 (0.030)	0.051 (0.004)	0.1064 (0.008)	-0.046 (-0.004)
Income	0.172 (0.188)	0.250* (0.048)	0.268* (0.096)	0.266* (0.136)	0.224* (0.251)	0.282* (-0.056)	0.062 (0.008)	0.043 (0.020)	0.018 (0.002)	0.026 (0.006)	0.002 (0.000)
Education	-0.138 (-0.058)	-0.307* (-0.022)	-0.299* (-0.041)	0.081 (0.037)	-0.135 (-0.013)	-0.092 (-0.016)	-0.210* (-0.025)	-0.055 (-0.032)	-0.125 (-0.020)	-0.111 (0.030)	-0.109 (-0.020)

Standardized regression coefficients. Numbers in parentheses are unstandardized regression coefficients.
* Significant at the .05 level or beyond.

TABLE 10.3

RESULTS OF MULTIPLE REGRESSION ANALYSIS BY GENERATION: WOMEN

Independent Variables	Older Generation (N=100)	Middle Generation (N=183)			Younger Generation (N=168)		
	Frequency of Drinking	Frequency of Drinking	No. of Drinks	Freq. x Volume	Frequency of Drinking	No. of Drinks	Freq. x Volume
Marital Satisfaction	0.088# (0.015)	0.025 (0.005)	-0.047 (-0.002)	-0.043 (-0.004)	-0.154* (-0.024)	-0.055 (-0.002)	-0.068 (-0.005)
Sex-Role Orientation	-0.082 (-0.022)	-0.003 (-0.001)	0.063 (0.005)	0.034 (0.005)	-0.171* (-0.043)	-0.125 (-0.009)	-0.130 (-0.016)
Second Marriage (or higher)	0.021 (0.056)	0.389* (1.013)	0.275* (0.174)	0.299* (0.328)	0.014 (0.047)	-0.013 (-0.124)	-0.007 (-0.011)
Language Scale	-0.026 (-0.075)	-0.108 (-0.034)	-0.121 (-0.009)	-0.132 (-0.017)	0.238* (0.077)	0.298* (0.027)	0.295* (0.046)
Age	-0.147 (-0.028)	-0.086 (-0.012)	-0.145* (-0.005)	-0.142* (-0.009)	0.016 (0.003)	-0.012 (-0.001)	-0.002 (-0.002)
Income	0.311* (0.256)	-0.078 (-0.030)	-0.007 (-0.001)	-0.016 (-0.003)	0.114 (0.035)	-0.078 (-0.007)	-0.067 (-0.010)
Education	0.007 (0.003)	0.128 (0.039)	0.096 (0.007)	0.089 (0.012)	-0.032 (-0.012)	-0.055 (-0.006)	-0.053 (-0.009)

Standardized regression coefficients. Numbers in parentheses are unstandardized regression coefficients.

* Significant at the .05 level or beyond.

SUMMARY: U.S. ALCOHOL USE IN ADULT POPULATIONS

This section has described the use of alcohol in several segments of the U.S. population. We have considered earlier the initiation of alcohol (Section 1: U.S. Alcohol Use by Adolescents). For the adult population, we must begin with the assumption that drinking is a behavior which is overwhelmingly common and accepted, to at least some degree. At what point does alcohol use become problematic and what are the implications of that for problem drinkers?

One theme which runs through these chapters is that of alcohol as anesthesia. Our authors examine a variety of stressors in their sample populations and describe the association of drinking with perceived high levels of stress.

Butler, Schuller-Friedman, and Shichor (Chapter 7) look at both of these issues with regard to the elderly. For them, aging and impairment are seen as stressors. The authors find that drinking declines with age, that men drink more than women, and that the non-impaired drink more than the impaired.

As we suggested in the Introduction to Section 3, the use of multiple drugs in this population holds the threat of serious potentiating effects. The findings for concomitant drug use among the elderly are therefore important. The most commonly used drugs are tranquilizers and barbiturates. Moreover, over one-third drink alcohol and use prescribed drugs. Though illegal drugs are not common, legal drug use is extensive at all ages but is greater among the non-impaired than among the impaired.

In this study, then, the notion of age and impairment as stressors leading to alcohol use is not borne out. Nevertheless, the authors identify a serious problem of multiple drug use among the elderly.

Fagan (Chapter 8) asks a very different question. He asks what the implications of being alcoholic are for the residents of skid row. He points out that skid row is not a place but a lifestyle, that only about 30% of the residents of skid row are alcoholic, and that only 20% to 30% of all alcoholics end up on skid row.

The problem for the skid row alcoholic is circular. Being alcoholic has placed him/her in the skid row lifestyle, but being in the skid row lifestyle makes rehabilitation and re-entry into "normal" society very difficult. For Fagan, the rehabilitation of these alcoholics requires a process of systematic re-socialization into the life of the community. It is not merely alcohol which is the problem of the skid row alcoholic but entrapment in a deviant subculture as well.

Smykla's (Chapter 9) treatment of drinking among the families of death-row inmates carries with it the implication of stress as a cause of drinking. He is careful to state the caveat that drinking may be a matter of subculture and not merely stress. Nevertheless, his respondents, in their own words, identify stress as the culprit. This again is a theme which we may come to expect: substance abusers have a rationale for their behavior that makes sense to them and that will be portrayed during any discussion of their problem. For these people, alcohol is reportedly anesthesia.

266

Markides and Krause (Chapter 10) examine dual stressors -- marital dissatisfaction and acculturation -- for a population of Mexican-Americans. Their findings are instructive. First, they find that drinking behavior is differently defined for men and for women. They add to our knowledge of the effect of culture the finding that drinking norms are sex-role specific. They go on to show an association between the stress of acculturation and drinking. They also show an association between marital dissatisfaction and drinking for men. For women, acculturation is associated with more drinking. Less acculturated women, however, do not respond to marital dissatisfaction with increased drinking.

We begin to see from these chapters that several things happen as adults drink substantial amounts of alcohol. There are effects on their biological functioning, as for example in the potentiating effects of alcohol and drugs. They may enter into subcultures and lifestyles which make the continuation of drinking possible but which make re-entry into "normal" society difficult. And they construct reasons for their behavior which "make sense" to them but do not mitigate either the biological risks which they run or their opportunities for exit from the drinking subculture and lifestyle. Finally, through this process, they begin to become labelled as "drunks" by non-alcoholics, which makes their re-entry into normal society all the more difficult.

SECTION 4
U.S. SUBSTANCE USE IN ADULT POPULATIONS

INTRODUCTION

As we have considered drinking behavior, we have been disciplined by the facts that alcohol is legal and readily available. Moreover, moderate use of alcohol is normatively prescribed in our society. It is only the continuation of use toward abuse that we need to ponder -- all other drinking is "normal."

Drug use is different. Most of it is illegal. Even those who are using drugs legally most often ultimately abuse the system and flirt with illegality to get their supply (Prather, Chapter 12). Why then do people use drugs?

Hoffman (Chapter 11) sets out the bounds of an explanatory theory but notes that the very complexity of the behavior defies easy conceptualization.

Beginning with Hoffman's conceptualization of drug, user, and setting as the key considerations in drug abuse, we commence an examination of the motivation to use drugs by suburban women (Prather, Chapter 12), women in the deviant under-class of New York (Goldstein, Chapter 13), physicians and nurses (Winick, Chapter 14), and a sample of heroin users (Wiebel, Chapter 15). The link between these reports is that each researcher has sought out an understanding of both the drug and the setting and has described the behavior of drug use in the user's own words.

We can analyze the phenomenon of drug use then on two levels: 1) we can look for the patterns of "footprints" which we have found earlier and 2) we can also view the behavior through the user's own rationale.

Several consistent themes emerge. In drug use, the user first has to be "loosened" from an anti-drug normative system either by association with an anti-normative subculture or by anomic isolation from a normative subculture. They then have to be present where the drug is available, to have access to it, to be able to learn to use it, and to learn to find it pleasurable. Very often, in the reports that follow, all of this is facilitated by a family member or friend who is already a drug user. As drug use continues, the user develops a rationale by which the behavior is made "rational."

Finally, in this section, Kaestner et al. return us to our focus on patterns with some quantitative data on just how widespread the phenomenon of drug use is in single-room-occupancy hotels in New York City (Chapter 16).

INTRODUCTION TO CHAPTER 11

The very complexity of the subject of drug use virtually defies clear conceptualization. In this chapter, Hoffman reviews attempts to conceptualize drug-use behavior (DUB). The author identifies problems in developing a theory of DUB and notes the key issues which any theory must address: 1) the delineation of cause, 2) the identification of types of users, and 3) specification of the level at which use of each particular drug becomes problematic.

In the course of her review of current theories of drug use, Hoffman identifies two basic types of drugs and five categories of use.

She goes on to conclude that a good theory must identify the interaction of three sets of variables: 1) a classification of users, 2) a classification of substances, and 3) a classification of settings.

There is one such integrated model which the author reviews for us. This is an especially useful exercise for us. It alerts us to the strengths and weaknesses of some of the theories of drug use which we will encounter and gives us a standard by which to evaluate them.

CHAPTER 11
CONCEPTUALIZATIONS OF DRUG-USE BEHAVIORS

Agnes L. Hoffman

ABSTRACT

Understanding drug-use behavior is important to professionals who handle the prevention and treatment of drug use, to the psychoactive drug user, to significant others involved in the immediate social context of use, and to the general public.

In this chapter, various definitions, types, patterns, and variables pertaining to drug-use behavior are discussed. Several theoretical approaches to explaining drug-use behavior derived from social, psychological, and biological sciences are summarized. Then

----
AGNES L. HOFFMAN is Associate Professor of Psychosocial Nursing at the University of Washington and a nurse.

an integrated model of drug use behavior
incorporating crucial elements from various
research findings is presented.

INTRODUCTION

Non-clinical psychoactive drug use or the use of
mind- and mood-altering substances (for example,
marijuana, alcohol, cocaine, or opiates) is widespread
in our society. Selected characteristics of users such
as age, sex, socioeconomic status, and ethnicity vary
considerably. Heterogeneity, rather than homogeneity,
marks the population of psychoactive drug users.

Knowledge important to understanding non-clinical
psychoactive substance use and its effects on the user
is broad and inclusive. Drug-use behavior is a
function of the interaction of the person with his/her
environment (Lewin, 1935). For example, drug
availability and resources for drug access are critical
to the occurrence of psychoactive drug use. To
understand the effects a given drug can have on a
user's behavior and health, it is necessary not only to
learn about the drug used but also to know much about
the drug user, the user's domestic and social
environment, and the user's previous and current
sociocultural background. Multiple factors must be
considered in understanding drug-user behavior: 1) the
vast array of both legal and illegal psychoactive
substances available to users today, 2) their
potential for interactive effects when used
simultaneously, 3) the heterogeneity of users, and 4)
the diversity of sociocultural contexts of use.

Given the complex and multiple factors involved in
non-clinical psychoactive drug use, it is important to

analyze and attempt to understand the phenomena. One concern is that treatment strategies are closely linked with how we conceptualize a given condition or disorder. For example, if we postulate that opiate addiction is a result of biological deficiency in the individual's supply of endorphins, then our intervention will be quite different than if we propose that drug dependence is learned behavior. From another perspective, if we view the cause of excessive drug use to be located in the user (from factors such as low self-esteem or narcissism) rather than in the environment (for example, from peer pressure or role modeling), then our intervention will be aimed primarily at the user's personality problems rather than at functioning in a social context. A second reason to understand substance use is its prevalence and potential harmful effects for members of society. Due to the escalation of non-clinical psychoactive drug use within the last two decades, it becomes increasingly important for us to understand the kind of drug use which has potential to lead to adverse consequences for both the user and for others. Conceptualization which enables us 1) to understand types and patterns of drug-use behavior, 2) to predict risk and adverse consequences of selected use patterns, and 3) to provide effective preventive approaches as well as treatment strategies are a critical contemporary need.

DEFINITIONS AND CRITERIA

Problems in defining drug abuse and dependence arise from theoretical views about deviance in general and about the non-clinical use of mind- and mood-altering substances in particular (Henderson, 1982). Definitions of deviance have included normative violations with respect to drug use in a given culture and the effects of being labeled "addict," "junky," "speed freak," and so on. Definitions of drug use/abuse have also included what has been referred to as "official" and "unofficial" versions. The official version defines drug abuse as the persistent and usually excessive self-administration of any drug which has resulted in the psychological or physical dependence on that drug or which deviates from approved social patterns of drug use in a given culture. Unofficial definitions define drug abuse as the use of a drug to the extent that it interferes with the individual's health, economic, or social functioning. Both of these attempts to define drug abuse have influenced public opinion and guided professional and lay action in the field of substance use/abuse.

Terms to designate type and level of drug use are often used interchangeably and easily lead to misunderstanding and confusion. For example, the terms use, misuse, abuse, dependence, and addiction are not clearly differentiated, and differences between psychological and physical dependence are not always delineated.

Linear and cyclic models can facilitate description of the extent and level of drug use/abuse/dependence. Peele (1981) has conceptualized drug-use behavior on a continuum which is a linear model of progress from "daily routines" (such as a daily cocktail hour) to "dependence" (drug use to maintain ordinary daily living activities) to "compulsions" (drug use required to function adequately) to "addiction" (drug use to avoid withdrawal symptoms where the drug becomes the focus of the users lifestyle). The model is diagrammed in Figure 11.1, page 275.

One cyclic approach to defining level and extent of drug use is based on the experience a drug provides to a user and the place this experience has in the individual's life. Initially, mind- and mood-altering substances are used to produce states of euphoria and/or to decrease dysphoria. When the amount of a drug consumed is sufficient to produce intoxication, the individual's ability to meet activities of daily living (ADL) is decreased. Then there is an increase in pain and discomfort associated with deficits in ADL. The negative states of pain and discomfort can, in turn, lead to additional drug use in order to deal with daily life events. The relationships between these potential cyclic aspects of psychoactive drug-use behaviors which can escalate to drug dependence or addiction are diagrammed in Figure 11.2, page 275.

Various signs may be identified which point to the development of drug dependence. They include:

1. inability to make alternative choices (inflexibility);
2. decrease in pleasure with preferred drug; and
3. diminished involvement in life events which are not drug-use related.

Diagnostic criteria of dysfunctional behaviors associated with abuse and dependence have been delineated by the American Psychiatric Association (1980). The diagnostic categories deal with behavioral changes associated with more or less regular use of substances that affect the central nervous system

FIGURE 11.1

A CONTINUUM OF DRUG-USE BEHAVIOR

Routine --- Dependent --- Compulsive --- Addictive
   Use   Use   Use   Use

FIGURE 11.2

PSYCHOACTIVE DRUG-USE BEHAVIOR (DUB) CYCLE


```
_____ Euphoria _____ Mind-State Alteration _
|        Dysphoria                             |
DUB                                       Deficits
|                                           ADL
|_____ Addiction _____|
```

(CNS). The behavioral changes would be viewed as extremely undesirable in almost all cultures and subcultures. Thus, the categories distinguish non-medical or recreational use on a continuum of "non-pathological" use to "pathological" use. The substance-use disorders (SUB) include maladaptive behaviors associated with regular use of a given substance (abuse or dependence) and substance-induced organic mental disorders (OMD) which describes the direct (acute or chronic) effects of these substances on the central nervous system. The diagnostic criteria for both SUD and OMD illustrated with cocaine and opiates are provided in Tables 11.1 and 11.2, pages 293 and 295 respectively.

TYPES AND PATTERNS OF DRUG USE
Various typologies have been used to differentiate individuals manifesting different types of drug abuse. Such a delineation can assist treatment professionals in tailoring care for specific clients as well as in providing guidelines for preventive strategies. Recent research findings by McLellan et al., reviewed by Alterman and McLellan (1981), suggest that a classification system of five sub-groups of substance abusers may be useful. Their classification system is based on the psychophysiologic effects of the drug and on the number of drugs used. The five sub-groups of substance abusers are: 1) single substance use -- psychodepressants, 2) single substance use -- psychostimulants, 3) multiple, similar substance use -- psychodepressants, 4) multiple, similar substance use -- psychostimulants, and 5) multiple, dissimilar substance

276

use -- psychodepressants and psychostimulants (Table 11.3, page 297).

Findings from a recent survey of types of drug use by 1,000 consecutive admissions to a Substance Abuse Treatment unit support the validity of the sub-groupings. Approximately 60% of the clients were found to be concurrently abusing two or more psychoactive substances, including alcohol. When the psycho-physiological effects of the substances being consumed were examined, it was found that 74% of the multiple substance abusers were using chemicals with similar effects. That is, concurrent use of amphetamines, cocaine, and/or hallucinogens were common, as was the concurrent use of heroin and alcohol, and of alcohol and barbiturates. A much lower percentage, 26%, of the multiple substance abusers reported concurrent use of drugs having psychophysiologically dissimilar effects. In a study of 56 cocaine users requiring clinical attention, one-half reported no drug use other than cocaine free base, which fits the category of single substance use (Cocaine free base-use, 1982). Sedative-hypnotic use by alcoholics and alcohol use by heroin addicts would fit the category of multiple, similar substance use (Barr et al., 1973).

Types of drug use may reflect systematic efforts by the user to induce particular psychophysiologic effects through the concurrent use of chemical agents having similar or dissimilar psychopharmacologic actions. While there are differences in the neuropharmacologic actions of similar substances, there are at least two categories of psychoactive agents which produce distinctive physiologic and behavioral effects. The categories are stimulants or psychic energizers (such as hallucinogens like LSD and Peyote, amphetamines, Ritalin, and cocaine) and depressants (such as opiates, sedative-hypnotics, and alcohol). Initial evidence suggests that individuals may use substances specifically related to their physiologic and behavioral needs for stimulation or for anesthetization.

The revised classificatory system proposed by Alterman and McLennan (1981) of the substance (stimulants or depressants), number of substances used (single or multiple), and similarity or dissimilarity of psychophysiologic effects in multiple substance use is provided in Table 11.3, Page 297. The model is currently being evaluated for its usefulness in designing specialized treatment strategies for the different sub-groups of substance abusers.

An individual's substance use pattern may indicate a level of substance use that places that person at risk for developing more serious substance-related health problems. When a hazardous level of substance use is assessed, health teaching is required such as teaching the warning signs of cancer to the tobacco smoker.

Although the diagnostic criteria for substance abuse and dependence have been operationally defined by the American Psychiatric Association DSM-III (discussed above), the clinical profile of drug-use levels which are hazardous has not been clearly delineated. Identifying the so-called "gray area" in which a transition from use to abuse occurs is critical to early intervention and subsequent prevention of substance-use disorders. One approach to understanding use patterns has been designated by the Shafer National Commission on Marijuana and Drug Abuse (1974), reviewed by the Liaison Task Panel on Psychoactive Drug Use/Misuse (Zinberg, 1980). The five use patterns include: 1) experimental use, 2) social-recreational use, 3) circumstantial-situational use, 4) intensified use, and 5) complusive use. This approach to delineating substance use patterns is based on the dose and duration of the substance used, the perceptual-cognitive-affective status or "set" of the user, and the physical and social environment or setting in which the drug use occurred.

Experimental use is defined as short-term, non-patterned use of a specific substance. Users are frequently motivated by curiosity and a desire to experience anticipated drug effects. The patterns of social-recreational use consists of users sharing social experiences with friends and acquaintances in a context of substance use (for instance, a cocktail party or a "free base party"). Circumstantial use is defined as a task-specific, self-limited use. The user consumes the substance to obtain an anticipated drug effect to cope with a specific condition or situation (for example, to increase work performance or to relieve depression). Intensified use is characterized by long-term patterned use of a substance which involves preoccupation with the drug-seeking and drug-taking behavior. Use is related to relief of stressful situations and to maintaining a self-prescribed level of performance. Finally, the pattern of compulsive use is defined as a level of substance use which is frequent, intense, and of prolonged duration and typically includes a substance specific dependence and withdrawal syndrome. The user is motivated to elicit positive drug effects (such as euphoria) and to avoid negative effects (like withdrawal symptoms).

The five patterns of substance use defined above can provide helpful markers or warning signs for substance use transitions. For example, a report of substance use that is determined by coping needs is evidence of potential dysfunctional use. Whether hazardous use levels continue or are reduced may well be related to the person's cognizance of his place on the continuum of substance use/abuse/addiction, as well as on available resources to address health-related concerns associated with current substance use levels.

MAJOR VARIABLES

So far no one single conceptualization has satisfactorily explained the diverse nature of alcohol and drug-abuse problems. Consequently, the most productive approach to studying these problems is one that takes into account multivariate theoretical approaches. The following conceptualization involves a multivariate framework which includes the interaction of three major variables: substance used, user, and setting of use (Hoffman and Heinemann, 1981). This conceptualization will be discussed next, followed by a discussion of five stages of substance-use behavior (initiation, continuation, transition of use to abuse, cessation, and relapse), and then of several theories proposed to explain drug-use behavior (psychological-intraphysic, psychological-social, sociological, and naturalistic-biologic).

User, Substance, and Setting

In order to understand drug-use behavior (DUB), the reciprocal interaction systems of user, substance, and setting need to be examined. The interactions of these three components comprise the major variables in the conceptualization of DUB. Study of the substance used includes its pharmocological properties (specific effects) and its non-specific effects attributable to the user and setting. The user is examined from biological and behavioral perspectives. The setting includes the social and physical environment in which the use occurs. Underlying this model -- which corresponds to the epidemiological health model of agent, host, and environment -- is the premise that at any one time, variables from each of the three systems interact in complex ways to determine who uses a psychoactive agent, how it is used, and what it affects. A paradigm of the reciprocal interaction of substance, user, and setting is provided in Figure 11.3, page 282.

Components of Drug-Use Behavior

Theoretical approaches proposed to explain drug use/abuse are diverse. For example, some explanatory approaches address the user only, while others address the user in a social context. Some viewpoints are based on one age group only (for example, youth or elderly), one substance only (such as alcohol or heroin use), or one sex (for example, males). If a theory is to have utility in explaining DUB, it must address the many variables involved in the complex person-drug-environment context. In a review of drug use/abuse

281

FIGURE 11.3

FACTORS AFFECTING OUTCOME
OF SUBSTANCE USE

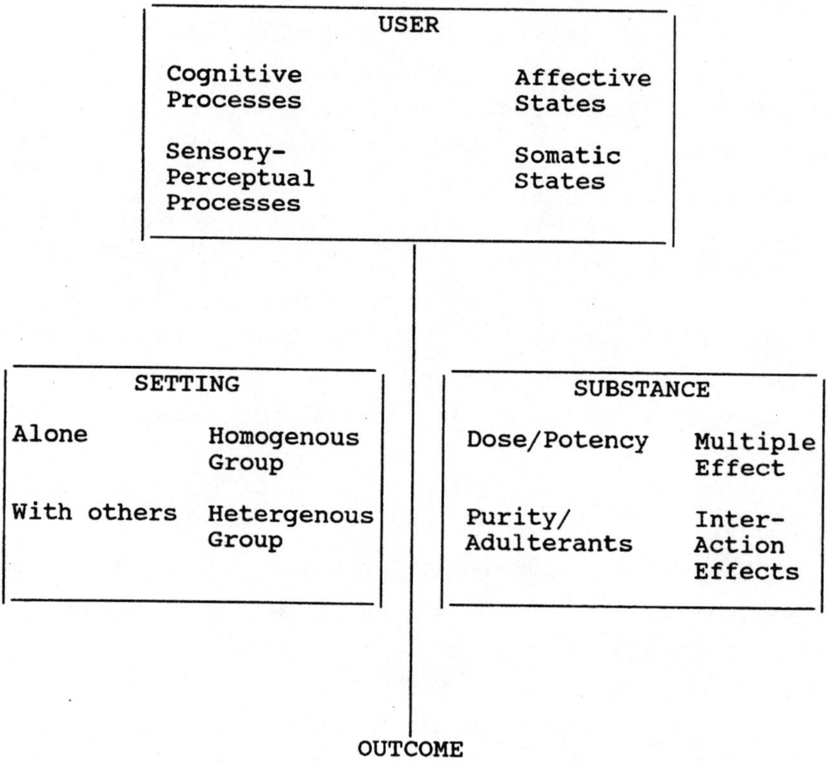

USER	
Cognitive Processes	Affective States
Sensory-Perceptual Processes	Somatic States

SETTING			SUBSTANCE	
Alone	Homogenous Group		Dose/Potency	Multiple Effect
With others	Hetergenous Group		Purity/ Adulterants	Inter-Action Effects

OUTCOME

theories, Lettieri, Sayers, and Pearson (1980) identified the five stages of drug use behavior for which factors have been identified: 1) initiation, 2) continuation of use, 3) transition from use to abuse, 4) cessation of use, and 5) relapse into use.

An example of a theory of drug use/abuse which addresses the five components of DUB from a sociological perspective is one proposed by Johnson (1980, 1973). He discusses four subcultures based on the primary drug of choice by the users: an alcohol-abuse subculture, a cannabis subculture, a multiple drug subculture, and a heroin-injection subculture. Each subculture has different norms of conduct associated with it. The particular norms of a given subculture govern the central activities of the group and of individual participants with respect to the five components of DUB.

Drug subcultures are seldom static. They change over time. While the central value (to get "high") and central roles (seller, buyer, and user) remain relatively unaltered over time, the conduct norms (expectations of behavior in a particular social situation attached to a status within the group) may shift considerably. Conduct norms may shift in response to social pressure, legal pressure, fads in drug preferences, and availability of drugs, especially in the illicit market.

THEORIES OF DRUG USE/ABUSE/DISORDER

The relative upsurge of various models and theories explaining the problems of drug abuse is one indication that this research domain has come of age. In 1980,

Lettieri, Sayers, and Pearson compiled a representative selection of contemporary social and biomedical perspectives in the drug-abuser research field. The compendium of perspectives includes categories to facilitate cross-theory comparisons. The categories include: 1) a list of the contributors and their theoretical affiliation (learning theory, role theory, family theory, and so on), 2) a classification of the theories into four broad categories (theories on one's relationship to self, to others, to society, and to nature), 3) classification of the theories by academic discipline (psychology, sociology, biology, neuroscience), 4) organization by the five components of DUB (discussed above) addressed by each theory, and 5) a comparative summary of each theory, including its drug focus, population to which the theory applies (age, sex, and ethnicity), and a list of the key variables inherent in the theory. Within the limits of this paper, only the classification of the theories into four broad categories as reviewed by Lettieri (1978) will be discussed.

Theories of drug use classified as "Humans in Relation to Nature" are derived from the biological sciences and address topics such as genetics, metabolism, and neural physiology in the causation of drug use. In contrast, theories of drug use classified as "Humans in Relation to Self" are derived from the behavioral sciences. Here the causation of drug abuse may be attributed to a personality disorder or to learned behavior. Application of selected theories of drug abuse classified as "Humans in Relation to Nature and Self" are provided in Table 11.4, page 298.

The classification of theories as "Humans in Relation to Others and Society" explains drug use from the psychosocial perspective. Theories which address "Humans in Relation to Others" view drug use as a function of the user interacting with his or her environment. In contrast, theories which address "Humans in Relation to Society" focus on sociological approaches to understanding drug use. That is, the focus is on the impact of cultural and social forces and their influences on the individual who uses drugs. Application of selected theories to drug abuse classified as "Humans in Relation to Others and Society" are provided in Table 11.5, page 300.

Drug abuse is a multifaceted problem. When the above theories are examined, the multiple factors which contribute to the initiation, continuation, and cessation of drug use may not be addressed in any single theory. A holistic model which encompasses all four relations of humans discussed above is needed. Such an integrated approach to understanding drug abuse should account for the many factors which contribute to it.

AN INTEGRATED MODEL

A model to explain the initiation, continuation, and cessation of substance use was proposed by the Society for the Study of Addiction to Alcohol and Other Drugs (1982). The model was developed not only for applied purposes but also because of the bearing a precise and integrated model might have on a variety of conceptual concerns. The model addresses the various components of drug-use behavior (DUB). Initial DUB is a response to one set of stimuli. The stimuli include both external (for example, social influences and situational cues) and internal (such as mood states) stimuli. Both biological (for example, genetic influences) and psychosocial (such as previous learning and peer group pressure) dimensions pertaining to the user are taken into account, as are drug-related factors (for instance, dose and route of administration) in initial drug use.

Once drug use occurs, a range of consequences may act as either deterrents or reinforcers for continuation of drug use and transition of drug use to abuse. The effects of DUB operate in at least three ways: 1) by direct impact on individual learning processes which have reinforcing or adversive effects for the user, 2) by external reactions either giving social approval or provoking disapproval from others, and 3) by the drug-related biological consequences. The development of tolerance to a particular drug and of withdrawal effects must be considered here as having both adversive and reinforcing consequences for the user. Relief of withdrawal symptoms by further drug taking can serve to strengthen the drug-seeking pattern.

In addition to the consequences cited above, the potential importance of a number of other learning processes in DUB which influence continuation of drug use need to be addressed. One process is stimulus generalization. The number of cues in the user's environment that may stimulate drug taking is likely to be increased through the process of generalization. For example, if anxiety is a component of drug withdrawal, then the general experience of anxiety may tend to excite drug taking. If a particular setting or circumstance has been associated with drug taking, these situations may subsequently become potential stimuli to a drug-taking response. As drug taking becomes a strongly reinforced response to a particular stimulus, the drug-taking response may lead to the lessening or extinction of other responses to that stimulus; the user may be left with few responses to anxiety other than drug taking. In addition, as drug taking becomes less exploratory and more determined by a complex set of cues, the pattern of drug taking will become narrowed and stereotyped.

Cessation of drug taking may be encouraged by a number of factors. One factor is lack of reinforcement for DUB. Lack of reinforcement may include such factors as biological changes that alter the immediate impact of the drug, psychological changes that alter the value placed on drug effects, or the use of drugs that block drug effect (for example, naloxane used to block effects of opiates). Adversive consequences of DUB also serve to suppress or extinguish drug-taking behavior. Such consequences may include a growing burden of negative responses from the environment, an increasing distress in withdrawal experiences, or increasing suffering occasioned by drug taking (for example, financial costs, interpersonal malfunctions, or occupational problems). Competitive reinforcement in response to a given stimulus can also alter the likely occurrence of drug-taking behavior. For example, engaging in non-drug-related social activities, or developing coping or self-control strategies to extinguish drug use. Finally, if drugs are not available, they cannot be taken. Reduced availability would be associated with both fewer cues to use a given drug and an increased cost of the response of drug taking related to the acquisition of the drug.

Relapse of drug-taking behavior after a period of cessation involves reinstatement of the events described above. Such reinstatement for the previous user will result in the user's reaching prior levels of use in a much shorter time than initially. This may be due partially to biological processes for re-acquisition of the neuroadaptive tolerance and withdrawal states. Learned responses with respect to drug taking may also be rather rapidly reinstated, and the external environment may also change to reinforce drug taking as the user associates with former drug-using friends. The process of reinstatement of drug-taking behavior involves an interacting system of events as depicted in Figure 11.3, page 282.

The authors (Society for the Study of Addiction, 1982) of the integrated model identify several limitations of the model's generality and circumscription. Strengths of the model include its identification of relevant events and their connections in the sequence of drug-taking behavior and drug dependence. However, no attempt was made to assign weights to each factor with respect to their significance in the sequence of events. The model is presented in general terms and does not provide specific applications to particular drugs. Analyses of the processes involved for any one variable or the nature of the relationships between variables was not attempted. Some important aspects of drug taking are not related to the DUB model at all. For example, the model does not attempt to describe events involved in the diffusion of drug taking within a population.

The usefulness of the model includes: 1) clarification and presentation of the current status of scientific understanding of DUB as a basis for scientific deliberation, 2) organization of factors for scientific research, 3) display of processes that may initiate DUB and serve to build the drug dependence system from which interventions can be derived, 4) representation of the likely impact specific interventions could have on the whole system, and 5) delineation of the relationships between drug-taking behavior and the development of drug dependence.

The model addresses the complexities and inter-actions involved in drug use/abuse/dependence. This integrated model, despite its complexities and limitations, has potential to lead to a more humane and effective understanding of drug-use behavior.

REFERENCES

Alterman, A. I. and McLellan, A. T. 1981. A framework for refining the diagnostic categorization of substance abusers. Addictive Behaviors 6:23-37.

American Psychiatric Association. 1980. Diagnostic and Statistical Manual of Mental Disorders, 3rd Ed. Washington, DC: The American Psychiatric Association.

Ausubel, D. P. 1961. Causes and types of narcotic addiction: A psychosocial view. Psychiatric Quarterly 35:523-531.

Ausubel, D. P. 1964. Drug Addiction: Physiological, Psychological, and Sociological Aspects. NY: Random House.

Barr, H., Rosen, A., Antes, D., and Ottenberg, D. 1973. Two-year follow up study of 724 drug and alcohol addicts treated together in an abstinence therapeutic community. Paper presented at 81st Annual Meeting of the American Psychological Association, Montreal, Canada.

Cocaine free base use. 1982. Journal of Psychoactive Drugs 14:311-319.

Crowley, T. 1972. The reinforcers for drug abuse: Why people take drugs. Comprehensive Psychiatry 13:51-62.

Dole, V. P. and Nyswander, M. E. 1962. Rehabilitation of the street addict. Archives of Environmental Health 14:477-480.

Freud, S. 1959. Further recommendations in the technique of psychoanalysis. In Vol. 2. Collected Papers, 1913. NY: Basic Books.

Gorsuch, R. L. 1976. Initial drug abuse: A review of predisposing social psychological factors. Psychological Bulletin 83:120-137.

Greaves, G. 1974. Toward an existential theory of drug dependence. Journal of Nervous and Mental Diseases 159:263-274.

Henderson, J. H. 1982. Substance use/abuse: Conceptualization, etiology, and treatment. Journal of Drug Issues 12:317-332.

Hoffman, A. L. and Heinemann, E. 1981. A conceptualization of alcohol and drug abuse nursing. Unpublished manuscript.

Johnson, B. D. 1973. Marijuana Users and Drug Subcultures. NY: Worley.

Johnson, B. D. 1980. Toward a theory of drug subcultures. In D. J. Lettieri, M. Sayers, and H. W. Pearson (eds.) Theories on Drug Abuse (NIDA Research Monograph 30, pp. 110-119). Washington, DC: U.S. Government Printing.

Jonas, D. F. and Jonas, A. D. 1977. A bio-anthropological overview of addiction. Perspectives on Biology and Medicine 3:345-354.

Khantzian, E. J., Mack, J. E., and Schatzberg, A. F. 1974. Heroin use an attempt to cope: Clinical observation. American Journal of Psychiatry 13: 160-164.

Lettieri, D. J. 1978. Theories of drug abuse. In D. J. Lettieri (ed.) Drugs and Suicide (pp. 31-46). Beverly Hills: Sage.

Lettieri, D. J., Sayers, M., and Pearson, H. W. 1980. Theories on Drug Abuse (NIDA Research Monograph 30). Washington, DC: U.S. Government Printing.

Lewin, L. 1935. A Dynamic Theory of Personality. NY: McGraw-Hill.

Lindsmith, A. R. 1947. A sociological theory of drug addiction. American Journal of Sociology 43:593-613.

Merton, R. K. 1957. Social Theory and Social Structure. Glencoe, IL: Free Press.

Misra, R. K. 1976. Drug addiction: Problems and prospects. Drug Forum 5:283-288.

Peele, S. 1981. How Much is Too Much: Health Habits or Destructive Addictions. Englewood Cliffs, NJ: Prentice Hall.

Rado, S. 1933. The Psychoanalysis of pharmacothymia (Drug addiction). Psychoanalytic Quarterly 2:1-23.

Seldin, N. 1972. The family of the addict: A review of the literature. International Journal of the Addictions 7:97-107.

Shafer, R. P. (Chairman). 1974. U.S. Commission on Marijuana and Drug Abuse. Drug use in America. Problem in Perspective. Washington, DC: MSS Information Corp.

Society for the Study of Addiction to Alcohol and Other Drugs. 1982. Nomenclature and Classification of Drug and Alcohol Related Problems: A shortened version of the WHO Memorandum. British Journal of Addiction 77:3-20.

Stanton, M. D. 1977. Drug use surveys: Methods and madness. International Journal of the Addictions 12:95-119.

Stanton, M. D. 1977. The addict as savior: Heroin, death, and the family. Family Process 16:191-197.

Stevens, B. J. 1979. Nursing Theory: Analysis, Application, Evaluation. Boston: Little, Brown.

Sutherland, E. H. and Cressey, D. R. 1960. Principles of Criminology. Philadelphia: Lippincott.

Weil, A. 1972. The Natural Mind. Boston, MA: Houghton, Mifflin.

Wikler, A. 1973. Dynamics of drug dependence: Implications of a conditioning theory for research and treatment. Archives of General Psychiatry 28:611-616.

Zinberg, N. 1980. Report of the Liaison Task Panel on Psychoactive Drug Use/Misuse. The Yearbook of Substance Use and Abuse. NY: Human Sciences Press.

APPENDIX

TABLE 11.1
DIAGNOSTIC CRITERIA FOR SUBSTANCE USE
DISORDERS (SUD) WITH ILLUSTRATION: COCAINE*

Diagnostic Criteria of SUD	Illustration: Cocaine
Substance Dependence	Cocaine Dependence**
Tolerance	Tolerance
Markedly increased amounts are required to achieve the desired effect or there is a markedly diminished effect with regular use of same dose.	Use continues until supplies are exhausted. Inability to titrate dose or to regulate dose regimens. Exhibition of syndromes of progressive psychopathology (for example, paranoid ideation, psychosis).
Withdrawal	Withdrawal
Substance-specific syndrome follows cessation of intake or reduction of intake of a substance that was previously regularly used to induce a physiologic state of mood alteration	Onset: 1 or 2 days following cessation of heavy dose regimens. Duration: 4 days or longer. Symptoms: depressed mood, fatigue, prolonged sleep disturbance, hyperphagia, chills, tremors, muscle pains, involuntary motor movements, severe craving, dreams involving themes of cocaine use.

----

* Adapted from American Psychiatric Association, Diagnostic and Statistical Manual of Mental Disorders, 3rd Ed, Washington, DC: The American Psychiatric Association, 1980.

** Adapted from a study of 56 cocaine free base users as reported in the Journal of Psychoactive Drugs, 14, (1982) 311-319. Reprinted by permission.

TABLE 11.1 (continued)

Substance Abuse	Cocaine Abuse
Pattern of pathological use.	Inability to reduce or stop use. Intoxication throughout the day. Episodes of cocaine overdose (occurrence of hallucinations and delusions).
Impairment in social and occupational functioning due to substance use.	Impairment due to cocaine use (for example, fights, loss of of friends, absence from work, loss of job, or legal difficulties).
Duration of disturbance of at least one month.	Cocaine-related use disturbances of at least one month.

TABLE 11.2

DIAGNOSTIC CRITERIA FOR SUBSTANCE-INDUCED ORGANIC
MENTAL DISORDER (OMD) WITH ILLUSTRATION: OPIOIDS*

Diagnostic Criteria for Substance-Induced OMD	Illustration: Opioids
Intoxication	**Opioid Intoxication**
Development of a substance-specific syndrome that follows recent ingestion and presence in the body of that substance.	Recent use of an opioid. Pupillary constriction (or pupillary dilatation due to anoxia from severe overdose). A least one of the following psychological signs: Euphoria, dysphoria, apathy, psychomotor retardation. At least one of the following neurological signs: drowsiness, slurred speech, impairment in attention or memory.
Maladaptive behavior during the waking state due to the effect of the substance on the CNS (for example, impairment of judgment, belligerence).	Maladaptive behavior effects (such as, impaired judgment, interference with social or occupational functioning).
The clinical picture does not correspond to any of the Specific Organic Brain Syndromes, such as Delirium Organic Delusional Syndrome, Organic Hallucinosis, or Organic Affective Syndrome.	Not due to any other physical or mental disorder.

* Adapted from American Psychiatric Association, Diagnostic and Statistical Manual of Mental Disorders, 3rd Ed. Washington, DC: The American Psychiatric Association, 1980.

TABLE 11.2 (continued)

Diagnostic Criteria for Substance-Induced OMD

Withdrawal

Development of a substance-specific syndrome that follows the cessation of or reduction in intake of a substance that was previously regularly used to induce a state of mental alteration.

The clinical picture does not correspond to any of Organic Brain Syndromes.

Illustration: Opioids

Opioid Withdrawal

A prolonged, heavy use of an opioid. At least 4 of the following symptoms due to recent cessation of or reduction in opioid use: Lacrimation, rhinorrhea, pupillary dilatation, piloerection, sweating, diarrhea, yawning, mild hypertension, tachycardia, insomnia.

Not due to any other physical or mental-specific disorder.

TABLE 11.3

TYPOLOGY OF SUBSTANCE ABUSERS AND
EXAMPLES OF SUBSTANCES USED

TYPOLOGY	EXAMPLES OF SUBSTANCES
Single substance - psychodepressants	Alcohol Heroin
Single substance - psychostimulants	Cocaine Amphetamines
Multiple, similar substances - psycho-depressants	Alcohol and Benzodiazepines Alcohol and Quaalude and Marijuana
Multiple, similar substances - psycho-stimulants	Cocaine and Amphetamines Amphetamines and Ritalin and Cocaine
Multiple, dissimilar substances - psychodepressants and psychostimulants	Heroin and Cocaine Cocaine and Barbiturates Ritalin and Quaaludes

TABLE 11.4

A CLASSIFICATION AND APPLICATION OF THEORIES
ON DRUG ABUSE: HUMANS IN RELATION TO SELF
AND NATURE (BIOPHYSICAL STATES)

Classification	Selected Theory/ Theorists	Application to Drug Abuse
Humans in relation to self	Psychoanalytic theory	Addiction viewed as narcissistic disorder; drugs are used regressively to satisfy libidinal drives.
	Existential theory (Greaves)	Antecedents to drug dependence include disturbances in pleasurable somatic feedback or sensory awareness, feelings of natural euphoria; drug use is substitute for primary source of pleasure.
	Learning theory (Winkler, Crowley)	Addictive behavior involves both classical and instrumental conditioning (for example, anxiety reduction); drugs are positive (that is, produce euphoria) or negative (that is, remove withdrawal symptoms) re-enforcers.
Humans in relation to nature	Genetic theory (Jonas and Jonas)	Addiction as part of overall natural (evolutionary) processes and focuses on gene pool. Addict possesses genetic trait of hypersensitivity, which produces need to narcotize self, thereby reducing stimulus overload; in a state of stimulus deficit, use of a stimulant drug to alter stimulus inputs in search of some optimal level of stimulation.

TABLE 11.4 (continued)

Classification	Selected Theory/ Theorists	Application to Drug Abuse
	Metabolic theory (Dole and Nyswander)	Addiction is the result of an unspecified metabolic deficiency (advocate methadone to correct deficiency).
	Neurological theory (Weil)	Drug use to alter consciousness is innate normal drive analogous to hunger or sexual drive; innate drive is rooted in neurological structures of the brain.

TABLE 11.5

A CLASSIFICATION AND APPLICATION OF THEORIES
ON DRUG ABUSE: HUMANS IN RELATION TO OTHERS
AND SOCIETY

Classification	Selected Theory/ Theorists	Application to Drug Abuse
Humans in relation to others	Coping theory (Khantzian, Mack and Schatzberg)	Addiction is an adaptive mechanism to deal with problems in interpersonal relations; drugs serve as substitutes for, and modifiers of interpersonal interactions; drug subculture affords addict a sense of interpersonal belonging with minimal individual effort.
	Interactive theory (Ausubel, Gorsuch)	Attribute drug use to personality (for example, dependency, low self-esteem) and to environmental (that is, social and peer influences, neighborhood acceptance of drug use) factors; three models of drug users: iatrogenic, non-socialized, and socialized (to pro-drug culture) users.
	Family Process theory (Stanton, Seldin)	Addiction is an individual's self-destructive behavior as an expression of pathology within addict's family constellation; suicide-equivalent behavior (addict is loyal, savior child who denies self to save family).
Humans in relation to society	Anomie theory (Merton, Misra) Jonas)	Addictive behavior is retreat from engaging in socially-sanctioned, goal-directed behavioral pathways; achievement anxiety theory (drug use is result of social pressure to achieve).

TABLE 11.5 (continued)

Classification	Selected Theory/ Theorists	Application to Drug Abuse
	Differential association theory (Sutherland and Cressey)	Drug use (deviant behavior) is function of ratio of exposure to deviant versus non-deviant values, definitions, and patterns which enhance or curtail deviancy.
	Social influence theory (Lindesmith)	Drug use is combination of peer influence, drug availability, and drug effects (after initiated to use).

INTRODUCTION TO CHAPTER 12

Hoffman has alerted us to the need for theories which integrate the interaction of drug, user, and setting. In Prather's description of tranquilizer use among suburban women, we have our first opportunity to use this three-part analysis.

The drugs being used are tranquilizers. In the strictest sense, these drugs are legally available to these women. They are taken as depressants, one of the two types mentioned by Hoffman.

Further, the users here are overwhelmingly female. If we look back to Markides and Krause's comments on sex-role differences (Chapter 10), we may note specific sex-role differences here in Prather's work as well. Not only is there a difference from male roles, but these women also have a specific interpretation of the place of "illness" in their female roles.

Finally, we must look at the setting. These drugs are legally available. Women who use them have learned to manipulate a medical setting to procure their drugs. It is clear in Prather's discussion that physicians are a willing and complicitous part of that setting. In addition, friends and family become players in the same setting. Prather also points out the role of the pharmaceutical industry in constructing a setting in which drug use occurs.

The in-depth interviews provide a view of how these women perceive themselves and their use of drugs.

CHAPTER 12
WHY WOMEN USE TRANQUILIZERS

Jane E. Prather

ABSTRACT

Beginning with adolescence and throughout adult life, women use more minor tranquilizers than men. In this chapter, various explanations for women's higher use of these drugs are explored: 1) women admit more psychological symptoms than men, 2) women indicate experiencing more depression episodes than men, and 3) physicians discount women's real symptoms and concentrate on treating neurotic or nervous symptoms. Results are presented from in-depth interviews with women, two-thirds of whom were identified in a previous study as tranquilizer users and one-third of whom claimed they had never used these drugs.

Differences between tranquilizer users and non-users were found in four areas: 1) users held self-images of being nervous, worrisome, anxious; 2) users, in contrast to non-users had positive attitudes towards medications of all kinds and believed in the efficiency of tranquilizers; 3) users had friends and family who shared their beliefs about drugs and supported their use; and 4) users perceived their physicians as supporting and encouraging the use of tranquilizers. Based upon the research findings, recommendations for prevention and treatment of tranquilizer dependency are suggested.

JANE E. PRATHER is Professor of Sociology and Coordinator of Women's Studies at California State University, Northridge.

INTRODUCTION

Among women, drug problems are most likely to occur with the use of legally prescribed drugs, notably minor tranquilizers. Common names for such drugs are Ativan, Centrax, Librium, Valium, Serax, and Xanax. Even though more men are involved in illicit drugs than women, the percentage of women using legitimate drugs is higher than the percentage of men using illicit drugs. Hence, the "at risk" population susceptible to drug problems is much higher among women than men.

When do women use these drugs? What problems are associated with their use? What factors can lead to prevention and treatment?

In this chapter, we will provide some answers to these questions as we explore the connection between women and these drugs. First, some relevant statistics about tranquilizer use and sex differences will help us to understand how a legally available medication can lead to drug problems:

1. At all stages of adulthood women use minor tranquilizers more frequently than men. In a national survey 42% of women and only 27% of men stated they had ever used these drugs (NIDA, 1977).

2. Among teenagers, more females than males report they use minor tranquilizers, often obtaining these drugs from their mothers (Chambers, 1982).

3. Most women report their source for tranquilizers is a physician's prescription. Prescription sources versus street sources for drugs leads to more frequent

and more consistent use of the drugs (Mellinger, Balter, Manheimer, 1971).

4. Minor tranquilizers account for most drug-related emergency room visits. When ingested in combination with alcohol, minor tranquil-izers are the fourth leading cause of drug-related deaths (DAWN, 1981).

5. Common reactions experienced by users of minor tranquilizers include: drowsiness, fatigue, loss of coordination, decreased ability to con-centrate, impairment of memory and learning, speech defects, sleep disturbance (Bargmann, Wolfe, and Levin, 1982).

Why sex differences occur in use of minor tranquilizers is subject to much debate. One explanation is that women, in contrast to men, feel freer to admit experiencing such psychological symptoms as nervousness, insomnia or anxiety, while men avoid disclosing these same symptoms, perhaps fearing this self-disclosure reveals weakness (Cooperstock, 1976). Women more frequently than men describe their physical health in conjunction with emotional symptoms and report suffering from depression more than men (Radloff, 1975). Finally, women admit experiencing more life crises than men, which may also account for their seeking relief through the use of tranquilizers.

Another explanation for the connection between women and tranquilizers focuses on the physician's role in prescribing these medications. Even though women make more physician visits than men, physicians also perceive male and female patient's symptoms differently. There is evidence that physicians are likely to ignore women's symptoms and consider them as complaints rather than as legitimate symptoms (Armitage, Schneiderman, Bass, 1979) or to label the female patient as a hypochondriac or hysteric (Schmidt and Messner, 1971). Physicians also report difficulty keeping abreast of new drugs and having limited knowledge about or training in psychopharmacology (Gottlieb, Nappi, Pharm, and Strain, 1978).

WOMEN'S PERCEPTIONS OF THEIR TRANQUILIZER USE

To understand why women use tranquilizers, we interviewed 100 women, two-thirds of whom identified themselves as current users of minor tranquilizers (taking at least six tranquilizers within the past four weeks) and one-third who defined themselves as non-users. The women selected for the in-depth interviews had been identified through a large survey of women residing in a predominantly white, middle-class suburb. The 90-minute interview included questions about health, use of drugs, life stress, marital and work roles, methods of coping with depression, boredom, and weight gain.

By analyzing the in-depth interviews, we learned how the tranquilizer users perceived their drug use in contrast to how non-users felt about using such drugs. In four significant areas, the tranquilizer users differed from the non-users.[1]

---

[1] The larger survey was a stratified random sample of women living in a suburban area sponsored by the National Institute on Drug Abuse (#DA00847) and conducted in collaboration with Linda Fidell.

Self Definitions

Users stated they frequently experienced such symptoms as nervousness, worry, and restlessness. They also reported suffering from more physical ailments than non-users and made more visits to physicians. Daily consumption of caffeine drinks, aspirin, and cigarettes was higher among users than non-users. The overriding explanation for taking tranquilizers was to relieve feelings of being nervous or tense, followed by reasons of inducing sleep or of relaxing muscles. Non-users, on the other hand, did not describe themselves as experiencing significant amounts of nervous symptoms.

Users could be further differentiated by the frequency and specificity of the situation in which they felt they needed a tranquilizer. Some users we labeled as "general" users because they suffered from various nervous symptoms in their daily lives:

> If I'm nervous that particular day, I'll take it maybe two or three times, next day it's over.

> I use Valium when I get a little uptight.

The vagueness of the symptoms is reflected in this view:

> Just a general type of thing -- something that comes and goes. I take Valium. I feel it does help me when I'm sort of down -- lifts my mood a little bit.

A "specific" user defined a situation or a limited time when the tranquilizer was needed:

> Things have to be very bad before I'll take a very mild tranquilizer. Last time was when

my niece passed away.

I took Valium when my child died.

I was going through a divorce and was very
nervous.

Not surprising, general users took tranquilizers more
often than a specific user.

Attitudes Towards Medications

Users held more positive attitudes towards all
medications and towards tranquilizers than non-users.
Users liked to have their medications readily available
and convenient. For example, they stored their
medications in a kitchen rather than a bathroom
cabinet. The significance of the kitchen may be that
this is an area of the home where the woman has power.
Users also kept tranquilizers in their purses, in
addition to their supply at home, so that wherever they
went they would have them available, as these users
explain:

I keep whatever I was using in my purse. I
would have been all panicky if I didn't have it
with me.

I liked to have it on hand in case I need
it....Well, if I'm nervous, or I get dizzy.

The power of having the tranquilizer in her
possession is revealed in this account of a respondent
who felt good just knowing she had her tranquilizer
with her regardless of whether she actually took it:

I feel if I need it, it's right here.
Sometimes even that helps, knowing I can take
it anytime I want to. I think it's
psychological ... just keep it in my purse,
right there if I need one. I just feel better
knowing that I have it.

308

Users believed it was better to take a tranquilizer than to continue to suffer, as this women explains:

> I feel it's better not to go through the day tense and uptight. I don't believe in that. I mean I'll take my Valium if it will calm me down to where I can cope with things. I can't take the screaming and yelling at the kids because I won't take something.

Users also had paradoxical beliefs about their own drug use. On the one hand, they believed that it was better not to take tranquilizers; but, on the other hand, they did not feel they should abstain. The following illustrates this paradox:

> I'd rather not have to take medication, but if there's a need for it, I'll take it. Doesn't bother me, there's no sense being a martyr about it.

Users recognized the hazards of using tranquilizers yet they stated with pride that even though tranquilizers had potential for abuse or harm, they know how to use them properly and safely:

> I feel that there is a time and place for it. I do not feel I overuse medication. I feel that if there is a need, and that I'm intelligent enough to know the difference, then I would take something.

The following user contrasts herself from an abuser on the basis of need:

> Well, I'm not a pill bug. But I do believe when you need it, take it, but don't abuse it. That's the way I feel.

Women who currently used tranquilizers usually did

not define themselves as abusers nor did they perceive that they took drugs too frequently or for non-medical purposes. Ex-users of tranquilizers, on the other hand, did define themselves as abusers or admitted they consumed too many, too frequently.

Users, unlike non-users, perceived tranquilizers as a rational, routine way of coping with stress, as this respondent who illustrates relieving nervousness as analogous to suffering from a cough:

If you don't abuse a pill, a pill's good for you. If you're nervous and you're tense and you take the Valium, it's good for you. It's like taking cough syrup when you have a bad cough.

Non-users, on the other hand, maintained very strong anti-medication attitudes, often stating with pride their stoic feelings. The most common statement among non-users about why they had never used a tranquilizer was, as this respondent stated, "I never even take an aspirin!" The most vociferous statement by a non-user was:

No! I think tranquilizers are terrible. I don't think they calm anybody down. I think tranquilizers should be outlawed! I don't think they help anyone. I think they make people more neurotic and nervous than anything else. And I think tran-quilizers are really bad for your nervous system.

Another non-user's explanation for not using tranquilizers was that use indicated a sign of weakness or lack of control:

I think I resist medication. I usually feel I can do without it. I also don't like

anything that removes control for me. I'm not
likely to take a tranquilizer because I don't
feel that I'm in control of myself, some other
force is taking over.

Just as some tranquilizer users expressed pride in
being responsible enough to handle a tranquilizer
prescription, the non-users took pride in their
abstinence.

In summary, not only did users have positive
attitudes toward tranquilizers and taking medication,
they also believed in the power or efficacy of the
drug. And they experienced tranquilizers as effective
in relieving their symptoms. The non-users, on the
other hand, held negative attitudes toward medications
and did not believe that tranquilizers were the most
effective way to cope with their symptoms.

**Family and Friends Attitudes Towards Their Tranquilizer
Use**

Although some tranquilizer users said they did not
discuss their use of the drugs with friends and family,
most users felt that spouses, children, and friends
supported their use of the drug and often directly
encouraged its use. Perhaps the most blatant example
of how a family can support drug use was this respondent's description of her young daughter's note:

Occasionally I'd find a note pinned to the
wall, 'Mommy, it's time to take a happy pill.'

Not infrequently, the user shares her tranquilizers
with her family, notably her daughter:

Yes, I gave her (daughter) half of one
(Valium). I felt she needed it, and she took

it. She was coming down with the flu and didn't realize what it was and neither did I, and her heart was really pounding....So I told her to take half a Valium and see if it was her nerves, see if she'd calm down, and see what happened.

Users transmitted their symptoms to their daughters. The following respondent reported problems with sleeping which she also identified in her 19-year-old daughter. Both used the same remedy -- the tranquilizer:

I do give it (Valium) to my daughter occasionally, but this again is on a doctor's instructions. She has been hyperactive, and it catches up with her once in a while. So occasionally I give her half. I don't know what it is that keeps her awake -- I think it tends to be stresses at school more than anything else.

Not only did users share tranquilizers with their family, but also with friends. Networks of users were common in which each member would share medications when another member had a need and no supply. When asked if she ever offered or suggested tranquilizers for others, this respondent replied:

Yes, if I know someone's going through a very trying period or some-thing like that. For instance, my brother-in-law and sister-in-law are going through quite a trying problem, and I would suggest that they take a tranquilizer, a Valium. I would even offer it to my sister-in-law. My sister-in-law would take it, but my brother-in-law wouldn't.

Perceptions of Their Physician's Attitudes Towards Medications

Most women believed their physicians supported their tranquilizer usage and felt they could continue to obtain the prescription from them. The physician's prescription, when perceived as an order, served as a powerful reinforcement. Users then justified their tranquilizer usage by shifting responsibility from themselves onto the physician:

> I think medications can be helpful if it's taken...uh by prescription. If a doctor prescribes...a person should take a pill four times a day, I think he should take it four times a day.

This respondent perceived that the orders were in fact commands beyond an individual's control:

> I really don't like it, but I feel like I have no choice, I have to accept it...the doctor told me if you have hypertension, basically you will have to take it the rest of your life.

Tranquilizer users believe their physicians support their use. The user's perception of the physician's attitudes toward their tranquilizer usage in turn reinforced their own attitudes towards tranquilizers and reinforced continuous use. In this example, the respondent believed her physician thought she should always have them (tranquilizers) available:

> My doctor -- his view of it was that you ought to have them -- just have them on hand.

Heavy tranquilizer users or ex-users frequently blamed the physician for any drug problems they encountered. They might even reveal, as this respondent, how they have duped physicians into prescriptions to support their dependency:

Well, I was going to a doctor for my headaches, and I told him that I didn't know what it was but I just felt drugged all the time. He gave me something to pep me up.... For 13 years I mean, I was on uppers and downers, and you name it, I took them all. In fact, it got to the point where -- that's when I worried -- if I didn't have a pill for the next day, I'd get tired and frantic and even to the point where I would play doctor against doctor. I didn't even use the same drugstore. I'd go to three or four doctors....I'd take five or six at a time. When you take so many, five, you have to go onto the next step -- higher one. I think I went as high as you can with Miltown. Then I couldn't get anything off of those. So I'd ask the doctor if I could change. He would say, 'Yeah.' Of course, it was always a new doctor, and he wouldn't say no. He'd say, 'Have you tried it before,' and I would lie and say, 'Yes.' Because I wanted it, and I had to have it.

RECOMMENDATIONS FOR TREATMENT AND PREVENTION

By understanding drug usage from the perspective of the user, we can make recommendations about treatment and prevention programs for female users of these drugs. This study of tranquilizer users suggests programs need to incorporate multi-faceted approaches

314

that recognize the roles a variety of people and institutions play in reinforcing tranquilizer usage.

First, the woman herself. If she perceives herself as nervous, anxious, and worrisome, she is likely to continue to seek relief through tranquilizers. When she finds these self-definitions reinforced by family, friends, and physician, a self-fulfilling prophecy occurs. She becomes the self that others reward. Reinforcement of her nervous self image from so many others perpetuates her drug use. Until she begins to perceive herself in new ways and identifies alternatives to drug therapy, treatment will remain ineffective. Programs must, therefore include modification of these negative self-images and selection of some methods for alleviating these anxieties, such as exercise, meditation, creative outlets, or nutritional changes.

Next, any effective drug program should include awareness of the roles that family and friends play in promoting drug usage. With women suffering from tranquilizer dependency, family and friends frequently form a drug milieu where tranquilizers are shared and encouraged. Family and friends recommend tranquilizers to alleviate the symptoms that, in turn, may impact upon them. In addition, family and friends may unwittingly be part of the situation that creates the anxiety, nervousness, or dependency traits for the woman.

The third and yet very significant person in the treatment process is the physician. Because the physician is usually the primary source for her tranquilizers, he[2] may not initially identify these drugs as causing problems, especially when taken as prescribed. And he may have been convinced by pharmaceutical and/or medical literature that these drugs are safe and, hence, warrant little concern about hazards or dependency. If he holds stereotyped views of women as nervous or emotional, he most likely feels the tranquilizer is legitimate treatment. As often happens in the patient-physician consultation, writing a prescription for a tranquilizer for relieving nervousness is much simpler than discussing alternative treatment for these symptoms. Moreover, writing a prescription corresponds to a traditional medical model. Both patient and physician have tangible evidence that something occurred during the consultation and the physician has an effective method for terminating the medical appointment (Muller, 1972).

Finally, drug prevention for tranquilizer dependency needs national awareness of the powerful role of the pharmaceutical companies. This industry spends more than a billion dollars each year advertising the efficacy and safety of these drugs (Nelson, 1976). Advertisements for tranquilizer ads often stereotype women as the patient requiring these drugs (Prather and Fidell, 1975). Drug manufacturers de-emphasize hazards of tranquilizer use that can occur even from so-called legitimate use. And pharmaceutical companies have a strong lobby against regulations that might prevent drug problems. For example, the industry

---

[2] The masculine pronoun is used in reference to physicians since over 90% of practicing physicians in the U.S. are male.

argued against Patient Package Inserts to be placed in all tranquilizer packages so a user could obtain information about the drugs and warnings about taking the drug in combination with other substances, especially alcohol (Bargmann, Wolfe, Levin, 1982).

Thus, effective drug treatment and prevention programs for tranquilizer users requires multi-dimensional approaches. Treatment for a user involves linking friends, family, and the physician to change the image and environment of the women. Any long-range prevention program for tranquilizer dependency requires cooperation of powerful groups in society -- the medical community and the pharmaceutical industry. All of these efforts together need to emphasize that not only can a woman become an abuser of these legitimate drugs but she can also be a victim of legitimate medical practice.

REFERENCES

Armitage, K. J., Schneiderman, L. J., and Bass, R. A. 1979. Response of physicians to medical complaints in men and women. The Journal of the American Medical Association 241(20):2186-2187.

Bargmann, E. M., Wolfe, S. M., and Levin, J. 1982. Stopping Valium. NY: Warner Books.

Chambers, C. D. 1982. The use and abuse of licit drugs in rural families. Chemical Dependencies: Behavioral and Biomedical Issues 4:153-165.

Cooperstock, R. 1976. Psychotropic drug use among women. Canadian Medical Association Journal 115: 760-763.

Drug Abuse Warning Network. 1981. 1980 DAWN Annual Report (DEA Contract #81-3). Washington, DC: U.S. Drug Enforcement Administration.

Gottlieb, R., Nappi, T., Pharm, D., and Strain, J. 1978. The physician's knowledge of psychotropic drugs: Preliminary results. American Journal of Psychiatry 135:29-32.

Mellinger, G. D., Balter, M. B., and Manheimer, D. I. 1971. Patterns of psychotherapeutic drug use among adults in San Francisco. Archives of General Psychiatry 25:385-394.

Muller, C. 1972. The over-medicated society: Forces in the marketplace for medical care. Science 16: 486-492.

National Institute on Drug Abuse. 1977. National Survey on Drug Abuse.

Nelson, G. 1976. Advertising and the national health. Journal of Drug Issues 6:28-33.

Prather, J. E. and Fidell, L. S. 1975. Sex differences in the content and style of medical advertisements. Social Science and Medicine 9:23-26.

Prather, J. 1981. Women's use of licit and illicit drugs. In J. Lowinson and P. Ruizx (eds.), Substance Abuse: Clinical Problems and Perspectives (pp. 729-738). Baltimore: Williams & Wilkins.

Radloff, L. 1975. Sex differences in depression: The effects of occupation and marital status. Sex Roles 1:249-269.

Schmidt, D. D. and Messner, E. 1971. The female hysterical personality disorder. Journal of Family Practice 4:573-577.

INTRODUCTION TO CHAPTER 13

Who is the female addict and what is her fate? We noted earlier that the common perception of the male alcoholic is the skid row bum (Fagan, Chapter 8). In the same way, one conceptualization of the female addict is the New York street prostitute. The streets of New York City are the setting in which Goldstein considers female drug use and violence.

Hoffman (Chapter 11) has alerted us to the need to consider drugs, users, and settings. Here, Goldstein looks at female addicts in New York City. He alerts us to the differential role that barbiturates and heroin play in producing violent behavior. Finally, he details the setting in which these behaviors occur.

His focus is on women, their drug use, and the violence which affects them -- both as perpetrators and as victims. Goldstein offers us a tri-partite model of drugs and violence: 1) psychopharmacological, 2) economic-compulsive, and 3) systemic. Using this model, he describes the lives of New York City female drug users in their own words.

CHAPTER 13
FEMALE SUBSTANCE ABUSERS AND VIOLENCE

Paul J. Goldstein

PAUL J. GOLDSTEIN is employed by Narcotic and Drug Research, Inc., a not-for-profit research affiliate of the New York State Division of Substance Abuse Services and is Principal Investigator of a NIDA drug-related violence research project.

ABSTRACT

In this chapter, relationships between drugs and violence are placed into a tripartite conceptual framework. The three types of drug related violence are 1) the psychopharmacological, 2) the economic-compulsive, and 3) the systemic. This chapter assesses the applicability of the conceptual framework for females, both with regard to perpetration of violence and to violent victimization. Descriptive data gathered from two separate studies confirm the strength and broad scope of the relationship between drugs and violence among women.

INTRODUCTION

The drugs/violence nexus is one of the most important criminological and health-care issues. Rigorously collected data of broad scope is currently unavailable. Several recent reports indicate the general magnitude of this issue. For example, Harwood et al. (1984) estimated that 10% of the homicides and assaults nationwide are the result of drug use. The authors include the caveat that their estimate should be viewed as a conservative approximation "in the face of inadequate empirical data to support an estimate derived in a systematic fashion" (1984:22).

Portions of this research were supported by the New York State Division of Substance Abuse Services, by a Public Health Service Award from the National Institute on Drug Abuse (RO1-DA01926), and by an Interagency Agreement between NIDA (RO1-DA02355) and the Law Enforcement Assistance Administration (LEAA-J-IAA-005-8). However, points of view or opinions in this document do not necessarily represent the official positions or policies of the United States Government or of the New York State Division of Substance Abuse Services.

320

In 1983, the New York City Police Department released a report entitled Homicide Analysis. This document is based on 1981 data. The report contains the following findings. Twenty-four percent of known homicides in 1981 were drug related. Drug-related homicides were the second most common form of homicide, following only the general category of "disputes". Handguns were used more often in drug-related homicides (84% of the time) than in any other form of homicide. In robbery-related homicide, which ranked second in this regard, handguns were used 61% of the time. In 94% of the drug-related homicides, the victim and perpetrator were friends or acquaintances. Similar findings were reported in Miami, Florida (McBride, 1983).

During the 1980's Los Angeles experienced a wave of violence that police attribute to drug trafficking. Law enforcement officials say that this violence, which has resulted in twelve homicides between October 12th and 28th, 1984, stems from competition between rival gangs to control the cocaine trade. Gang members are alleged to be as young as thirteen years old. The city's Director of Criminal Justice Planning stated the following:

> The rash of killings that's occurred is not really gang initiated, it's drug initiated. Those who are involved are executioners and dealers. (Cummings, 1984:A1,A10)

A recent report concluded that violence was one of the primary causes of drug-related mortality and morbidity. It estimated that in the United States in 1980 over 2,000 homicides and over 460,000 assaults resulted from drug-related causes. It further estimated that in more than 140,000 of the assaults, the victims sustained physical injury. These injuries led to nearly 50,000 days of hospitalization in 1980 (Goldstein and Hunt, 1984).

Drug-related violence strikes disproportionately among the young. Assuming an average life span of sixty-five years, it was estimated that drug-related homicides in 1980 resulted in nearly 70,000 years of life lost (Goldstein and Hunt, 1984). Clearly, the drugs/violence nexus constitutes a major social, health, and criminological problem area.

In an earlier paper, I introduced a tri-partite conceptual framework in order to explain the relationship between drug use and violence (Goldstein, 1982). This conceptual framework will now be briefly summarized. The three types of relationships were dubbed: 1) the psychopharmacological, 2) the economic-compulsive, and 3) the systemic.

The psychopharmacological model suggests that some persons, as a result of short-term or long-term ingestion of specific substances, may exhibit violent behavior. Alcohol is the substance most often associated with psychopharmacological violence. Other substances associated with this form of violence include stimulants, barbiturates, and PCP.

The category of psychopharmacological violence encompasses both perpetrator and victim behavior. Drug use may contribute to a person behaving violently, or it may alter a person's behavior in such a manner as to bring about that person's violent victimization. Previous research has found high frequencies of alcohol consumption in rape and homicide victims (Rada, 1975; Amir, 1971; Wolfgang, 1958; Shupe, 1954). Public intoxication may invite a robbery or mugging. One study found that in rapes where only the victim was intoxicated, she was significantly more likely to suffer physical injury (Johnson et al., 1975).

The economic-compulsive model suggests that some persons engage in violent crime, such as robbery, in order to support costly drug use. The primary motivation of the actor is to obtain money to purchase drugs. Heroin and cocaine are the substances most frequently associated with this form of violence because of their relative costliness and their compulsive patterns of use.

It should be noted, however, that most heroin and cocaine users avoid violent acquisitive crime if viable, non-violent alternatives exist. Drug users frequently obtain cash or drugs by working within the drug business, as dealers, touts, or steerers, or by engaging in petty theft, prostitution, and a wide variety of other hustling activities (Goldstein, 1981). Most drug users eschew violent acquisitive crime because it is physically dangerous and embodies the threat of prison and because they may lack a basic orientation towards violent behavior.

In the systemic model, violence is intrinsic to involvement with any illicit substance. Systemic violence refers to traditionally aggressive patterns of interaction within the system of drug use and distribution. Examples of systemic violence include fights over territory between rival drug dealers, assaults and homicides committed within dealing hierarchies as a means of enforcing normative codes, robberies of drug dealers, violent retaliation that follows such robberies, elimination of informers, punishment for selling alterated or phony drugs, and punishment for failing to pay one's debts.

Most of the data from which this conceptual framework was generated were gathered from males. It has been suggested that many of our so-called "general" theories of deviance are actually theories of male deviance (Harris, 1977). This is because the empirical work upon which such theories have been based may have focused disproportionately on male subjects. If so, these studies may have overlooked social processes or situations that are unique to females and, hence, created theories that are unique to males. The purpose of this chapter is to assess the applicability of the above framework for females.

The data that will be used in this examination of females' substance use and violence were gathered in the course of several studies. Sixty women were interviewed between 1975 and 1977 for a study of the relationship between drug use and prostitution (Goldstein, 1979). An additional 51 women were interviewed on repeated occasions between 1978 and 1982 as part of an ethnographic study of the economic behavior of street drug users in Harlem (Johnson et al., 1985).

The discussion to follow will be divided into two main sections. Part one will focus on females as perpetrators of violence. Part two will focus on females as victims of violence.

An important caveat is necessary. Neither of the studies which provide the data for this report was designed to investigate the issue of drugs and

324

violence. Because violence is such a ubiquitous part of the drug scene, much descriptive material was gathered. However, these data were not gathered in a systematic fashion, and no statistical analysis is possible.

Further, the nature of the studies was such that more data are available on females as perpetrators than as victims of drug-related violence. This is unfortunate. There is a critical need to generate data on the nature, scope, and consequences of the violent victimization of women. This need will be further discussed below.

FEMALES AS PERPETRATORS OF VIOLENCE

Data were not collected in such a fashion as to allow rigorous statistical comparison between males and females. However, it appears that a far greater proportion of violent events among females were of the psychopharmacological variety. Women exhibited lesser magnitudes of both systemic and economic-compulsive violence when compared to males.

Within the psychopharmacological context, the two substances most often mentioned by women when describing acts of violence that they had committed were barbiturates and heroin. In the former case, it was the presence of barbiturates that led to the psychopharmacological violence. In the latter case, it was the absence of heroin and the resultant withdrawal stress and irritability that they blamed for their violent behavior.

Most subjects, males and females alike, described the barbiturate "high" as a tremendous feeling of omnipotence. An example unrelated to violence, but one which aptly characterizes the sensation, was reported by a young women who had smuggled drugs into the country several times. She stated that she could never have accomplished this without being high on barbiturates each time. She claimed that she just would have been so nervous that the customs agents would certainly have detected her. However, after ingesting barbiturates, she "knew" that there was "no way" that she would be apprehended.

Another subject described her experience with barbiturates in the following way:

Barbiturates had me on an up head.... Mostly every time I got arrested was behind barbiturates. Because I just wasn't afraid to do anything. I would just go ahead and do whatever I wanted. It gave me false courage. ...You just do anything that maybe you would want to do when you were straight, but you were scared to do. When you are high on pills, you just go ahead and do it. And you have no fear at all. None at all.

She stated the following later in the interview:

I have gotten into a lot of fights behind barbiturates, not with one person, but like maybe with ten. I was in the car one time, and I was really high, me and someone else, and we had stopped on the street....It was a street with all Spanish and Black....I had gotten out of the car. I don't remember if we had went through the light. All I know is that we were wrong, and the next thing I knew I was around twenty or thirty people, and I pulled a knife on them. Thank God the cops pulled up....and they had taken me in the car and said, 'Hey, what are you trying to do?' I said, 'Wow! I don't know what I was doing.'

I would get into fights with anybody. I had fights with my mother. I had a very bad understanding on pills.

A women reported that the following experiences began when she was seventeen years old and continued for about ten years:

Barbiturates, that was my first high...the first really heavy drug I got into....They use to make us rowdy, wanted to fight....I had a crew that I use to run with. There were three of us. We use to get into fights....It makes you do that. Because I'm not a fighter....We weren't troublemakers. We got along with everybody. It was only when we got pilled up that we got argumentative...wanted to fight. ...People were telling me, 'You need to stop taking them pills because you break, you go berserk.'

Another women reported serving ten months for a vehicle homicide that occurred after she had taken barbiturates. She was twenty-six years old at the time.

I was taking pills. I was high. I was in a car, and the guy that owned the car was with me, and we were both high, and there was a man killed. I don't know whether I was driving or not. He had a license. He was cut loose, and I took the weight.

Another woman reports getting into shoving matches, and occasionally more serious altercations, on the line at the Welfare Office if she had previously taken barbiturates. A young woman recalls the time that she and her boyfriend felt that they had been cheated on a drug transaction by a "big dealer." One night when they were high on barbiturates, they decided to "take him off." The woman said that it was four or five o'clock in the morning, and by the time they got out of bed, got dressed, and got about halfway there, the effects of the pills must have worn off because they decided that they would probably get themselves killed. They decided to return home.

These sorts of accounts are a recurring theme in the transcripts of interviews with barbiturate-using women. It should be noted that the last account contained elements, albeit only potentially, of both psychopharmacological and systemic violence. The young couple sought revenge on a drug dealer whom they felt had cheated them. Such an act is in the realm of systemic violence. But it was only because they were high on barbiturates that they tried to carry out their plan for revenge. Therefore, the act also belongs in the realm of psychopharmacological violence.

Most of the heroin-related psychopharmacological violence was perpetrated by addicted prostitutes. Before describing these sorts of events, a few words on the nature of prostitution are in order. The essence of street prostitution is the "gentle con." Prostitutes try to "sweet talk" a customer out of as much money as they possibly can. Elaborate stories may be concocted to arouse sympathy, thereby increasing generosity. Successful achievement of these cons requires patience, tact, and good intuitive probing of the customer.

Addicted prostitutes who are "sick"; that is, in need of heroin and suffering from withdrawal symptoms, find it difficult to practice the gentle con. The following account is offered to illustrate this point:

I couldn't work when I was sick because I would be irritable and impatient, and I had to have the drugs to cope with those moments with the tricks....(With heroin) I wasn't irritable, and my patience wasn't short where I might push him; say, 'hurry up' or curse him, make him irritable. I might have a fight or argument with him...and just make more trouble for myself. Otherwise I'd be patient....I'd be all right, if I wasn't sick.

Most heroin-addicted street walkers that were interviewed described this phenomenon in similar terms. Another woman stated the following:

Without the drugs, I didn't even want these men to touch me....If I hadn't been sick, I'd have gotten more. But, I had to be in a hurry. I couldn't wait to con him.

Many of the instances where addicted prostitutes robbed and/or assaulted customers occurred during these times of withdrawal distress. Several women even reported that they might rob their first "trick," use that money to purchase heroin and "get straight," and then return to the "ho stroll" to truly engage in prostitution. More will be said later in this chapter about the intervening effects of prostitution on the relationship between drugs and violence among women.

329

The aforementioned situation where addicted prostitutes robbed clients while suffering from withdrawal symptoms might be classified as economic-compulsive violence. After all, these women were committing robberies and assaults in order to get the money to support their drug use. However, most of these women intended to obtain money by practicing prostitution. They did not intend to commit violence. A state of mind induced by withdrawal distress seemed to be the primary factor motivating the violent behavior. For this reason, the events were classified as psychopharmacological.

There were relatively few accounts of women engaging in economic-compulsive violence. Women who were "strung out" on costly drugs usually found alternatives to robbery to support their drug use. Prostitution and shoplifting were the most common. Females also worked in the drug business, usually in lower-level capacities and also received gifts of drugs from men. Bartering sexual favors for drugs was not uncommon.

In the few cases where females did engage in economic-compulsive violence, it was usually in concert with a male partner. At times these women acted as lures, pretending to be prostitutes in order to entice a male into a hallway or room where her male confederate would be waiting to relieve the would-be "trick" of his wallet. Occasionally, a female would join a man in a strong-arm mugging. Some women acted as lookouts on robberies directly perpetrated by men. These events, however, were relatively infrequent.

It was previously stated that females appeared less likely than males to engage in systemic violence. Few females wished to be involved in violent confrontations with armed males. For example, a young white heroin-using female who copped her drugs in Harlem was asked if she would do anything if she was cheated in a drug transaction. She replied as follows:

> Me personally, no. Being female, no. Being a white female, no. Especially up there. But I know people who will. Crazy guys with a gun will go back.

Several females who were employed in the drug business were robbed or otherwise victimized while working. Such a situation normally calls for a violent retaliation. These retaliations did take place but were never done by the women involved. Rather, male members of the organization "took care of business" and sought out the guilty parties for normatively appropriate retribution.

FEMALES AS VICTIMS OF VIOLENCE

It was previously stated that the data on female victimization is not as complete as the data on perpetration. However, many rich and provocative accounts were obtained. New dimensions of drugs/violence relationships become apparent.

A major category of psychopharmacological violence involves physical abuse of wives or girlfriends. In most of the accounts in this category, the substance involved was alcohol. In several cases, however, PCP was reported. For example, one young man was known as a mild-mannered and loving husband and father to his infant son. Yet, one day we received the news that the man had been arrested for severely beating his wife and son. The son was in the hospital fighting for life. The wife told us that her husband had taken PCP and then appeared to go out of his mind.

Drug use may influence a person's behavior in such a manner as to bring about that person's violent victimization. A young women reported being raped on two different occasions while she was high on barbiturates. She described one of those experiences.

> I was aware what was happening, but there was nothing I could do. I was too zonked out to go to a policeman and say I got raped. He probably wouldn't believe me because I couldn't remember what the persons looked like. I was in the elevator. I was going upstairs in the project, and there were about fourteen to fifteen young fellows, and they took me up on the roof....There is really nothing you can do. Because after it happened, I got my brother and his friends, but I couldn't remember what any of them looked like. That's really pathetic.

The above account raises an important issue. Drug-using women who may be exceptionally vulnerable to violent victimization may also be disproportionately unlikely to report these victimizations. A variety of factors may contribute to this unwillingness. The young woman cited above felt shame at not being able to remember what any of her attackers looked like and, also for this reason, felt that reporting the offense was useless. Another reason why drug-using females may not report victimizations is the reluctance to inform authorities that they were involved in an illicit activity. If these speculations are correct, then official statistics may seriously underestimate the magnitude of violent victimization of women.

Females were victimized by economic-compulsive violence, but they appeared to have a lower probability of victimization than demographic statistics would indicate. An analysis of 183 robberies committed by a sample of 201 Harlem opiate users revealed that females were the victims in only about 11% of the robberies (Goldstein and Johnson, 1983). However, street prostitutes reported frequent robberies or attempted robberies by street "junkies." Several addicted prostitutes said that the situation was so bad that they were afraid to carry any money on their persons. They would turn a few tricks and then go to cop and inject their heroin before they could be robbed of their earnings.

Females were also the victims of systemic violence. For example, one young women worked as a "house connection". Every morning "The Man" would arrive at the apartment in which she worked with the day's supply of drugs. She would inject some of the shipment to determine its potency and how much diluent could be added. She would then mix and bag the drugs. About five or six "runners" worked for her. Their job was to take orders and cash from prospective customers, go to the apartment, pass her the cash, and receive the drugs for delivery to the customer. This women lived in the same building, in a different apartment, with her young daughter. On several occasions, addicts waited outside the building to rob her. They hoped that she might have quantities of cash or drugs with her. The situation became so bad that the woman first sent her daughter to live with her mother and then eventually moved to another apartment.

Another aspect of systemic violence refers to the dangerous locations in which many women go to purchase their drugs. Most women addicts report at least one experience of attempted rape or robbery that took place when they were copping. Predatory males may seek vulnerable victims in known copping areas. The following account is from a young woman who was raped after buying some pills:

> I was walking, and a nice looking dude started talking to me and naive me, I'm gonna talk back. He said, 'Let's go have a cup of coffee and talk.' I didn't think there was anything wrong in it. So I went with him and we got in this room....He shut the door, and I saw other people there....He pulled a knife and, you know, what can you do? To boot it all, he took my pills.

For this reason, many women employed other drug users to cop their drugs for them or teamed up with a male friend when buying drugs.

Another aspect of systemic violence refers to the previously mentioned bartering phenomenon where women may exchange sexual favors for drugs. This process may be fraught with danger, as the following account illustrates:

> This was my very best friend. She couldn't wait to get the dope for herself. I said, 'No,

no man....How would I know it was dope? Can I
test it first?' I said, 'Don't go with him.
Something's wrong.' She wouldn't listen. She
goes with the trick. The trick takes care of
business....He gets dressed. He gives her the
bag. She shoots it. It's rat poison. I come
into the room, she's gagging. I took her over
to...(the hospital),...but it was too late.

Another aspect of systemic violence, the slaying of
an innocent bystander, affects both males and females.
This assertion was tragically documented recently on
the lower east side of Manhattan. A young women, the
mother of two children, was killed by a stray bullet
fired during an altercation over a drug transaction.
Her husband was killed the same way three years
earlier.

Some aspects of the relationship between drugs and
violence as it occurs among prostitutes have been
discussed above. However, there are several classes of
events that have not yet been introduced because they
do not really fit into the framework of
psychopharmacological, economic-compulsive, or systemic
violence. Actually, these events are a form of
systemic violence, but the system in which they belong
is not the system of drug use and distribution.
Rather, it is the system of contemporary street
prostitution.

The current social organization of prostitution is
such that the narcotics-using prostitute is an
outsider. Massage parlors, houses, escort agencies,
and "professional" pimps reject addicted prostitutes.
This is because such women are deemed unreliable, poor
money-makers, and certainly liabilities.

Unreliability signifies that addicted prostitutes cannot be trusted to keep appointments, to appear looking appropriately appealing, or to render the sort of service demanded by the organization. Poor money-making ability refers to poor physical appearance caused by inadequate personal hygiene, improper care of clothes and makeup, body scarring and abscesses related to needle use. Also, pimps complain that addicted women shoot as much money into their arm as they make on the streets, and, hence, they can make little profit from them. One pimp stated the following when asked about addicted prostitutes:

> I wouldn't have a junkie broad. All my women that I've had were square to the drug game. Because if a drug babe makes a hundred dollars tonight, she'll pop thirty dollars on you. She'll tell you...like Joe Blow ran up on her and so-and-so trick ran out on her and all this crap. Where a square broad, square to the drug game, she's going to pop your bread too. Dig what I mean? But she won't bring you thirty dollars out of a hundred dollars. She'll bring you eighty dollars. (Goldstein, 1979:107)

Addicted prostitutes are viewed as liabilities for various reasons. It is believed that they are likely to become police informants because of their fear of being locked up and deprived of their drugs. Prostitution entrepreneurs, such as madams and massage parlor managers, claim that addicts may antagonize established clientele or even attempt to rob them. These entrepreneurs also know that in case of a police raid, it is very difficult to make a prostitution case hold up in court, but, if drugs are found on the premises, they are in much greater danger.

When women working in houses or massage parlors are discovered to be using narcotics, they are usually fired, though a few women reported being beaten. The latter, however, appears to be the norm with pimps. A street walker had the following comments on the behavior of pimps towards any of their women who begin to use narcotics:

> Usually he'll try to help her, and, if he sees where he can't help her, he'll put a whipping on her. He'll fix her up real good and proper. And then, if he sees its no good, he'll just give her a real good ass whipping and throw her out, and she can't take no clothes with her. She can't take nothing that she had obtained while she was with him.
> (Goldstein, 1979:105)

The situation of addicted prostitutes becomes more terrifying in the next account by another street walker.

> They don't want her. They can't get any money from them....She's strung out....She's sneaking, dipping and dabbing. They don't want that. They beat 'em up....Try to make her kick. Everybody fucks her. His friends. I heard some stories of girls being locked in a closet and only let out to be fucked in the ass ...to make them kick. To learn: be right, stay in line, or this is what's going to happen. Riding girls down when they run away...in their

337

car....Beat their ass on the street. Usually
it's one of their girls that points up, 'Janey
is over on such and such.' 'Cause she's got to
come up. She may run and hide, but they figure
she's got to go back to make money....That's
when they catch her. (Goldstein, 1979:105-106)
The terror continues in the following response by a
pimp when I asked him what he would do if one of his
women did start to get into narcotics:

If she didn't know that much about me, I
would just fire the bitch. But, if she had a
lot of information to different little things
that I do, what I'm into, and they could
criminalize me, I would probably take her out
(that is, kill her). I'd probably give her a
hotshot (that is, a fatal dose of narcotics).
(Goldstein, 1979:107)

Further drug-related violence occurs in occasional
fights over territory between addicted and non-addicted
street prostitutes. A great deal of antagonism was
reported between these two groups. Each group accuses
the other of "going lower"; that is, charging lower
rates and bringing the general price structure down for
everybody. Non-addicted street walkers claim that
addicts are more criminalistic, frequently robbing
tricks, thereby bringing police "heat" into the
neighborhood and making it more difficult for them to
work.

CONCLUSION

Descriptive data gathered from interviews with drug-
using women were presented. These data clearly showed

the strength and broad scope of the relationship between drugs and violence among women. Drugs were shown to strongly influence both the violence that is perpetrated by women and the violence that is directed at women.

A conceptual framework for classifying drug-related violence was tested for its applicability with females. This framework categorized drug-related violence as being psychopharmacological, economic-compulsive, or systemic. Most cases were classified within the framework. In this sense, its generalized utility was demonstrated. Notable exceptions that failed to fit into the framework were related to the role of drug use within the social organization of prostitution.

The nature of the data did not permit detailed statistical comparison between males and females. However, impressionistic observation suggest that males and females vary in the nature of the drug-related violence that they commit. Females committed less economic-compulsive or systemic violence, and, hence, psychopharmacological violence comprised a greater proportion of their total violent behavior.

The need for more rigorously collected and detailed data on the violent victimization of females, and the relationship of those victimizations to drug use and distribution, was clearly apparent. Drug-using women are a population at special risk for violent victimization. Further, several accounts suggested that this highly vulnerable population may be especially unlikely to report such events.

The physical and mental health consequences of the violent victimization of women are enormous. They impact on the total life of both the victim and relevant others, including children, spouses, parents, other relatives, and friends. They affect the ability of the victim to work and function in society. They affect the likelihood that a drug-using victim will successfully graduate from a drug treatment program. Increased research in this area is needed to better specify the parameters of the problem and to develop promising intervention strategies that may be employed in physical, mental health, and drug treatment programs.

REFERENCES

Amir, M. 1971. Patterns in Forcible Rape. Chicago: University of Chicago Press.

Cummings, J. 1984, October 29. Increase in gang killings on coast is traced to narcotics trafficking. New York Times.

Goldstein, P. J. 1979. Prostitution and Drugs. Lexington: Lexington Books.

Goldstein, P. J. 1981. Getting over: Economic alternatives to predatory crime among drug users. In J. Inciardi (ed.), The Drugs/Crime Connection. Beverly Hills: Sage Publications.

Goldstein, P. J. 1982. Drugs and Violent Behavior. Paper presented at annual meetings of the Academy of Criminal Justice Sciences.

Goldstein, P. J. and Johnson, B. 1983. Robbery Among Heroin Users. Paper presented at annual meetings of the Society for the Study of Social Problems.

Goldstein, P. J. and Hunt, D. 1984. Health Consequences of Drug Use. Emory, GA: Centers for Disease Control and the Carter Center of Emory University.

Harris, A. R. 1977. Sex and theories of deviance: Toward a functional theory of deviant typescripts. American Sociological Review 42:3-15.

Harwood, H. et al. 1984. Economic Costs to Society of Alcohol and Drug Abuse and Mental Illness. Rockville, MD: Alcohol, Drug Abuse, and Mental Health Administration.

Johnson, B. et al. 1985. Taking Care of Business: The Economics of Crime by Heroin Abusers. Lexington: Lexington Books.

Johnson, S. et al. 1975. Alcohol and rape in Winnepeg, 1966-1975. Journal of Studies on Alcohol 39:1887-1894.

McBride, D. 1983. Trends in Drugs and Death in Miami. Paper presented at annual meetings of the American Society of Criminology.

Rada, R. 1975. Alcoholism and forcible rape. American Journal of Psychiatry 132:444-446.

Shupe, L. M. 1954. Alcohol and crime: A study of the urine alcohol concentration found in 882 persons arrested during or immediately after the commission of a felony. Journal of Criminal Law, Criminology and Police Science 44:661-664.

Wolfgang, M. E. 1958. Patterns in Criminal Homicide. Philadelphia: University of Pennsylvania Press.

INTRODUCTION TO CHAPTER 14

There are three elements of alcohol and drug use which we have discussed which become salient in a consideration of the substance-abusing behavior of physicians and nurses. We have identified the comparative availability of alcohol and drugs as an issue (Introduction to the book), we have talked about the development of subcultural patterns of use (Introduction to Part 1), and we have discussed particularly stressful situations which are related to use (Smykla, Chapter 9, and Markides and Krause, Chapter 10). Medical professionals are vulnerable to abuse on all of these grounds. First, drugs are commonly available in a medical environment. Both physicians and nurses have access to drugs by dint of their professions and access to alcohol by dint of their incomes. In addition, both professions work with drugs on a moment-by-moment basis. They prescribe them, administer them, talk about them, handle them as a routine function. Thus, they lose the awe for drugs which we find more commonly among lay persons. For both these reasons, medical professionals are vulnerable to abuse. Finally, medical professionals see themselves as being under extreme stress.

These are issues which we have mentioned previously (Clark et al., Chapter 6). In that earlier discussion, we took a developmental approach. We examined the changing prevalence of substance use among medical students as an indicator of the growth of norms for behavior.

In this chapter, Winick takes a situational approach. Using the words of physicians and nurses, he creates categories of use/abuse among medical

342

professionals. Of particular importance here is the distinction that he makes between the reasons that people begin using substances and the reasons that they continue.

Do they themselves perceive the risks? And what do they propose are the reasons for their use/abuse? Winick uses self-report data to inform us. From these beginnings, Winick goes on to describe programs for the apprehension and treatment of physicians and nurse abusers.

CHAPTER 14
SUBSTANCE DEPENDENCE AMONG PHYSICIANS AND NURSES

Charles Winick

ABSTRACT

Alcohol and drug dependence affects a substantial number of physicians and nurses. The concern about these health professionals being able to function effectively and without drug impairments has aroused communities, peer groups, professional associations, and regulatory agencies. Interviews with 281 physicians and 243 nurses who are or were dependent on alcohol or drugs identified overwork, ailments, mood modification, magical thinking, family problems, fatigue, benchmarks, level of aspiration, situation of work, stress, misinformation, re-integration, access

---

CHARLES WINICK is Professor of Sociology at City College and the Graduate Center, City University of New York and Co-director of the Behavioral Sciences Training Program in Drug Abuse.

343

to and awareness about drugs, and career ending as factors in the condition's genesis.

The outlook for successful treatment of impaired physicians and nurses is good, although few of the professionals enter treatment voluntarily. Treatment typically involves a period of detoxification, out-patient counseling, and participation in some form of group therapy or AA session. In most states, the medical society has established a program for helping impaired physicians. The problem is getting more attention, and professional education is giving young nurses and physicians better information about drug misuse.

INTRODUCTION

The use of and especially the abuse of alcohol and other mood-modifying substances by health professionals, like physicians and nurses, has attracted the attention of professional groups and regulatory agencies and is of special interest and concern to the community. Society has a stake in these professionals' ability to use their skills and training for the good of the community and in their ability to function in an effective manner. In recent years, a number of factors have combined to give prominence to society's handling of the problem of alcohol and other drug dependence by physicians and nurses: 1) expansion of the consumer movement to considerations of health services, 2) some widely publicized cases of physician alcohol and drug abuse, 3) huge jury awards against drug abusing physicians in malpractice suits and resultant pressure for professional accountability, 4) a crisis in malpractice insurance and large increases in its premium costs, and 5) a movement toward peer assistance for impaired physicians and nurses.

The use of alcohol and other drugs by physicians has received special attention as an important contributor to physician impairment (Morrow, 1982; Stroedel, 1982; Arena, 1982). Although physicians and nurses become impaired in a variety of ways, such as aging, emotional illness, physical ailments, and for many other reasons, alcohol and other forms of substance dependence represent the largest single contribution to impairment among those professionals who come to the attention of their colleagues.

The impaired physician or nurse is unable to practice their profession with reasonable skill and with safety to patients because of their symptoms, including deterioration of functioning, inaccurate diagnosis, and lack of motor skill, which are among the effects of excessive use or abuse of drugs including alcohol (Hugunin, 1977). Perhaps one-tenth of the 470,000 physicians and of the 1,375,000 nurses currently in the United States will develop an alcohol or drug problem in the course of their careers. Society is concerned when the nurse or physician becomes dependent on these substances but not, of course, in ordinary recreational drinking or appropriate use of legal substances. Society's concern is based, of course, on the life or death nature of the daily professional activities of health care providers, like physicians and nurses. The concern arises because someone for whom substance dependence has become central may be unable to function acceptably. If we estimate conservatively that the average physician will treat 500 new patients and that the typical hospital nurse will provide service to 500 patients each year, it is clear that even one substance dependent physician or nurse has the potential for causing substantial harm.

This chapter will deal with the findings of a continuing study of alcohol and other substance dependence among health professionals. Where appropriate, reference is made to relevant studies conducted by others. We shall discuss the method of the study, some characteristics of the physicians and nurses interviewed, factors contributing to substance use, how drug-dependent professionals are discovered, and treatment and outcome.

METHOD OF STUDY

The current investigation of alcohol and other drug dependence among health professionals began 25 years ago (Winick, 1974; 1961). Through a variety of sources, it was possible to interview 281 physicians and 243 nurses who were or had been alcohol or other substance abusers. They were interviewed in seven states (New York, New Jersey, Pennsylvania, Massachusetts, Rhode Island, Connecticut, and Indiana). They had been taking a broad range of substances, including alcohol. Over half (56%) were taking or had taken more than one substance. Every subject interviewed was either alcohol or drug dependent and had used a mood modifying substance at least daily for at least two months. Some, who were involved with addicting substances like opiates or barbiturates, were addicted and others, who were involved with non-addicting substances like cocaine or amphetamines, were psychologically dependent on the drugs.

The physicians interviewed were 97% male and ranged in age from 27 to 78, with an average age of 47. There was a bimodal age distribution, with one peak between

29 and 35 and another cluster between 48 and 57. One physician was Hispanic, 278 were White, and two were Black. The range of their drug or alcohol dependence prior to the interview had extended from three months to 22 years. All the physicians had been trained in the United States.

The nurses interviewed were all female and ranged from 21 to 62 years of age, with an average of 44. There was also a bimodal age distribution, with a cluster of cases between 24 and 29 and another peak between 50 and 54. Eighteen were Hispanic, 215 were White, and 10 were Black. Pre-interviewing drug or alcohol dependence ranged from six months to 14 years.

Access to the physicians and nurses was obtained through a variety of non-law enforcement sources. Some were in treatment, others were in treatment for non-drug related conditions, some were located as part of a larger study of drug-dependent persons not known to the authorities, others were identified in the course of the author's presentations to hospital and medical or nursing groups, and another group was part of a follow-up investigation of "maturing out" of narcotic addiction (Winick, 1962).

The interviews averaged two hours and covered the personal, family, social, professional, and alcohol- and other substance-use dimensions of the respondents' lives. Complete confidentiality was, of course, assured to all subjects.

SOME CHARACTERISTICS OF THE PHYSICIANS AND NURSES

The physicians came from a range of specialties: general practice (28%), obstetrics/gynecology (11%), surgery (9%), psychiatry (8%), pediatrics (7%), emergency medicine (7%), pathology (5%), and other (26%).

The drug of choice of the physicians was: Demerol (31%), Talwin (19%), alcohol (12%), cocaine (9%), Fentanyl (8%), Seconal and other barbiturates (8%), Dalmane (6%), amphetamines (5%), and other (2%).

The persons who primarily took alcohol tended to be over age 45. Persons taking either amphetamine or Seconal tended to have taken alcohol first, but there was no clear pattern of specific previous substance use or alcohol-drug interaction in the case of the narcotic analgesic-dependent group. There was a tendency for persons using barbiturates to replace them with Dalmane, because it was believed to be less dangerous. Persons under 35 who took drugs tended to use more than one substance. Four percent of the spouses of the physicians but none of the nurses' spouses were also involved in drug or alcohol abuse; efforts to conceal the situation from spouses were common.

In the case of both physicians and nurses, alcohol use tended to be concentrated in the upper-age cluster and to be of less interest to the younger persons. In both professions, about a third of the users interviewed, mostly under age 40, had had some experience with marijuana, but its causal relationship to the taking of other substances was not clear. In three-fifths of the cases, the marijuana use preceded the taking of other substances, but in the other two-fifths, it was parallel with involvement with other substances.

Both nurses and physicians tended to use the same range of substances with a few exceptions. Fentanyl, a narcotic analgesic, was primarily used by physicians, all of whom were anesthesiologists. Percodan and codeine, which are relatively weak narcotic analgesics, were only used by nurses.

Forty-five percent of the alcohol users, mostly under 40, also took other substances, often as a way of coping with the effects of alcohol. Thus, someone who had been drinking in the evening might take tranquilizers the next morning and then take a stimulant in the afternoon; each substance would be intended to deal with the effects of the previous substance.

FACTORS CONTRIBUTING TO SUBSTANCE USE

Why do high-status professionals, like doctors and nurses, take substances which can lead to personal, social, vocational, career, and even legal difficulties? Relatively few of the professionals interviewed in the current study could answer such a question directly, but analysis of their answers to a wide range of other questions permitted a reasonable estimate of the causal factors involved in genesis of the condition.

The comments of the physicians and nurses interviewed were coded in terms of a series of content categories which had been established on the basis of previous interviews. For both physicians and nurses, it was possible to establish twelve categories to summarize the factors contributing to the beginning of substance use. Ten of these categories were only applicable to physicians, and two other contributors were unique to nurses. The ten shared categories and those which are unique to each profession are summarized below and in Table 14.1, page 366, Factors Contributing to Substance Use, with an indication of any differences between the two professions on each dimension.

Overwork

The most frequently cited reason for physicians' substance use was overwork (38%). These physicians tended to be working in large cities and to be professionally responsible and committed. They took the substances in order to be better able to cope with their duties. They tended to push themselves to their limit. In younger physicians, "moonlighting" at more than one job in order to increase their income was common. The overwork had different meanings to different physicians; some were driven, others could not decline responsibility, some worked very hard because other gratifications were not important, others were very patient-oriented.

Overwork, cited by 35% of the nurses, included working extra shifts, accepting more duties, and assuming tasks which were experienced as difficult and onerous.

Ailments

Ailments of various kinds, which the physician was treating without outside assistance, figured in 32% of the cases. Among the conditions included were gastrointestinal disorders, migraine, and depression. These physicians had difficulties in assuming the role of a patient. They might medicate themselves with one substance and then take something else to counter the effect of the original drug. Most physicians do not get a regular physical examination and rely heavily on "corridor consultations" with colleagues and on self-diagnosis (Stoudemire and Rhoads, 1983). Previous studies suggest that 90% of physicians recommend annual physicals to their patients, but only 30% get one themselves (Schreiber, 1978). It is especially difficult for physicians to become patients in the hospitals or clinics in which they work.

Many of the nurses who had ailments (29%) which they were self-medicating had conditions, like menstrual pains or headaches, which they did not think would be very responsive to physicians' intervention. A positive experience in easing symptoms via alcohol or a medication, often an analgesic, would lead to increasing the amount ingested and then to increasing its frequency.

Mood Modification

In the physicians (27%) and nurses (24%) for whom mood modification was a factor, there had usually been some pre-professional experience with recreational drug use. Most of these persons tended to be relatively young. Before or during professional training, they had often been involved as members of a sub-group, the lifestyle of which tended to accept use of psychoactive substances. They tended to be interested in expanding their sensibility and expanding consciousness.

Magical Thinking

For 26% of the physicians and 12% of the nurses, there was a strong belief that the substances ingested, though potentially hazardous to other people, would not pose problems to them. "I would know when to stop," or "I would be able to control the use and avoid getting addicted," were frequent comments. Particularly in the physicians, their attitudes were often expressions of a larger omnipotent worldview and an inability to accept restrictions. The nurses handled analgesics so frequently that many had developed very casual and

351

emancipated attitudes toward the drugs, which they believed they could control.

Family Problems

Family problems were slightly more important for nurses (27%) than for physicians (24%). Many nurses were working mothers, some were single parents, others were dealing with a child's or husband's illness, and a number were experiencing substantial problems with spouses or children. The physicians reported a range of difficulties with wives and children and con-siderable deterioration in the quality of their family lives.

Fatigue

For both physicians (20%) and nurses (14%), fatigue was important. Some younger physicians reported work situations requiring 18 or 24 hours without sleep. Other physicians were so overtired that they could not fall asleep. Interns and residents were socialized into a situation without normal rest periods and sleep which was interrupted frequently. Older physicians worked so hard and for such long hours that they became very tired. Many of the nurses were always tired because of the demands of their job and/or a personal or professional role conflict and also suffered from insomnia. With other nurses, their fatigue made it difficult to achieve a fulfilling sleep.

Benchmark

For physicians (14%) and nurses (11%), approaching a significant personal or professional benchmark or career milestone was related to the commencement of their substance use. This might be a promotion or a movement from a staff to private practice situation or some change in the structure of a practice, in the case of a physician. With nurses, it was often a change to a supervisory from a direct service position or to a different kind of duty.

Situation of Work

For some physicians (12%) and nurses (17%), the special dimensions of the work situation posed overwhelming problems. Young physicians commented on the "brutal meat grinder" and triage aspects of a hospital situation, involving choices of who would get scarce medical resources. These young doctors often saw a contrast between the administrative demands of the institution on young doctors and the ideals with which they had entered medicine as well as the competitiveness among the house staff. The enormous range of what the young physician was expected to know and the pressure not to make mistakes were, to many of these physicians, overwhelming. For nurses, the great responsibilities they were shouldering which could not easily be shared, and the daily need to face suffering and death, were very disturbing.

Stress

Especially for younger physicians (11%) and nurses (26%), situational stress was a ubiquitous feature of their work. The shift from the predictable situation of medical school to the sub-optimal conditions of a training hospital was often very stressful. Some older physicians found themselves facing the stress of the increasing demands of patients, litigation by patients, and the hazardous shoals of malpractice suits. Despair characterized some of the nurses who faced near-intolerable stress on the job because they did not feel

353

they were able to meet the demands of their patients. Recent investigations have documented the wide range and many types of stress in nursing (Numerof, 1983). Both physicians and nurses spoke of the stresses related to the insulation and intensity of their work, which made it difficult for them to relax with non-colleagues.

Misinformation

About a tenth (10% of physicians and 9% of the nurses) of the subjects felt that they did not have valid and accurate information about the implications of drug use and dependence. The physicians were especially likely to note that their courses in pharmacology did not include enough material on drug abuse and even less on alcohol.

There were two factors which characterized physician, but not nurse, substance users: levels of aspiration and re-integration.

Level of Aspiration. These physicians (13%) had a substantial record of achievement within medicine, often combined with ambivalence toward the profession and ailments with a range of physical symptoms. Expressing disaffection toward medicine was difficult for these subjects and their drug use could have drained off some of their aggression and ambivalence, which perhaps contributed to their physical symptoms.

Re-integration. In 9% of the physicians, encountering difficulties and problems in their mid-career years when they were in their forties and fifties resonated with their experiences a few decades earlier when they had been able to ease some problems by alcohol or other drug use. By recalling the favorable consequences of such use in the past -- re-integration -- they were encouraged to try the alcohol or drug use again. The seeds of later substance use may not have germinated in these physicians for a few decades.

Two factors were not relevant to doctors, but were discussed by nurses: access and awareness to drugs and career ending.

Access and Awareness. About a sixth (16%) of the nurses mentioned as a possible factor in their own use of drugs their growing explicit awareness in the course of their professional work that specific drugs were effective in blocking or enabling people to cope with or defer physical and emotional pain and other symptoms. When they felt themselves approaching or facing such pain and symptoms, it was easier for them to consider taking the drugs. Because nurses have such easy access to drugs, it was also easy to obtain the substances.

Career Ending. One-tenth of the nurses seem to have begun drug use as they approached retirement and realized that their careers were ending. Their lack of a network of family and non-work interpersonal relationships made various physical symptoms more urgent. Self-medication of these symptoms increased as the implications of the ending of the nurse's career became more significant to her.

Thus, there are ten dimensions which apply to both physicians and nurses beginning drug use, and a few which are unique to each profession. On the average, each drug- or alcohol-dependent physician or nurse was involved with more than two of the factors relating to the genesis of substance dependence. Their substance behavior was likely to be a result of more than one factor and was thus over-determined. The multiple genesis of this substance dependence among physicians and nurses should not be surprising since drug or alcohol use is not a unitary phenomenon and has different meanings and implications for different people. Many different kinds of people become physicians and nurses and their differing backgrounds may contribute to some sub-groups being over-represented among alcohol- and drug-using health professionals.

It is possible to combine a number of these dimensions into a smaller number of factors which lend themselves to a sociological theory of the genesis of drug dependence. Such a theory proposes that substance dependence will be high in groups with 1) access to drugs, 2) disengagement from negative proscriptions about their use, and 3) role strain and/or deprivation (Winick, 1980). Physicians and nurses certainly have access to drugs and are not bound by negative proscriptions about their use. The many specific factors cited above document the high degree of role strain and/or role deprivation which is to be found in these professions.

In the case of those physicians and nurses who were or had been in treatment on whom there were psychiatric profile data, there was no clear evidence either of a particular psychiatric syndrome or of a specific pro-morbid personality. However, a study of 50 addicted physicians treated at the Menninger Foundation in Topeka, Kansas concluded that those under 40 were more likely to exhibit serious psychopathology in the border-line range, while those over 40 were more likely to have organic brain impairment and depression (Johnston and Connelly, 1981).

Another consideration is the psychological principle of the functional autonomy of motives, which holds that a particular course of action may begin because of one set of reasons but can continue for other reasons. Some of the physicians and nurses interviewed could have begun their alcohol or drug use in response to, or along with, some of the factors cited above. Their continued use of the substance might be so reinforcing that its genesis might have become less consequential. Thus, they might have begun for a specific reason but continued because drug use became attractive in its own right.

HOW DRUG-DEPENDENT PROFESSIONALS ARE DISCOVERED

Some physicians and nurses may be alcohol or drug dependent for their whole careers and not be discovered by colleagues, supervisors, or law enforcement officials. Others, however, are discovered or, in a small minority of cases, voluntarily report themselves.

A physician or nurse can be reported by a spouse, colleagues, or patients. State prescription monitoring offices may detect an unusually heavy or erratic pattern of prescriptions on the part of a physician and investigate him or her. A physician or nurse may be observed stealing drugs from a hospital or diverting a patient's drugs to private use.

Another avenue to detection is an abrupt change in the person's dress or mood or social behavior, irritability or erratic behavior, lateness, extended lunch hours or breaks or other absences, a decline in work performance or some other interference with professional functioning. Someone who drinks may have very recognizable alcohol breath.

Generally speaking, it is much easier for a drug or alcohol dependent nurse to avoid detection and its consequences than for a physician to do so. Even if she is detected and is dismissed, she can often get another job fairly easily. There is no onus attached to a nurse changing jobs, whereas a physician who moves around professionally is much more likely to be viewed with suspicion. There are fewer sanctions for drug- or alcohol-dependent nurses, and the demand for their services is so great that employers might be relatively eager to overlook some aspects of the nurse's background. Some kinds of nursing duty, such as service with terminal patients who require heavy analgesic medication, or night duty, can facilitate a nurse's access to drugs with minimal fear of detection.

Supervisors and colleagues will take action against substance-dependent colleagues because drugs and alcohol can cloud perceptions, thinking, and decision-making. The easiest way of handling alcohol- or drug-impaired colleagues is to terminate their employment, but professional societies and supervisors usually try to get them into treatment, voluntarily or, if a danger is posed to patients, by coercion. Colleagues and supervisors usually avoid confronting the impaired nurse or physician until ready to provide some assistance to them. In spite of the importance of relieving an alcohol- or drug-dependent physician or nurse of their duties, existing federal regulations which protect the confidentiality of people in treatment for alcohol and drug problems must be observed.

In the sample of substance dependent physicians and nurses discussed above, 28% of the nurses and 42% of the physicians had, as of the time of the interview, gotten into difficulties related to their substance use. Another 23% of the nurses and 21% of the physicians were known to at least one colleague or friend or family member to be involved in drug or alcohol use.

Until recently, it was the older impaired physician or nurse who was likely to be detected. During the last decade, there has been a special concern about impairment in medical students and young physicians in training. One investigation of interns found that their anger and hostility increased during the training (Uliana, 1984). A survey of 247 programs to train anesthesia residents and nurse anesthetists in the United States found that 74% had at least one suspected incidence of drug dependence to report (Ward, Ward, and Saidman, 1983). The country's largest union of young physicians established a program to provide treatment for its alcohol- and drug-dependent members (Winick, 1983). In one medical school, alcohol had become an equal or more serious problem than drug use among the students (Thomas, Luber, and Smith, 1977). Medical students were found in one study to experience about as much stress related to personal relations, academic requirements, time pressures, and money as law and graduate students (Heins, Fahey, and Leiden, 1984).

TREATMENT AND OUTCOME

A physician or nurse who enters treatment is likely to do so in a hospital or community other than the one in which they have been working for reasons of maintenance of confidentiality. After treatment, a third person, often a psychiatrist, is usually asked to evaluate their fitness to return to work in the last and re-entry phase of treatment.

Most treatment involves a residential in-patient and out-patient detoxification, typically from 5 to 30 days, and 6 to 24 months of out-patient treatment, usually including some group therapy activity. Attendance at a therapy group, often composed entirely of health professionals with similar disorders, is common in cities or areas serviced by a medical center. Attendance at Alcoholics Anonymous (AA) is usually urged for persons with an alcohol problem and there are many AA groups specifically for physicians and nurses (Bissell and Haberman, 1984). Every effort is made to involve other members of the family in treatment, especially after detoxification. The most difficult part of a treatment involves not detoxification from alcohol and other drugs but staying off. In order to confirm that a formerly drug-dependent physician is actually drug free, there is widespread use of urine testing, often at unannounced intervals. The physician's or nurse's assurance of non-drug use is not sufficiently valid to be acceptable to the treatment authorities, who are concerned about the consequences of returning a drug-dependent person to work.

Every single state has passed a bill to regulate the impaired physician since the American Medical Association (1972) first issued a report on the subject. The goal of such legislation is to provide procedures for identifying impaired physicians, relieving them of clinical duties, getting them into treatment, insuring the safety of their patients, and facilitating their return to practice once they are again able to function.

There is a strong preference for giving the responsibility for managing impaired physicians' programs to the state medical society rather than to the official licensing and professional regulatory agency on the assumption that peer control of such matters is preferable to bureaucratic supervision. In 47 states, the state medical societies have actually implemented programs to assist and rehabilitate impaired physicians. California (Gualtieri, Cosentino, and Becker, 1983), Wisconsin (Herrington et al., 1982), Oregon (Shore, 1982), Georgia (Talbott et al., 1981), and New York (Carone and Nagy, 1979) have established well-known programs to assist impaired physicians. Every program which has published its results has reported that at least 60% of the physicians treated have successfully returned to the practice of medicine and the proportion of successful outcomes has been over 90% in some jurisdictions.

At the country's largest program for treatment of addicted health professionals, the Ridgeview Institute of Smyrna, Georgia, alcohol and other drug dependencies are treated in the same way. In six years, the program has successfully treated 635 physicians and 300 other health professionals. The program, which is sponsored by the Georgia Medical Society, includes four months of in-patient and halfway house treatment and 20 months of follow-up care (Talbott et al., 1981).

In 1981, the American Nursing Association (ANA) implemented a Task Force on Addiction and Psychological Disturbance to help in establishing procedures for impaired nurses. In 1982, the ANA House of Delegates passed a resolution accepting the profession's responsibility for dealing with the problem by providing access to treatment before any disciplinary action is taken. Professional nursing journals have carried information on various state programs and approximately half the states have or are planning such programs.

One innovative approach which applies compulsion to physician and nurse drug abusers involves the abuser preparing a letter to the appropriate licensing board, confessing renewed drug abuse and surrendering his or her license (Crowley, 1984). The patient and therapist sign a contract in which the latter is directed to collect frequent urine samples and to mail the letter if any urine sample contains traces of drug use. The physician and nurse patients who signed such contracts improved dramatically. Other programs are adapting this modification of the contract approach to therapy. Other treatment programs have also reported success. The most important consideration in all such programs is overcoming the physician or nurse's tendency to deny the problem often by using a constructive confrontation with them.

The outlook for physicians and nurses who are drug or alcohol dependent and enter treatment is very positive. Every single nurse or physician who had been in treatment in the current study had returned to professional functioning and had experienced no reoccurrence of symptoms. In any alcohol- or drug-treatment situation, the prognosis for a patient with a job, who is highly motivated, and who has a series of relationships or other support systems is likely to be positive. Most of the subjects interviewed were, like other drug-dependent health professionals, high achievers who had a strong drive toward vocational success.

One special problem in the treatment of the physician or nurse who is drug dependent is that they have usually been taking relatively pure drugs, so that the physical consequences of their drug use are likely to be more intense than is the case with street addicts, who are using diluted-strength drugs.

In the case of a young drug- or alcohol-dependent physician in training, it is usually possible to have them experience detoxification and other in-patient treatment and return to work, without losing any significant part of their training experience or department rotations. Like a resident who takes time out for hepatitis or a pregnancy, vacation and other extra time can be used to offset the physician's absence during treatment. The later in the training cycle a resident enters a treatment situation, the easier will it be to make up the time.

It is much easier to relieve drug- or alcohol-dependent nurses or physicians of their duties than to return them to work. The supervisor who certifies that such a person can return to work has assumed a major responsibility. As more health professionals enter treatment and as such treatment continues to return larger numbers of professionals to effective functioning, supervisors will be more willing to assume the responsibility. If nursing and medical education includes more instructional content relating to alcohol and drugs, there should be fewer health professionals involved with such problems. There are growing signs that the health professionals are slowly recognizing the importance of such content in the professional curriculum.

REFERENCES

American Medical Association Council on Mental Health. 1972. The sick physician. Journal of the American Medical Association 223:684-687.

Arana, G. W. 1982. The impaired physician: A medical and social dilemma. General Hospital Psychiatry 4:147-154.

Bissell, L. and Haberman, P. 1984. Alcoholism in the Professions. NY: Oxford University Press.

Carone, P. A. and Nagy, B. R. 1979. Medical discipline: Dealing with physicians who are unscrupulous, disabled, and/or incompetent. New York State Journal of Medicine 79:108-141.

Crowley, T. J. 1984. Contingency contracting treatment of drug-abusing physicians, nurses, and dentists. In J. Grabowski, M. L. Stitzer, and J. E. Henningfield (eds.), Behavioral Intervention Techniques in Drug Abuse Treatment (pp. 66-83). Rockville, MD: Government Printing Office.

Gualtieri, A. C., Cosentino, J. P., and Becker, J. S. 1983. The California experience with a diversion program for impaired physicians. Journal of the American Medical Association 249:226-229.

Heins, M., Fahey, S. N., and Leiden, L. I. 1984. Perceived stress in medical, law, and graduate students. Journal of Medical Education 59:169-179.

Herrington, R. E., Benzer, D. G., Jacobson, G. R., and Hawkins, M. K. 1982. Treating substance-use disorders among physicians. Journal of the American Medical Association 247:2253-2257.

Hugunin, M. B. 1977. Helping the impaired physician. Proceedings of the AMA Conference on the Impaired Physician. Chicago: American Medical Association.

Johnston, R. P. and Connelly, J. C. 1981. Addicted physicians: A closer look. Journal of the American Medical Association 245:253-257.

Morrow, C. K. 1982. Sick doctors: The social construction of professional deviance. Social Problems 30:92-108.

Numerof, R. E. 1983. Managing Stress: A Guide for Health Professionals. Rockville, MD: Aspen Systems Corporation.

Schreiber, S. C. 1978. The sick doctor: Medical school preparation. Psychiatric Forum 7:11-16.

Shore, J. H. 1982. The impaired physician: Four years after probation. Journal of the American Medical Association 248:3127-3130.

Stoudemire, A. and Rhoads, J. M. 1983. When the doctor needs a doctor: Special considerations for the physician-patient. Annals of Internal Medicine 98:654-659.

Stroedel, R. C. 1982. Thy brother's keeper: Responsibility for the impaired physician. Legal Aspects of Medical Practice 10:1-8.

Talbott, G. D. et al. 1981. The Medical Association of Georgia's Disabled Doctors Program--A 5 year review. Journal of the Medical Association of Georgia 70:545-549.

Taylor, J. and Benson, E. B. 1980. Impaired physicians: The dilemma of identification. Postgraduate Medicine 68:56-64.

Thomas, R., Luber, S., and Smith, J. 1977. Survey of alcohol and drug use in medical students. Diseases of the Nervous System 38:41-43.

Uliana, R. L. 1984. Mood changes during internship. Journal of Medical Education 59:118-123.

Ward, C. F., Ward, G. C., and Saidman, L. J. 1983. Drug abuse in anesthesia training programs. Journal of the American Medical Association 250:922-925.

Winick, C. 1961. Physician narcotic addicts. Social Problems 9:174-186.

_____. 1962. Maturing our view of narcotic addiction. United Nations Bulletin on Narcotics 14:1-7.

_____. 1974. Drug dependence among nurses. In C. Winick (ed.), Sociological Aspects of Drug Dependence (pp. 155-162). Cleveland: CRC Press.

_____. 1980. A theory of drug dependence based on role, access to, and attitudes toward drugs. In D. Lettieri (ed.), Theories of Drug Dependence (pp. 225-236). Rockville, MD: Government Printing Office.

_____. 1983. Healing the physician. Committee of Interns and Residents News 12(5):5-6.

APPENDIX

TABLE 14.1

SOME FACTORS CONTRIBUTING TO SUBSTANCE USE

Physicians	Percent*	Nurses	Percent*
Overwork	38%	Overwork	35%
Ailments	32%	Ailments	29%
Mood Modifications	29%	Family Problems	27%
Magical Thinking	26%	Stress	26%
Family Problems	24%	Mood Modification	24%
Fatigue	20%	Situation of Work	17%
Benchmark	14%	Access and Awareness	16%
Level of Aspiration	13%	Fatigue	14%
Situation of Work	12%	Magical Thinking	12%
Stress	11%	Benchmark	11%
Misinformation	10%	Career Ending	10%
Reintegration	9%	Misinformation	9%

---
* More than one factor may contribute; therefore, totals exceed 100%.

INTRODUCTION TO CHAPTER 15

In the previous chapter, Winick described for us the reasons that medical professionals give for their use of alcohol and drugs. This is a population for which drugs are quasi-legitimate and easily accessible. They are available in the environment and the users deal with them on a routine basis.

In this next chapter, Wiebel gives us a glimpse into the self-reports of another drug-abusing population -- heroin users. Like Winick, he employs the drug users' own words and own rationale as a data base to describe their reasons for using drugs. The difference, of course, is that these users have not found these drugs readily available, nor are they legal.

How then do people come to be heroin users in a society in which heroin use is generally reviled? Wiebel takes us along the path of socialization into the drug subculture, describing how people came in contact with the drug, why they first used it, and what they felt like. He notes the central role of a significant relative or friend, the importance of a supply, and the process of learning to use the drug.

In his discussion, Wiebel gives us the flavor of life in the heroin-using subculture. We can compare this with the description of life on skid row offered earlier by Fagan (Chapter 8) and the violent life of female drug users in New York City (Goldstein, Chapter 13). All of these represent subcultures in which use of alcohol is an accepted part of life, the substance is freely available, and participants have well-established rationales for using it.

CHAPTER 15

FACTORS INFLUENCING PERSONAL DECISIONS TO USE HEROIN

W. Wayne Wiebel

ABSTRACT

As part of the ongoing monitoring of patterns and trends of drug abuse at the National Institute on Drug Abuse (NIDA), a study of "new heroin users" in Chicago was authorized. This chapter examines that portion of the Chicago study dealing with the factors involved in decisions to experiment with and use heroin.

A snowball sample of twenty individuals who had begun using heroin in the past two years provided the data base. Subjects were recruited from ethnographic street contacts, drug-abuse treatment programs, and criminal justice referral programs. In open-ended interviews, respondents discussed childhood attitudes toward heroin, introductions to the drug and its users, progressive patterns of use, and related life situation factors.

Almost everyone interviewed recalled having very negative sentiments toward heroin during their youth. By the time they considered experimenting with heroin, a significant shift in attitude had taken place. Access to a known user was a necessary condition but not sufficient in itself to explain this transition. Analysis suggested that the most important factor was previous involvement in a drug-using network. Though heroin use might remain unacceptable, other drugs were appreciated as intoxicants, and a conceptual

----

W. WAYNE WIEBEL, formerly Manager of Community Assistance and Information at the Illinois Department of Alcoholism and Substance Abuse, Chicago, Illinois, is currently Principal Investigator for the AIDS Outreach Intervention Project, School of Public Health, University of Illinois, Chicago.

framework was developed which allowed heroin to be imagined and evaluated as an intoxicant. For most subjects, this change in perspective seemed crucial in explaining the transition which allowed heroin to be eventually considered as an option for experimentation.

Whether the drug was asked for or offered, nearly everyone was introduced to heroin by a user who provided information, reassurance, and expertise. First use of heroin was often casually dismissed, but decisions to continue were justified by practical considerations. The desirable effects of heroin use in conjunction with stimulants and the effectiveness of heroin in reducing emotional stress were most often cited as reasons for continued use.

INTRODUCTION

Drug abuse and patterns of abuse are in a constant state of change. The entire range of drugs which are subject to abuse, including drug combinations, go through cycles of increasing and decreasing popularity. Because the public health issues associated with the abuse of different substances are constantly changing, the importance of trend data can be appreciated.

The scientific perspective utilized in studying drug trends is based upon the medical model used for following the spread of disease. The study of epidemics, called epidemiology, may at first seem inap-

---

I gratefully acknowledge the encouragement and support of Nick Kozel and his colleagues at the Division of Epidemiology and Statistical Analysis at the National Institute on Drug Abuse. Edgar Adams and Dr. Raquel Crider deserve special thanks for help in developing this study. Recognition is also extended to friends at the Dangerous Drugs Commission who provided the support needed to complete the study.

propriate to the study of drug abuse because of the obvious differences between the voluntary use of drugs and the involuntary spread of disease, yet closer examination proves otherwise. For example, although the spread of most disease is involuntary, people are often exposed to infectious bacteria or virus while engaged in voluntary activity. Once exposed, the physical predisposition of some individuals to contract a disease can be compared to the susceptibility of others to experiment with a drug and accept its use when it is made available to them. Thus, it can be seen that when a drug becomes available within a community, it is introduced from one person to another, and its spread in use is largely dependent on the predisposition of those exposed to accept the substance. If a drug is not available, or users do not introduce the drug to novices, or experimenters do not accept the new substance, then there is no spread in use and no epidemic.

While researchers use the same model for studying drug trends as is used for monitoring other public health problems, there are numerous factors relating to the abuse of drugs which significantly complicate this procedure. The source of most difficulties can be attributed to the simple fact that drug use itself is an illicit and criminal behavior. As a consequence, there is no official record-keeping system which maintains direct information on the public's use of controlled substances. Most drug trend data is based on indicators which are believed to reflect the use of various substances rather than actually measuring their use. For example, overdose deaths for heroin are believed to go up or down in relation to the numbers of people using heroin, but they do not actually measure the number of users.

Having set the stage with a very brief overview of drug trend analysis, I will proceed to the specific circumstances of this study. Data collected through the Division of Epidemiology and Statistical Analysis at the National Institute on Drug Abuse (NIDA) had shown a general decline in heroin indicators across the country since the mid-1970's. Then, beginning in New York City and Washington, D.C. at the end of the decade, heroin indicators reversed direction. Over the next few years, other major metropolitan areas on the East Coast and then the West Coast, began to show definite signs of increasing heroin trends. By 1983, only a few metropolitan Midwest cities had shown clear indications of increasing heroin use.

With an apparent heroin epidemic in progress on both coasts and declining or stable trends throughout most of the Midwest, drug-abuse policy-makers were in a distinct predicament. If heroin addiction continued to spread, then it would be important to gear intervention strategies and treatment capabilities to the particular requirements of a heroin epidemic. If, however, the spread in heroin addiction was not destined to include the rest of the country and lasted for only a short period of time, the re-allocation of resources would be unnecessary and inappropriate.

In an attempt to fill in the missing gaps of information required for planning purposes, Federal authorities determined that additional research was warranted. One component of the additional information required was data on new heroin users. By focusing on new users, investigators were expected to provide insight into the nature of the current epidemic. An analysis of present patterns would allow comparisons with existing data on previous epidemics. This would help determine whether the present situation was merely an extension of established cycles and relationships or whether new, intervening factors had emerged to alter the formula used in making projections.

By late 1983, a study of new heroin users was initiated in Chicago to address issues of concern to substance abuse professionals and policy-makers. A description of the investigation and its major findings follows.

THE STUDY

The first issue to be addressed was how to define or operationalize a "new heroin user" for the purposes of the study. It was decided that anyone who had begun using heroin in the past two years and had established at least some minimal pattern of continued use would qualify as a research subject. Thus, one-time or two-time users were excluded, but subjects did not have to be physically addicted nor were they required to consider heroin their preferred drug or drug of choice in order to qualify as a research subject. It was reasoned that these selection criteria would provide the broadest base of information regarding introductions to heroin use even though some individuals interviewed might never progress to the point of physical dependence associated with actual addiction to the drug.

Given the short time frame allotted for completion of the study and the difficulty of identifying potential subjects, a target number of twenty new users was established as a reasonable goal. Any attempt to randomly sample from the larger population of all new heroin users was dismissed as being infeasible. Quite simply, there was no practical way to identify everyone in the Chicago area who may have begun using heroin in the proceeding two years. Instead, a "snowball" sampling technique was adopted utilizing a large network of sources known to have connections with new heroin users. Snowball samples utilize the social networks of eligible subjects to build up the sample, through referrals, to an acceptable size. Anyone able to enlist a research subject was offered a $10 referral fee upon verification of eligibility and completion of the interview. The subjects themselves were paid a $20 participation fee at the conclusion of the interview. Throughout the course of the study, everyone approached to participate in an interview agreed to do so once the purpose of the research was explained and the confidentiality of information collected was guaranteed. Before being interviewed, all subjects were required to have their heroin histories confirmed by at least one independent source.

Included in the sampling network for potential subjects were a wide array of street research contacts, drug-abuse treatment programs, and screening programs for criminal justice or treatment referral. Street contacts included both heroin users and heroin dealers who were part of a field network developed over the past ten years of research on drug problems in natural settings. Treatment programs provided access to new clients with less than two-year heroin histories and to other clients who could refer subjects from their neighborhoods or personal networks. The screening programs identified eligible subjects from their client loads and referred anyone willing to be interviewed. In all, six subjects were identified through street contacts, seven from screening programs, and seven from drug-treatment programs.

An attempt was made to secure as diverse a group of subjects as possible. Thus, while the sample could not claim to be representative of all the city's new heroin users, the selection process did seek to include a broad range in user characteristics. This, it was hoped, would minimize the possibility that a major category of new user would be excluded. Judging from the research subject's more prominent characteristics, the efforts to sample a broad spectrum in types of new users was largely a success. Included in the sample were a middle-class advertising executive and a South American revolutionary; a street "drag queen" and a disabled, middle-management supervisor introduced to heroin after his physician stopped prescribing a legitimate narcotic for the control of pain; an alienated, upper-middle-class 25 year old who found relief from her severe depression in heroin; and a lower-class, violence-prone, career criminal with a history typical of most people's notions of an addict lifestyle. Also interviewed were a high-class call girl, a street hooker, and a male prostitute. The sample included one addict who claimed never to have paid to supply her habit and eight other subjects who became heroin dealers in order to generate income and/or to pay for their own habits. In short, given the small sample of only twenty respondents, the subjects included a remarkably diverse cross section of personal characteristics, experience, and situation.

FINDINGS

Each research subject completed both a questionnaire and an interview. The questionnaire covered personal background and drug history information. The interview provided subjects an opportunity to discuss their opinions of heroin prior to exposure, as well as their initial contact with the drug, progressive patterns of use, means of supporting use, and related life-situation factors. Given limitations of space and scope, this chapter will focus on the results of the interview portion of the study.

Subjects were asked about their opinions of and attitudes toward heroin prior to coming into contact with the drug or its users. Nearly everyone interviewed recalled having negative sentiments about the drug when they were younger. Many of these harsh judgments, recalled by the subjects in retrospect, were associated with the more commonly portrayed consequences of addiction such as overdose death, moral decay, slavery to addiction, and lives of prostitution or crime to support a habit. As one subject remembered thinking as a child, "It's a horrible drug that only hopeless losers use." For others, what they heard about heroin was so inconsistent with their lives at the time that it was not even really perceived as being a threat. For example, one of the middle class subjects recalled, "It was bad, but actually (it was) something that was beyond the realm of my imagination or comprehension. You know? Starvation is horrible too, but I didn't even know what it's like to be hungry." Although a few subjects had recollections which they considered to be relatively neutral or non-judgmental concerning heroin, only one person recalled being favorably predisposed to the drug as a child. Even in this case, however, the positive attitude could not be attributed to the youngster having heard good things about the drug. On the contrary, the subject recalled hearing only negative things about heroin, but, being very rebellious and anti-social even in youth, he figured that anything adults would bother to describe as being so terrible must in fact be "pretty good."

Almost everyone interviewed in the study came into first contact with a heroin user through friends or family. Often, someone with whom the subject had already developed an acquaintance revealed themselves to be a heroin user. In most cases, a personal involvement in the drug-using subculture was already firmly established before those interviewed developed any relationships with heroin users. The most common exception to this pattern was when the first heroin user known to the subject was a member of his own family. Among the 25% of the sample with heroin-using relatives, one Puerto Rican addict remembered watching his father "shoot up" ten years before he tried the drug himself. In other instances, it was an older brother or uncle who were discovered to be users. In two cases, families reacted negatively towards the addict, but, in each case, the close personal attachment of the respondent to the relative brought to question how horrible the drug could actually be.

In reviewing the interviews, it became apparent that for almost everyone, a significant change took place between the subject's negative impressions of the drug in youth and the situation which led to their experimenting with it. Though becoming acquainted with a known user was often a necessary condition, it was not sufficient to explain the attitudinal shift which made taking heroin a desirable alternative. The missing link which emerged in analysis as being the most important factor in changing the previously unthinkable to a viable possibility was involvement in the drug subculture. The only exceptions to previous participation in a drug scene were the revolutionary who had virtually no history of recreational drug use and the middle-aged foreman who was placed on narcotics by his doctor following a serious automobile accident. Everyone else reported increasing involvement in friendship networks where drug use was a frequent and accepted group activity. Because the use of drugs in general became desirable, the user of heroin, though still unacceptable, was brought into a conceptual framework where its effects as an intoxicant could be imagined and evaluated. Given this change in perspective, it is easier to see how something once inconceivable could slowly, over a period of years, become an option for experimentation.

Though respondents indicated that their attitudes towards heroin had changed before they considered taking it, this shift was not complete or without reservation. In the process of seriously considering experimentation, nearly everyone sought assurance that such risk-taking would not result in addiction or inadvertent overdose. Once convinced that the immediate consequences of their experimentation did not exceed acceptable levels of risk, the subjects were only then willing to try heroin. Even after having decided to try it for the first time, many still described feelings of anxiety and had second thoughts about their decisions. At the age of twenty, the Puerto Rican subject described buying a "quarter bag"

377

($25) of heroin and taking it to someone he knew who could "cook it up" into an injectable solution and "run it" (inject it) for him. He said that at the last minute he wanted to back out and forget the idea but that he could not because of his pride and the fear that others would discover that he had "chickened out."

Having reached a point where experimentation with heroin was a distinct possibility, the subjects required only a situation where their option could be exercised. In half of the cases, the individuals interviewed actively pursued the opportunity to try heroin. Like the Puerto Rican described above, they were responsible for creating a situation which made their first experience possible. The remaining half of the sample was offered the drug as a friendly gesture, at no cost, and placed in the position of having to decide whether they, in fact, wished to try it. For those individuals who had already injected other drugs, the decision to try heroin seemed the least significant. For many of the others, the needle itself was an issue of discomfort, and, as a consequence, many opted to snort the drug instead of having it injected.

With the exception of the South American revolutionary who proved to be an exception to almost every general finding, the respondents were given their first opportunity to try heroin through a friend or relative who was a user and with whom they had an established relationship. Whether the heroin was asked for or offered, this individual served as the agent of introduction providing information, reassurance, and knowledge regarding the proper dose, preparation, administration, and anticipated effects of the drug. In the one instance reported where the available expertise was not utilized, the consequences of failing to do so proved quite undesirable. The career criminal who had expected that he would like heroin from his youth was provided with his first opportunity when a friend asked him if he wanted to "get off." They went to a "shooting gallery" where addicts purchase and inject drugs. He decided that he did not want to appear inexperienced, so instead of admitting his ignorance, he watched the others and tried to mimic their procedures. His lack of experience resulted in his missing the vein while injecting, and he later complained to his partner that his lower arm was very painful. The friend informed him that he had obviously missed the vein and made fun of him because he had been unwilling to accept assistance.

A significant minority of the sample was introduced to heroin, not because of the effect of the drug itself, but because of the effect produced when it was used in combination with another substance. Two of the subjects, the male prostitute and the transsexual, were intravenous users of Preludin, a powerful pharmaceutical stimulant. They had both heard independently that heroin was a good drug to "come down on" after a period of extended stimulant abuse. The third subject, a North side pimp, was introduced to heroin in conjunction with cocaine as a "speedball" and was told that the high was better than either of the drugs alone. Another respondent also used heroin in conjunction with cocaine, but, in this case, it was not because he preferred the combined high. In fact, he preferred the high of cocaine, but he would also take heroin because he found that this reduced the anxiety and paranoid thoughts he got when only using cocaine. Other cocaine-dependent respondents, however, would only use heroin at the conclusion of extended periods of chronic cocaine administration.

Three other individuals interviewed attributed their initiation to heroin as a direct consequence of their preferred drug being unavailable. In its place, heroin was either offered or available. One twenty-eight year old black had been addicted to Talwin and Pyribenzamine, known on the streets as "T's and Blues." Talwin (T's) is a synthetic narcotic and Pyribenzamine (Blues) is a blue antihistamine pill. The abuse of this drug combination, which is "cooked" and injected much like heroin, originated in Chicago's black neighborhoods and grew to epidemic proportions during the mid- to late 1970's. One evening this addict was unable to find any T's and Blues from his established connections. Faced with the alternative of not getting high at all, he and his friends decided to try heroin since that was available. The second individual found to follow this pattern was an auto repairman who had been approached by a drug dealer to fix a car for a bag of cocaine. When the dealer came to pick up his car, he told the repairman that he was out of cocaine but that he did have a bag of heroin he was willing to substitute as payment. Fearing that if he refused the heroin he might never receive payment for his work, the respondent accepted it. He then split the heroin with a co-worker who was experienced and willing to initiate him. The final subject to be introduced to heroin as a substitute drug was the middle-aged trucking supervisor. After failing to convince his doctor that he should continue to receive narcotics for his accident-related injuries, the respondent contacted some "shady" relatives who were known to be trafficking in heroin. When approached, they agreed to supply the drug and inject him as required.

The subjects' reactions to heroin after first trying it were on the whole quite positive although some complained about side effects and others, while enjoying it, were not particularly impressed. The latter was most often the case with those who snorted rather than injected the drug. The advertising executive, after giving into curiosity, snorted a few "lines" and remembered it as being "all right" but nothing very impressive. Likewise, the psychologically unstable, upper-middle-class female snorted heroin four separate times during her first evening's experimentation. She recalled feeling a pleasant, relaxed, floating sensation, but at the time she did not think that it was the kind of thing she would go out of her way to try again.

Individuals who injected the drug the first time were much more likely to notice significant drug effects. Although about half of those injecting felt nauseous, only a few actually vomited. The most frequently experienced effects were the "rush" of the drug's onset, a feeling of relaxation, itching, and a sense of well-being. For some of the users, the relief from strain and problems was an especially desirable part of the experience. One user said, "I liked not thinking about stuff that bothered me; I felt good." Another subject summed up his reaction when he related, "All of a sudden all the bullshit, ya know, nothin' was that important any more. I didn't care if the house burned down." Only three of the intravenous (IV) experimenters mentioned negative aspects about their experience. One did not like the itching sensation he felt, and another found the nausea and vomiting distasteful. The third subject, the chronic cocaine abuser, liked the different high produced by combining heroin with cocaine as a speedball injection and particularly appreciated the reduced sense of paranoia. However, in comparison to cocaine alone, he did not care for the less intense rush produced by a speedball nor did he like the reduced sense of awareness.

Given the number of individuals who had expressed concern over the possibility of becoming physically addicted prior to experimentation, it was surprising to note how quickly many of these subjects developed patterns of intensive use. Most ironic was the fact that the issue of addiction seemed a more prominent concern among those who began using heavily from the start. One of the more extreme examples was the career criminal who, after learning that it might take months to develop a habit, began compulsively using. He reasoned that he might as well get in all the highs he could at first before having to slow down to avoid addiction. Before the end of the first month he did, in fact, slow down his use, but after convincing himself that he was not addicted, he resumed daily use. Following an extended period of denial, he was forced to realize that the occasional withdrawal symptoms he experienced were not a "touch of the flu," but were, in fact, heroin related.

Similar, though less dramatic, examples were described by the Puerto Rican youth and the Latino street hooker. Both started using daily and then slowed down after a week to avoid addiction. Daily use was resumed, however, because the hooker found it difficult to turn tricks when not high on heroin and the Puerto Rican simply lost concern over becoming addicted. Only one subject began using heroin heavily from the start without concern about addiction. This twenty-four-year-old white user told his friends to mind their own business when they warned him of the consequences of his intensive use. He did not bother to seriously consider the outcome of his regular heroin consumption until an addict he knew recounted the personal trauma of addiction. Regretfully, the initiate recalled, "it was already too late." The youngest member of the sample, an eighteen-year-old high school dropout, remembered thinking that it would be "cool" to try heroin but feared that his parents would see the holes in his arms and that he might become addicted. These reservations were apparently short-lived, however, as he commenced a daily pattern of use throughout the first month. In the second month, he was introduced to speedballing, which he preferred and switched to. Two months later, he was arrested and placed in jail where he went through withdrawal. The facts were clear to him upon reflection. He had been using heroin daily for three months, both alone or in combination with cocaine, and he had suffered distinct discomfort upon discontinuation. Nevertheless, he said it was hard for him to believe that he had really been addicted. In an obvious demonstration of denial and disregard for the problem of addiction, he resumed his speedball habit upon release from jail.

Those individuals who established slow to moderate patterns of heroin use tended to fall into two categories. The first group maintained a pattern of use which minimized the risk of addiction, while providing some degree of desired effects. Irregular patterns of heroin use, called "chipping," can be pursued for recreational or other more practical ends. An example of the latter case is found among the chronic stimulant abusers who learned that heroin is a very effective drug for coming down from a long period of continued stimulant abuse. Among this variety of user, the occasional taking of heroin is not considered to be a problem itself. This was clearly the case for a twenty-eight-year-old black male who entered treatment for a cocaine problem. In his extensive drug history, he had abused numerous drugs both alone and in combination. He liked heroin but found that it inhibited his self-perception as a very "up," lively, and active person. After becoming dependent on cocaine, he learned that a speedball at the conclusion of his cocaine "run" reduced his craving for more cocaine and enabled him to go to sleep. Because his use of heroin was incidental to that of cocaine, the heroin was not perceived by him to be a problem requiring treatment.

The second type of slow to moderate beginning user differed from the previous category in that they were not able to maintain a moderate and irregular pattern of consumption. For some unexplained reason, they tended to conclude the initial moderate pattern of use with a period of abstinence. This was followed by a resumption of use at a frequency exceeding previous levels of consumption. This pattern of progression was most common among female respondents. One of the women in the sample first tried heroin at a time when she was already dependent on Tuinal, a central nervous system depressant. She recalled liking the heroin high even though it negated the effect of the Tuinals she had taken. She used heroin a number of additional times before deciding that she should stop. The expense of heroin was more than she could afford at a time when it was difficult enough for her to attend to her addiction to depressants. Following a few months of hard times, a heroin dealer she knew offered to set her up with a steady flow of customers if she would deal for him. For one month, she dealt heroin without using any herself but then started testing batches and later developed a heavy habit. The high-class call girl in the sample demonstrated a similar pattern. She experimented with heroin four times in as many months before quitting. After six months of booming prostitution business, she was making huge sums of money but feeling very strained. She took heroin again "for the heck of it" and rapidly progressed to a heavy habit, which depleted all of her money.

Three quarters of the sample interviewed developed a physical addiction to heroin in their brief, less-than-two-year histories of use. Those who had never been addicted were much more inclined to believe that their use of heroin might extend on indefinitely. As one recreational user stated, "I did like it, and I don't want to stop. I'll probably use it the rest of my life. I don't want to get strung out, but I can enjoy it without going to extremes." In contrast, among those who had become addicted, the desire to stop using or to remain abstinent if they had stopped, was much more common. For one quarter of the sample, their experiences had created a series of problems which they clearly related to heroin. The obvious means of addressing these difficulties was to stop using heroin. In two cases, the discovery of the subject's addiction by a family member resulted in decisions to discontinue use. In both cases, the family had played a very supportive role and helped the respondents stay heroin free. In their cases, being arrested and bottoming out financially were strong incentives to terminate addiction. The advertising executive recalled that upon realizing she was addicted and that she had gone through her entire savings, an evaluation of her situation and future were necessary. The decision to quit heroin was motivated, in part, by her realization that the idea of being a "junkie" did not fit into the way she wished to think of herself.

DISCUSSION

In reviewing both the drug histories and personal accounts of these new heroin users, a number of distinct, though not necessarily independent, motivations and patterns of use become apparent.

Perhaps most crucial in setting the stage for heroin experimentation was an involvement in social networks where drug use was a common and integral component of social relations. While the groups which these individuals were first associated with rarely included heroin among the drugs which were acceptable to use, the orientation toward altered consciousness and the criteria developed to evaluate the relative merits of various intoxicants are central to understanding the phenomena investigated. As previously discussed, this change was also crucial in explaining the gradual attitudinal shift away from earlier considerations of heroin as a highly stigmatized substance that they would never use.

The patterns of drug use reported by this sample represent a full spectrum of possible drug combinations from single drug abusers to heavy multiple drug abusers. Traditionally, the most common pattern of abuse among the drug dependent was largely confined to the individual substance that an addict preferred. Although a heroin addict would substitute another narcotic for heroin when he was unable to obtain his preferred drug, such switching was based on practical necessity rather than choice. Within this traditional pattern, a user who discovered a new drug of preference would tend to substitute it completely over his old drug of choice. Over the past ten to fifteen years, patterns of multiple drug consumption have become much more prominent. In this more recent pattern, users have grown to accept a variety of drugs they are willing to take on a regular basis. When a new drug is discovered, it tends not to replace another, but is added to the assortment of substances regularly consumed as part of a multiple drug repertoire. A prominent feature of this new trend is the combined use of intoxicants to produce a wide array of different highs based on the interaction effects of drugs being mixed at any given time. Within this sample of new heroin users, multiple drug-using patterns were clearly evident among three quarters of the group. At the extremes of the spectrum, however, an equal number of users (25%) were categorized within the single-drug and heavy multiple-drug (five or more drugs regularly consumed) patterns. As a consequence, the numbers of drugs normally consumed by these users did not seem to impact on decisions relating to heroin experimentation.

In explaining and/or justifying their decisions to try heroin, most respondents adopted a carefree attitude once their major concerns had been satisfactorily addressed. Most often, the rationales were expressed as variations on the theme of, "What the hell?" For example, "I'll try anything once, so I figures, what the hell, I'll see what it's like," or "I was curious and had the opportunity, so what the hell, I tried it."

In contrast to the curious or adventurous posturing used to explain their initial heroin experimentation, decisions to continue using were usually justified by some variation of practical considerations. For the eight subjects who used heroin in conjunction with a stimulant (either cocaine or Preludin), the practical consideration was the interaction effect of the two drugs. Though it is not possible to know how many of these individuals might have progressed to using heroin independent of their established fondness for stimulants, it is clear that their abuse of stimulant drugs was a primary factor contributing to the use of heroin at the time of introduction. Those individuals who used heroin in conjunction with a stimulant drug accounted for the largest sub-group of new heroin users in the Chicago sample.

Other practical rationales used to explain continued heroin use included that it made them feel good (they liked the high) and that it enhanced their status among friends who were also users. Second only to those respondents who liked heroin because of its interaction effect with stimulants, continued heroin use as an effective means of coping with or escaping from feelings of alienation or disenchantment was a common and recurring theme. The fact that the long-term effects of using heroin aggravated rather than alleviated problems seemed to have no impact on perceptions of the drug's desirability as a self-medication for depression. Though it is not clear to what degree underlying self-destruction impulses may have reinforced the use of heroin among those seeking to escape emotional strain, it did appear that significant additional problems had to accumulate before these individuals began to question the advisability of continued heroin use.

This study has attempted to provide insight into the variety of characteristics to be found among Chicago's new heroin users and, through analysis of the subject's own accounts, suggest some of the more important factors contributing to decisions to use the drug. Though design and sampling limitations do not allow for conclusive comparisons of this group with previous generations of new users, some general observations are possible. In most respects, there does not appear to be a dramatic difference in the composition of this group as compared to the range in characteristics found among older generations of Chicago heroin users. The single factor which may significantly differentiate this group from previous cohorts is the prominence of stimulant abuse in conjunction with heroin during the introductory stages of heroin experimentation. It seems likely, at least over the short term, that heroin trends in Chicago will be influenced to a considerable degree by trends of stimulant abuse. The impact of increasing heroin purity which has been associated with the epidemics in other metropolitan areas has not been noted as yet in Chicago. With an average purity of only 1-2% heroin in street samples, the subjects included in this study were not influenced by any change in improved heroin quality. In comparing Chicago's stable trends to the epidemic trends in other urban areas, it appears likely that heroin purity is a crucial variable in accounting for the presence or absence of a current epidemic.

The data from this study, in conjunction with numerous other independent data sources from across the country, were reviewed by analysts at NIDA during the first half of 1984. Although each source of data provided only a limited view of the national picture, like pieces of a puzzle, they were linked together to form a broader perspective. Having participated only in the local analysis of the Chicago study, it is not possible to include a discussion of the national overview here. It can be reported, however, that the evidence indicated that the current changes in heroin availability and use, unlike earlier epidemics, were regional in scope and, in large part, limited to the country's northeast metropolitan corridor which originally and later emerged in selected areas of southern California and mid-central United States.

REFERENCES

Akins, C. and Beschner, G. 1980. Ethnography: A Research Tool for Policy Makers in the Drug and Alcohol Fields. (Department of Health and Human Services Publication No. (ADM) 80-946). Washington, DC: U.S. Government Printing Office.

Hughs, P. 1977. Behind the Wall of Respect: Community Experiments in Heroin Addiction Control. Chicago: The University of Chicago Press.

Lindesmith, A. 1947. Opiate Addiction. Bloomington, IN: Principia Press.

Richards, L. and Blevens, R. (eds.). 1977. The Epidemiology of Drug Abuse: Current Issues (Monograph 10). Washington, DC: National Institute on Drug Abuse Research.

Weppner, R. (ed.). 1977. Street Ethnography. Beverly Hills, CA: Sage.

Wiebel, W. 1984. Patterns and trends of drug abuse in Chicago and Illinois. In National Institute on Drug Abuse, Epidemiology of Drug Abuse: Research and Treatment Issues, Volume I. Rockville, MD: Author.

Wiebel, W. 1984. Chicago report: New heroin users study. Unpublished mimeograph.

Zinberg, N. 1984. Drug, Set, and Setting. New Haven, CT: Yale University Press.

INTRODUCTION TO CHAPTER 16

Fagan (Chapter 8) showed us that skid row is not only a place, it is a culture and a way of life. In this chapter, Kaestner and co-authors use survey methodology to quantify the degree of drug and alcohol use in a similar place and through a similar way of life -- the single-room-occupancy (S.R.O.) hotel in New York City.

The magnitude of the drug and alcohol use problem is alarming. Nearly one-third of these people are dependent on one or more drugs. Fifteen percent have been treated for addiction of one type or another. Sprinkled throughout the chapter are the patterns or "footprints" we have learned to look for: young people use different drugs than do older people; women use different drugs than do men; drug use differs from Hispanics to blacks to whites.

We learn then that the S.R.O. hotel in New York City is not only a place and a way of life, it is also the locale for a number of sub-groups with different drug- and alcohol-using habits. The drug-using problems of a large city, such as New York, are not just composed of places such as skid row and the S.R.O. hotel nor specific lifestyles, these are problems of diverse populations which have gathered in identifiable communities. It is only when we understand the differences between communities such as the S.R.O. hotels and skid rows that we can begin to construct preventions and treatments for those who participate in their cultures.

CHAPTER 16

DRUG USE AMONG TENANTS OF SINGLE-ROOM-OCCUPANCY HOTELS IN NEW YORK CITY

Elisabeth Kaestner, Rozanne Marel,
Blanche Frank, James Schmeidler,
and Michael Maranda

ABSTRACT

Procedures and findings are presented for a major survey of drug use among residents of single-room-occupancy (S.R.O.) hotels in New York City conducted by a state agency as part of a statewide survey of drug use. These hotels provide modest facilities and often accommodate the unemployed, the poor, the elderly, ex-offenders, and mental patients released to the community. S.R.O. residents in New York City are predominantly young men from minority groups with annual incomes below $7,000. A random sample of 236 S.R.O. residents, 12 years and older, were interviewed by telephone. The interviews probed the use of illicit drugs and prescription drugs. The sample was then projected to reflect drug use among an estimated 23,100 S.R.O. residents in New York City.

ELISABETH KAESTNER is Senior Research Scientist at the New York State Division of Substance Abuse Services; ROZANNE MAREL is Head of Survey Research for the New York State Division of Substance Abuse Services; BLANCHE FRANK is the Chief of Epidemiology for the New York State Division of Substance Abuse Services; JAMES SCHMEIDLER is Special Lecturer in Mathematics at the New Jersey Institute of Technology and Associate Statistician at the New York State Division of Substance Abuse Services; MICHAEL MARANDA is a member of the Epidemiology Research Unit of the New York State Division of Substance Abuse Services.

Drug use is a significant problem among S.R.O. residents. In the six months prior to the survey, 12,700 S.R.O. residents (55% of S.R.O. residents) have used illicit drugs and/or prescription drugs non-medically. Of these, 7,000 residents (31%) are considered to be serious abusers of drugs, many of whom have used seven or more drugs in the six months prior to the survey. An estimated 5,100 S.R.O. residents (22%) see themselves as dependent on one or more drugs. This does not include dependency on alcohol or on pre- scription drugs used medically.

An analysis of characteristics of drug-using S.R.O. tenants reveal that females have higher rates of use than males, that young adults, as well as older adults, are drug users, and that blacks and Hispanics have higher use rates than Whites. A comparison with household residents in New York City show that S.R.O. residents have rates of drug use that are significantly greater than the rest of New York City's residents.

INTRODUCTION

The New York State Division of Substance Abuse Services periodically surveys the household population as part of a continual monitoring of the drug abuse problem within the state. The Division of Substance Abuse Services is the single state agency that is responsible for planning, funding, and coordinating drug abuse treatment and prevention in New York State. The purpose of these surveys is to determine the extent of drug use in New York State; that is, what drugs are used, by whom, and with what frequency. The surveys are empirical in nature. We, the research staff of the agency, are responsible for the design and imple- mentation of the surveys. The type of work we do is applied social science research. Freeman and Rossi (1984) point out in their discussion of applied sociology that applied sociologists are focused on practical payoffs in contrast to conventional sociologists who tend to defend the theoretical significance of their work.

Unlike our previous household surveys, the 1981 survey included residents of single-room-occupancy (S.R.O.) hotels in New York City. These residents constitute a varied population, many of whom have drug-abuse problems. Residents of S.R.O. hotels generally lack the financial resources to afford more traditional housing. The S.R.O. type of housing usually provides modest facilities including a room in which to sleep, a communal kitchen, and shared bathrooms; rent is within public assistance limits. In the past, these hotels provided temporary hosing for the working poor and the student. Today, these hotels also accommodate the unemployed, the elderly, ex-offenders, and mental patients released to the community.

Previous studies of S.R.O. tenants in New York City, where the largest concentration in the state resides, have focused on segments of that population (New York State, 1980; Siegal, 1978). This study has attempted to survey a probability sample of the S.R.O. population throughout the city, while also surveying the household population. Inferences can, therefore, be made to the general S.R.O. population in New York City as they can be made to the household population.

METHODOLOGY OF THE SURVEY

The central focus of this report is drug use among the S.R.O. population.[1] The assessment of drug use among S.R.O. hotel residents in New York City was the first effort at surveying this population. Since this study was part of the 1981 statewide household survey, areas of inquiry covered in the interviews were those that applied to the New York State population at large. While previous surveys used face-to-face interviewing, the 1981 survey was conducted by telephone from a central location. A private research organization did the actual interviewing.

A list of 199 lower-priced hotels located in New York City provided the universe of hotels. Hotels were stratified by the five boroughs, by price (under $36 per week, $36 to $50 per week, over $50 per week, lodging house), and by neighborhood. From this stratified universe, 47 S.R.O.'s were randomly selected with a probability proportional to the size of the hotel.

Letters were sent to the managers of the hotels selected for the study which informed them of the purposes and procedures of the study and promised them a monetary incentive for their cooperation. Specially trained field workers were assigned to work in the hotels. The first step was to enlist the cooperation of the manager and to list all the rooms within the selected S.R.O. for the purpose of sampling. Using

---

[1] Two other reports have been issued by the New York State Division of Substance Abuse Services from its 1981 household survey: Preliminary Report: Drug use Among New York State's Household Population and The Use of Psychoactive Prescription Drugs Among New York State's Household Population.

396

specific procedures, a total of eight rooms were selected per hotel in an effort to get five completed interviews per S.R.O. Upon contacting the specific room selected, the field worker determined the primary occupant, asked him or her to participate in the study, and walked the respondent to a pay phone, except in the rare situations where respondents had phones in their rooms. A call to a toll free number was placed to the consulting firm by the field worker. A trained interviewer then immediately recontacted the respondent and proceeded with the interview. At the end of the interview, the field worker contacted the interviewer to determine whether, in fact, the interview had been completed.

In cases where the field workers did not obtain cooperation from management, another S.R.O. was selected from the list of S.R.O.'s within the same borough, price, and neighborhood. The final number of S.R.O.'s included in the sample was 43 from which 236 interviews were obtained. Results from these 236 interviews were projected to reflect drug use among an estimated 23,100 S.R.O. residents in New York City.

POPULATION CHARACTERISTICS: A COMPARISON

S.R.O. residents are predominantly young men from minority groups with self-reported annual incomes below $7,000 (Table 16.1, page 413). Often referred to as a transient population, they are indeed far less settled than the New York City household population. While 58% of S.R.O. residents lived at three or more addresses during the past five years, only 9% of New York City household residents moved that often. S.R.O. residents are typically single (59%); divorced, separated or widowed (26%); leaving 15% who are married or living together. In contrast, nearly half of the New York City household population are married.

There are also marked differences in employment status. More than three-quarters of S.R.O. residents (77%) and 70% of household residents have worked full-time at some point in their lives. Current full-time employment, however, is much less common among S.R.O. residents (25%) than among New York City householders (46%). Unemployment and disability are extremely high among S.R.O. residents -- 35% and 10% respectively -- while only 6% of household residents are unemployed and 2% are disabled. Part-time employment is more common, though (16% among S.R.O. residents versus 8% among householders).

New York City household residents are somewhat more educated than S.R.O. residents -- 13% went beyond 2 years of college compared to 5% of S.R.O. residents. S.R.O. tenants also were more likely to have dropped out of high school in or below the 11th grade (49%) than household residents (38%).

The majority of S.R.O. residents are between 18 and 34 years old (64%) and male (71%), whereas the majority of household residents are 35 years or older (57%) and female (53%). Furthermore, most S.R.O. residents are from minority groups (40% black, 27% Hispanic, 29% white, and 4% other), whereas the majority of New York City household residents are White (57%). Finally, while 53% of S.R.O. residents have an annual income of less than $7,000, 58% of household residents report annual incomes of $15,000 or more.

DRUG USE AMONG S.R.O. TENANTS: MAJOR FINDINGS

The interview asked about the use of a variety of drugs. These included illegal or illicit drugs, such as marijuana, cocaine, heroin, illicit methadone (that is, not medically prescribed), PCP, and other hallucinogens. Questions were also asked about the non-medical use of prescription drugs, such as stimulants, tranquilizers, sedatives, analgesics, and cough medicine with codeine. Non-medical use is defined as the acquisition of these drugs through ways other than one's own prescription or the use of drugs in amounts beyond those prescribed or for purposes other than prescribed.

The sections that follow describe the extent or prevalence of use of these individual drugs, new use or incidence of use of these drugs, the combinational use of drugs, and a summary index or hierarchy of the intensity of drug use.

Prevalence of Substance Use

Marijuana and cocaine are by far the most widely used drugs among S.R.O. residents in New York City (Table 16.2, page 414). For example, two of every five S.R.O. residents used marijuana in the month prior to the survey, and one of every five residents is using cocaine. Non-medical use of psychoactive prescription drugs is less prevalent, though fairly common. Among prescription psychotropics, tranquilizers and sedatives are used most frequently; 10% of S.R.O. residents used tranquilizers non-medically and 13% used sedatives in the previous month. Stimulants and anti-depressants are used, non-medically, each at a rate of 7%.

Perhaps, the most important finding is that 15% of S.R.O. residents have used heroin and 8% have used illicit methadone in their lifetime. Another narcotic, codeine contained in cough medicine, has been used non-medically by 13%. The S.R.O. population in New York City thus contains a high proportion of persons who have been exposed to narcotic use. About one-third of the heroin users and half of the illicit methadone users report use in the month prior to the survey.

In contrast to the drugs discussed so far, use of PCP, other hallucinogens, and inhalants is less common among S.R.O. residents. Rates for lifetime use are 5% for PCP, 12% for hallucinogens, and 11% for inhalants.

Combinational Substance Use

Substances can be used singly or in combination, that is, two or more drugs, or drugs and alcohol, can be used together so that they affect the individual at the same time. The effects of one or more substances may modify or amplify the effects of another. Many mental and physical health risks are associated with using drugs in combination. In view of the potential dangers of using combinations, the finding that 42% of the S.R.O. population in New York City have recently used combinations is alarming (Table 16.3, page 416).

The substances most often used in combination by S.R.O. residents in New York City are alcohol, marijuana, and cocaine. During the six months prior to the survey, 32% of the S.R.O. residents have taken marijuana together with alcohol. The second most prevalent combination is marijuana and cocaine, used by 15% of the S.R.O. residents. Cocaine and alcohol are used in combination by 11% of the S.R.O. population.

Marijuana is also combined with other drugs. During the six months prior to the survey, 7% have used marijuana together with heroin or illicit methadone. Use of marijuana and sedatives is far more common among the S.R.O. population (8%) than use of marijuana and stimulants (3%) or use of marijuana and hallucinogens or PCP (2%). Combinations of marijuana with alcohol and a third drug are fairly prevalent (7%).

While this survey did not inquire into motives for combinational use of drugs, a previous survey of the New York State household population indicates that users either combine drugs to reduce or enhance the effects experienced from one substance, or simply take several substances together because they are readily available, as in the case of alcohol and marijuana. (New York State, 1979).

New Substance Use

New substance use, or incidence, indicates the extent to which drug use is spreading in a population. For the purpose of the study, incidence is defined as the number of residents in New York City S.R.O.'s who have started using a given drug between January 1980 (somewhat more than a year prior to the survey) and the date of the survey. The number of new users, therefore, gives some indication of the spread of drug use in the S.R.O. population in New York City.

A major finding is that cocaine attracted the largest number of new users (Table 16.4, page 417). An estimated 1,800 S.R.O. residents (8%) are new users of cocaine. The new users account for one in every five S.R.O. residents who have ever used cocaine. Non-medical use of stimulants is also spreading at a high rate among these residents. There are 1,000 new non-medical users of stimulants (4% of the S.R.O. population); nearly one in every four residents who had used stimulants was a new user. The non-medical use of sedatives, cough medicine with codeine, and the use of marijuana each increased by 3% in the S.R.O. population.

Of particular importance is the use of heroin and illicit methadone. Nearly twice as many S.R.O. residents have used heroin in their lifetime than have used illicit methadone, and 28% of the illicit methadone users started using in the year prior to the survey, compared to 12% of the heroin users.

The drugs that are spreading at the slowest rate include PCP and other hallucinogens, inhalants, tranquilizers, anti-depressants, and analgesics. Each of these drugs has spread at a rate of 1% or less among the S.R.O. population; there is no indication of a significant spread in the use of these drugs.

Substance Use Hierarchy

In order to summarize substance use and to determine the probable need for services, a hierarchy was devised that reflects the seriousness and recency of non-medical drug use (Table 16.5, page 418). The criteria used to assign each person to the highest applicable level of the hierarchy are listed below:

No Use: those who have never used drugs non-medically.

Prior Use: those who have not used any drugs during the six months prior to the survey, but used at least one drug prior to that time.

Infrequent Use:	those who have used one drug in the past six months. In the case of marijuana, use in the past month should not exceed nine days; in the case of a drug other than marijuana, use in the past month should not exceed three days.
Regular Use:	those who used two or three drugs in the past six months, or those who used marijuana between 10 and 24 days in the past month, or those who used a drug other than marijuana between four and seven days in the past month.
Substantial Use:	those who used four drugs in the past six months, or those who used marijuana at least 25 days during the past month, or those who used another illicit drug between 8 and 11 days during the past month, or those who used a prescription drug non-medically between 8 and 14 days during the past month.
Extensive Use:	those who used five or more drugs in the past six months, or those who used an illicit drug other than marijuana at least 12 days during the past

month, <u>or</u> those who used a prescription drug non-medically at least 15 days during the past month.

The higher the category in which the person is placed, ranging from "no use" to "extensive use," the more likely the person is to have used many drugs and to have used them frequently during the past month.

At least one of every seven S.R.O. residents in New York City is an extensive user, having used five or more different drugs during the six months prior to the survey, or having used drugs other than marijuana frequently in the month prior to the survey. There are slightly more S.R.O. residents who are substantial users: 16% of the population or 3,600 persons.

Compared to extensive or substantial use, regular or infrequent use is less common. Of the S.R.O. population, 11% are regular users and 13% are infrequent users. Another 15% have used drugs in the past, but have not used during the six months prior to the survey. Finally, there are 30% of the S.R.O. population in New York City who have never used drugs non-medically.

DRUG-RELATED PROBLEMS, DEPENDENCY, AND SEEKING TREATMENT

This part of the report discusses problems that have resulted from drug use, the users' perception of being physically or psychologically dependent on drugs, the willingness to seek treatment, and current or past treatment.

Problems Associated With Drug Use

Questions in the survey addressed problems of

functioning in everyday life as well as physical health. Users were asked whether their drug use ever caused problems in the areas of family, friends, work and school, health, accidents, or the law. Almost half (48%) of S.R.O. residents report having experienced one or more problems in these areas as a result of using drugs (Table 16.6, page 419).

The most common type of problem was experienced in relationships with family and friends; one of every four S.R.O. residents reports having experienced such problems. These problems are as often attributed to the non-medical use of prescription drugs as they are attributed to the use of marijuana or of other illegal drugs. Nearly one of every five S.R.O. residents says that he or she has had problems with the law as a result of using drugs, especially with illegal drugs.

Many S.R.O. residents state having health problems as a result of using drugs which is nearly one of every five persons. A large number of S.R.O. residents also report problems in the area of work or school (17%). Accidents were mentioned less frequently; however, 1% of S.R.O. residents have had automobile accidents and 8% have had other accidents they attributed to drug use.

Perceptions of Drug Dependence

Drug dependency may include physical aspects, such as the appearance of withdrawal symptoms after sudden cessation of drug use, or it may include psychological factors, such as the inability to function without the mood-altering effects of the drug. In this survey, users were asked whether they saw themselves as dependent on certain drugs or were using them too much in the course of the past year. The findings show that one of every five S.R.O. residents sees himself or herself as dependent. This figure does not include drug-dependent persons who use prescription drugs as prescribed, nor does it include persons dependent on alcohol.

S.R.O. residents are more likely to feel dependent on illegal drugs than on prescription drugs. For example, 9% mentioned prescription drugs, whereas 11% mentioned marijuana, and 11% mentioned other illegal drugs. Specifically, 6% mentioned heroin, 6% mentioned cocaine, and 4% mentioned illicit methadone.

Another measure of dependency that could be seen as more objective is the level of drug use; that is, the extent and frequency of drug use as developed in the drug-use hierarchy. Using this criterion, close to one-third of the S.R.O. residents in New York City could be seen as dependent on one or more drugs used non-medically (31%). This is an alarming figure indicating that a large part of this population is in need of treatment.

Seeking Treatment

Of the 23,100 S.R.O. residents, 3,400 or 15% have received treatment for drug abuse, including 1,500 who are currently in treatment. Most of the 3,400 S.R.O. residents went to drug treatment programs (67%). Some went to hospitals (9%) or mental health clinics (3%), to private doctors (3%), or to self-help groups (6%). The remaining 12% received treatment in other settings. Of the 5,100 S.R.O. residents who reported having felt dependent on drugs or using too much, 51% have received treatment or are currently in treatment.

When S.R.O. residents were asked whether they would seek some form of treatment if they had a drug problem and needed help, 97% stated that they would seek help. The treatment settings, in order of preference, are: private doctor (35%), self-help groups (24%), drug treatment program (23%), hospital (13%), and mental health clinic (5%).

Thus, while 35% of the S.R.O. residents' first choice is to see a private doctor for a drug problem, only 3% of the 3,400 S.R.O. residents who received treatment actually saw a private doctor. Two-third of those who received treatment went to drug programs; however, less than one-quarter of the S.R.O. population would select this setting as treatment of first choice.

CHARACTERISTICS OF DRUG-USING S.R.O. TENANTS

Though S.R.O. residents are frequently regarded as a homogeneous group, there are sufficient differences among residents to warrant examination of drug use by sub-groups of S.R.O. residents. The discussion that follows describes findings by age, by sex, and by ethnicity.

Drug Use By Age

Young adults (18 to 34 years old) show the highest rates of drug use among S.R.O. residents. About two-thirds have taken drugs non-medically in the six months prior to the survey. The most popular drug, marijuana, has been used by 59% of residents in this age group, and cocaine by 31%. Older S.R.O. residents (above 34 years) are far less likely to have recently used marijuana (25%) or cocaine (18%).

Recent use of heroin and illicit methadone, the narcotics most often used by the addict, is most

407

prevalent among those 25 to 34 years old (10% each).
Recent use of these narcotic drugs is more common among
the older residents (above 34 years) than among younger
adults (18 to 24 years). Non-medical use of prescription drugs is also common among adult S.R.O.
residents, with recent use being generally more
prevalent among those age 25 to 34 years old.

Drug Use By Sex
Drug use varies by sex, especially among S.R.O.
residents where a higher proportion of women are
involved in drug use than are men. For example, 58% of
women in S.R.O.'s have recently used marijuana and 38%
have used cocaine, whereas among men, 43% have used
marijuana and 22% cocaine. Non-medical use of
prescription drugs is also more prevalent among women.
Examinations of levels of drug use also showed marked
differences between men and women in S.R.O.'s, with
more women using at high levels.

There is one clear reversal in the pattern
described so far: more men than women have used heroin
(8% versus 5%). However, consistent with the overall
trend, more women than men have used illicit methadone
(9% versus 4%).

Drug Use By Ethnicity
Drug use rates vary somewhat between ethnic sub-
groups. Generally, Hispanic and black S.R.O. residents
are using more than do white residents. In fact,
findings for use in the six months prior to the survey,
for example, show that use rates for marijuana and
cocaine are higher among Hispanics than among blacks
(marijuana, 57% versus 54%; cocaine, 33% versus 27%)

and both groups have higher rates than whites (marijuana, 30%; cocaine, 17%).

Considering recent use of heroin and illicit methadone among S.R.O. residents, blacks have the highest rates (heroin, 10%; illicit methadone, 8%), followed by Hispanics (8% and 6% respectively), and whites (3% and 2% respectively).

Patterns of non-medical prescription drug use vary by drug, but use rates differ only slightly between S.R.O. residents of various ethnic groups, and differences are largely inconsistent.

COMPARISON OF DRUG USE BETWEEN S.R.O. TENANTS AND HOUSEHOLD RESIDENTS

To put the findings for S.R.O. tenants in perspective and to appreciate the extent of drug use in this special population, overall comparisons are made with the New York City household population. In addition, a second comparison is made between young adult Black males in the S.R.O. population and in the New York City household population. Young Black males constitute an important sub-group of S.R.O. tenants.

An Overall Comparison With Household Residents

Comparisons were separated for selected demographic variables such as age, sex, ethnicity, and income. Without exception, use rates are much higher among the S.R.O. population than among the New York City household population. For example, 55% of S.R.O. residents have used drugs non-medically during the six months prior to the survey, compared to 16% of the household population.

New use of drugs, especially, spread at a higher rate among the S.R.O. residents. For example, during the year prior to the survey, 8% began using cocaine, 2% began using heroin and 2% began using illicit methadone, while among the household population, 1% began using cocaine and few (less than 0.5%) began using illegal narcotics. Combinational drug use is also more widespread among S.R.O. residents, reflecting their greater involvement in drug use. Levels of drug use, as indicated by the hierarchy, are also much higher among S.R.O. residents. For example, 15% of S.R.O. residents are extensive users, compared to 1% of New York City household residents. Substantial users comprise 16% of S.R.O. residents compared to 2% among household residents.

Other important aspects of drug use also show that S.R.O. residents are, overall, more deeply involved in using drugs than are household residents. For example, among S.R.O. residents, 22% admit to feeling dependent on drugs (3% among householders), 48% state having experienced problems as a result of using drugs (14% among householders), 15% have sought treatment for drug abuse problems (1% among householders), and 6% are currently in treatment (0.1% among householders). In summary, on the major aspects of non-medical drug use examined in the survey, S.R.O. residents show considerably greater involvement than household residents. The extent of the differences in use rates, however, varies considerably depending on the specific drugs and the specific sub-groups of the population that are examined.

A Comparison Between Young Black Men in the S.R.O. Population and in the Household Population

Many S.R.O. residents are young adult black men within the low-income groups. In order to evaluate the

410

findings of the survey even further, drug-use rates for this sub-group of S.R.O. residents are compared to drug-use rates of household residents who had similar demographic characteristics. The comparison group consisted of black men, ages 18 to 34 years, whose annual incomes were less than $15,000, and who resided in New York City. While 16% of the S.R.O. population met these criteria, only 2% of the household population did.

In the comparison of this sub-group with similar household residents, S.R.O. residents are three times as likely to have used drugs recently as are New York City householders. During the six months prior to the survey, 75% of this sub-group of tenants have used drugs, as compared to 25% of this sub-group of household residents.

When use of drugs in the past six months is compared, S.R.O. tenants are also using at higher rates than are householders of similar demographic characteristics. For example, 69% of young black men among S.R.O. tenants recently used marijuana, compared to 25% of the respective householders. Cocaine is the only drug which has the same rate of recent use, 18%.

When levels of drug use are considered, it becomes apparent that a large proportion of this sub-group of householders are substantial or extensive users (17%); however, a much higher proportion of the sub-group of S.R.O. tenants use at substantial or extensive levels (32%). It appears that the young black men who are household residents either use at high levels or do not use at all. Among the young black men who are S.R.O. tenants, most are users.

A second important aspect of the findings is that young black men among New York City household residents

411

are five times more likely than household residents at large to use at substantial or extensive levels (17% versus 3%). Among S.R.O. tenants, however, substantial or extensive levels of drug use are as common among the young black men as they are among the S.R.O. population at large (32% versus 31%).

In conclusion, non-medical drug use is significantly greater among the S.R.O. population than among New York City's household population. When the modal S.R.O. group (that is, young Black men) is compared to the similar group in the household population, drug use rates remain significantly greater.

REFERENCES

Freeman, H. E. and Rossi, P. H. 1984. Furthering the applied side of sociology. American Sociological Review 49:571-580.

New York State Department of Social Services. 1980. Survey of the Needs and Problems of Single Room Occupancy Hotel Residents on the Upper West Side of Manhattan, New York City. Albany: Author.

New York State Division of Substance Abuse Services. 1979. Polydrug Use among the New York Household Population. New York: Author.

New York State Division of Substance Abuse Services. 1981. Preliminary Report: Drug Use among New York State's Household Population. New York: Author.

New York State Division of Substance Abuse Services. 1982. The Use of Psychocative Prescription Drugs among New York State's Household Population. New York: Author.

Siegal, H. 1978. Outposts of the Forgotten. New Brunswick, NJ: Transaction Books.

TABLE 16.1
DEMOGRAPHIC CHARACTERISTICS

	New York City			
	S.R.O. Tenants		Household Residents	
	Number	Percent	Number	Percent
Age				
12-17	400	2%	630,000	11%
18-24	6,600	29%	737,000	13%
25-34	8,200	35%	1,120,000	19%
35+	7,900	34%	3,243,000	57%
Sex				
Male	16,500	71%	2,680,000	47%
Female	6,600	29%	3,050,000	53%
Ethnicity				
White	6,600	29%	3,246,000	57%
Black	9,300	40%	1,412,000	25%
Hispanic	6,200	27%	884,000	15%
Other	1,000	4%	183,000	3%
Unknown	0	—	5,000	—
Income				
None	600	2%	86,000	2%
Less than $7,000	11,600	51%	831,000	15%
$7,000 to $14,999	7,500	33%	1,375,000	25%
$15,000 or more	3,100	14%	3,126,000	58%
Unknown	300	—	312,000	—
Total for each section	23,100	100%	5,730,000	100%

TABLE 16.2

SUBSTANCE ABUSE AMONG SINGLE-ROOM-OCCUPANCY (S.R.O.) HOTEL RESIDENTS IN NEW YORK CITY

23,100 SRO Hotel Residents – Spring 1981

Type of Substance#	Never Used		Lifetime Use (Used at Least Once)		Response Unknown		Recent Use (Used in Past 6 Mos.)		Current Use (Used In Past 30 Days)	
	N	%	N	%	N	%	N	%	N	%
Marijuana	8,800	38	14,300	62	0	0	10,900	47	9,900	43
Cocaine	14,700	64	8,400	36	0	0	6,000	26	4,700	20
PCP (Angel Dust)	22,000	95	1,100	5	0	0	300	1	**	*
Hallucinogens#	20,300	88	2,800	12	0	0	300	1	100	*
Inhalants	20,500	89	2,600	11	0	0	400	2	300	1
Heroin	19,700	85	3,400	15	0	0	1,600	7	1,200	5
Methadone (Illicit)	21,300	92	1,800	8	0	0	1,200	5	900	4
Tranquilizers##	19,200	83	3,900	17	0	0	2,700	12	2,400	10
Sedatives##	18,300	79	4,800	21	0	0	3,500	15	3,000	13

Note: The numbers reported in the table are low estimates since they do not include the non-respondents.

* Less than 0.5%.   ** Less than 50.

\# Hallucinogens such as LSD, mescaline and psilocybin; inhalants such as glue/solvents, sprays, nitrous oxide and Amyl Nitrite; tranquilizers such as Valium and Librium; sedatives such as barbiturates and methaqualone; stimulants such as amphetamines and diet pills; anti-depressants such as Elavil and Imipramine; analgesics such as Demerol and Darvon.

\## Refers only to the non-medical use of prescription drugs, defined as use other than according to a physician's direction (that is, in amounts beyond the prescribed dose and/or obtained from a non-medical source).

TABLE 16.2 (continued)

Type of Substance#	Never Used		Lifetime Use (Used at Least Once)		Response Unknown	Recent Use (Past 6 Mos.)		Current Use (Past 30 Days)	
	N	%	N	%	N	N	%	N	%
Stimulants##	19,000	82	4,100	18	0	2,800	12	1,500	7
Anti-Depressants##	20,800	90	2,300	10	0	1,800	8	1,600	7
Analgesics##	21,000	91	2,100	9	100	1,400	6	900	4
Cough Medicine with Codeine##	20,200	87	2,900	13	0	1,100	5	700	3

Note: The numbers reported in the table are low estimates since they do not include the non-respondents.

* Less than 0.5%.   ** Less than 50.

Hallucinogens such as LSD, mescaline and psilocybin; inhalants such as glue/solvents, sprays, nitrous oxide and Amyl Nitrite; tranquilizers such as Valium and Librium; sedatives such as barbiturates and methaqualone; stimulants such as amphetamines and diet pills; anti-depressants such as Elavil and Imipramine; analgesics such as Demerol and Darvon.

Refers only to the non-medical use of prescription drugs, defined as use other than according to a physician's direction (that is, in amounts beyond the prescribed dose and/or obtained from a non-medical source).

TABLE 16.3

RECENT USE* OF COMBINATIONS OF SUBSTANCES
AMONG SINGLE-ROOM-OCCUPANCY (S.R.O.) HOTEL
RESIDENTS IN NEW YORK CITY

23,100 S.R.O. Hotel Residents - Spring 1981

Combination of Substances	Number	Percent
Marijuana and Alcohol	7,500	32
Marijuana and Sedatives**	1,800	8
Marijuana and Stimulants**	700	3
Marijuana and Cocaine	3,400	15
Marijuana and Hallucinogens or PCP***	400	2
Marijuana and Heroin/Methadone	1,700	7
Sedatives** and Alcohol	1,000	4
Stimulants** and Alcohol	900	4
Cocaine and Alcohol	2,500	11
Marijuana, Alcohol, and a Third Substance***	1,700	7
Other Combinations	3,600	16
Any Combination	9,600	42

Note: The numbers reported in the table are low estimates since they do not include the non-respondents.

* Recent use refers to use in the six months prior to the survey.

** Refers only to the non-medical use of prescription drugs, defined as use other than according to a physician's direction (that is, in amounts beyond the prescribed dose and/or obtained from a non-medical source).

*** Hallucinogens such as LSD, mescaline and psilocybin; inhalants such as glue/solvents, sprays, nitrous oxide and Amyl Nitrite; tranquilizers such as Valium and Librium; sedatives such as barbiturates and methaqualone; stimulants such as amphetamines and diet pills; anti-depressants such as Elavil and Imipramine; analgesics such as Demerol and Darvon.

416

TABLE 16.4

NEW SUBSTANCE USE SINCE JANUARY 1980
AMONG SINGLE-ROOM-OCCUPANCY (S.R.O.) HOTEL
RESIDENTS IN NEW YORK CITY

23,100 S.R.O. Hotel Residents - Spring 1981

Type of Substances	Number	Percent
Marijuana	700	3
Cocaine	1,800	8
PCP (Angel Dust)	100	*
Hallucinogens**	200	1
Inhalants**	100	*
Heroin	400	2
Methadone (Illicit)	500	2
Tranquilizers***	300	1
Sedatives***	800	3
Stimulants***	1,000	4
Anti-Depressants***	100	*
Analgesics***	300	1
Cough Medicine with Codeine	700	3

Note: The numbers reported in the table are low estimates since they do not include the non-respondents.

* Less than 0.5%.

** Hallucinogens such as LSD, mescaline and psilocybin; inhalants such as glue/solvents, sprays, nitrous oxide and Amyl Nitrite; tranquilizers such as Valium and Librium; sedatives such as barbiturates and methaqualone; stimulants such as amphetamines and diet pills; anti-depressants such as Elavil and Imipramine; analgesics such as Demerol and Darvon.

*** Refers only to the non-medical use of prescription drugs, defined as use other than according to a physician's direction (that is, in amounts beyond the prescribed dose and/or obtained from a non-medical source).

TABLE 16.5

LEVEL OF SUBSTANCE USE AMONG
SINGLE-ROOM-OCCUPANCY (S.R.O.) HOTEL
RESIDENTS IN NEW YORK CITY

23,100 S.R.O. Hotel Residents - Spring 1981

Level of Use*	Number	Percent
No Use	7,000	30
Prior Use	3,400	15
Infrequent Use	3,100	13
Regular Use	2,600	11
Substantial Use	3,600	16
Extensive Use	3,400	15
Total	23,100	100

---

* Level of substance use or substance-use hierarchy is a
classification of S.R.O. hotel residents which reflects the
history and recency of drug use as well as the extent and
frequency of use (see detailed explanation in text).

TABLE 16.6

PROBLEMS ATTRIBUTED TO DRUG USE
AMONG SINGLE-ROOM-OCCUPANCY (S.R.O.) HOTEL
RESIDENTS IN NEW YORK CITY

	Problems Due to the Use of:							
	Any Drugs#		Marijuana		Other Illegal Drugs##		Prescription Drugs###	
Problem Area:	N	%	N	%	N	%	N	%
Family/Friends	5,900	25	2,600	11	2,700	12	3,000	13
Work/School	3,900	17	1,800	8	2,000	9	2,000	9
Motor Vehicle Accidents	200	1	**	*	100	*	200	1
Other Accidents	1,800	8	100	*	600	2	1,400	6
Health	4,500	20	1,300	6	2,100	9	1,900	8
Law	4,300	19	1,600	7	2,500	11	1,800	8

_____

Note: The numbers reported in the table are low estimates since they do not include the non-respondents.

*   Less than 0.5%.   **   Less than 50.

Any drugs refers to marijuana, other illegal drugs, and prescription drugs.

Other illegal drugs include cocaine, PCP, hallucinogens, inhalants, heroin, and methadone (illicit).

Prescription drugs include tranquilizers such as Valium and Librium; sedatives such as barbiturates and methaqualone; stimulants such as amphetamines and diet pills; anti-depressants such as Elavil and Imipramine; analgesics such as Demerol and Darvon.

SUMMARY: U.S. SUBSTANCE USE IN ADULT POPULATIONS

It is difficult for the non-drug user to understand substance-using behavior. The authors of these chapters have taken a twofold approach toward providing us such an understanding: 1) the development of abstract theories of substance use and 2) the reporting of user's life experiences and motivations.

The development of theories is a crucial issue. As Hoffman (Chapter 11) points out, our theories of cause are intimately related to our methods of treatment. Hoffman begins this work with definitions of the continuum of drug use from daily routines to dependence to compulsions to addictions. She alerts us to psychiatric definitions of abuse and creates for us a typology of abusers (Table 11.3, page 297). She then goes on to a typology of patterns of use. Having created a terminology, she instructs us that to understand drug use, we must understand the user, the substance, and the setting -- elements in the traditional epidemiological model. In Tables 11.4 and 11.5, pages 298 and 300 respectively, she summarizes existing theories of human behavior and their relationships to drug use. Finally, she explicates the model of substance abuse developed by the Society for the Study of Addiction to Alcohol and Other Drugs.

Prather's work (Chapter 12) on women's use of tranquilizers is a good application of Hoffman's paradigm. The drugs are tranquilizers, the users are women, and the setting is, by and large, medical. Only by understanding each of these variables can we comprehend the behavior.

Prather notes that this is a female behavior, re-enforcing the conclusion we reached in our consideration of the work of Markides and Krause (Chapter 10). Normative patterns of behavior differ by sex-role. Thus, it is not surprising that we find sex-role differences in drug-using behavior.

The setting in which the drug use by females occurs is overwhelmingly medical. This brings on to the scene other role players such as physicians and pharmacists, as well as others who must come to accept the behavior as "treatment" and the drug as "medication." Prather goes on to report users' understandings of their behavior in their own words. As we have seen with alcohol use (Section 3, Summary), the users have developed a coherent rationale for their behavior. We also see here that once the behavior is in place, self-definitions change, and the definitions that others, such as physicians and family, make of the user change. The use of the drug becomes part of their social identity, making it even more difficult to alter the behavior.

Finally, Prather notes, in passing, the role of the pharmaceutical industry and governmental regulation. Though this is an issue which is not central to the author's concerns in this chapter, it will surface later in Chapter 17 in a consideration of power relations in substance abuse.

A contrast to Prather's suburban, tranquilizer-using women are Goldstein's New York City prostitutes (Chapter 13). Here also, we can apply Hoffman's paradigm of drug, user, and setting. Goldstein suggests that the violence associated with "the life" may be a product of: 1) the drug and its physiological actions, 2) the economic compulsion which comes from

421

the addiction, or 3) the nature of the illegal system for distributing drugs. Like Fagan's skid row alcoholics (Chapter 8), these women are immersed in a subculture from which escape is very difficult.

In Winick's study (Chapter 14), population is also a specific subculture and a specific setting: doctors and nurses. Winick finds that the drugs used are many, especially alcohol, amphetamines, and barbiturates. The reasons for their use are given by self-report data and include overwork and fatigue, illness, recreation, family problems, and stress. Access and awareness were also issues described by these professionals as leading to drug use. These are issues which we have seen associated with drug and alcohol use very early in the careers of medical students (Clark et al., Chapter 6). Again, we must consider carefully that the reasons given by users are rationales.

This issue of rationale is written large in Wiebel's work on personal decisions to use heroin (Chapter 15). The author looks at new heroin users and asks them to describe their entry into the habit. Almost all described the key role of family or friends. Returning to Hoffman's paradigm, we see that the drugs vary but are related to one another in effects as reported by users. The settings invariably include places where drugs are present. And the users all have rationales for their use as well as social supports.

The final chapter in this section is of a different kind. Kaestner, Marel, Frank, Schmeidler, and Maranda (Chapter 16) describe a survey of residents of single-room-occupancy hotels in New York City. Assessing drug use in this population, the authors find that it is widespread. Moreover, 42% of these people are using a particular drug in combination with other legal and illegal drugs or alcohol. Additionally, 48% report having problems as a result of using drugs. We can assume from what we have learned about other settings that the S.R.O. hotel is a setting, in Hoffman's terms (Chapter 11), in which drug use is accepted and in which drugs are readily available.

We conclude then that attention to prevention or treatment will have to take into account the factors of drug availability, user characteristics and beliefs, and the social setting of use.

SECTION 5
INTERNATIONAL SUBSTANCE USE

INTRODUCTION

To this point in our deliberations, we have considered alcohol and drug use only in an American context. As we expand our view to consider an international perspective, there are two changes which we might expect.

First and most obvious, we might expect that the patterns of alcohol and drug use may differ from the U.S. We have made a strong argument in these pages that substance use varies with culture. To the extent that other countries have cultures which are different from our own, we should expect associated differences in substance use.

Second, and more subtly, we might expect that investigators in other countries will have perspectives which differ from American perspectives. The chapters which follow illustrate this point.

In Forster's work (Chapter 4), we considered early use of drugs by U.S. adolescents. In Chapter 17, Javetz and Shuval ask similar questions about adolescent drug use in Israel. Their experience is different from the U.S. experience for two major reasons: 1) the prevalence of the behavior is lower and 2) the normative context is stronger. Nevertheless, some of the same conflicts emerge; that is, the conflict of cultural influences between negative norms and positive peer attitudes and behaviors.

The work by Teichman, Rahav, and Barnea (Chapter 18), done in Israel also, is social psychological in character. The authors provide a thorough review of theories of substance abuse and build their own conceptual model. They provide a limited test of this model and then go on to discuss its implications for prevention of substance-abusing behavior.

Adding to our understanding of substance use in Israel, Toch's work (Chapter 19) examines the place of alcohol and alcoholism in a society where the behavior is relatively new. As Markides and Krause (Chapter 10) found for Mexican-Americans, patterns of alcohol use in Israel may be affected by the process of acculturation. Additionally, Toch raises for us the issue of genetic differences, a problem which we have not discussed previously.

Sargent (Chapter 20) provides an analysis of alcohol use in Australia which is quite different from what we have seen previously. In Prather's chapter (Chapter 12) on use of tranquilizers by suburban women, we have gotten the first hint that industry (pharmaceutical companies, in this instance) and government are complicitous in the use of drugs. Sargent uses this form of analysis of power relations to great advantage to pose provocative questions for us.

Finally, moving into the realms of heroin addiction in international perspective, we note the work of van de Wijngaart (Chapter 21). The author adds to our knowledge a historical perspective which is new for us. He goes on to chronicle the approach of the Dutch government to opiate addiction. Their approach is rather different from our own and bears careful consideration.

Use of alcohol (or drugs, for that matter) is not a peculiarly American phenomenon. With this chapter, we begin an examination of use of alcohol and drugs in other countries. This is a very useful exercise. Obviously, we may get ideas on new forms of prevention and treatment from other nations. More important in this section, however, we get new ideas on the causal factors associated with alcohol and drug use.

In Chapter 4, Forster chronicled for us the very early use of drugs by pre-teens in an American middle-class suburb. She also provided us with a test of some of the theoretical explanations for early drug use. Here, we see a similar study, only now in an Israeli context. Overall, the approach that Javetz and Shuval use is an interesting parallel to Forster's work.

The situation in Israel is somewhat different than it is in the U.S. Substance use among adolescents is less prevalent. As a result, peer use of drugs is less frequent for drug-using individuals.

These authors, as others we have discussed earlier, see the beginnings of substance use in availability, use by others, a "loosening" of normative attachments, and some behavioral pathology (Forster, Chapter 4). To test some of these hypotheses, they have devised a very sophisticated survey methodology and have questioned a large sample (5,914) regarding their drug-using behavior and their attitudes toward drugs.

As with most good research, Javetz's and Shuval's conclusions raise more interesting questions: Do these adolescents' attitudes predispose toward drug using or are the attitudes themselves a product of a society in which drug use is increasing? The authors find that these young people are in a quandary. For those who use substances, there is the normative pressure against this behavior -- a pressure which must somehow be reconciled with their own anti-normative behavior.

CHAPTER 17

NORMATIVE CONTEXTS OF DRUG USE
AMONG ISRAELI YOUTH

Rachel Javetz and Judith T. Shuval

ABSTRACT

The normative-motivational context of illicit drug use among high school students in Israel is analyzed on the basis of a two-dimensional conceptual model: one dimension relates to levels of actions -- attitudes about drug use and other deviant behavior and actual drug use; the other deals with frames of reference -- personal characteristics and attitudes attributed to others. The 5,914 students studied were in grades 7 to 12 (ages 12 to 18) in all types of schools in Israel, including working youth who study in part-time programs. The data was collected by means of an anonymous, pre-coded questionnaire completed by students in classrooms.
The findings indicate that the distribution of attitudes among students is compatible with prevailing norms in Israel which regard drug use as deviant. By peers, whom they perceive as relatively controlling

----

RACHEL JAVETZ is Research Associate in the Programme in Medical Sociology at the School of Public Health, the Hebrew University, Jerusalem, Israel; JUDITH T. SHUVAL is Professor of Sociology at the School of Public Health and Department of Sociology, Hebrew University, Jerusalem, Israel.

for drug behavior it becomes evident that this distribution is char- acteristic of non-users who comprise the majority of the students. Those who have used drugs show less consensus, reflecting the normative cross-pressures to which they are subject. While non-users attribute to significant others attitudes similar to their own, users tend to differentiate between permissive adults and those who are perceived as conforming more to the general norm. The motives concerning drug use are also seen differently by users and non-users: while the latter emphasize the negative effects of such motives as curiosity, users point to curiosity as the principal positive motive for drug use. Attitudes concerning other types of deviant behavior are correlated with actual use or non-use of drugs. Moreover, users' tendency to attribute to their friends considerably more permissive attitudes toward other deviant behavior, points to their need to reconcile the cross-pressures they face. The data sheds light on the normative meaning of illicit drug use within the general anti-drug-use atmosphere in Israel.

INTRODUCTION

Drug use in Israel is manifested in two basic patterns: 1) there is the traditional use of hashish known for centuries in this part of the world; and 2) more recently, the phenomenon has been observed in the Jewish population among criminal groups, the bohemia, and young people and adults in more broadly based groups. The use of drugs, with the exception of alcohol and tobacco, is illegal in Israel, unless prescribed by a physician.

In an effort to understand the phenomenon of illicit drug use, sociological and social-psychological studies have analyzed behavioral as well as motivational and attitudinal correlates of the phenomenon. Studies focusing on youth have identified certain behavior patterns, fashions, and norms which are related to the tendency of adolescents to experiment with drugs or to use them regularly (Johnston, Bachman and O'Malley, 1979; Horowitz, 1977; Kandel et al., 1976; Lucas, Grupp, and Schmitt, 1975; Johnson, 1973; Sadova, 1973). Despite the fact that the correlations established are not able, in most cases, to determine cause and effect in the process, the analysis of such interrelationships is crucial in understanding the phenomenon of drug abuse as perceived by the population studied (Johnston, Bachman, and O'Malley, 1979; Jessor and Jessor, 1978).

Norms and values as reflected in young people's attitudes are crystallized through differential internalization of messages received from the social environment. In distinguishing between the micro-environment closest to adolescents -- their peers, family, and other significant adults -- and the wider macro-environment -- the society at large -- it could be expected that the former would be more influential. In addition, with respect to such a normatively problematic issue as illicit drug use, we might expect the micro-environment to be differentiated by the age of significant others: the peer group is likely to have a stronger effect than adults (Ginsberg and Greenley, 1978).

Several studies have investigated drug-use patterns among adolescents in Israel during the past decade. The findings have consistently shown that, between 1971 and 1979, the average life-time prevalence of use of any kind of illicit drug was approximately 5% for the 14 to 18 age group, a low rate when compared to many Western countries (Javetz and Shuval, 1984; Javetz and

Shuval, 1982; Kandel, Adler, and Sudit, 1981; Barnea, 1978; Shoham et al., 1974; Peled and Schimmerling, 1971a, 1971b).

Yet, the prevalence of drug use among specific sub-populations in Israel was found to be higher than the average rate, although these sub-groups are also characterized by lower rates than parallel groups in other countries, particularly in the U.S. Thus, high school students in Israel who use drugs tend to be relatively concentrated among males, older age groups, working youngsters who study only part-time, students in boarding schools, and children from broken homes (Javetz and Shuval, 1984).

Research in Israel has confirmed other findings which indicate that adolescents who have used drugs tend to express more favorable attitudes toward such use and are more knowledgeable about the subject (Barnea, 1978; Shoham et al., 1978; Shoham et al., 1974; Peled and Schimmerling, 1971b). Such attitudes appear to be part of a wider complex of individualistic, less conforming normative perceptions concerning more general societal values related to family, achievement, and sexual relations. Young people who reveal more openness toward non-conforming attitudes and behaviors, also express a stronger tendency to use drugs. From a psychological point of view, it has been noted that Israeli students who tend to use drugs are characterized by situational and personal anxiety and a stronger tendency for sensation-seeking (Barnea, 1978).

The present analysis focuses on the attitudinal-motivational aspects of drug use among secondary school students in Israel. In a previous analysis of the behavioral complex associated with drug use (Javetz and

430

Shuval, 1984), a "syndrome of vulnerability to drugs" was identified which pointed to an ordered pattern comprising the behavioral correlates of drug use. The syndrome of vulnerability includes the following groups of variables which are listed from high to low correlation with drug use: 1) exposure to drugs and drug use by others; 2) use of legal substances (tobacco, alcohol, and psychoactive medicine); 3) petty delinquency, and 4) tension and problems in the home and school environments.

THEORETICAL APPROACH

The present analysis is based on a two-dimensional model describing the structure of a set of relevant variables and their interrelationships:

1. The action dimension: includes a behavioral level concerning subjects' patterns of behavior in various social domains and an attitudinal level referring to subjects' attitudes and motivations with regard to relevant normative issues; and

2. The frame-of-reference dimension: includes subjects' personal frames of reference and that of various significant others.

The joint relationship of these two dimensions defines four areas of research interest (Figure 17.1, page 432). Analysis of the interrelationships among these areas is our central objective beyond the separate investigation of each area.

In analyzing the behavioral level, a comparison was undertaken of young people's presentation of their own behavioral patterns with those of significant others (Javetz and Shuval, 1984; Javetz and Shuval, 1982). Thus, adolescents' own drug behavior (1 in Figure 17.1, page 432) was examined in relation to their reports

FIGURE 17.1

CONCEPTUAL MODEL

<u>Type of Action</u>   <u>Frame of Reference</u>

                        Personal   Significant Others

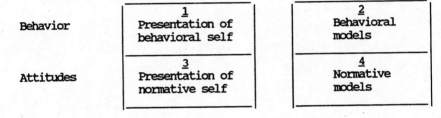

Behavior

Attitudes

about drug use among peers and friends (2 in Figure 17.1, page 432). Similarly, with respect to legal substances such as tobacco and alcohol, the analysis examined the effects of the behavior of friends and family members on the subjects' own tendency to use these substances. This approach considered the subjects' presentation of behavioral self in relation to their perception of the behavior of significant others who act as models.

The present chapter focuses on the normative-attitudinal level of drug behavior, relating the subject's attitudes, the presentation of the normative self (3 in Figure 17.1, page 432), to attitudes he or she attributes to various significant others (4 in Figure 17.1, page 432). Values and normative perceptions regarding drug use will be examined and considered in terms of their relation to the actual tendency to use or not use illicit drugs (that is, in relation to 1 in Figure 17.1, page 432). Young people's degree of self-criticism concerning drug use, as reflected in the relationship between their expressed attitudes and actual behavior, is of interest in view of the widespread norm in Israel which is generally opposed to drug use on the formal-legal as well as the public-moral levels.

The comparison of personal attitudes with those attributed to others is of special interest when "sensitive" issues, such as illicit drug use, are examined. In such a case, it may be expected that the adolescent's "real" positions will more reliably be reflected in the attitudes they attribute to others. Such projection, however, may also reflect a difference between the perception of peers' attitudes and attitudes of adults (Kandel et al., 1976).

A comparison of the prevalence rates of drug use among high school students in Israel and parallel rates in Western countries shows, as noted, that the former are low (Johnston, Bachman, and O'Malley, 1979; Kosviner and Hawks, 1977; and Kosviner and Hawks, 1974). Hence adolescents who use drugs, or who contemplate such behavior, are part of a small minority in Israel, while in other countries such users often are part of a large segment of the population and in certain sub-populations, such as college students, are even in the majority. In such contrasting macro-contexts, the drug user finds him or herself under different pressures with regard to salient reference groups which approve or disapprove of the behavior. In both types of society, the micro-environment, consisting of immediate friends, is, in most cases, likely to be supportive of deviant behavior because of associative processes which cause people to select like-minded friends. But, the combined effect of the macro- and the micro-contexts is likely to place the individual drug user in Israel under greater cross-pressures than counterparts in other Western countries.

The analysis will focus on the following hypotheses:

1. Attitudes and behavior of young people will be positively related: non-users will express the generally accepted anti-drug norm, while drug users will show attitudes which are more compatible with their behavior in an effort to reduce dissonance;

2. Young people's perception of the attitudes of various significant others will differ in terms of the latter's location in a) the micro- or macro-environments and b) peer or adult groups;

3. Motives for and against drug use will be perceived differently by users and non-users;

4. Drug behavior and attitudes will be associated with attitudes concerning other types of deviant behavior; and

5. In view of the normative sensitivity of the issue of illicit drug use, young people will attribute to others, particularly to peers, more permissive anti-normative attitudes than they attribute to themselves, thereby reflecting the value conflict involved in the presentation of self.

METHOD

The population studied included Jewish students in grades 7 to 12 (ages 12 to 18) in all types of schools in Israel. A national sample of 5,914 students was drawn by a multi-stage procedure and represents two sub-populations:

1. Full-time students in all schools under the auspices of the Ministry of Education; and

2. Students in various part-time study programs for working youth under the auspices of the Ministry of Labor.

The latter sub-population is generally from a lower socioeconomic background than the former. Young people not registered in some school framework were not included in the sample. The latter population, which includes youngsters between 16 and 18 years of age, comprises approximately 15% of these cohorts and is likely to include relatively high proportions of drug users. However, in view of the difficulty in sampling this sub-population, the present study focuses only on full-time and part-time students.

The data was collected in 1979 by means of an anonymous pre-coded questionnaire completed by students in classrooms. The questionnaire included a wide battery of items concerning various aspects of the student's family, leisure, and school life as well as use of legal substances and petty delinquency. Students also reported on exposure to drug use, life-time prevalence of drug use, types of drugs used, age of first use, and circumstances of drug use.

Satisfactory reliability is assured by low overall non-response rates for all items including those concerning illicit drug use (less than 1.5%). Furthermore, there is high internal consistency among various items designed to measure similar conceptual dimensions (Amsel et al., 1976). The Crowne and Marlowe Social Desirability Scale (Crowne and Marlowe, 1964), utilized as an additional tool for assessing reliability, does not change the basic relationships among the variables reported even in sub-groups showing high "social desirability."

In an attempt to construct a composite drug-use index which could serve as the principal predicted variable, the specific items measuring drug behavior were analyzed by factor analysis. The results which yield a single factor with an eigenvalue of 0.96 demonstrate the uni-dimensionality of the behavior measured. An average score was thus constructed for these variables and called the "Drug Use Index." It was divided in terms of profiles defining two principal types of drug behavior: 1) users, who used some kind of illicit drug at least once and 2) non-users, those who have never used any kind of drug. The Drug Use Index distribution shows that the users comprise 2.4% of the full-time student population and 8.5% of the part-time student sample.

The decision to divide the Drug Use Index into two categories was based on the finding that only a minority of the students in both samples have actually used drugs. The reader should bear in mind, however, that those who did use drugs range from one-time users to students who reported regular use of drugs including "hard" drugs. The latter, however, comprise only a tiny minority of the users.

FINDINGS

The analysis of the data follows the conceptual model presented in Figure 17.1, page 432, and focuses on the subjects' own attitudes and perceptions and on those they attribute to various significant others. Three principal types of data are considered:

1. Attitudes directly concerned with drug use;

2. Opinions regarding the reasons, or motives, for use or non-use of drugs; that is, positive motives encouraging use or negative motives discouraging drug use; and

3. Attitudes regarding other types of deviant behavior, including use of legal substances and petty delinquency.

ATTITUDES CONCERNING DRUG USE

A person's attitudes and actual behavior concerning a certain domain of action constitute two dimensions which are related, although often imperfectly. According to dissonance theory, the two factors tend to converge, yet, in reality, the degree of compatibility between them varies. When normatively problematic issues, such as illicit drug use, are considered, there is particular interest in examining the degree of compatibility between the respective attitudes and behavior. Since the general societal stand on drug use in Israel tends to view it as deviant, our aim is to assess the degree of acceptance of this position among adolescents, particularly among those who have used drugs.

In addition to their own response, students were asked to classify the positions of five types of significant others in response to the question: "What, in your opinion, do the following people think about drug use?", The positions presented were: 1) "there is nothing wrong with it", 2) "quite bad," or 3) "very bad."[1]

We shall first focus on the personal frame of reference; that is, the interrelationship between the subjects' own attitudes and their drug behavior. The latter is operationalized by the Drug Index cut on a dichotomous basis distinguishing between users and non-users. Table 17.1, page 454, presents the distribution of attitudes expressed by the students in the two populations. The data referring to the students' own attitudes, shown in the first row of each sample, demonstrated the almost complete consensus opposing drug use among the non-users, especially among full-time students. By way of contrast, among users in both samples, there is less consensus, although over 50% still maintain that drug use is either "quite bad" or "very bad." Thus, while the presentation of self among

---

[1] No overtly positive positions were included as the findings of the pilot study showed that only a negligible percentage of the respondents chose such a position, and even the originally mid-scale position (category 1 above) was adopted by only a small fraction of the sample.

non-users demonstrates an almost complete congruence between attitudes and behavior (less than 2% of this population do not oppose drug use), among the users a sizeable segment, but still a minority, are not opposed to drug use (29% among full-time students and 39% among part-time students). The distribution of opinions among the users apparently reflects the normative cross-pressures which they feel.

When we controlled for sex, it became clear that compatibility between attitudes and behavior is sex-related only among the users. In others words, no significant differences were found between the attitudes expressed by males or females who have never used drugs. Among the users, on the other hand, males tend to express more permissive attitudes, compatible with their behavior, than females whose attitudes show more conformity with the generally accepted norms. Thus, among the males, 31% of the full-time students and 42% of the part-time students thought there is "nothing wrong" with drug use, yet only 22% of the females in the first sample, took this position.[2]

Similar results were obtained when we controlled for age. The distribution of opinions among the non-users was basically the same for all age groups, whereas among the users attitudes were age-related. The higher the age of the users the less negative are their attitudes concerning drug use.

Turning to the relationship between students' presentation of self and their perception of the attitudes of significant others sheds further light on the nature of the normative atmosphere prevailing among

----
[2]   The data concerning the part-time female students are not reliable due to the small size of the drug-user groups.

adolescents.

The data for non-users underline the strength of the anti-normative perception of drug use (Table 17.1, page 454). Within the micro-environment, adults are perceived to hold the most negative views, but student's own attitudes are, on the average, very close to those of the adults. Attitudes attributed to friends are more permissive yet still largely negative. The last two groups, representing the macro-environment, are perceived by the respondents to hold positions which are significantly less negative.

The data pertaining to the users reveal a different perceptual stand. In this case, the distinction between micro- and macro-environments is not meaningful; the major difference is between adult groups (parents and teachers) and the adolescents, including the respondents themselves. The society in general is perceived, especially by the full-time students, to take an intermediate position. By and large, users tend to attribute to others, even to adults, considerably more permissive views than the non-users. This inclination to perceive the social environment as less critical of their behavior is seen specifically in the attitudes attributed by users to their friends, presenting them as even more permissive than themselves.

MOTIVES FOR DRUG USE

The motives for drug use were operationalized through items concerning conceptions people ostensibly hold regarding drug use. Since, in a society characterized by strong anti-drug norms, it is problematic to probe directly for student's motives, the strategy used involved evaluation of motives

440

attributed to generalized others. The respondents were requested to express their agreement or disagreement with these conceptions, some of which were phrased in a direction favoring drug use while others were phrased as opposing it. The respondents' position would thus indicate the perceived social relevance of each motive as affecting the tendency to use or not use drugs.

The motives encouraging drug use included curiosity, social involvement, pleasure, relaxation, and escape from problems. The negative motives concerned the dangers supposedly involved in drug use to the user's health, danger of addiction, and loss of self-control. In order to analyze systematically the students' positions, we compared those who agreed "strongly" or "somewhat" with the motives which encourage drug use to those who disagreed with the motives discouraging drug use. Table 17.2, page 455, presents the motives in their original form, but the data refer to the students who expressed agreement with pro-use motives (a,e,f,g in Table 17.3, page 457) and those who disagreed with anti-use motives (b,c,d in Table 17.3, page 457).

The results demonstrate (see right-hand column of Table 17.3, page 457) that the order of the relative effect of the various motives is virtually identical for both samples. Both full-time and part-time students tend to agree that curiosity (motive a) is not a good motive for drug use. The three anti-use motives (b,c,d) are also perceived as discouraging factors; only a small minority, especially among the full-time students, perceive drug use as being harmless. As to the last three motives, all pro-use (e,f,g), there is somewhat more agreement that they might encourage drug use, although most subjects disagree with them, particularly with the social motive (e).

The order of the motives remains mostly unchanged when controlling for sex. The differences between males and females are generally negligible, except for concerns about addiction and loss of control for the first sample and social motives (e,f,g) for the second. It is interesting to note that over 40% of the females, in both samples, agree that drugs help in escaping problems.

Analysis by age reveals a clear correlation between age and perceived motives only in the case of three items: 1) curiosity, 2) the pleasure motive, and 3) the motive of escaping problems (a,f,g). The rates of subjects agreeing with these pro-use motives rise with age. In other words, the effect of these motives is weaker among younger students and increases significantly by age 16 to 17. The perception of the rest of the motives (b-e) do not vary significantly with age.

The motivational variables were further analyzed in relation to respondents' actual drug behavior. The differences in perceived motives among drug users and non-users are shown in the right-hand columns of Table 17.3, page 457.

The outstanding finding concerns the curiosity motive, which, as noted above, was perceived by the smallest minority of students as encouraging drug use. Yet, by comparing the majority who have not used drugs with the minority who have, it becomes apparent that this motive is by far the factor most strongly associated with drug behavior. The respective difference between users and non-users is between 2 and

10 times larger than the rest of the differences. Similar findings have been reported in the U.S.

A comparison of the two samples with regard to differences in perceived motives of users and non-users shows different perceptual patterns: the positive motives (e,f,g) are more highly correlated with drug behavior than the negative motives (b,c,d) among the part-time students; for the full-time students, on the other hand, two of the negative motives -- the danger of addiction and loss of self-control -- are more strongly associated with drug behavior. In view of the finding that the two populations differ in their degree of involvement in drug use and exposure to drugs as well (Javetz and Shuval, 1984; Javetz and Shuval, 1982), the difference in motivational patterns may reflect the degree of deviance attributed to illicit drug use by each. These data suggest an additional hypothesis: the relative prevalence of drug use within a given population affects the perception of its level of deviance, causing differential emphases on the relevant motives for use or non-use. More specifically, the higher the prevalence the less deviant it is perceived to be, and, therefore, it is associated with pro-use motives. When prevalence is lower, drug use is viewed as more deviant, and a stronger emphasis is placed on anti-use motives.

Controlling for sex as well as use and non-use indicates motivational differences, though these are not entirely consistent for the two samples. Again, the curiosity motive (a) plays the major differentiating role for males and females alike. Yet, males who used drugs generally tend to express more anti-normative views which are consistent with their behavior; this is less true of females who used

443

drugs.[3] In comparing the males of both samples, the highest correlations with drug behavior for the full-time students involve pleasure, loss of self-control, and danger of addiction motives (f,d,c), while the part-time students emphasize the social motive, escaping problems, and pleasure (e,g,f). As to the females, in both samples, the only motive, in addition to curiosity, which clearly differentiates between users and non-users is the danger of addiction (c).

ATTITUDES CONCERNING OTHER TYPES OF DEVIANT BEHAVIOR

Following the analysis of attitudes and motives regarding drug use and their association with drug behavior, we turn to an examination of a wider context of conformity or non-conformity. Students' drug behavior and attitudes are analyzed in relation to other deviant behaviors: use of legal substances (tobacco and alcohol) and petty delinquency.

Correlations, based on this data, between drug behavior and use of legal substances as well as involvement in petty delinquency have been reported (Javetz and Shuval, 1984; Javetz and Shuval, 1982). Our aim here is to examine the extent to which drug use is related to other social norms which are salient to adolescents: Is anti-normative action regarding illicit drugs associated with wider non-conforming attitudes, or is drug behavior perceptually detached from conformity in other areas?

Table 17.4, page 459, presents the relationship between students' drug behavior and their attitudes

----
[3] See footnote (**) in Table 17.3, page 457, regarding the data for part-time students.

444

towards the use of tobacco and alcohol and selected forms of petty delinquency. Examining the data concerning personal stands (columns a and b), and differentiating again between users and non-users of illicit drugs, it can be seen that the non-users are practically unanimous in opposing such behavior. Only with respect to cheating on exams and cigarette smoking does the percentage of those who do not condemn such behavior approach 10%.

Among the users, the rates of students expressing negative positions towards this behavior are consistently lower than among the non-users. Yet, even in this group, a considerable majority express views which conform to the generally advocated norms. At the same time, there is a clearer differentiation among these variables as the users perceive them. Tobacco use, in particular, is opposed by only 57% of the full-time student users and 62% of the part-time student users. This finding is hardly surprising in view of the strong correlation, established earlier, between the use of tobacco and illicit drugs. Among the regular tobacco smokers 25% have also used drugs, and over 70% of those who have used drugs smoke tobacco at least occasionally (Javetz and Shuval, 1984; Javetz and Shuval, 1982).

When the two samples are compared, the difference column (a-b) shows that beyond cigarette smoking, among the full-time students, cheating on exams and alcohol use are more associated with drug behavior than petty delinquency; for the part-time students the picture is reversed.

When the relation between students' own drug behavior and the attitudes they attribute to their friends is considered, the data shed light on the hypothesis that people tend more easily to project anti-normative positions on others rather than present them as their own. Comparing column a and b with c and d in Table 17.4, page 459, makes it clear that the students in both samples, users and non-users, project fewer negative positions on their friends. The users' tendency to project anti-normative stands is stronger than the non-users' (compare difference columns c-d with a-b). Attitudes attributed to friends can be taken as more validly reflecting the normative atmosphere among adolescents. It, thus, appears that the atmosphere in users' reference groups is significantly more permissive than in those of non-users.

Columns a-c and b-d present differences between the rates of respondents who expressed personal negative positions towards deviant behavior, and the rates attributed by them to their friends. The differences, controlling for drug behavior, are smaller among non-users than among users, which suggests greater reliability in the normative stands taken by the non-user population. The only exception occurs among full-time students regarding the issues of cheating on exams, which is apparently perceived as less deviant than other types of behavior. There is, on the other hand, a strong consensus among the non-users condemning shoplifting and breaking into cars.

Among the users of drugs, the large differences between personal and attributed attitudes point to the weaker normative consensus existing in this population. The findings, in line with other conclusions, suggest that these students are subject to greater cross-pressures. On the one hand, the prevailing social norms pressure against deviant

446

behavior and even against expressing attitudes condoning such behavior; yet, their involvement in illicit drug use requires taking positions consonant with their behavior in order to reduce dissonance.

SUMMARY AND CONCLUSION

This research concerns norms relating to illicit drug use among high school students in Israel. The general model on which the present analysis is based included two cross-cutting dimensions. One relates to levels of action: attitudes and behavior. The other deals with frames of reference: self and others including friends, parents, teachers, and wider groups. (Figure 17.1, page 432).

This chapter focuses on attitudes concerning both frames of reference. However, in an attempt to understand the working of the full model, these attitudes were also related to drug behavior. Thus, the students' presentation of their normative selves are examined in relation to their perception of the attitudes of others. In addition, the same relationships are controlled for students' own drug behavior.

The distribution of attitudes concerning drug use confirms the assumption that the norm opposing it is indeed widely accepted in Israel. The non-user population, comprising the vast majority of high school students, shows overwhelming consensus in this direction over all age and sex categories. The attitude distribution among drug users is different, showing less consensus within this group.

Perceived attitudes of significant others is affected by respondents' actual drug behavior. Non-users tend to differentiate between their immediate

447

circle of others, whose positions are seen as basically negative, and less personal reference groups in the society, who are perceived to hold less negative views. Users of drugs, on the other hand, perceive their peer group as more permissive than the wider groups and considerably more permissive than their parents and teachers. The latter findings suggest that users may see themselves and their friends as deviant.

The data on motives concerning drug use also show differences between non-users and users: the majority of non-users emphasize the anti-use effect of motivations, especially curiosity and motivations concerning the dangers in drug use; users point to curiosity as the principal motivation for use, while the rest of the motives carried less pro-use effect yet are not viewed as negatively as among the non-users.

Analysis of normative perceptions with regard to other types of deviant behavior -- use of legal substances and petty delinquency -- shows that drug behavior is not a detached pattern of behavior. This conclusion concerning attitudes, complements previous findings in Israel, which showed drug behavior to be associated with other types of deviant behavior. In other words, the syndrome of vulnerability to drugs, showing drug behavior as a component in a wider range of problematic behavioral tendencies, can now be extended to include normative perceptions along with behavioral patterns.

Attitudes toward deviant types of behavior attributed by students to their friends enabled further understanding of the different normative atmosphere prevailing among users and non-users of drugs. While users tend to view their friends as considerably more permissive than they presented themselves, non-users saw their friends as only slightly more permissive. The conclusion points again to the users' need to reconcile the normative cross-pressures they face. One solution is the projection of less conservative stands on their peer group.

Figure 17.1, page 432, presents the conceptual model of the study which was based on two dichotomous dimensions: 1) types of action including behavior and attitudes and 2) frame of reference including personal or significant others. The present analysis concentrated on the attitudinal level controlling for the personal presentation of the behavioral self. The findings indicate that the model requires differentiation for the two critical sub-populations with which the study has been concerned: 1) non-users and 2) users of illicit drugs.

Figure 17.2, page 450, based on the original model, summarizes the principal findings for each of these populations. The model thus serves to explicate the difference between users and non-users in terms of both action levels and frames of reference.

The non-users population presents a normative context characterized by consensus opposing drug use. Consistency between the behavioral and attitudinal levels of action, as well as between self and the great majority of others, provides a reflection of the normative context concerning illicit drug use in Israel in general.

Within the user population, on the other hand, consistency between behavior and attitudes is markedly lower, as is the consensus concerning drug use. The results point to the conflictural normative context in which youngsters using drugs in Israel find themselves. The great majority which condemns illicit

FIGURE 17.2

CONCEPTUAL MODEL APPLIED: DRUG
USE IN TERMS OF THE RELATIONSHIP
BETWEEN TYPE OF ACTION
AND FRAMES OF REFERENCE

<u>Type of Action</u>   <u>Frame of Reference</u>

<u>Non-Users</u>	Personal	Significant Others
Behavior	<u>1</u> Presentation of normative behavior	<u>2</u> The majority as a model for conformity
Attitudes	<u>3</u> Conforming consensus* normative self	<u>4</u> Distinction between conformingf majority and non-conforming minority

<u>Users</u>

Behavior	<u>1</u> Presentation of anti-normative behavior towards majority normative in minority	<u>2</u> Conforming versus non-conforming minority which reduces dissonance
Attitudes	<u>3</u> No consensus: normative cross-pressures (evidence of dissonance)**	<u>4</u> Projection of more non-conforming attitudes providing consonance

_____

*   Not affected by age and sex.

** Affected by age and sex; higher age groups and males are less conforming.

450

use of drugs encompasses not only remote social circles of the adult segment of the society but also the majority of their peer group. In order to resolve the conflict, users may either turn to the minority group of other users for normative and motivational support or abandon drug use altogether.

In fact, some seem to search for intermediate solutions, such as holding to the accepted views despite actual drug use, by limiting their involvement with drugs[4] or by projecting more anti-normative views on their friends than they were willing to report as their own. Such variety of possible reactions highlights the confrontation process involved in the problem of conformity to a sensitive issue.

REFERENCES

Amsel, S. et al. 1976. Reliability and validity of self-reported illegal activities and drug use collected from narcotic addicts. International Journal of Addictions 11:325-336.

Barnea, Z. 1978. A multiple model of readiness to use drugs by adolescents. Society and Welfare 1:359-383 (in Hebrew).

Crowne, D. and Marlowe, D. 1964. The Approval Motive. NY: John Wiley.

Ginsberg, I. J. and Greenley, J. 1978. Competing theories of marijuana use. Journal of Health and Social Behavior 19:22-34.

Horowitz, I. L. 1977. The politics of drugs. In P. E. Rock (ed.), Drugs and Politics (pp. 155-166). NY: Transaction Books.

Javetz, R. and Shuval, J. 1982. Vulnerability to drugs among Israeli adolescents. Israel Journal of Psychiatry 19:97-119.

---
[4] The majority of users actually reported a very limited experience with drugs.

Javetz, R. and Shuval, J. 1984. Drug use among high school students in Israel: A syndrome of social vulnerability. Youth and Society 16: 171-194.

Jessor, R. and Jessor, L. 1978. Theory testing in longitudinal research on marijuana use. In D. B. Kandel (ed.), Longitudinal Research on Drug Use (pp. 41-71). NY: John Wiley.

Johnson, B. D. 1973. Marijuana Users and Drug Subcultures. NY: John Wiley.

Johnston, L. D., Bachman, J. G., and O'Malley, P. 1977. Drug Use Among American High School Students 1975-1977. Washington, DC: National Institute on Drug Abuse.

Johnston, L. D., Bachman, J. and O'Malley, P. 1979. Drugs and the Class of 1978: Behaviors, Attitudes, and Recent National Trends. Washington, DC: U.S. Department of Health Education and Welfare.

Johnston, L. D., O'Malley, P., and Eveland, L. 1978. Drugs and delinquency: A search for causal connections. In D. B. Kandel (ed.), Longitudinal Research on Drug Use (pp. 137-156). NY: John Wiley.

Kandel, D. B. et al. 1976. Adolescent involvement in legal and illegal drug use: A multiple classification analysis. Social Forces: 55:438-458.

Kandel, D. B., Adler, I., and Sudit, M. 1981. The epidemiology of adolescent drug use in France and Israel. American Journal of Public Health 71:256-265.

Kosviner, A. and Hawks, D. 1974. Cannabis use among British University students, I: Prevalence. British Journal of Addiction 69:35-60.

Kosviner, A. and Hawks, D. 1977. Cannabis use among British University students, II: Patterns of use and attitudes to use. British Journal of Addiction 712:41-57.

Lucas, W. L., Grupp, S., and Schmitt, R. 1975. Predicting who will turn on: A four year follow up. International Journal of Addictions 10:305-326.

Peled, Z. and Schimmerling, H. 1971a. Attitudes of School Youth to the Topic of Drugs. Jerusalem, Israel: Institute of Applied Social Research.

Peled, Z. and Schimmerling, J. 1971b. The Drug Culture Among the Youth of Israel: The Case of High School Students. Jerusalem, Israel: Institute of Applied Social Research.

Sadova, S. W. 1973. Initiation to cannabis use: A longitudinal social psychological study of college freshmen. Canadian Journal of Behavioral Sciences 5:371-384(a).

Shoham, S. et al. 1974. Drug use among Israeli youth: Epidemiology pilot study. Bulletin on Narcotics 26:9-28.

Shoham, S. et al. 1978. Differential patterns of drug involvement among Israeli youth. Bulletin on Narcotics 30:17-32.

TABLE 17.1

STUDENTS' PRESENTATION OF OWN AND OTHERS' ATTITUDES ON DRUG USE,
BY DRUG BEHAVIOR (FULL-TIME AND PART-TIME STUDENTS PERCENTAGES)

Attitudes Concerning Drug Use	Non-Users Percentages					Users Percentages				
Frames of Reference	Very Negative	Quite Negative	Nothing Wrong	Total %	Total N*	Very Negative	Quite Negative	Nothing Wrong	Total %	Total N*
Full-Time Students										
Student respondent	89.5	9.4	1.1	100	4524	31.4	35.3	33.3	100	99
Close friends	79.2	18.6	2.2	100	3900	21.8	39.6	38.6	100	101
Parents	94.2	5.5	.3	100	4523	73.0	21.1	5.9	100	102
Teachers	93.4	5.7	.9	100	4232	71.9	16.6	11.5	100	96
Other young people in Israel	46.4	43.6	10.0	100	3165	22.1	52.3	25.6	100	86
Israelis in general	51.8	39.8	8.4	100	3642	48.9	37.0	14.1	100	92
Part-Time Students										
Student respondent	84.3	13.6	2.1	100	535	34.0	24.5	41.5	100	53
Close friends	76.3	18.0	5.7	100	460	28.6	30.6	40.8	100	49
Parents	88.4	10.3	1.3	100	534	66.7	20.8	12.5	100	48
Teachers	87.3	10.3	2.4	100	496	45.5	43.1	11.4	100	44
Other young people in Israel	65.4	24.1	10.5	100	390	20.5	31.8	47.7	100	44
Israelis in general	63.7	26.9	9.4	100	427	30.8	35.9	33.3	100	39

* N varies because of changing numbers of "don't know."

TABLE 17.2

PERCEPTION OF MOTIVES CONCERNING DRUG USE BY SEX AND AGE (FULL-TIME AND PART-TIME STUDENTS PERCENTAGES)

Perceived Positive and Negative Motives Concerning Drug Use*	Sex Percentages		Age Percentages			Total Percentages
	Males	Females	12-15	16-17	18	
Full-Time Students						
a Worth trying at least once	12.1	9.5	6.1	16.2	22.7	10.7
b May cause harm to user	13.2	9.7	12.4	9.9	9.2	11.3
c May cause addiction	14.9	9.2	12.5	10.8	12.5	11.8
d May cause loss of self-control	15.1	11.3	13.3	12.4	13.1	13.3
e A way of being "one of the gang"	22.3	21.4	20.9	23.5	23.3	21.9
f Enjoyable and relaxing	34.9	33.8	29.1	42.3	40.2	34.3
g Helps to escape problems	37.9	44.7	35.9	49.3	51.8	41.6
Total N	2253	2651	2931	1688	329	

* The categories range from 1 (agree) to 4 (disagree). For simplicity of presentation, only the positive, encouraging end of the continuum is presented. For items a,e,f,g, the encouraging categories are agreements with the statement, and for items b,c,d, the encouraging categories are disagreements with the statement.

TABLE 17.2 (continued)

Perceived Positive and Negative Motives Concerning Drug Use*	Sex Percentages		Age Percentages				Total Percentages
	Males	Females	12-15	16-17	18		
Part-Time Students							
a Worth trying at least once	13.8	13.1	9.7	13.8	21.3		13.7
b May cause harm to user	19.8	18.2	22.9	17.4	21.0		19.4
c May cause addiction	22.3	20.6	20.8	21.0	26.0		21.9
d May cause loss of self-control	20.7	21.9	22.5	19.9	22.0		21.0
e A way of being "one of the gang"	23.3	28.5	23.5	25.1	23.5		24.6
f Enjoyable and relaxing	36.5	28.9	27.8	35.4	47.6		34.8
g Helps to escape problems	36.3	41.6	29.7	40.1	43.2		37.6
Total N	520	156	176	429	82		

---

* The categories range from 1 (agree) to 4 (disagree). For simplicity of presentation, only the positive, encouraging end of the continuum is presented. For items a,e,f,g, the encouraging categories are agreements with the statement, and for items b,c,d, the encouraging categories are disagreements with the statement.

TABLE 17.3

PERCEPTION OF MOTIVES CONCERNING DRUG USE BY SEX
AND DRUG BEHAVIOR (FULL-TIME AND PART-TIME STUDENTS
PERCENTAGES)

Perceived Positive and Negative Motives Concerning Drug Use*	Male Percentages			Female Percentages			Total Percentages		
	Non-Users	Users	Difference	Non-Users	Users	Difference	Non-Users	Users	Difference
Full-Time Students									
a Worth trying at least once	10.2	61.9	51.7	8.8	62.5	53.7	9.4	62.1	62.7
b May cause harm to user	12.5	30.9	18.4	9.6	19.3	9.7	10.9	27.7	16.8
c May cause addiction	13.9	40.3	26.4	8.9	32.2	23.3	11.2	38.1	26.9
d May cause loss of self-control	14.0	43.9	29.9	11.2	22.6	11.4	12.5	38.1	25.6
e A way of being "one of the gang"	20.3	34.2	13.9	21.3	35.4	14.1	20.8	34.5	13.7
f Enjoyable and relaxing	33.7	67.0	33.3	50.3	48.4	- 1.9	42.7	61.9	19.2
g Helps to escape problems	37.1	58.5	21.4	44.7	46.9	2.2	41.2	55.3	14.1
Total %	96.3	3.7		98.8	1.2		97.6	2.4	
N	2158	84		2604	32		4762	116	

* The categories range from 1 (agree) to 4 (disagree). For simplicity of presentation, only the positive, encouraging end of the continuum is presented. For items a,e,f,g, the encouraging categories are agreements with the statement, and for items b,c,d, the encouraging categories are disagreements with the statement.

TABLE 17.3 (continued)

Perceived Positive and Negative Motives Concerning Drug Use*	Male Percentages			Female Percentages			Total Percentages		
	Non-Users	Users	Difference	Non-Users	Users	Difference	Non-Users	Users	Difference
Part-Time Students									
a Worth trying at least once	8.0	70.9	62.9	10.5	71.4	**	8.6	71.0	62.4
b May cause harm to user	18.7	33.6	14.9	18.4	14.3	**	18.6	23.6	5.0
c May cause addiction	21.0	33.4	12.4	19.6	42.8	**	20.7	37.9	17.2
d May cause loss of self control	19.4	32.0	12.6	21.6	28.5	**	19.9	31.6	11.7
e A way of being "one of the gang"	20.1	55.1	35.0	28.5	28.5	**	22.2	51.8	29.6
f Enjoyable and relaxing	34.0	63.3	29.3	28.9	28.6	**	32.7	58.9	26.2
g Helps to escape problems	33.5	65.4	31.9	42.0	33.3	**	35.6	61.8	26.2
Total %	90.6	9.4		95.6	4.4		91.8	8.2	
N	462	48		135	7		615	55	

* The categories range from 1 (agree) to 4 (disagree). For simplicity of presentation, only the positive, encouraging end of the continuum is presented. For items a,e,f,g, the encouraging categories are agreements with the statement, and for items b,c,d, the encouraging categories are disagreements with the statement.

** Small number of cases; hence also the omission of the differences.

TABLE 17.4

ATTITUDES ATTRIBUTED TO SELF AND FRIENDS CONCERNING DEVIANT BEHAVIOR BY DRUG BEHAVIOR (FULL-TIME AND PART-TIME STUDENTS PERCENTAGES)

Types of Deviant Behavior	Disapproving Respondents Percentages		Attribution of Disapproval to Friends Percentages		Differences in Percentages			
	Non-User (a)	Users (b)	Non-Users (c)	Users (d)	(a)-(b)	(c)-(d)	(a)-(c)	(b)-(d)
Full-Time Students								
Cheating on exams	90.4*	71.7	59.5	36.2	18.7	23.3	30.9	35.5
Smoking cigarettes	91.7	57.6	73.3	27.1	34.1	46.2	18.4	30.5
Drinking alcohol	96.5	76.1	86.0	60.7	20.4	25.3	10.5	15.4
Sneaking into movies or football games	97.0	83.9	84.5	52.0	13.1	32.5	12.5	31.9
Pilfering	98.7	88.0	92.3	63.5	10.7	28.8	6.4	24.5
Breaking into cars	98.9	86.3	96.1	71.4	12.6	24.7	2.8	14.9
Total N	4812	113	3979	89				
Part-Time Students								
Cheating on exams	93.5	80.7	75.7	54.4	12.8	21.3	17.8	26.3
Smoking cigarettes	89.4	62.7	72.3	30.2	27.4	42.1	17.1	31.8
Drinking alcohol	96.3	83.1	85.5	59.5	13.2	26.0	10.8	23.6
Sneaking into movies or football games	96.3	73.7	84.0	57.1	22.6	26.9	12.3	16.6
Pilfering	97.7	80.7	90.8	60.0	17.0	30.8	6.9	20.7
Breaking into cars	98.2	79.7	94.2	62.2	18.5	32.0	4.0	17.5
Total N	645	55	484	42				

* Categories range from 1 (approve) to 4 (disapprove). For simplicity, only the two negative categories (3,4) are presented.

INTRODUCTION TO CHAPTER 18

The following chapter by Teichman, Rahav, and Barnea is a conceptual bridge. It brings us from a consideration of substance abuse into logical deductions about prevention. It is exactly this type of conceptual bridge which we hope to make in the mind of the reader when we conclude our consideration of patterns of substance use and of the factors associated with substance use.

Indeed, Teichman, Rahav, and Barnea argue that the only effective treatment for substance abuse is prevention. The authors begin a thoughtful consideration with a social-psychological theory of drug use. It is a well-thought-out analysis of the literature. Its focus is on the individual, in contrast with the type of societal analysis we will see later in this section by Sargent (Chapter 20) and by van de Wijngaart (Chapter 21).

The authors then test their social-psychological theory in a survey of 228 Israeli youth. Based on the findings from their survey, they attempt to construct principles for preventive intervention. Their target group is teenagers, aged 13 to 15. From our reading of Forster (Chapter 4), this would seem to be the latest appropriate age at which such intervention might take place.

CHAPTER 18

A MULTI-DIMENSIONAL MODEL OF PSYCHOACTIVE SUBSTANCE USE BY ISRAELI ADOLESCENTS

Meir Teichman, Giora Rahav, and
Zipora Barnea

ABSTRACT

Recent research suggests that adolescent
use of drugs and alcohol presents a complex
multi-dimensional phenomenon, not necessarily
related to psychopathology or deviance. An
emerging view is that it represents cognitive,
emotional, and behavioral patterns that inter-
relate with various social and developmental
elements characterizing adolescence.
    Research in this area shows that the
likelihood of alcohol and drug use among
adolescents in general, and among Israeli
adolescents as well, increases as a function of
the following conditions: 1) peer use of
alcohol and drugs, 2) positive attitudes toward
these substances, substance use, and substance
users, 3) positive attitudes towards substances
attributed to peers and parents, 4) substance
availability at home, 5) personality variables
such as sensation-seeking, anxiety, depression,
and "moodiness," and 6) availability of the
drugs in the community at large.
    Based on these findings, a multi-
dimensional model of adolescent substance use
was developed, which incorporates personality
variables, cognitive processes, interpersonal
and societal factors, and the availability of

MEIR TEICHMAN is a Senior Lecturer of Psychology at Tel Aviv
University Institute of Criminology, Tel Aviv, Israel; GIORA RAHAV
is Associate Professor of Sociology at Tel Aviv University, Tel
Aviv, Israel; ZIPORA BARNEA is a Research Associate at the
Institute of Criminology, Tel Aviv University, Tel Aviv, Israel.

substances within a given community. This
theoretical model has been tested in Israel for
its validity and applicability.

A comprehensive alcohol and drug education
program is based on this theoretical model.
The proposed educational program consists of
four phases. The first phase consists of a
value/attitudes clarification workshop. The
second part of the program is the
information/knowledge phase. The third
phase, labeled "substance-temptation-inocula-
tion," focuses on skills needed to resist
interpersonal situations in which an adolescent
or a group of youngsters entice one another
into the use of substances. The fourth phase
is "parents-training sessions," which include,
for parents, general knowledge about alcohol
and drugs and presentations of effective
methods of coping with their adolescent
children, especially, when a drug-related
crisis arises.

INTRODUCTION

One of the alarming characteristics of the drug
scene in the Western world is the decrease in age of
substance users and the rising frequency and quantity
of drug and alcohol use. Today, more juveniles use
drugs and alcohol; they frequently consume larger
quantities, and they begin with that habit at an
earlier age than did adolescents of the 1960s and the
early 1970s (Mills and Moyes, 1984; Huba, Wingard, and
Bentler, 1981; Kandel, 1980; Johnston, Bachman, and
O'Malley, 1979).

It is particularly important to understand the
developmental aspects of adolescents' substance use.
Numerous reports and studies have indicated that the
most effective policy of coping with the epidemic of
substance use is the primary prevention approach, and
therefore, the target population should be adolescents

who, so far, have not been initiated into using drugs. Substance abuse tends to be a cumulative process -- few seem to drop out of the users' ranks despite the efforts and the resources invested in treatment (Galanter and Panepinto, 1980; Backeland and Lundwall, 1977). The body of the research, dealing with relapse into alcohol and drugs, further indicates that it is very difficult to induce changes among substance users (for example, Teichman, 1987; Teichman, 1986; Marlatt, 1979; Nace, 1978).

A complicating factor in current adolescent drug use stems from a wider cultural change in attitudes toward use of drugs to affect mental states. The new classes of medications (such as tranquilizers and anti-depressants) that primarily affect the central nervous system and offer effective therapeutic interventions in cases of psychological hardships, have brought a thorough change in public attitudes towards these conditions, as well as in the acceptance of use of pharmaceutics in order to control mental states. If chemicals can be used to cure the mentally ill, they may just as well be used for the benefit of the healthy, helping them to be "happier," more "relaxed," more "creative" or more "self-conscious." The analogy made by many youths is quite simple: "drugs make you feel good, therefore, drugs are good." Chambers, Inciardi, and Segal (1975) termed the concept of "chemical coping," which describes individuals, or groups, using alcohol and drugs habitually in order to cope better (or easier) with the pressures of life.

INITIATION

For the purposes of the present discussion, we shall divide the adolescent drug-use phenomenon into two separate issues: first, why juveniles try drugs, and second, what is it that makes them continue using drugs once they have tried them. We shall discuss the initiation issue first.

The problem with initiation lies in the fact that even at the very first moment they try them out, most juveniles know that the substances they are about to experiment with involve some danger: risks of painful dependence, illegal and deviant behavior, and risks to the juveniles' social relationships. Psychologically, one may explain the readiness to take these risks with a self-destructive tendency (Wurmser, 1978, 1974). However, this unitary explanation seems to over-simplify a complex phenomenon.

Our position is that drug or alcohol use is the result of many separate processes. In order to simplify, we distinguish among three types of causal factors: 1) social factors, 2) personal and interpersonal factors, and 3) drug-related factors.

Social factors. Drug use usually occurs within an accepting, or even encouraging, environment of values and interpersonal relationships in the family and other reference groups, particularly the adolescent peer group. Parents who often relieve their own headaches with over-the-counter medication and who frequently use chemicals for the relief and remedy of disease in their children, "teach" and encourage patterns of chemical coping. The same effect is produced by a society which cultivates a hedonistic lifestyle in which psychoactive substances, such as caffeine, nicotine, and alcohol, play a major role. The social environment and the mass media provide most adolescents in modern society with a multitude of role models who demonstrate the use of beer, wine, tobacco, and hard liquor. In such a society, liberalism may involve approval and tolerance not only of the more legitimate drugs but of marijuana and, perhaps, cocaine as well. This social environment provides a general background which renders the initial drug experience only a relatively small step.

Parental attitudes towards psychoactive drugs (Fawzy, Coombs, and Gerber, 1983; Smart and Fejer, 1972) as well as the parents' actual consumption of these substances (Smith, 1980; Kandel, Kessler, and Margulies, 1978) were found by several investigators to be associated with drug abuse by their children. This is precisely what one should expect, according to social learning theory (Akers, 1977; Bandura, 1977).

But the family has other roles as well. First, several studies (Napier et al., 1983; Penning and Barnes, 1982; Kandel et al., 1976) found that the prevalence of drug use is higher among children of broken or tension-ridden families. This may be explained both by the strains that the malfunctioning family produces in its members and by their members' behavior.

Social learning theory (and its variant in criminology, "differential association" theory) predict a strong peer group influence, too. The adolescent, trying to develop along the lines provided by a variety of role models, often imitates the behavior of his or her peers. Thus, several studies show that the more one is exposed to drug-using peers, the more likely he or she is to use drugs, even if such substances were never used before (Smith, 1980; Akers, Krohn, Lanza-Kadure, and Radosevitch, 1979).

The step from readiness to actual use is largely dependent on the availability of the right drug. This availability includes both the physical presence of drugs in an easily accessible environment and the adolescents' knowledge of the accessible drugs, prices, and the procedure for obtaining them. This is precisely where law enforcement has its major effect. Thus, in countries like Israel, laws and law enforcement agencies render cocaine a rare, expensive drug, while alcohol is easily available.

The value orientation of the adolescent and his or her involvement in the activities of a religious community may be very important factors. Khavari and Harman (1982) found a significant association between the intensity of religious beliefs and the consumption of drugs and alcohol among adolescents and adults: subjects who described themselves as religious consumed significantly lower quantities of these substances. Similar findings were reported by McIntosh, Fich, Wilson, and Nyberg (1981); Singh, Broota, and Singh (1983); and Kirk (1979). Fischler (1976) found that even those subjects who used drugs only occasionally were lower in their religious values than non-users. It seems, then, that religion with its absolute values and highly internalized control mechanisms provides effective barriers against deviant behavior.

Personal and Interpersonal Factors. Gendreau and Gendreau (1970) coined the term "Addiction Proneness." This term denotes a personality who is predisposed, or susceptible, to addiction. One of the major research directions of psychologists in the substance abuse domain has been the attempt to discover and identify those personality traits which mark the addiction prone. Once this goal is achieved and reliable indicators of risk are provided, it may be possible to identify and direct intensive prevention programs at specific, high-risk populations.

Work in this area has been directed by several theoretical assumptions. Conger (1956) considers drug and alcohol consumption a type of drive-reducing behavior. This approach is supported by a number of studies which found that drug abuse among adolescents was associated with anxiety and depression (Penning and Barnes, 1982; Kilpatrick, Sutker, and Smith, 1976; Cockett, 1971). Interestingly, this was found for users of different drugs, regardless of the drug's specific pharmaceutical effects.

These findings, however, are not universal. Other investigators, particularly those who looked not only for the presence of anxiety-reduction effects but for their relative contribution, suggest that these effects, although present, are marginal. Only a few of the adolescents using drugs do so primarily as a means for overcoming anxiety and depression (Kaestner, Rosen, and Appel, 1977).

Several investigators suggest that adolescent drug use is largely an expression of rebellion and rejection of established norms and a desire to have fun and exciting experiences (Iutcovich and Iutcovich, 1982; Jessor and Jessor, 1977). This mode of explanation relies heavily on the personality trait that Zuckerman (1972) and Zuckerman et al. (1972) identify as "sensation seeking." Sensation seekers are, by definition, more likely than others to manifest risky, unusual, and non-conforming behaviors. Barnea (1978) found that (Israeli adolescent) sensation seekers are higher in their readiness to use drugs, and Segal, Huba, and Singer (1980) suggest that this association is produced by a direct, causal link. This link is dual: first, the direct neural stimulation provided by psychoactive drugs would be gratifying for sensation seekers. Second, being an illegal act, drug use involves its own risks and excitement which, in turn, would satisfy sensation seeking.

The expectation of a satisfying substance experience has become a part of the adolescent's attitude toward drugs. Several studies found that the approaches toward drugs are positively related to drug behavior and behavioral tendencies (Andrews and Kandel, 1979; Barnea, 1978). Christiansen and Goldman (1983), following Fishbein's earlier work, have suggested that when adolescents' expectations are reinforced by a group's positive norm towards alcohol, there is a high probability that actual drug consumption ensues.

The Multi-dimensional Approach

It is now obvious that drug related behavior is influenced by many different factors. Modern studies generally refute the once-accepted assumption that adolescents use drugs as a consequence of certain psychopathological conditions. A variety of social and psychological processes bring the adolescent to that stage in his life in which he or she makes up his/her mind and decides whether or not to use drugs. Figure 18.1, page 469, presents the major drug-use factors and their interrelationships.

At first, consumption is generally associated with pleasure and, at the same time, it may aid in coping with stressful personal situations. But, with

FIGURE 18.1

A MULTI-DIMENSIONAL MODEL OF ADOLESCENT SUBSTANCE ABUSE

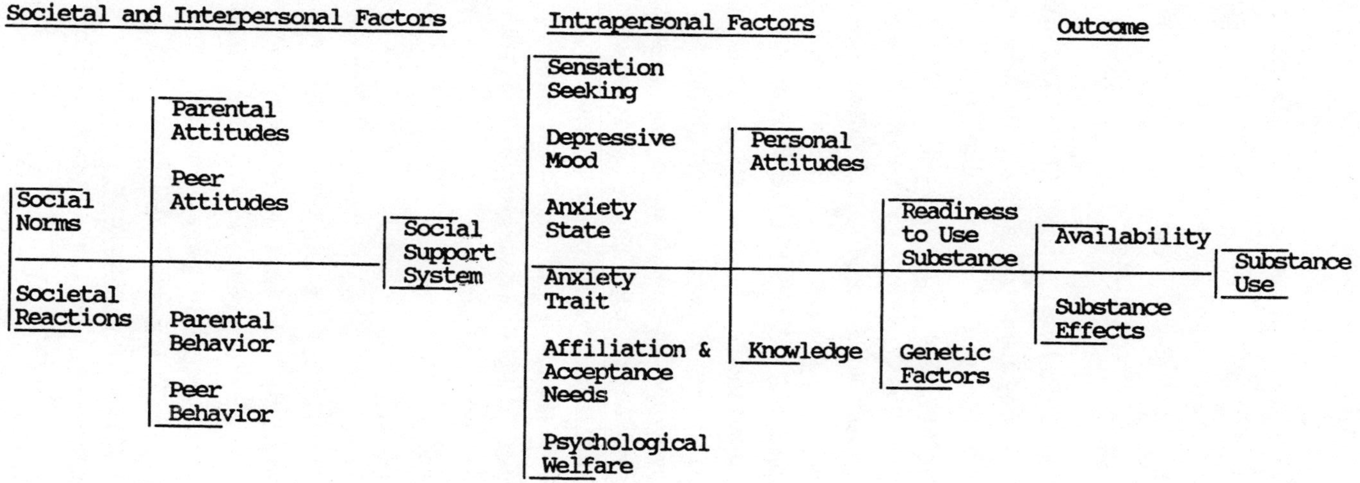

Societal and Interpersonal Factors

Social Norms
- Parental Attitudes
- Peer Attitudes

Social Support System

Societal Reactions
- Parental Behavior
- Peer Behavior

Intrapersonal Factors

- Sensation Seeking
- Depressive Mood
- Anxiety State

Personal Attitudes

- Anxiety Trait
- Affiliation & Acceptance Needs
- Psychological Welfare

Knowledge

Genetic Factors

Readiness to Use Substance

Outcome

Availability

Substance Use

Substance Effects

progressive consumption, the nature of the process changes. The expectation of a hedonistic and pleasurable experience diminishes and fear of withdrawal symptoms grows as a dominant motivation. It is at this stage that addictive patterns of substance use are developed and the adolescent's lifestyle takes a "down-the-road" turn.

Empirical Validation of the Multi-dimensional Model

A study testing a part of the above-described model was conducted. Two hundred twenty-eight Israeli juveniles, 108 males and 120 females, whose ages ranged from 15 to 17 years, served as subjects. The following variables were studied: Sensation seeking, state-trait anxiety, the need for social approval, knowledge about substances, attitudes towards the various substances and substance use, and the dependent variable which was labelled by us "the readiness to experiment with and use drugs." The purpose of the study was to examine the effects of these variables upon adolescents' readiness to use drugs. As Figure 18.2, page 471, shows (based on a two-step multiple regression analysis), the readiness is affected by two cognitive variables and three affective factors. The major affective factors are sensation seeking and the need for social acceptance. However, only sensation seeking has a direct effect upon the "readiness to use drugs," while the effect of the need for social approval is mediated by its influence on attitudes and knowledge.

It is interesting to note that anxiety state has effects on readiness, while anxiety trait has not. This may imply that A-state may be related to initial use only as a transient, situational factor; A-trait as an inherent, perhaps, pathological, personality trait

Figure 18.2

PATH ANALYSIS FOR READINESS TO USE DRUGS

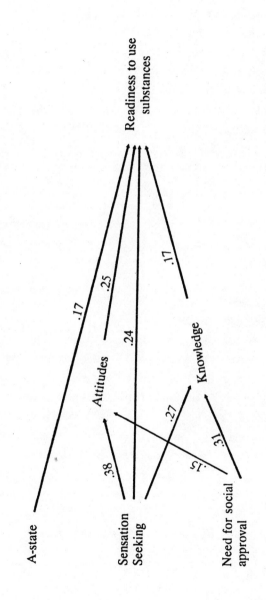

has hardly an effect (at least when emphasis lies on a large-scale view of the problem).

A rather surprising finding is that knowledge, while it is affected by personality traits, has a positive (rather than negative) effect upon "readiness." That is to say, that individuals who express high "readiness to use drugs" usually know more about drugs than those who are not willing to experiment with them.

Following this study, a longitudinal investigation was designed and implemented in Israel. The preliminary findings further support the proposed multi-dimensional model of adolescents' substance use in Israel.

Let us now discuss prevention of adolescent substance use, in particular, an experimental substance-education program which is based on our multi-dimensional model.

PREVENTION

Preliminary Considerations

Several assumptions concerning the nature of educational prevention programs and our target population underlie our thoughts.

Our first assumption is that educational programs should be directed towards "demand reduction." The alternative approach, "supply reduction," is more appropriately achieved by law enforcement.

Secondly, it is assumed that prevention should begin as early as possible. It is generally accepted that juveniles who start their drug use at an early age tend to be heavier, more persistent users than late starters. Indeed, Rotter (1977) found in Israel that over 75% of the Israeli opiate addicts had started their drug-use career during adolescence. Our preliminary findings in a recent longitudinal study, also indicate that about half of the substance-using adolescents started their involvement with substances before they reached the age of sixteen. Yet, educational programs in Israel tend to be oriented towards the period of late adolescence. Therefore, in line with the recommendations of Newman et al. (1984), it is suggested that in order to achieve their optimal effects, educational programs should be aimed at the 13- to 15-year-old age levels.

The third assumption is related to the social setting in which the program is applied. We assume that adolescents are using substances within a given encouraging social environment. Thus, prevention should be exercised within such social environments. Applying it within the social setting has an additional advantage. As we indicated, one of the major factors that determine substance use among adolescents is the attitudes and values of the adolescents, which, in turn, are significantly affected by the attitudes the adolescent ascribes to his or her peers. Staging the educational program in this setting and exposing all of the adolescents to it is expected to affect group attitudes towards alcohol and drug use in the desired direction. Thus, group influence and pressure are serving the purpose of prevention rather than of initiation. In Israel, substance education programs are primarily applied in schools.

Among the educational programs, one may distinguish three major approaches: Knowledge/Attitudes, Values/Decision-Making, and the Social Competence (Moskowitz, 1983).

The Knowledge/Attitudes approach assumes that substance use is at least partly the result of lack of information or of decisions based on misinformation. The misinformed adolescent develops false positive attitudes towards the drugs. Thus, educational programs undertake to correct wrong beliefs by supplying true, reliable information. It is hoped that this information will cause attitude change and, consequently, a change in drug-related behavior.

The Values/Decision-Making approach is based on the assumption that drugs or alcohol abuse are the consequences of a faulty decision-making process. The fault may be either in the logical process or in the values underlying it. Thus, these programs focus on the clarification of major social values and their logical implications, demonstrating the various undesirable aspects of alcohol and drug use.

Social malfunctioning is assumed by the Social Competence approach. Presumably, adolescents tend to use drugs either as a coping mechanism, or as a consequence of group pressure. Either way, acquiring social skills would reduce the need for drugs. Programs following this approach emphasize the ability to stand firm and resist group pressures and try to "inoculate" the participants against social climates which encourage alcohol and drug use.

While alcohol and drug education programs have been operating for over twenty-five years, attempts to evaluate them systematically started only recently. A survey of several evaluation studies leads to the following conclusions:

1) Most programs succeed in improving the participants' knowledge about drugs. However, they hardly show any effect as far as behavior change is

concerned. This finding is consistent with one of our early findings in Israel (Barnea, 1978): drug-related knowledge was positively related to readiness to use drugs.

2) Most studies suffer from a variety of methodological inadequacies. Primarily, these include small, selected (and hence biased) samples, high drop-out rates, inappropriate control groups, and fuzzy criteria for success.

3) Most studies provide only a sketchy, superficial description of the program, its operators, and the participants. Yet, it seems that the success of a program may largely depend upon the persons who actually operate it (Moskowitz et al., 1984; Goldstein and DiNitto, 1982; Schaps et al., 1981).

The Prevention Program

One major implication of the theoretical and empirical model presented above is that an effective prevention program must take a multi-level approach. It should address intra-personal factors, such as self-awareness and understanding, improvement of self-concept, and self-reliance to allow responsible decision-making.

The program should be directed at the interpersonal level, including some explication of interpersonal interactions and communication skills. Finally, the program must involve the extra-personal level: the subject's social attitudes and values, the development of environmental mastery skills, and the inter-dependence within his or her community.

A second implication, derived mostly from our empirical finding, is that information alone is not preventive and may, in fact, bring more harm than

475

benefit. Better information (or knowledge) about drugs will reduce their consumption only when it is combined with negative attitudes and with lowered anxiety.

Given these findings, we suggest that substance education programs should include the following elements:

1) Information from several areas. Those areas should include human development and how it is affected by unbalanced consumption of different substances (sugar, caffeine, medications, alcohol, and so on). A second topic should be the psychoactive drugs and their physiological and psychological effects. A third topic should involve relevant regulations, laws, and penal policy. And, finally, information should be provided about local services and agencies which may be helpful to users and their families.

2) Clarification of values and attitudes. As we have already emphasized, attitudes may have a major role in the formation of an individual's drug-related behaviors. Thus, a clear, consistent presentation of values and attitudes is crucial in order to shape the attitudes in the desired direction.

3) An inoculation workshop. Inoculation is well known in the fields of attitude change and propaganda, on one hand, and stress management, on the other hand. Duryea (1983) developed it into a prevention method. Assuming that a youngster may be trained to withstand pro-drug-use opinions and to cope with peer pressures, Duryea (1983) introduced a preventive alcohol education program, which was based on the inoculation theory. He was able to demonstrate that knowing the pro-substance-use arguments, awareness of these pressures, and being trained in role-playing resistance to them have actually reduced alcohol use.

4) <u>Alternatives</u>. As we have shown in our findings, drug use may satisfy certain individual needs. If one wishes to reduce it, alternative modes to the satisfaction of these needs must be supplied. Many of the users tend to ascribe to the drug of their choice properties such as anxiety and tension reduction, increased creativity, sensory stimulation, and so on. These individuals may develop a feeling of helplessness in the absence of the psychoactive substance. One of the major functions of any prevention program is to provide the adolescents with viable socially approved alternatives. It seems reasonable to expect that once these juveniles find alternative ways to achieve satisfaction, meaningful activities, and acceptable excitement, substances will lose at least some of their attraction.

5) <u>Specific relevant topics</u>. There are a number of alcohol- and drug-related topics which may be of particular significance for adolescents. They include a topic like sexual relationships. Since many adolescents mistakenly believe that psychoactive drugs may serve as aphrodisiacs and improve sexual performance, the topic should be thoroughly clarified.

Another topic involves the effects of drugs upon perception, thoughts, and creativity. However, the most significant topic in our program is the effect of drugs and alcohol upon driving. We are facing a universal trend in which the minimum age of drivers is becoming lower and lower. At the same time, alcohol and drug consumption among adolescents increases, thus producing a significant growth in the number of driving accidents (Douglas, 1983; Damkot, 1982). Any prevention program should, therefore, focus on facts related to driving while intoxicated. This means the development of responsibilities beyond those implied by the basic issue of whether or not to use alcohol (or any other drug). Responsibility, in this issue, means "don't drive after you drink," "warn your friends not to drive while intoxicated," and so forth.

Two additional target populations were incorporated by us into the educational program. The two groups are parents and teachers. We have already mentioned the parental role in the initiation process. However, this role may be reversed and parents may actively participate in prevention and rehabilitation. Parent's organizations are already actively involved as lobbying groups, but their roles may be expanded. Parents may be subjects of programs increasing their responsiveness to the needs of youths, and they may serve as models for appropriate, responsible behavior (for example, by avoiding driving after drinking). Although early studies in this area did not yield any clear conclusion, we advised school systems to involve parents in the programs (Albert, Simpson, and Eaglesham, 1983; Bandy and President, 1983; Klein and Swisher, 1983; Shain, Suurvali, and Heather, 1980).

As for teachers' involvement, they may be particularly relevant, since the school may be the optimal organizational or communal setting for conducting educational prevention programs. Newman, Mohr, Badges, and Gillespie (1984) and Rose and Duer (1978) found that teacher training was a central factor in the effectiveness of their programs. Slaven (1980) and DiCicco (1978) found that in addition to acquiring training skills following a training program, teachers also change their attitudes and show more understanding towards adolescents who have experimented with substances. This attitudinal change, as well as the information and training acquired, may significantly increase the teacher's effectiveness.

CONCLUSION

In view of the rising use of cigarettes, alcohol, and legal and illegal drugs, our starting point is that consumption and its patterns are largely matters of individual choice. Our theoretical model, and the empirical findings validating it, present a number of factors which may affect the individual's choice.

Our approach to prevention is based on demand reduction and attempts to combine various resources toward the achievement of this goal. We believe that a program should be considered as an integration of elements, rather than a mere collection of unrelated approaches. This combination should involve information as well as attitude change, participation of significant others, and provision of alternative channels for the satisfaction of adolescents' needs.

REFERENCES

Akers, R. L. 1977. Deviant Behavior: Social Learning Approach, 2nd Ed. Belmont, CA: Wadsworth.

Akers, R. L., Krohn, M. D., Lanza-Kadure, L., and Radosevich, N. 1979. Social learning and deviant behavior. American Sociological Review 44: 635-655.

Albert, W. G., Simpson, R. I., and Eaglesham, J. A. 1983. Evaluation of a drinking and parenting educational program in six Ontario communities. Journal of Drug Education 3:327-336.

Andrews, K. H. and Kandel, D. B. 1979. Attitude and behavior: A specification of the contingent consistency hypothesis. American Sociological Review 44:298-310.

Backeland, F. and Lundwall, L. K. 1977. Engaging the alcoholic in treatment and keeping him there. In B. Kissin and H. Beglieter (eds.), Treatment and Rehabilitation of the Chronic Alcoholic. NY: Plenum.

Bandura, A. 1977. Social Learning Theory. Eaglewood Cliffs, NJ: Prentice Hall.

Bandy, P. and President, P. A. 1983. Recent literature on drug abuse prevention and mass media: Focusing on youth, parents, women, and the elderly. Journal of Drug Education 13:255-272.

Barnea, Z. 1978. A multi-dimensional model of adolescents' drug use. Society and Welfare 4:359-383 (Hebrew).

Chambers, C. D., Inciardi, J. A., and Siegal, H. A. 1975. Chemical Coping. NY: Spectrum.

Christiansen, B. A. and Goldman, M. S. 1983. Alcohol-related expectancies versus demographic/background variables in the prediction of adolescents' drinking. Journal of Consulting and Clinical Psychology 51:249-257.

Cockett, R. 1971. Drug Abuse and Personality in Young Offenders. London: Butterworth's.

Cockett, R. and Marks, V. 1969. Amphetamine-taking among young offenders. British Journal of Psychiatry 115:1203-1204.

Conger, J. J. 1956. Alcoholism: Theory, problem, and challenge II: Reinforcement theory and the dynamics of alcoholism. Journal of Studies on Alcoholism 17:291-324.

Damkot, D. K. 1982. Alcohol incidence in rural drivers: Characteristics of a population and clue for counter measures. Drug and Alcohol Dependence 3:305-324.

DiCicco, L. 1978. Evaluating the impact of alcohol education. Alcohol Health and Research World 3(2).

Douglas, R. L. 1983. Youth, alcohol, and traffic accidents: Current statutes. Recent Developments in Alcoholism 1:347-366.

Duryea, E. J. 1983. Utilizing tenets of inoculation theory to develop and evaluate a preventive alcohol education intervention. Journal of School Health 53:250-256.

Fawzy, F. I., Coombs, R. H., and Gerber, B. 1983. Generational continuity in the use of substances: The impact of parental substance use on adolescent substance use. Addictive Behaviors 8:108-114.

Fischbein, M. 1967. Attitudes and the prediction of behavior. In M. Fischbein (ed.), Reading in Attitude, Theory, and Measurement. NY: Wiley.

Fischler, M. L. 1976. Drug usage in rural, small town New England. Journal of Altered States of Consciousness 2:171-183.

Galanter, M. and Panepinto, W. 1980. Entering the alcohol out-patient service: Application of a systems approach to patient drop out. In M. Galanter (ed.), Currents in Alcoholism, Vol. II. NY: Grune and Stratton.

Gendreau, P. and Gendreau, L. 1970. The "addiction-prone" personality: A study of Canadian heroin addicts. Canadian Journal of Behavioral Science 2:18-25.

Goldstein, H. K. and DiNitto, D. 1982. Some method-ologocial problems, solutions, and findings from evaluating risk reduction projects. Journal of Drug Education 12:241-253.

Huba, G. J., Wingard, J. A., and Bentler, P. M. 1981. A comparison of two latent variable causal models for adolescent drug use. Journal of Personality and Social Psychology 40:180-193.

Iutcovich, J. M. and Iutcovich, M. 1982. Just for fun Alcohol and the college student. Chemical Dependencies: Behavioral and Biomedical Issues 4:167-185.

Jessor, R. and Jessor S. L. 1977. Problem Behavior and Psycho-Social Development. NY: Academic Press.

Johnston, L. D., Bachman, J. G., and O'Malley, P. M. 1979. Drugs and the Nation's High School Students: Five Year National Trend. Rockville, MD: National Institute for Drug Abuse.

Kaestner, E., Rosen, L., and Appel, F. 1977. Patterns of drug abuse: Relationships with ethnicity, sensation seeking, and anxiety. Journal of Consulting and Clinical Psychology 45:462-468.

Kandel, D. B. 1980. Drug and drinking behavior among youth. Annual Reviews in Sociology 6:235-285.

Kandel, D. B., Kessler, R., and Margulies, R. 1978. Antecedents of adolescent initiation into stages of drug use: A developmental analysis. In D. B. Kandel (ed.), Longitudinal Research on Drug Use: Empirical Findings and Methodological Issues. Washington, DC: Hemisphere.

Kandel, D. B., Treiman, D., Faust, R., and Single, E. 1976. Adolescent involvement in legal and illegal drug use: A multiple classification analysis Social Forces 55:438-458.

Khavari, K. A. and Harman, T. M. 1982. The relationship between the degree of professed religious belief and use of drugs. International Journal of the Addiction 17:847-857.

Kilpatrick,. D. G., Sutker, P. B., and Smith, A. D. 1976. Deviant drug and alcohol use: The role of anxiety, sensation seeking, and other personality variables. In M. Zuckerman and C. D. Spielberger (eds.), Emotions and Anxiety: New Concepts, Methods and Applications. Hillsdale, NJ: Lawrence Erlbaum Association.

Kirk, R. S. 1979. Drug use among rural youth. In G. M. Beschner and A. S. Friedman (eds.), Youth Drug Use. Lexington, MA: Lexington.

Klein, M. A. and Swisher, J. D. 1983. A statewide evaluation of a communication and parenting skills program. Journal of Drug Education 13:73-82.

Marlatt, G. A. A cognitive-behavioral model of the relapse process. In N. A. Krasnegor (ed.), Behavioral Analysis and Treatment of Substance Abuse (Research Monograph 25). Rockville, MD: National Institute on Drug Abuse

McIntosh, W. A., Fich, S. D., Wilson, J. B., and Nyberg, K. 1981. The effect of mainstream religious social control on adolescent drug use in rural areas. Review of Religious Research 23:54-75.

Mills, C. J. and Noyes, H. L. 1984. Patterns and correlates of initial and subsequent drug use among adolescents. Journal of Consulting and Clinical Psychology 52:231-243.

Moskowitz, J. 1983. Preventing adolescent substance abuse through drug education. In T. Glynn, C. Leukefeld, and J. Ludford (eds.), Preventing Adolescent Drug Abuse (Research Monograph 47). Rockville, MD: National Institute on Drug Abuse.

Moskowitz, J. M., Malvin, J. H., Scharffer, G. A., and Schaps, E. 1984. An experimental evaluation of a drug education course. Journal of Drug Education 14:9-22.

Nace, E. P. 1978. The Use of Craving in the Treatment of Alcoholism. Paper presented at the 32nd International Congress of Alcoholism, Warsaw, Poland.

Napier, T. L., Bachtel, D. C., and Carter, M. V. 1983. Factors associated with illegal drug use in rural Georgia. Journal of Drug Education 13:119-140.

Newman, I. M., Mohr, P., Badges, B., and Gillespie, T. S. 1984. Effects of teachers' preparation and student age on an alcohol and drug education. Journal of Drug Education 14:23-36.

Penning, M. and Barnes, G. E. 1982. Adolescent marijuana use: A review. International Journal of the Addiction 17:749-791.

Rose, S. E. and Duer, W. R. 1978. Drug/alcohol education -- A new approach for schools. Education 9:198-202.

Rotter, A. 1977. Epidemiological Approach to the Israeli Drug Problem. Jerusalem: Hebrew University. Unpublished M. A. thesis.

Schaps, E., DiBartolo, R., Moskowitz, J., Palley, C., and Churgin, S. 1981. Primary prevention evaluation research: A review of 127 impact studies. Journal of Drug Issues 11:17-43.

Segal, B., Huba, G., and Singer, J. 1980. Drugs, Daydreaming, and Personality: A Study of College Youth. Hillsdale, NJ: Lawrence Earlbaum.

Shain, M., Survali, H., and Heather, L. K. 1980. The Parents Communication Project. Toronto: Addiction Research Foundation.

Singh, S., Broota, K. D., and Singh, J. G. 1983. Value patterns and drug use behavior. Personality Study and Group Behavior 3:81-85.

Slaven, T. M. 1980. Evaluating professional education in drug use and abuse. Journal of Drug Education 10:313-318.

Smart, R. G. and Fejer, D. 1972. Drug use among adolescents and their parents: Closing the generation gap in mood modification. Journal of Abnormal Psychology 79:153-160.

Smith, G. M. 1980. Perceived effects of substance use A general theory. In O. J. Lettieri, M. Sayers, and H. W. Pearson (eds.), Theories on Drug Abuse: Selected Contemporary Perspectives (Research Monograph 30, pp. 50-59). Rockville, MD: National Institute on Drug Abuse.

Teichman, M. 1986. Dealing with the relapse: A relapse inoculation training. In S. Einstein (ed.), Drugs and Alcohol: Issues and Factors. NY: Plenum.

Teichman, M. 1987. An inoculation training for recovering alcoholics. Alcoholism Treatment Quarterly 10:29-40.

Wurmser, L. 1974. Psychoanalytic considerations of the etiology of compulsive drug use. Journal of the American Psychoanalytic Association 22:820-843.

Wurmser, L. 1978. The Hidden Dimensions: Psychodynamics in Compulsive Drug Use. NY: Aronson.

Zuckerman, M. 1972. Drug usage as one manifestation of a sensation seeking trait. In E. Keup (ed.), Drug Abuse: Current Concepts and Research. Springfield, IL: C. C. Thomas.

Zuckerman, M., Neary, R., Mangelsdorff, D., and Brustman, B. 1972. What is the sensation seeker? Personality trait and experience correlates of the Sensation Seeking Scale. Journal of Consulting and Clinical Psychology 39:308-321.

INTRODUCTION TO CHAPTER 19

In this chapter, Toch chronicles the modern Israeli experience with alcohol abuse where alcoholism was virtually unknown until recently. However, it is developing rapidly. Why?

The author addresses two problems simultaneously: 1) what is the cause of this rise in alcoholism and 2) where must the society intervene?

Toch suggests that the disease is imported along with immigration to Israel. But, fascinating questions emerge here: Is it imported as a cultural trait or as a genetic trait? Or, alternatively, is it the stress of social disintegration which accompanies migration that is responsible for increasing rates of alcoholism? The issue of cultural differences was seen earlier in the work of Hanson and Engs (Chapter 3). The issues of cultural differences and the stresses of acculturation were also raised previously in the work of Markides and Krause (Chapter 10). Though the author of this chapter does not provide definitive answers to these questions, she provides us some interesting methodologies by which current studies are attempting to find answers.

CHAPTER 19

RAPIDLY DEVELOPING ALCOHOLISM IN ORIENTAL JEWS: A PILOT STUDY OF ENZYMES AND ATTITUDES

Evelyn Toch

ABSTRACT

The purpose of the pilot project in this chapter was to explore the factors contributing to the rapidly developing alcoholism seen in a high percentage of Oriental Jews living in Israel. It is planned to use this knowledge to improve treatment, which, until now, has been an almost complete failure in this ethnic group.

Because earlier studies had implicated physiological reasons for alcohol sensitivity in other Oriental groups, the first step was to ascertain whether problems with alcohol metabolism could also be found in this group. Hair root analyses were run to detect the presence of an atypical form of the enzyme aldehyde dehydrogenase which has been found to play a key role in the elimination of alcohol and its degradation product acetyl aldehyde, which is much more toxic than the parent compound.

In this preliminary study, 46 Ashkenazi and Oriental Jews were used. Subjects were further divided into alcoholics randomly selected from a newly opened alcoholism treatment center in Ashdod, Israel, and non-alcoholic port workers, who were matched to the patients in origin and age. The results showed no difference in enzyme composition, either between alcoholics and non-alcoholics or between the different groups of origin. It is, however, premature

----

EVELYN TOCH began and administered the first alcoholism treatment center in Israel located in Ashdod.

to come to any conclusions from this small
sample, and further studies involving a larger
number of subjects are being carried out at
present.

In addition to an enzyme factor in
alcoholism, the stress of moving to Israel and
the inability to cope in a very heterogeneous
society has been implicated. The subjects
answered a "sense of coherence" questionnaire. This instrument was developed in Israel
to test the relationship between the effects of
stress and coping in determining health
outcomes. Both alcoholic and non-alcoholic
Oriental Jews showed a decreased coping
capacity, but alcoholic Oriental Jews showed
the most deficit. This finding suggests that
poor stress handling may lead to use of alcohol
as "relief."

ALCOHOLISM IN ISRAEL

Alcoholism in Israel is of relatively recent
origin. In 1950, Glatt (1970) on his visit to Israel
could not find any cases of alcoholism. By 1962,
however, according to Shuval and Krasilowksy (1968),
there were 25 Jewish alcoholic patients in the Talbieh
Hospital in Jerusalem. By 1976, Perina Eldar (1976),
who later was instrumental in starting a large network
of alcoholism treatment centers throughout Israel,
noted that some 1,500 heads of large households
receiving social assistance in Israel suffered from
alcoholism.

By 1979, several sources began to remark on the
"steadily growing problem of alcohol addiction" (Sagiv,
1979:280), and by early 1980, when Snyder arrived to
begin field work in Israel, the Jerusalem Post had
published an estimate of Israel's alcoholic population
as approaching 6,000 (February, 1980). Although the
available data continues to point to a rate that is

487

comparatively low among modern societies, it can no longer be said that Israel has no alcoholism problem. As a matter of fact, in an article in the Jerusalem Post, Dr. Krasilowksy quoted the number of 12,000 alcoholics in Israel and predicted that "within 15 years the rate of alcoholism in Israel will equal that of France or of the United States" (October, 1984).

INFLUENCES ON DRINKING PATTERNS

The socio-cultural factors relating to alcoholism in modern Israel have been only scantily studied to date. Attention has been drawn through research to possible links between alcoholism and immigration and the socio-cultural origins of alcoholic patients. It was found that alcoholics from Asia or Africa were most numerous (Wislicki, 1967).

For Jews of Asian or African origin, who are said by some to have exhibited a pattern of heavier drinking the in the first place, the dissolution of community and an exacerbation of drinking problems may be connected with the nature of the migration and the process of resettlement itself.

When considering the pre-immigration pattern of relatively heavier drinking among Jews in Middle Eastern countries, Asia, or North Africa, it is relevant to bear in mind that Islam required of its followers total abstinence from drinking alcohol. Against this background and the contrasting situation of Europe over the centuries, many observers see a dialectic in which Jewish minorities have inverted the dominant norms of the surrounding population regarding alcohol use, being sober when the majority drink heavily and more permissive about drinking when the surrounding population was abstinent (Bales, 1946).

Glad (1947) contends that comparative freedom from alcohol problems many be characteristic of so-called Ashkenazi Jews with roots in Europe but by no means necessarily of Jewish communities, resident for centuries in regions of the world where the surrounding majorities had quite the opposite norms regarding alcoholic beverages and their use. Jews in Europe, especially later in Poland and Russia, were surrounded by heavily drinking gentiles (Cossaks). Drinking often led to pogroms and was, therefore, especially abhorred by the Jews of this region, and this led them to invert the norms of the dominant heavy-drinking majority by despising drunkenness.

On the other hand, during Gandhi's time, Jews in India lived under strictly enforced prohibition. Even after his death, alcohol was expensive, difficult to get, and entirely forbidden to the surrounding Moslem and Buddhist population. Jews, at that time, were the only ones able to transport and sell alcohol, and in this way were more in contact with it than their neighbors.

After moving to Israel, these Jews found every type of alcohol freely available, and, furthermore, came into contact with other already heavily drinking immigrants. In addition, the male who had been a venerated patriarch in the rural family was often ill-equipped to cope with industrialized western society and frequently lacked the skills to find employment. The female could find work as a cleaning woman, and, because of the change of roles and other adjustment problems, the family structure disintegrated. It seemed that the unemployed male began to use alcohol to find "relief" from his anxiety and failure to deal with his problem.

BACKGROUND OF THE STUDY

For the purpose of this study we used a classification of Jews widely used by geneticists which recognizes three major ethnic communities of world Jewry: the Ashkenazi, the Sephardi, and the Oriental.[1] This classification has been especially useful in demonstrating the thesis that while Jews as a whole have more genetic traits in common with one another than the surrounding non-Jewish populations, there are, nevertheless, identifiable genetic communities within world Jewry exhibiting differences in the frequency of

----

[1] Ashkenazi Jews. Ashkenazi Jewry developed out of the Palestinian branch of Oriental Jewry. There was a slow and steady migration into Europe under Roman rule, and by the Middle Ages, Jews had established themselves in substantial numbers in what is now France and Germany. Eventually, they were forced largely to abandon these areas and to move into Eastern Europe, where they were to become the largest of world Jewry's ethnic communities. The main language of Ashkenazi Jewry was Yiddish (Judeo-German).

Oriental Jews. After the destruction of the first temple, one segment of the Jewish community remained in Israel (Palestinian branch). Being nomads, part of their group gradually drifted into Arabia. (In 1950, the entire Jewish population of Yemen and Aden were flown to Israel in the famous "Magic Carpet.") The other segment was taken into captivity to Babylon (Iraq) and some migrated to Iran, Kurdistan, Afghanistan, Bukhara, the Caucasian Mountains, and India. (This last sub-group is now called the Bene Israel.) They kept their Jewish identity but accepted much of the cultural and dietary habits of the surrounding population; for example, many wear saris. With the rise of the Greco-Roman Empires, some Oriental Jews also began to migrate westward and settle in parts of North Africa.

Sephardi Jews. This is a part of Oriental Jewry who migrated westward within Islam. Sephardi in Hebrew means "Spanish" and came into general use as a designation when, centuries later (during the Inquisition), these Jews were driven from what had then become Catholic Spain. Several sub-groups evolved and the main language spoken was Ladino (Judeo-Spanish).

certain known genetic traits (Goodman, 1979). There are certain diseases of known genetic origin with relatively high frequency among Ashkenazi Jews but seldom encountered among Sephardim and Orientals, while others virtually unknown in Ashkenazim are frequent among the Sephardim.

Reference to these ethnic communities as genetic communities should not obscure the fact that they are divergent from one another in social-historical experience, surrounding peoples and civilizations, special cultural and religious emphasis, and language.

Because of this unclear genetic picture, there was considerable speculation whether alcoholism in Oriental Jews in Israel had a physiological component similar to that found in the Orientals studied by Ewing et al. (1974) at the University of North Carolina.

In clinical studies, he found Oriental subjects to be significantly more sensitive to alcohol than Occidental subjects. The Orientals showed significantly more skin flushing, increased heart rate, drop in blood pressure, and general discomfort with alcohol than Occidental subjects. In addition, the Orientals more frequently reported family histories of flushing. He reported, at this time, that evidence suggests that the low rates of alcohol abuse and alcoholism commonly found among Oriental people may have physiological rather than cultural origins. Ewing further found that the overall blood acetylaldehyde levels of the Oriental subjects after ingesting alcohol did exceed those of the Occidental subjects. He felt that there was a relationship between the flushing syndrome and the presence of a high level of acetylaldehyde in a person's body, and stated that "it does seem clear that physiological factors are at work here and that cultural explanations will not suffice to explain the phenomena we have observed" (1974:135).

In his study, all of the subjects lived in the U.S. and most were eating an American diet, and he, therefore, doubted that diet was a significant factor in this particular research project.

While both Ewing and Yoshida found that the discomfort accompanying alcohol ingestion kept alcohol abuse at a low level in some Oriental subjects (Yoshida, 1982), other researchers took additional factors into account. Wolff wrote that "conceivably the prevalence of the highly visible flushing response will inhibit these groups from drinking as long as their social structure is intact and exercises sanctions against intoxication. When the social cohesion of a culture is destroyed, as it has been in the case of the American Indians, a greater susceptibility to alcohol intoxication may act as one of several predisposing factors for alcoholism" (1973:195). It was for this reason that our pilot study took a two-pronged approach.

First, the physiological component was studied (enzyme analysis) by hair root analysis, and, second, the social disintegration concept was tested by exploring the coping mechanisms of the subjects ("sense of coherence" questionnaire).

THE PHYSIOLOGICAL COMPONENT

Two major enzymes, alcohol dehydrogenase (ADH) and aldehyde dehydrogenase (ALDH) play an important part in alcohol metabolism. Most data so far collected show that the initial alcohol sensitivity quite common in many Oriental subjects might be due to a delayed oxidation of acetylaldehyde (Goedde et al., 1979). No significant differences between Orientals and Caucasians was found in the rate of alcohol degradation (action of alcohol dehydrogenase). However, the second major enzyme, aldehyde dehydrogenase, may possibly be a determining factor in alcohol sensitivity (Goedde et al., 1983). Acetylaldehyde, which is more toxic than alcohol itself, has been shown to produce alcohol intoxication symptoms and has been implicated in causing possible organ damage in chronic alcoholics. Using sensitive micro-methods, both alcohol and aldehyde dehydrogenase have been detected in human hair root cells. The use of hair root follicles to study enzyme variants and metabolic defects was developed and described extensively by Goedde, Agarwal, and Harada in Hamburg (1983, 1980, 1978). They reported studies on Europeans and a variety of Oriental subjects which showed that their hair-root-analysis methods detected a relationship between the presence of an unusual aldehyde dehydrogenase enzyme and a flushing response, coupled with a high level of acetylaldehyde in the blood of Oriental subjects (Goedde et al., 1980).

Using the above studies as a guide, hair root samples were collected from 43 alcoholic subjects registered for treatment at a newly opened alcoholism treatment center in Ashdod, Israel. The subjects were then matched for age and ethnic group with port workers who volunteered to participate in the project. Altogether, 86 subjects were tested.

The hair roots were analyzed by Professor Goedde in Hamburg. The results of this preliminary sample showed no difference between either ethnic group or between alcoholics and non-alcoholics.

Because of the small number of respondents, a larger study including Ashkenazi, Sephardi, and Oriental Jews divided into alcoholics and non-alcoholic subjects is now in progress.

SENSE OF COHERENCE

Because of the implications of social and environmental factors in alcoholism, a questionnaire was also administered to alcoholics and non-alcoholics to determine whether there was a different response in coping with stress between the groups.

This instrument was developed at the Department of Sociology at Ben Gurion University of the Negev (Antonowsky, 1982) to determine a person's location on the health-disease continuum. The sense of coherence is defined as: "A global orientation that expresses the extent to which one has a pervasive, enduring through dynamic feeling of confidence that one's internal and external environments are predictable, and there is a high probability that things will work out as well as can reasonably be expected" (Antonowksy, 1982:4). The model regards stress as ubiquitos in human existence and emphasizes coping as decisive in determining health outcomes. Themes such as manageability, comprehensibility, and meaningfulness of one's life are explored.

The responses to these questionnaires were analyzed, and the results showed significantly lower scores for alcoholics than non-alcoholics. The 38 alcoholic respondents included 15 Ashkenazis, 16 Sephardis, and 7 Orientals. The 38 non-alcoholic members of the control groups were 18 Orientals, 13 Sephardis, and 7 Ashkenazis.

The mean "sense of coherence" had been set at 55 to 60 by tests among various populations and ethnic groups. The non-alcoholics tested in this study showed a mean of 56.6, which, even if somewhat on the low side, was within the norm established. The alcoholics, however, showed a mean of 47.4, which is a significant difference.

Overall, the sense of coherence was lower in Oriental Jews than in Ashkenazi Jews. Non-alcoholic Ashkenazis rated 58.3, while non-alcoholic Oriental Jews rated 52.8 on the sense of coherence scale. Alcoholic Ashkenazis rated 48.8, while alcoholic Orientals rated 47.0. Therefore, Oriental Jews exhibited a smaller capacity for coping with life's problems, and those Oriental Jews who are alcoholic show even lower coherence. This reduced ability to cope may lead to a sense of failure that could be one of the factors increasing the likelihood of their looking for "relief" in alcohol.

Other studies found that higher levels of anxiety and/or lower levels of assertiveness predispose an individual toward the development of alcoholism (Schuckit, 1983). Both of these traits can be said to be present in many Oriental Jews, and they certainly are not conducive to good coping in a society composed of many ethnic groups with severe economic and political problems. Lastly, it is essential that dietary habits be studied in more detail. The suggestion has been made that the metabolism of aldehyde toxicity is associated with "a rice diet" and/or lower protein intake than is typical in the United States (Ewing, 1983). Therefore, studies in this area are being undertaken and results should be forthcoming soon.

REFERENCES

Ackerman, R. 1983. _Children of Alcoholics_. Holmes Beach, FL: Learning Publications, Inc.

Antonowksy, A. 1982, August. _The Sense of Coherence: Development of a Research Instrument_. Paper presented to the Research Committee on the Sociology of Mental Health at the International Sociological Association World Congress, Mexico City.

Asmussen, E. _et al_. 1948. The pharmacological action of acetylaldehyde on the human organism. _Acta Pharmacologica Toxicologica_ (K.b.h.) 4:311-320.

Bales, R. 1946. Cultural differences in rates of alcoholism. _Quarterly Journal of Studies on Alcohol_ 6:480-499.

Black, C. 1982. _It Will Never Happen to Me_. Denver, CO: M.A.C. Printing and Publications Division.

Eldar, P. 1976. _An Israeli Experiment in the Treatment of Alcoholism_. Jerusalem: Israel Ministry of Social Affairs, Department of International Relations.

Ewing, J. 1983. Biomedical aspects of alcohol sensitivity. _Advances in Alcoholism_ II (17):2.

Ewing, J. _et al_. 1974. Alcohol sensitivity and ethnic background. _American Journal of Psychiatry_ 131:2.

Glad, D. 1947. Attitudes and experiences of American-Jewish and American-Irish male youth as related to differences in adult rates of inebriety. _Quarterly Journal of Studies on Alcohol_ 8:406-472.

Glatt, M. 1970. Alcoholism and drug dependence among Jews. _British Journal of Addiction_ 64: 297-304.

496

Goedde, W. et al. 1980. Genetic studies on alcohol metabolizing enzymes: Detection of isozymes in human hair roots. Enzyme 25: 281-286.

Goedde, W. et al. 1983. Pharmacogenetics of alcohol sensitivity. Pharmacology, Biochemistry and Behavior 18: 161-166.

Goedde, W. et al. 1978. Racial differences in alcohol sensitivity: A new hypothesis. Human Genetics 51: 331-334.

Goodman, R. 1979. A perspective on genetic diseases among the Jewish people. In R. R. Goodman and A. G. Motulsky (eds.), Genetic Diseases Among Ashkenazi Jews. NY: Raven Press.

Pickens, R. 1983. Children of Alcoholics. Holmes Beach, FL: Learning Publications, Inc.

Sagiv, M., 1979. The problem of alcoholism in Israel. Archives of International Medicine 39:280-281.

Schuckit, M. 1983. Anxiety and assertiveness in the relatives of alcoholics and controls. Journal of Clinical Psychiatry 43:238.

Shuval, R. and Krasilowsky, D. 1968. A study of hospitalized male alcoholics. Israel Annals of Psychiatry 1:277-292.

Snyder, C. et al. 1982. Alcoholism among the Jews in Israel: A pilot study. Journal of Studies on Alcohol 43(7).

Wislicki, L. 1967. Alcoholism and drug addiction in Israel. British Journal of Addiction 62:367-373.

Wolff, P. 1973. Vasomotor sensitivity to alcohol in diverse mongoloid populations. American Journal of Human Genetics.

Yoshida, A. 1982. Molecular basis of differences in alcohol metabolism between Orientals and Caucasians. Japanese Journal of Human Genetics 27:55-70.

INTRODUCTION TO CHAPTER 20

Sargent begins her discussion of drinking in Australia with a mini-review of some theories of alcohol use. Her agenda, however, is to test the applicability of one specific theory -- a power relations theory of drinking. This requires that she examine the role of the state .in promoting drinking behavior. If she finds that the state does promote drinking, she must then ask why it does so.

This is not a type of theorizing that is well known in the United States, and it bears careful scrutiny. Sargent adds a perspective on the consumption of alcohol not seen before in this volume. Where previously we have focused upon use of alcohol by individuals, Sargent focuses on the state. She argues that there is an alcohol industry, which includes producers, sellers, tax collectors, and alcohol therapists among others, that is dependent upon alcohol consumption and alcoholics. Her argument is impressive and not to be taken lightly. She contrasts the economic benefit to the state of high alcohol consumption versus the costs to individuals and families of alcoholism.

In examining why the state should encourage alcohol use, we are led to recall the comments of Hanson and Engs in Chapter 3 about the encouragement of black slaves to drink in America. Sargent makes a similar argument here about the role of alcohol in promoting and maintaining social inequalities in Australia.

Further, she argues that alcohol is used to create and maintain categories of deviants such as the skid row alcoholics, which we have seen in Fagan (Chapter 8), and in Kaestner et al.'s S.R.O. occupants (Chapter 16).

Sargent's is a unique perspective. It does not explain all drinking behavior, but it adds a valuable insight -- the state and deviance are interconnected.

CHAPTER 20

DRINKING AND THE PERPETUATION OF SOCIAL INEQUALITY IN AUSTRALIA

Margaret Sargent

ABSTRACT

In this chapter, various social science explanations to alcohol use through cultural, social deviance, and political economy approaches are critically reviewed. A macro-sociological power relations perspective is used. Drinking is regarded as one behavior of many through which subordinate groups in society are managed by dominant groups and social inequality is created and perpetuated. Pressures to drink operate when people are participating in social processes of achieving acceptance, equality, and social mobility. Drinking norms of subordinate groups permit them less freedom, legitimize social control, and maintain racial barriers.

Australian society is described in illustration. The Alcoholism Industry is an unorganized alliance of government, business,

---

MARGARET SARGENT is Consultant to the New South Wales Ministry of Education in Australia.

upper professions, and media -- the dominant
groups. They employ thousands in alcohol
manufacture and distribution, treatment,
correction and insurance, and they produce
"alcoholics." The results of drinking in terms
of social control and psychological regard are
compared with those of sexual activity,
gambling, and use of other drugs.

INTRODUCTION

The social sciences have used a number of different
approaches to explaining the causes and consequences of
the drinking of alcohol. There was the cultural
approach in which societies were studied and compared
to discover how drinking might be causally related to
social organization, cultural anxiety level, cultural
integration, religious ritual, psychological dependency, social attitudes to drinking, and so on. The
greatest benefit of this approach was the way it
bypassed the moralistic, "blame the individual,"
interpretations of psychological and medical perspectives. Its greatest defect was to postpone consideration of the role of the state, and of political
and economic aspects of drinking.

Secondly, there was the social deviance approach.
The subject matter of sociology has in the past been
conveniently divided between sociologists of "deviance"
and sociologists of "normal" life. The former accepted
the responsibility for explaining various dramatic
forms of deviance, such as crime, drug dependence,
alcoholism, mental illness, and sexual deviation all
assumed by definition to be abnormal. Their
explanations were framed in functionalist terms, being
based on the notion that the health of a society
depended like a biological cell on its parts

functioning efficiently to contribute to the health of the whole, and that any deviation from this normal process was unhealthy and pathological, to be "corrected," "treated," and returned to its previous healthy state. It was not perceived until the labelling theorists' and phenomenologists' work that society might create deviance by its so-called attempts to bring people back into conformity with norms (Lemert, 1967). Meanwhile, conflict theorists in general ignored deviance as such, implicitly equating it with the economic inequality inevitable in any class society. They made little effort to analyze the more subtle and disguised processes through which continued social inequality for some is effected.

Thirdly, the political economy approach is emerging and offering insights into the relationships between political and economic organization and aspects of alcohol use. At last, we seem to have a framework for developing macro-sociological theory in alcohol studies. Yet, again, there is a danger of a limited perspective being taken. One tendency is to focus too closely on alcohol control policy and its relationship to alcohol problems, thus, ignoring the opportunity to relate the whole picture of the relation of the state, and its political and economic organization, to broad aspects of social inequality. A second danger is to view the state in narrow terms. For example, as if it is an independent power which governs and balances relationships between business interests and consumer interests. From this assumption arises a second, which is that it is the state's role which determines which consideration will predominate: the economic freedom of producers or the maintenance of people's health and quality of life generally. But, in monopoly capitalism, the state is no longer an independent power for its interest in maintaining political and economic control is the same as the producers. By requiring revenue payments from producers, the state becomes economically dependent and subject to their influence in its enactment of law and application of policy. How much consideration is given to non-economic values?

Makela and Viikari (1977:160) have listed four interests of the capitalist state with regard to alcohol: 1) fiscal, 2) industrial, commercial, and agricultural policy, 3) social policy, and 4) public order. They point out that the political economy approach focuses on the first two interests and usually regards them as unrelated to the consequences of drinking. Other workers concentrate on the last two interests and confine their attention to drinking as a problem. However, if macro-sociological theory is to be developed, all four interests must be considered and seen in the historical and cultural context of a given society. They need to be studied in relation to the whole gamut of drinking behavior from abstaining to "alcoholism." There is nothing pathological about the extremes of a behavioral continuum like drinking except when society defines it so, and we cannot afford to ignore the ideological aspects of how social problems are defined.

The perspective advanced in this chapter is that drinking patterns in all status groups and social classes can be analyzed in relation to structural inequality. Drinking is one behavior among many through which social inequality is created and perpetuated by means of social control. Social control is exercised by the more powerful groups to manage subordinate groups which might, through discontent with their inferior social and economic position, disturb the status quo. The subordinate groups are not simply the working class, but include women, blacks, the young, the unemployed, the mentally ill, drug users, and counter-cultural or any other groups which might conceivably present a challenge to the position of the more powerful groups. From the point of view of the dominant groups, it has to be possible to control or discredit the subordinate groups as a whole in some way in order to allay possible threats to order. The maintenance of law and order is necessary for the preservation of the arrangements through which the more powerful sections of society benefit.

Other behaviors which could be considered to function in a similar way are sexual behavior, use of other drugs, gambling, acquisition of consumer goods, religion, education, and so on. Most of the theory development remains to be done, and, at present, the analysis cannot be continued at a macro-sociological level. I will retreat to the examination of a single cultural context, Australian society, and hope to provide an example which will illustrate how a power relations theory of drinking can be applied in this particular instance (Sargent, 1979).

A Marxian analysis which describes existing social inequality as stemming from the relations of social classes to the means of production does not explain how inequality is perpetuated. On the contrary, classical Marxist theory holds that it is impossible for the inequality to continue, since there is an inevitable historical process towards increased class conscious-ness, revolution, and a more equal redistribution of wealth. Such a process cannot, however, necessarily be discerned in a given country such as Australia. It would seem probable that inequality will be maintained and even increased in future years. The question is, therefore, what is the nature of the social processes which perpetuate inequality in Australia?

THE STATE AND THE ALCOHOLISM INDUSTRY

The state is typified by what I shall call the Alcoholism Industry,[1] insofar as the economic interests of a number of dominant groups coincide and bring about a powerful unorganized alliance. These groups include government, big business, the upper professions, and the media, who have a common relationship to the means of production, and in whose interests it is to maintain the present power relationships in Australia.

Both the federal and the state governments in Australia derive a significant proportion of their income from alcohol and drugs. In the form of excise revenue, the federal government received from manufacturers of beer and spirits over $8,000 million in 1984, the equivalent of 4% of the G.D.P. (A.B.S., 1984). State governments obtain funds through requiring payment for licenses, permits, and fines by retail liquor outlets. In this way, in 1982 the state government of New South Wales derived an income of $1,197 million (NSW Liquor Administration Board, 1983). In the meantime, the level of drinking is

---

[1] The term "Alcoholism Industry" is not used in the same sense as in Trice who defined it as "a group of formal organizations, both voluntary and governmental, that have grown up to promote treatment and education" (1966:113). Nevertheless, Trice's work has been influential in the development of my thinking.

maintained through advertising and continued expansion of the liquor industry. (The enormous economic power of these companies lies in their allied interests and diversification in oil, mining, and so on.)

The official reason for this area of government activity, apart from the need for revenue, would include the necessity for control of possible harmful effects on the consumer of unrestricted liquor interests. However, as a result, through being financially dependent on big business, governments, in turn, are controlled by business lobbies. In a very real economic sense, it is in the interests of both government and business for the Australian population to drink as much alcohol as possible. It is important to see the measures taken by governments against high consumption, alcoholism, traffic accidents, and other alcohol problems in this context. It has to be asked, in areas such as laws controlling availability of alcohol and the provision of treatment, how much is actually done rather than merely perceived as being done? Which exercises more influence on the government, business lobby groups or the needs of the comparatively few individuals and families who have alcohol problems? In purely economic terms, the answer is clear. Similarly, treatment programs in industry, said to help workers handle their alcohol problems, can be seen as another means of control for employers wishing to maintain profits through a docile hard-working body of employees.

In the liquor industry itself, a large number of people are employed: over 13 thousand in the production and distribution of beer, wine, and spirits, thousands of others in primary production, and 210 thousand in retail outlets, such as hotels, clubs, and liquor stores (A.B.S., 1975). Now that the number of available jobs is so much less than the number of workers seeking employment, it can be seen that the liquor industry economically and socially exercises control over the people they employ.

It might be thought that there is an attempt to counter-balance these economic pressures behind drinking in the activities of the "helping professions" to remedy individual alcohol problems. Yet, the interests of these professions, both as groups and individuals, lie in the continued expansion of treatment, correction, education, and research programs and in the maintenance of the flow of clients, old and new, through the system. The interests involved concern not only income but also, especially for the elite within certain occupations, professional status and career progression. Yet, comparatively few professional people and other "experts" appear to experience any sense of conflict. Perhaps this is because most of them have social origins in the middle class (Boreham et al., 1976) and, therefore, expect their interests to coincide with people in big business and in government who also originate in that social class (Encel, 1970). It needs to be recognized that even in road crashes which are partly due to alcohol, there are people who benefit. For example, the motorcar manufacturers, insurance companies, and the people engaged in correction of offenders and treatment of the injured.

Might it be, though, that the operation of these economic pressures against the welfare of the needy must eventually be exposed? Not so, for all these bodies, government, business, and professions have recourse to legitimation for their actions.

Furthermore, each may divert the blame to the others, and each takes precautions in anticipation of possible accusations. The government, for example, could be blamed for diverting insufficient funds into treatment or showing lack of concern. Government counters such accusations through making funds available in response to the expression of public opinion (without mentioning that, between these occasions, funds may have been withdrawn, as in the case, for example, of the community health program and the budget for Aboriginal programs). If the government is charged with lack of concern, they can point to innumerable inquiries, committees, and royal commissions, government appointed and financed.

In the case of manufacturers, they are sometimes blamed for profiting from others' misfortunes, but they can point to their contributions to research and treatment, and to their increasing responsibility in advertising now that there is a threat of outside control of it. The public does not usually realize that the particular research projects funded generally support manufacturers' business activities. Big business can also point to their contribution to the flourishing of the economy through revenue and through the creation of employment. The assumption is explicitly that what is good for the economy is good for all the Australian people, but it is clear that profits are not distributed to the unemployed, to the poor, or to most employees, except reluctantly in response to their demand.

The professionals, if blamed, can always point to deficient facilities, insufficient research, and lack of funds to finance the treatment programs they have themselves proposed. They are protected also by the mystique of professionalism that experts are always upright and ethical, altruistic, and rigorously trained to reach standards of excellence and expertise. In any case, a diversion of focus is always possible. For example, the New South Wales Commission of Enquiry into Drugs (1979) brought about a crackdown on marijuana growers (resulting in grass being less available on the streets than heroin, and, therefore, in bigger profits for those engaged in heroin trafficking).

The media play a part in the diffusion of true and false information, and in intensifying emotional reactions in consumers. Sensationalism helps sales, and, again, profit is generally the prime motive. All the television and radio stations, and the newspapers, in Australia are almost entirely owned by four large business corporations, so their interests also coincide with those of the groups already discussed -- government, big business, and professional groups.

FRAGMENTATION AND INEQUALITY
Fragmentation

Subordinate groups who are perceived as threatening the power of the dominant group are managed in various ways. One method of management is to fragment their members into smaller groups and individuals through a variety of wage awards, different degrees of occupational status, and variable rates of unemployment. Thus divided, members of subordinate groups see their interests as being in conflict and fail to perceive the unity of their class interests vis-a-vis the dominant group. Australian Aborigines are ascribed the lowest status of all and have had little or no chance to compete for economic rewards on an equal basis with whites. Foreign language-speaking immigrants also experience discrimination (for example, by non-acceptance of their qualifications and lack of consideration for language problems) and are forced to take the jobs and housing which no one else wants. Recently, in the name of "multi-culturalism," there is promotion of the rights of each separate ethnic group, but the good effects are marred by the fragmentation of "migrants" into separate ethnic groups in competition with each other. Women also experience the results of the segmentation of the labor market and work in predominantly low-paid occupations. Women and young people have high rates of unemployment compared with others, but are set against each other by the viewpoint conveyed by government and media that married women hold the jobs which would otherwise be occupied by young people. In fact, most of the jobs occupied by women are in different segments of the labor force from jobs undertaken by young people. Women who are "only housewives" are further fragmented, each into her separate kitchen.

Inequality and Drinking

In the above ways, many varying degrees of inequality are created. By "victim socialization" certain groups learn how to behave like persons of inferior status and to believe in their own inferiority. At the same time, the dominant group ideology purveys the notion that, no matter how unequal our status may seem, really we all have equal opportunity to achieve greatness if only we work hard and strive for greater economic rewards.

Drinking patterns are an integral part of socialization. One learns how to use alcohol both as symbolizing acceptance as an equal in peer groups and as a tool for achieving upward social mobility. On skid row, alcohol has come to symbolize downward mobility. In Australia, alcohol has traditionally been used convivially as part of the "mateship" philosophy and in order to support the solidarity of the male adult group. The ritual of "shouting" (or buying rounds of drinks) involves reciprocal exchange of drinks according to certain unspoken rules (Barbara, Barnes, and Usher, 1978; Sargent, 1973), and is most frequent in male working-class drinking groups. It indicates the acceptance of each other as equals to all members of the group which is drinking together. For those seeking upward mobility, it is possible for them to arrange to be included in drinking sessions of the group to which they aspire to belong and thus to initiate a process of acceptance.

It is because different status groups are ascribed different drinking patterns that alcohol can be viewed as maintaining the present social inequalities. Few status groups are ascribed drinking patterns with as much freedom to drink heavily and get drunk as the dominant male middle-class group in Australia. For example, women's norms (standards) of drinking behavior do not generally allow getting drunk, especially in a public place. Usually the sanctions against women's heavy drinking are much more punitive than against men's. Young people similarly experience the social expectation that they will not appear to be usurping adult power by drinking as much and as freely as adult men. Working-class men may appear to drink and get drunk as freely as middle-class men, but they experience much greater sanctions; for example, in being arrested as drunk by the police, while the middle-class drunk drives home in his car. Since white

Australians introduced alcohol, Aborigines have learned to use it in various ways, including attempts to achieve equality with white men by drinking with them in the pub. Alcohol has been used politically to maintain racial barriers. Aborigines were prohibited by law for many years from buying alcohol or entering the pub. But, white men used alcohol to purchase sexual favors from Aboriginal women and to weaken the resistance to colonial domination of the blacks.

In all these examples, status is confirmed, degraded, or raised by particular drinking patterns, the sanctions applied, and related behavior.

Fragmentation and Drinking

Fragmentation probably increases the need for the promotion of group solidarity and the sense of belonging. A great degree of fragmentation may also increase the individual's tendency to satisfy his personal needs by drinking. Bales (1946) described how the "convivial" attitude typical of mateship drinking, easily "breaks down" into the "utilitarian" attitude in which drinking is oriented towards individual self-satisfaction. The utilitarian attitude, he considered, was the most conducive to alcoholism. It seems likely that the greater the dividedness, competition, struggle for acceptance, and striving to obtain material rewards, the more widespread the utilitarian attitude will be. (Although typical under capitalism, this does not mean that the utilitarian attitude cannot exist in other types of state economic organization.)

Fragmentation makes it possible for the medical model "blame the individual" approach to prevail. The solidarity of the male, heavy-drinking, working-class group is divided by the belief that some of their members have the self-inflicted condition of alcoholism. For the model assumes that certain individuals are in some way predisposed to the disease or, in other words, have some individual weakness. Moreover, the disease is held to be progressive and incurable, which implies that intervention of any kind is useless. Myths surround the concept of addiction which make it seem that, even when drugs are totally eliminated from the body, there is still a physical dependence, a mysterious "craving," which prevents the addict from becoming a normal human being. (The view put forward here is not at all incompatible with the operation also of individual psychological factors in drinking and alcoholism.)

One social consequence of utilitarian drinking is the pacification of subordinate groups. Their management is assisted, and the perceived threat they offer is reduced. The consolidation of the discontented is affected so that they do not act to achieve social change but, through inaction, allow the status quo to continue and social inequality to be maintained.

SOCIAL CONTROL AND DRINKING

Social control is viewed by functionalists as essential for maintaining order in society and for correcting non-conforming behavior. It is viewed here primarily as a method of managing subordinate groups who might seek to reduce the power of the dominant group. "Older sociology tended to rest heavily upon the idea that deviance leads to social control. I have come to believe that the reverse idea; that is, that social control leads to deviance, is equally tenable and the potentially richer premise for studying deviance in modern society" (Lemert, 1967:v).

Creating Social Problems

Deviance is created by the defining by powerful people of certain kinds of behavior as deviant or constituting a social problem, thus implying a need for social control. Some of these definitions are formalized through legislation, and control of what is called "crime" is effected by the application of legal sanctions (Quinney, 1974). These processes perpetuate deviance as already described and also institute a "revolving door" process by which individuals go from hospital to half-way house to clinic, only to be readmitted and passed through the system again and again. The need for rehabilitation is the rationale for the game, for the ideology does not permit outright condemnation of the individual until attempts at "correction" and "treatment" have been made. Becoming expendable is a long, drawn-out but thorough process. This is where the Alcoholism Industry is important. In the name of rehabilitation, professions have been set up to provide care or at least custody, facilities have been financed, and institutions have been built. There has grown up an industry whose interests are served by creating and perpetuating deviance. The victims created by these processes come to be seen as "crims" and "addicts" who are irretrievably deviant and have become socially expendable.

Labelling Individuals and Discrediting Groups

The resulting social rejection and exclusion of certain individuals is perpetuated by selecting them for labels such as "alcoholic," "addict," "bum," or worse, assigning them deviant roles and instituting them in a deviant career (Goffman, 1960). Social expectations are low for behavior as a "down and out drunk," a "no hoper." "Deviants" are segregated from people in general and thrown into association with other deviants in hospital or jail, thus giving them every encouragement to continue in the deviant role assigned to them. At the same time, their individual self-concept is damaged and brought into line with the expectations of others, thus making the role almost irreversible.

The final result is, however, to discredit whole status groups of people through scapegoating individuals who may be representative members of them. For example, all the young unemployed are discredited by the exposure by the Department of Social Security of a few individuals as "dole bludgers."

There are also some less-direct techniques which are employed to manage subordinate groups including normalization, conversion, containment, and the support of organized crime (Spitzer, 1975). Normalization is where an excessive number of deviants has been created and so some are redefined as normal or at least as not in need of hospitalization or imprisonment. An excessive number of troublemakers can also be reduced by converting some, by the provision of job opportunities and training schemes, into, for example, police, social workers, or alcohol or drug counsellors (especially, in the case of ex-addicts). A proportion of the subordinate groups can be managed by containment; that is, by isolating them geographically into skid row hostels or into communes and then ignoring them. An alternative to imprisonment for some groups is to allow organized crime to offer an opportunity structure for people choosing illegitimate means of achieving social goals. Organized crime thus lends a "cooling-out" function, which eases hardships and pacifies some troublemakers.

Management and control is likely to increase group and individual tensions, which may find an outlet through drinking. There is an element of protest and expression of feelings of rebellion in some drinking groups -- for example, among blacks against white domination, working class men against the bosses, men against women, women against men, young people against adults. The rebellious feelings may be affected by alcohol in a number of ways. Their expression may be facilitated by the release of inhibition, for example, and this may be followed by immediate aggressive behavior, or by the formation of an organized group for future action, or by pacification of feeling and action through the tranquilizing effects of alcohol. From the point of view of managing subordinate groups, the expression of rebellious feelings may have a cooling-out function, reducing discontent in the future. It also enables the control processes to begin with the identification of troublemakers and then the application of sanctions leading to the discrediting of the whole status group involved.

One of the reasons why management of subordinate groups through alcohol is possible is that the social expectations for drinking in every case put greater limitations on subordinate groups than on dominant groups -- for example, women's drinking is more limited than men's, Aboriginals receive greater negative sanctions than whites, and so on. Therefore, striving for greater equality by women, blacks, and others tends to involve drinking behavior which emulates that of the dominant groups. The whole ethos of drinking in Australian society determines that there are <u>initially</u> social pressures on many people to drink fairly frequently and heavily and sometimes to get drunk. Yet the ethos, when people's drinking goes beyond the limits of their group norms, then punishes them severely and excludes them from the group. It is a "Catch 22" situation.

ALTERNATIVES TO ALCOHOL

In Australia, alcohol plays a central role in the various social processes described above: 1) These processes bring about striving for social acceptance as equals in peer groups, participating in peer-group solidarity, striving for upward social mobility and/or greater economic rewards, and striving by certain status groups for greater equality in relation to other status groups; 2) Alcohol is also central in enabling subordinate-status groups to be managed so as not to create a threat to the dominant group's power position. At the same time, the psychological tensions created a) by striving for status and b) by being controlled are assuaged by the tranquilizing effects of alcohol. Alcohol rather than religion is the opium of the people. Individual consolation and group pacification are psychological rewards which are always available.

Are there alternatives available which could offer the rewards without making people subject to control? Most other suitable drugs are illegal and, therefore, make their users liable to control. Legally prescribed drugs are available only to individuals and are not socially approved in Australian society as substitutes in drinking situations. Sexual activity could be largely equivalent to alcohol as a striving for status, but it also has had limitations imposed historically, which make it liable to control. Gambling is the most socially available alternative and is very popular in many different forms in Australia. The greatest limitation is that for gambling, one constantly needs money, and our society permits the obtaining of money, especially by members of subordinate groups, only in narrowly specified ways. The social processes involved are similar in all these activities. There are economic and social pressures to participate in all these in ways which vary according to group membership, but, in all of them, strict limitations on excessive participation exist. Control can be exercised on subordinate groups through both their everyday participation and through their excessive participation. If alcohol and all the alternatives make subordinate groups liable to control as described, the result is to reinforce pressures to use the legitimate ways of striving for social acceptance and equality; that is, through hard work and family stability. Present power relationships are thus maintained and the present inequality perpetuated.

CONCLUSION

An interpretation of drinking in Australian society has been offered as an illustration of a possible macro-sociological perspective for alcohol studies. The perspective combines aspects of the cultural approach, social deviance theory, and the political economy approach and attempts to overcome the restricted viewpoints which have limited the usefulness of each one of these. The perspective, as it stands, can be applied only in a context where a power relations

theory is appropriate and where the interests of the
state can be seen as coinciding with those of the
politically and economically powerful groups in a given
society. Plain pluralists and conservative capitalists
will need to invent an alternative perspective.

REFERENCES

Australian Bureau of Statistics. 1975. Census of
Retail Estimates and Selective Estimates, 1973-74.
Canberra: Author.

Australian Bureau of Statistics. 1984. Quarterly
Estimate of National Income and Expenditure, Sept.
Quarter 1984 (No. 5206.0). Canberra: Author.

Barbara, F., Barnes, N., and Usher, J. 1978. Rules of
"Shouting" groups in Sydney public bars.
Australian Journal of Social Issues 13:119-128.

Boreham, P., Pemberton, A., and Wilson, P. 1976. The
Professions in Australia: A Critical Appraisal.
St. Lucia: University of Queensland.

Encel, S. 1970. Equality and Authority. Melbourne:
Cheshire.

Goffman, E. 1960. Asylums. London: Penquin.

Lemert, E. M. 1967. Human Deviance, Social Problems,
and Social Control. NJ: Prentice Hall.

Makela, K. and Viikari, M. 1977. Notes on alcohol and
the state. Acta Sociologica 20:155-179.

New South Wales Liquor Administration Board. 1983.
Annual Report, 1982. Sydney: Government Printer.

NSW Royal Commission into Drug Trafficking. 1979.
Report (Woodland). Sydney: Government Printer.

Quinney, R. 1974. Critique of Legal Order: Crime
Control in Capitalist Society. Boston: Little
Brown.

Sargent, M. J. 1975. Drinking and Alcoholism in
Australia: A Power Relations Theory. Melbourne:
Longman Cheshire.

Spitzer, S.   1975.   Toward   a   Marxian   Theory   of
    Deviance.   Social Problems 22:638-651.

Trice, H. M.   1966.   Alcoholism in America.   NY: Mc-
    Graw-Hill.

INTRODUCTION TO CHAPTER 21

Toch and Sargent have offered us rather different
perspectives on alcohol use than we have seen
previously in this volume. Partly as a result of their
different perspectives, they have developed theoretical
foci on the causes of the alcohol-abuse problem. Toch
has suggested the need to assess genetic factors and
the stress of acculturation in the use of alcohol, and
Sargent has alerted us to the role of political and
economic power relations. In this next chapter, we
examine the problem of drug addiction, in this case
heroin, in yet another country, the Netherlands.

Van de Wijngaart is unusually thorough here.
Beginning with a detailed description of the geography
and economy of the Netherlands, he next takes us on a
historical tour of opiate use from its early origins to
the current situation in the Netherlands. In the
course of his description van de Wijngaart notes
cultural differences among users, the effect of the
law, and the relationship to other drugs.

From this rather comprehensive beginning, the
author then discusses issues of treatment. One of the
fascinating aspects of opiate addiction in the
Netherlands is the role of the Junkie League, a virtual
union of drug addicts which works cooperatively with
the government. The contrast between van de
Wijngaart's description of the Junkie League and the
U.S. experience with its addicts is remarkable. In the
latter case, addicts are deviants and criminals and are
treated for an individual pathology. The approach in
the Netherlands is different.

Among other policy differences, which the author discusses, is the provision of heroin for addicts. This is a policy which has been attempted in Great Britain and has been mentioned, but not tried, in the U.S.

Van de Wijngaart's conclusions provide no great discoveries about the management of opiate addiction. The Dutch labor with the problem just as any other society. Nevertheless, his appraisal of the problem is insightful and realistic.

CHAPTER 21
HEROIN ADDICTION IN THE NETHERLANDS

Govert F. van de Wijngaart

ABSTRACT

In Europe, on the borders of the North Sea, the Netherlands, or as many people say incorrectly, Holland, is located. It is a rich and highly developed country with a strong currency and many ports. In other words, an inviting place to import and trade drugs like heroin.

The Netherlands has a long tradition as a place where people from abroad like to stay and live because of its colonial history and liberal climate. It has known opium for a long time, partly because the Dutch traded it in Southeast Asia (Dutch Indies, now Indonesia, and China) and partly because it had a Chinese "colony" in the capital city of Amsterdam,

----

GOVERT F. VAN DE WIJNGAART is Associate Professor of Psychology at the University of Utrecht in the Netherlands.

where the use of opium was permitted connivently.

After the "hashish culture" of the sixties, heroin was introduced on a large scale. In a period of 12 years since 1972, the number of people using heroin rose to about 20,000.

Developments in the Netherlands are described with a special focus on those issues that can be considered "typically Dutch": 1) the divergent "opium-act," 2) the methodone buses, 3) the Junkie League, and 4) the plans for heroin maintenance. Also, the important role of the Dutch Government in the organization of the relief work system is discussed.

THE NETHERLANDS IN BRIEF

The Netherlands is a small, but densely populated, and highly developed country situated in Western Europe on the North Sea. The most important economic activities are shipping, commerce, and transit trade. The surface area is 37,313 square kilometers and the country has a little over 14.3 million inhabitants; that is, 423 inhabitants per square kilometer. The most densely populated area is the 'Randstad' conurbation in the west of the country, which comprises Amsterdam, Rotterdam, The Hague, and Utrecht. The labor force is 4.8 million: 63% in the services sector, 31% in industry, and 6% in agriculture and fisheries. Approximately 40% of employees are members of trade unions. More than half the country lies below sea level and the many dikes and pumping installations are therefore essential to keep the land dry. The Netherlands is a constitutional monarchy with a parliamentary system. The seat of the government is The Hague; Amsterdam is the capital.

The Netherlands was one of the largest colonial powers until World War II. The colonies became independent fairly soon after the war ended. Indonesia severed all its links with the Netherlands; Surinam and the Dutch Antilles, situated in the Caribbean, became equal partners with the Netherlands in 1945. Surinam became an independent republic in 1975.

Since the early sixties, there has been an influx of foreign guest workers from the Mediterranean area. Besides, there has also been a relatively large influx of immigrants from Surinam after its independence in 1975. The immigration of foreign workers has now virtually ceased, but relatives of those already here are still admitted on humanitarian grounds, that is to say, for purposes of family reunion.

According to figures from the Central Bureau of Statistics, the percentages for the various denominations are: Roman Catholic 40%, Protestant 33%, None 24%, and Others 3%.

In comparison with many other countries, the Netherlands has a very good system of social provisions and health care. There is a wide range of social provisions, which is regarded as a major achievement. The 5-day working week has been standard for quite some time now, and, since 1975, the 40-hour week has become common. The minimum holiday is 15 working days, though, generally 22 days are given. Wages and salaries continue to be paid during holidays, in addition to which a lump sum of holiday allowance is paid, the legal minimum being 7.5% of the annual gross salary. As from July 1, 1982, the minimum wage for employees, aged 23 and over, is 2,028 guilders ($900) per month. After deductions for social security contributions and wages and salaries tax, this leaves a net monthly income of about 1,500 guilders ($600) for a married employee. If one is unable to work as a result of sickness, disablement or accident, the Sickness Benefit Act assures 80% of his/her basic wage for up to 52 weeks. The same percentage is also given for unemployment due to circumstances beyond someone's power. Apart from many other Social Acts, there is the National Assistance Act that entitles every Dutch citizen to assistance when it is impossible to support him/herself financially anymore.

It is the government's responsibility to create the necessary legal framework and facilities to prevent diseases and accidents and to promote the treatment, nursing, and care of those who need it. Under the Health Insurance Act, every Dutch citizen is entitled to medical, pharmaceutical and dental assistance, and hospital treatment. One of the greatest problems facing the health service is a financial one. In 1973 costs were over 12 billion guilders and, by 1981, they had risen to almost 28 billion; that is, 2,000 guilders per head of the population. Health care facilities are mainly financed by the insurance system. The state makes a contribution which includes the provision of services such as the Municipal Health Service and the Food and Commodity Inspectorates. Much preventive medicine, medical research, and the training of health workers is paid for by the state. But, after all, health is the concern of the entire population.

There are about 240 hospitals with roughly 73,000 beds. In addition, there are the general psychiatric hospitals with over 26,000 beds, the institutions for the mentally and physically handicapped with roughly 25,000 beds, and the nursing homes with over 46,000 beds.

THE HISTORY OF OPIATE ADDICTION
Introduction

In this chapter, the notion of drugs is used in a "narrow" sense. Generally speaking, drugs can be defined as substances that can influence human consciousness and are used for this reason. In this broad definition, drugs are considered to be the same as any other stimulants, whereas tobacco, coffee, and tea are not commonly regarded as drugs, which is made clear by the statement: "drugs are stimulants that are not used by decent people."

The use of drugs and, especially their incidental use, is not the same as drug addiction. Neither does drug usage automatically and irrevocably lead to addiction to drugs. Besides being addicted to drugs, a person may also develop a dependence on gambling, home computers, watching television, eating candy, or even on work (a "workaholic").

In the following chapter, we will limit ourselves to illegal drugs. The emphasis is on opiates and, especially, on heroin. Although alcohol and other drugs are also mentioned several times, it isn't our intention to describe the policy regarding these substances.

Opium

The poppy is a plant that has been known to humans for centuries. The Greek writer Homer mentioned it in his epic poem of the Trojan War, the Iliad (8th century B.C.). Its marvelous qualities as a "remedy" is probably the reason that it has been known for such a long time. The famous Greek physician Hippocrates spoke highly of the qualities of opium ("opion") some 2500 years ago. The milk juice of the "Papaver

Somniferum" is gathered for the preparation of opium by cutting the unripe ovary of the plant. Drops of white milk then form that dry in the open air and then become brown. The plant can be grown in all kinds of soil and under various climatological circumstances. The origin of the poppy probably was in Asia Minor.

The qualities of opium were also known in Egypt, and later the Arabs took over the usage of opium from the Egyptians. The Arabs probably were responsible for making the usage of opium known as a stimulant to humans. The extension of the poppy culture for the production of opium followed the trail of Islam.

In the Middle Ages opium was prescribed on a large scale as a medicine by Arab physicians. They introduced it to European doctors. Since the twelfth century opium was increasingly used as a medicine. It became an essential part of numerous medicinal drinks and derivations at that time. Opium was believed to be beneficial to nearly all diseases.

When the usage of opium in history is discussed, it is usually wrongly connected with China. However, in China the poppy was grown as an ornamental plant until far into the nineteenth century. The import of opium was forbidden by the Chinese government until then. This prohibition was the cause of the First Opium War (1833-1842) in which Great Britain tried to force open the Chinese ports so that opium could be imported from its colony, British India. The British were successful because a short time after this war, there were millions of addicts in China. Only since 1853 has opium been produced in China itself.

The use of opium as a stimulant dates back to the end of the eighteenth century in Europe. The habit spread fast in England due to supplies from its colony,

India. Information about the "opium-scene" at the time can be found in the famous book by Thomas de Quincey: "Confessions of an English Opium-Eater." According to its author, the use of opium occurred in all sections of the population (de Quincey, 1822). The chemists complained that they could not make out whether the clients used the opium as medicine or as a way to commit suicide. There were hardly any access problems for the users of opium at the time. Opium was cheap and not illegal; thus, its user did not commit any criminal offence. Opium did not cause any damage to organs or tissues, while aggression under influence did not occur like it did with alcohol.

In contrast to England, where opium was usually eaten or drunk, the substance was smoked in France. The French had taken over the smoking habits from the Far-East, and, in particular, from the Chinese. The custom of smoking opium was also known in the colony of the Dutch Indies, where a lot of poppies were cultivated (Tan Tong Joe, 1929). At the start of the twentieth century, most of the opium came from China, British India, Turkey, and Persia (Iran).

Chemical Research

During the last century, analytical chemists managed to separate out a number of pure substances from opium, which are called alkaloides. The chemical research on opium and acquaintance with its structure and effective components date back to 1803 when Denrose isolated a substance that he named "opium salt." In 1805, the German chemist Serturner also managed to produce this chemical substance. He called it "Morphium." Besides morphine, many other alkaloides have also been isolated, like codeine and narcotine.

Morphine is the actual somnolent part of opium and was soon applied in the medical science because of its pain-killing and soothing properties. Morphine, however, was also used as a stimulant, like opium.

In 1874, the English chemical analyst Wright developed a half synthetical morphine derivation called "diacetylmorphine." The German analyst Dreser continued to test this new substance. He called it "Heroin" after having discovered its powerful properties. In practice, it appeared to be a very efficient pain-killing remedy. At first it was thought that heroin was not addictive at all. The opposite proved to be true; particularly in the United States, countless persons have become addicted to this substance since about 1915.

The use of heroin in itself has no or hardly any harmful consequences for the physical health of a person -- except in the case of an overdose. Yet, many diseases do occur in heroin users. They can be ascribed to a number of factors that seem to be indissolubly connected with the use of heroin: bad hygienics, the use of non-sterile syringes, bad food, an unhealthy life pattern, the use of dirty mixtures, and so on. In short, the use of heroin has no or hardly any direct effects on one's health. The consequences are indirect. In modern western society, heroin addiction nearly always leads to a serious interference of one's social well-being.

It wasn't only the discovery of heroin that made an important contribution to the rapid spread of addiction to opiates but also the development of the syringe. It became possible to bring the substance much faster into the bloodstream through hypodermic injections or injections into the veins than with smoking or eating.

The most recent development in the chemical field that is important for the following sections is the development of the synthetic opiate "Methadone." The drug was originally synthesized by the German firm I. G. Farben in 1941 and appropriatly named "Adolphine." Since Morphine was unavailable in Germany during World War II for the relieving of pain in battlefield injuries, Methadone was developed as a synthetic substitute on orders from Hitler (Bellis, 1981).

Recent Developments

In the Netherlands, there were a few opium users in the large cities from early days. It was mainly a group of old Hong Kong Chinese who maintained the traditional use of opium. It was smoked by means of a special pipe. Most pipes were made of bamboo, the expensive ones of ivory or jade. This opium culture was known to the police but was condoned. The Dutch who used opium or morphine were doctors, chemists, and "artists." Besides these groups, there was also the group of persons who became addicted because of medical reasons: patients who had received morphine for some kind of painful complaint over a long time and who had become addicted.

In the 1960's, the Dutch drug scene was especially marked by the use of marijuana and hashish. This "hashish culture" showed influences from the student movement and "Flower Power." It was during this period that Amsterdam came to be the hippie capital of Europe. Cannabis products, marijuana and hashish, became the most used stimulants after alcohol and tobacco. In the beginning of the 1970's, the use of cannabis products also found general acceptance outside circles of the youth culture.

In 1969, a report was published about the backgrounds of the increased (illegal) use of substances that came within the Opium Law (Cohen, 1969). The report showed that many experimentations with drugs took place in those days. However, any real addiction was hardly found. Its users mainly came from the higher middle classes. Sixty-eight percent had started with cannabis products, marijuana and hashish, and 32% with opium, amphetamines, and LSD. The use of drugs by friends or acquaintances quite often was the reason for trying drugs, but it often did not lead to a repeated use.

In the middle of the 1960's, the injecting of opium and amphetamines took place for the first time. Before 1968, amphetamines could still be obtained legally. In 1968, however, they were placed under the law of medicine distribution. Later, around 1970, there was a strong increase of the use of amphetamines ("speed," "pep"), but, like in other European countries such as Sweden, it declined after 1974.

Heroin

Before 1972, there was hardly any demand for heroin in the Netherlands. In 1971, it is said that sailors from Singapore brought small quantities of "brown sugar" (an opiate with 70% heroin) to Holland.

In 1972, heroin appeared on the market in Amsterdam during the summer for the remarkably low price of 25 to 50 guilders ($10 to $20) per gram. A few months later, the results of a more professional way of marketing appeared: the price suddenly had risen to 200 guilders ($80) per gram and the market had established itself. An analysis of the heroin showed that it was so "pure" that it must have originated from large, well-equipped laboratories.

The departure of Americans from Vietnam meant that an important market for dealers had disappeared. A new market in West Europe was sought and found. Three large Chinese syndicates from Hong Kong and Singapore found their way to the port of West Europe: the Netherlands. It was an affluent country with hard currencies and an excellent intermediate station to other countries, especially to West Germany, where many U.S. soldiers were stationed. In a number of publications, it has been remarked that an important role was played by the CIA in cooperation with "organized crime" in the marketing of heroin (Kruger, 1980; McCoy et al., 1982).

In 1977, the number of heroin addicts was estimated to be 5,000 in Holland. Much of the heroin comes from the "Golden Triangle" of Thailand, Laos, and Burma. At the end of the 1970's, Turkish heroin appeared on the market that was transported by way of old cannabis routes to Holland. Currently, much heroin comes from Afghanistan, Iran, and Pakistan.

At the moment, Holland has probably between 15,000 and 20,000 heroin addicts. According to the authorities, the number of heroin addicts appears to be stabilizing, but certain shifts in the population of drug addicts can be acknowledged. An increasing number of addicts are of non-Dutch origin and are usually members of the second generation of guest workers. More than 50% of all addicts reside in the western part of Holland in the four major cities: Amsterdam, Rotterdam, The Hague, and Utrecht. By far the greatest number -- between 4,000 and 7,000 -- live in the capital city of Amsterdam. The number of addicts among

persons of Surinam origin (180,000) and among persons
with a Moluccan background (30,000) is estimated to be
2%.

Presently, mere heroin addiction does not occur.
More and more heroin addicts use any drugs they can
obtain, especially tranquilizers. Since the price of
cocaine equals heroin, we can observe a rising use of
cocaine, often alternated with heroin. Nevertheless,
the expectation is that "coke" will never be as popular
in Holland as in "speedy" countries like the U.S.A.,
Sweden, and Japan (van de Wijngaart, 1983b).

PEOPLE FROM ABROAD

Since the introduction of heroin in the
Netherlands, the composition of the user group has
gradually changed. Research indicates that persons who
have few possibilities of improving their social
situation increasingly become addicted to heroin,
persons who have a low level of education and who
experience a bad housing situation (Janssen and
Swierstra, 1982). The number of persons taking heroin
who belong to ethnic minority groups is strongly
increasing, particularly persons of Surinam and/or
Moluccan descent. The children of foreign guest
workers ("second generation youths") are an additional
risk group.

The drug problem among cultural minorities began
with Surinam youths in Amsterdam and Rotterdam. The
profound cultural differences required a specific
approach. Therefore, initial help is given by people
from a similar cultural background because only they
have a sufficient knowledge of the language and
cultural background of users. The first steps in
starting the relief work for Surinam persons came from

groups of former drug users with the support of Surinam welfare institutions. This led to the development of different programs and projects.

The Moluccan youths generally live in more than 60 closed communities in the Netherlands. Most communities are situated in areas with a high level of unemployment. The drug use and the resulting consequences are often dealt with within the Moluccan communities.

It is of significance to note that among Surinam and Moluccan addicts hardly any heroin is used by means of injecting. Most of the time, they smoke the heroin or "chase the dragon."

In 1978, the Surinam society "Srefidensie" counted 2,400 chronic heroin addicts of Surinam origin. This number has probably increased since then, but no one can give an accurate estimate.

The Moluccan society "Tjandu" calculated that there were 626 Moluccan hard drug users in 1977. Some estimates, which have recently been made, claim that there is one addict in every two Moluccan families, while others state that 10% of the Moluccan population is involved in hard drug use.

DRUGS AND THE LAW

In Holland, the first Opium Act was enacted in 1919. This law has been changed a number of times, the most recent alteration being in 1976. Internationally speaking, Holland has ratified the 1962 Single Convention on Narcotic Drugs of New York. The convention stipulates the taking of effective measures against the abuse of narcotics. The possession of narcotics has to be limited to medical and scientific purposes.

533

At the end of the 1960's, a reconsideration of prosecution was advocated by a growing number of groups. They insisted on a decrease of punitive measures for the use of cannabis products or for deleting marijuana and hashish from the Opium Law entirely, basing this on the theory that the harm of the danger of certain substances is an insufficient motive for interfering with the privacy of a person by means of punishment.

This is not to say that all supporters of a revision of the policy as regards cannabis products were in favor of a deletion of these substances from the Opium Law just like that. They wanted to prevent the Netherlands from becoming a center of trade of these substances if other countries did not adopt the same attitude. Furthermore, they also wanted to prevent an undesired situation of heroin use if there were no restrictions at all. In 1969, Denmark decided not to make use of any punitive measures against cannabis users. However, officially the use of cannabis remained forbidden by law (Schiler, 1983; van de Wijngaart, 1983a).

In the Netherlands, cannabis products are generally seen as drugs that cause little harm. One of the reasons is that the so called "stepping stone hypothesis" -- the theory that the use of a certain substance, for example, hashish, can lead to the use of more dangerous substances -- has been largely rejected by experts. That is why the Netherlands do not wish to see the use of cannabis as a crime. This tolerant attitude is frowned upon by the International Narcotics Control Board of the United Nations and of countries like the United States, France, Sweden, and West Germany (Vernooy and van de Wijngaart, 1984). The 1971

Convention on Psychotropic Substances was not ratified by the Netherlands. In 1976, a distinction was made in the law between high-risk drugs and drugs with a lower risk. The last group consists of the products of the hemp plant.

It happens regularly that a foreigner asks us what the consequences have been of the alteration of the law for cannabis products. Did that measure lead to any increase of the use of hashish and marijuana at all? The answer to this question is that this alteration did not have any such effect. To the contrary, even at the present time, the use of the products is a bit "out of fashion," and it appears that a decreasing number of students use hashish and marijuana.

An investigation by Sijlbing (1984) showed that 12% of students used marijuana and hashish now and then and this is considerably less than the 59% that was found for the same group in the United States (Johnston et al., 1984). The percentage in general of those who use cannabis products is also quite a bit lower in the Netherlands than in the United States: 5.4% against 29% (Sijlbing, 1984; Johnston et al., 1984).

The penal provisions for drugs with an unacceptable risk have been more rigidly enforced since 1976. The following distinction has been made for punishable behaviors:

- the possession or presence of drugs;
- the import and export to and from Holland;
- the selling, delivering, transporting, or supply of drugs; and
- the production of drugs.

The much-occurring phenomenon in other countries of "under cover" agents, who provoke punishable acts, is not permitted under the Dutch law. Another difference between the Netherlands and other countries consists of the distinction between what the law formally prescribes and the directives of the Public Prosecutor. The latter, in fact, govern the prosecution policy. No actual prosecution and detention will take place if only "a small amount meant for personal use" is concerned.

RELIEF WORK

The history of relief work and social security in the Netherlands is marked by an ever-increasing network of services. This was the reason that the name "welfare state" was introduced. It meant that each Dutch person could ask for financial help from the cradle to the grave, if necessary.

During the last couple of years, this has changed again. The changing situation of the world economy, the growing number of unemployed, and the ever-increasing health care costs have led to a number of cuts in the Social Security system. Besides, a discussion was also started about the subject of "care" itself and the dependence of the clients on relief work. It could even be said that a large number of persons became "addicted" to professional relief work. An author like Illich, who has written much about this problem, had an important influence in the Netherlands (Ingleby, 1985; Illich, 1976).

Before summarizing the relief work for heroin addicts in Holland, it is necessary to bring forward two discussion points. The first point centers upon the question of whether the heroin addict will take the initiative in solving his addiction problem. The second point in question is whether or not the supply of relief determines the demand or the other way around.

The care for alcohol addicts originated in organizations which were set up by total abstainers in the beginning of the century. An important task of the consultation came to be the aftercare of discharged prisoners. Many alcoholics were provided with relief work after having come into contact with the law (for example, traffic violations). After World War II, the aftercare of discharged prisoners became less prominent and the focus of attention shifted from alcohol to other kinds of addiction. This led to the set-up of the present consultations centers for alcohol and drugs (CAD's).

Presently, there are 18 CAD's (with 65 establishments) and a total of about 900 staff members. Around 500 of them only deal with drug addicts. The CAD's cover areas which, to a large extent, coincide with the jurisdiction of Dutch courts because of the close organizational ties with the judiciary in the past. The CAD's are financed through government subsidy.

The CAD's can be contacted directly or indirectly (through referral) and their work is conducted in multi-disciplinary teams (psychologists, doctors, social workers, and so forth). Prevention and information form an important part of the task. In 1979, nearly 6,000 drug users visited the centers at least once.

Traditionally, an addict could only receive in-patient help in a psychiatric clinic. The increasing number of persons in need of aid and the particular aspects of relief work have led to the establishment of a growing number of clinics for drug addicts. The first Dutch drug-free therapeutic community,

Emiliehoeve, celebrated its 10th anniversary in the spring of 1982.

Independent clinics for addicts, as well as specialized departments of psychiatric hospitals, are financed out of public funds by means of "AWBZ" -- the Exceptional Medical Expenses (Compensation) Act. It is estimated that about 6,000 drug users are helped by ambulant programs, the semi-mural help about 2,000 and the intra-mural about 250 persons. About 2,000 formation places for drug relief were subsidized by the government, of which 1,500 are for direct care. The fact that about 2,000 persons are employed for this type of work is due to the preference of a growing number of social workers to work part-time.

In addition, the number of (often small-scale) institutions is increasing. These institutions, which often have religious backgrounds, derive their money from various sources (gifts, funds, and local subsidies). They are characterized by a combination of initial care, treatment, aftercare, and other means of help that might be needed afterwards. Many volunteers work in these institutions.

Finally, we will also give some facts about methadone on the basis of experience of Dole and Nyswander (1965). The Netherlands started to work with methadone in 1968. Initially this took place with little organization and on a small scale. In the middle of the 1970's, however, more official methadone programs were set up. These programs formulated new objectives and methods of work. Generally stated, there are two kinds of methadone programs in the Netherlands. With one type, the emphasis is to reduce the use of opiates; the other type aims at stabilizing the use. In the last case, there may be certain regulations concerning the permission to also use opiates.

In large cities, the phenomenon of the "methadone bus" is known since the end of the 1970's. The advantage of providing methadone from a mobile bus is that it does not cause a great annoyance to people who live nearby. This type of bus has a number of fixed halts in town. At certain times, the clients can come and fetch the methadone. The fluid kind of methadone, however, has to be used at the place of help (Vernooy and van de Wijngaart, 1982).

PROMOTION OF THE INTERESTS: THE JUNKIE LEAGUE

The Dutch policy takes into account the advice of the addict's parents and the addict himself. The Foundation "Parents of Drug Addicts" is nationwide. It was established in 1980 as a result of the cooperation between contact groups for parents of drug addicts in The Hague and Amsterdam. The Foundation's aims are to organize the parents of drug addicts and to combine their ideas and interests. Besides, Holland has known groups like "Drug Anonymous" and "Anonymous Families" for a long time.

In 1980, the first Dutch "Junkie League" was set up. The direct cause for this were plans that were proposed from particular quarters to force addicts to abstain from drug use. Traditionally, the national authorities in the Netherlands have always taken a negative view concerning the forced treatment of drug addicts. The Junkie League observed the ever-increasing problems and the deterioration of the situation of addicts and cited these and other reasons as the cause for their foundation.

The increasing number of local organizations are united in the Federation of Dutch Junkie Leagues. Their main aim is in the development of a policy, in consultation with the junkies and the decision-makers, directed towards the acceptance of hard-drug users.

The starting point of the Junkie League is representing the interests of the user of heroin. Most important is combating the deterioration of the user, or to put it in another way, improving the housing and general situation of the addict. Improvements in relief care and participation are based on the philosophy that the users of heroin know best what the problems are.

The work of the Junkie League involves discussions with government officials about things like the distribution of methadone, the policy of the law makers and police, and housing problems. In Rotterdam, the so-called "Broad Movement" has been set up, in which the Junkie League, doctors and other relief workers, parents of addicts, and members of the city council participate. This discussion has as its aim to review the problems from various viewpoints and to seek solutions for these problems. Another aspect of the work of the Junkie League is clearly directed towards the "scene." If, for instance, there is bad heroin on the market, members of the Junkie League will make a pamphlet which is handed out in the "scene" to warn addicts. The same happens when an outbreak of Hepatitis B occurs. The project group of "Pharmacy and Society" has published a report "Adulterations of Heroin." This group from the University of Utrecht wrote the report at the request of the Junkie League, based on the questions: "What can a user do when he has used bad heroin and what can be done against bad heroin being sold?"

Finally, the Junkie League also publishes a periodical in which the activities of the League and the experiences of addicts are described. The inaccurate information given by the media is also analyzed.

What is striking after first reading of the above-mentioned statements is the positive tone of the aims. The Junkie League does not criticize only -- it also has its own objectives. The aims are mainly centered on the promotion of the interests of the heroin user. The Junkie League has given much attention to the analysis of the existing relief care situation and the formation of proposals for reorganizing relief care.

Ideas from the Junkie League Concerning Improvement of Relief Care

The basis of all criticism is the fact that altogether the relief programs are able to reach only 15% of all addicts. The larger part of addicts is not helped, and their situation therefore deteriorates without anything being done about it.

Fundamental criticism has also been made of the doctrine of freeing oneself from the use of heroin that is part of the philosophy of the relief workers. Because there are insufficient facilities for the addicts, this can quite soon lead to false or unreal motivations and feelings of impotence with the addicts.

In many cases, a junkie has to accept a form of relief care which he/she does not ask for. The Junkie League thinks it is not correct that heroin users are in an unfavorable, exceptional situation in comparison with other users of stimulants (such as alcohol, sleeping pills, tranquilizers). The Junkie League, in general, sees relief care as follows: the relief worker always knows the situation of a user better than the user him/herself; the relief care is not part of the daily reality. In that sense, a user will think of the relief care as a failure because the daily reality (environment, circle of friends, daily routine, and so on) does not change and the user will have to return there. Relief care which only teaches a different approach to one's feelings will never be able to offer a different daily reality.

The starting point of the League is that life without the use of stimulants is best. The Junkie League is aware of the danger that exists in the use of stimulants to suppress problems that are caused by society. The Junkie League finds that heroin users deteriorate at a certain point into junkies. This is not because of the heroin itself but because of the fact that the usage is illegal. This is the reason why it is so expensive, and everything has to be done to get it. A junkie is not all that different from other persons. There is, for example, a similarity with a housewife who has become addicted to Valium. However, she does not have to "score" because her addiction is tolerated or even supported by her environment. So, she is no junkie, but the user of illegal substances is.

The heroin addict does not find his/her position deteriorating because of heroin itself, but because of the public order perspective. Traditional relief care, according to the Junkie League, states that addiction is a problem of the victim and that he/she should do something about it him/herself. However, the problems are a combination of factors, uniquely belonging to the user and his or her environment; they are social problems, especially when a user has become a junkie.

The relief plan of the Junkie League has, as its first aim, the prevention of further deterioration and the realization of the social rights for a normal life. The starting points for adequate help are:

- the help has to be accessible at places where the problem exists; that is to say in the areas where the users live;
- it will have to be first-line aid: the distribution of methadone (or other substances) and relief care, in general, should be carried out as close as possible to the area in which the user lives; that is to say, through one's own doctor or chemist. It is necessary that one can call on the relief worker who lives in one's own neighborhood;
- no conditions can be formulated beforehand and the aim is primarily to combat deterioration; to free oneself from the use of drugs should not be the goal of relief work; and
- the addict should also be responsible for the treatment.

The Junkie League states that relief care cannot be held solely responsible for the problems. Another genuine problem is legislation. The penal system and relief care cannot be integrated in an acceptable manner. Current policy is set on achieving political results and not on a good relief care; preserving the public order is more important for the decision-makers. Therefore, a modification of the Opium Law is advocated by the League. The fact that drugs are illegal has as a result that very important secondary problems may arise. The Opium Law often creates more problems than it prevents.

MODIFICATIONS IN GOVERNMENT POLICY

In the meantime, it has become clear in Holland that there is no ideal solution. That is why it is a good thing that experts, although they have quite different disciplines, are prepared to listen to each other and think about a policy that is suited to the Dutch situation. Significant for this development was the two-day symposium sponsored by the Erasmus University of Rotterdam in 1982 about the drugs policy of the future. Discussions were held by representatives of the local and national government, social workers, policy-makers, politicians, academics, members of the clergy, civil servants from the Justice Department, researchers, persons from the Junkie League, and other ex-users.

After the symposium, everyone must have gone home with a satisfied feeling that a set-up like this was possible. These and other meetings influenced the policy of the government. The policy of 1984 is based on several assumptions.

First, the fact that there are addicts who cannot live without drugs cannot be denied. The Dutch government also feels that these individuals are entitled to proper care.

Second, it often appears that the addict's lifestyle was "different," with a divergent viewpoint of society, before he/she became addicted to drugs. The use of heroin fits into this frame of reference and becomes an instrument for expressing a particular lifestyle. In this lifestyle, the use of heroin offers the addict the possibility of being part of a group in which he/she is given more status and prestige. In accordance with this viewpoint, not every youth is "in danger" of using heroin. At present, there is a

544

growing need for relief work aimed at a better social and physical functioning of addicts. In this type of relief work, the addict does not necessarily have to be free from drugs. Drug usage can have such an important meaning for some addicts that this may account for their inability or unwillingness to stop using drugs.

Third, a healthy alcohol and drug attitude can be achieved by letting persons regulate their use themselves in a manner that does not have many negative consequences. Structural measures should also be enforced, which should create a climate that does not stimulate too much drug abuse.

Finally, self-regulation can be improved through information and education. In informing users, it is important to explain one's knowledge of drugs and to influence the users attitude and behavior. A starting point with the provided information should be to stop broadening the norms for alcohol and drug use. Handling drugs and alcohol should be taught at home. Information about drugs and alcohol should be part of other subjects at school. Isolated alcohol and drug information usually does not have an important preventive function.

PROVISION OF HEROIN

An often recurring subject in the discussion about the heroin addiction problem is the possibility of providing addicts with heroin. In 1983 the city council of Amsterdam suggested providing a number of persons who had been addicted for a long time with a daily dose. The national government's reaction was very reserved.

The similarity between this development and earlier developments in the U.S. is quite striking. In the beginning of the 1970's suggestions were also made to begin a heroin-maintenance project in New York. The Nixon Administration opposed these plans: "The administration is opposed to any program of heroin maintenance as a means of solving the problem of drug abuse" (Robinson 1978:10). The discussion about the concept of "heroin provision" shows many opposing viewpoints. There are some who say: "If the heroin users cause that much trouble to get their heroin, just give it to them then." Others say: "My neighbor is an alcoholic, does he also have to be provided with alcohol each day?" There are some people who reject any form of heroin maintenance without further discussion. They think that all available means, including the judicial, should be employed as much as possible to prohibit the possibility of procuring heroin.

The groups of supporters can roughly be divided into two categories. There are some who think that heroin should be sold at an acceptable price in a shop; others are in favor of a kind of provision of heroin that is, medically speaking, carried out in a responsible way. The supporters of a heroin-maintenance program have two starting points: a normal life with heroin addiction should be made possible and, secondly, a reduction in crime and alarming situations in general.

The system that is advocated by the first group of supporters has advantages as well as disadvantages. Heroin criminality will disappear, but drug crimes in that case will center on other illegal drugs like cocaine. This situation implies that these drugs

546

should also be offered for sale. The number of addicts then would probably increase but to estimate the number would be impossible. The relief care for addicts would very likely become less complex, however. The great disadvantage of this system, however, is the practical impossibility of carrying it out due to reasons of international politics. Even if all international criticism would be ignored, a situation can be envisaged where the Netherlands would become a haven for all European addicts. This does not seem to be a very desirable situation. With a system of heroin maintenance that is responsible from a medical viewpoint, foreigners and non-addicts would not be induced to come to Holland.

The problems that arise from this type of heroin provision are especially of an ethical and organizational kind. The ethical side seems to be the same with the handing out of methadone. To go into all practical consequences would lead too far in this case (Noorlander, 1984).

To conclude, we can state that in the near future, there will not be any regulated form of heroin maintenance in the Netherlands.

In this context, it is also interesting to go into the opinion of the consumer. The Junkie League doesn't have an official viewpoint, but that clients think in a quite differentiated way about heroin maintenance is illustrated by the results of an investigation that was carried out by us in cooperation with clients of the methadone-maintenance program in Utrecht. We asked the clients if they preferred receiving heroin instead of methadone in case this would be possible. Sixty-two percent answered positively. We also asked them to choose between a strongly regulated heroin-maintenance program or a less-regulated methadone-maintenance program. In that case, a larger group of respondents (51%) preferred methadone to heroin. The remaining 11% did not have an opinion on this matter (van Elzakker and Steinbusch, 1982).

CONCLUSION

It seems that the heroin problem cannot really be solved. In our opinion, it is useless to suggest models for a solution. The medical model sees the addict as a patient, the psychiatric model sees him as mentally deranged, and the model of the law sees him as a criminal. Society will have to live with the heroin problem, whether it wants to or not. Discussions about a viable approach should emphasize elements of compassion as well as of control. A human approach to the addicts and their environment is needed. Control is also needed in the sense of an as great a reduction as possible of the negative consequences of addiction -- negative consequences for the addict himself and his environment, as well as for the society in which the addict lives (Vernooy and van de Wijngaart, 1984).

REFERENCES

Bellis, David J. 1981. Heroin and Politicians: The Failure of Public Policy to Control Addiction in America. Westport, CT: Greenwood Press.

Brecher, Edward M. 1972. Licit & Illicit Drugs -- The Consumers Union Report. Boston/Toronto: Little, Brown and Company.

Cohen, J. 1969. In C. Wijbenga (ed.), Soft Drugs: Sociale, Medische en Juridische Aspecten. Amsterdam: Van Gennep.

De Quincey, Thomas. 1822. Confessions of an English Opium-Eater.

Dole, V. P. and Nyswander, M. A. 1965. A medical treatment for Diacetylmorphine (Heroin) addiction. Journal of the American Medical Association 193: 646-650.

van Elzakker, A. and Steinbusch, M. 1982. Heroineverstrekking? Utrecht: CAD.

van Epen, J. H. 1983. Drugverslaving en Alcholisme. Amsterdam/Brussels: Elsevier.

Illich, Ivan. 1970. Medical Nemesis: The Expropriation of Health. NY: Pantheon Press.

Janssen, Otto and Swierstra, Loert. 1982. Heroinegebruikers in Nederlandeen Typologie van Levensstiglen. Groningen: RUG.

Joe, Tan Tong. 1929. Het Internationale Opiumprobleem. 's-Gravenhage: Gerretsen.

Johnston, L. D., Bachman, J. G., and O'Malley, P. M. 1984. Monitoring the Future: Questionnaire Responses from the Nation's High School Seniors, 1983. Ann Arbor: MI: Institute for Social Research.

Kruger, Henrik. 1980. The Great Heroin Coup. Utrecht: South End Press.

McCoy, Alfred W. et al. 1982. The Politics of Heroin in Southeast Asia. NY: Harper.

Ministry of Foreign Affairs. 1983. The Netherlands in Brief. Amsterdam: The Author.

Noorlander, Els. 1984. Heroineverstrekking -- En overzicht van (on) -- mogelijkheden. Medisch Contact 39:151-152.

Robinson, Cyril D. 1978. A proposal for a heroin maintenance experiment in New York City: The limits of reform strategy. Contemporary Crises 1:1-26.

Schiler, P. 1983. Almen Stoflaere. Kobenhavn: G.E.C. Gads Forlag.

Sengers, W. (ed.), Engelen, P., and Veuger, T. 1982. Verslag van tien Gesprekken Tussen Martien Kooyman en Leden van de Junkiebonden. Rotterdam: Erasmus University Press.

Sijlbing, G. 1984. Het Bebruik van Drugs, Alcohol en Tabak. Amsterdam: SWOAD.

United National Division of Narcotic Drugs. 1982. The United Nations and Drug Control. NY: United Nations.

van der Vaart, J. M. 1981. The Treatment of Drug Users in Custody: An Experiment. Paper presented at the 11th International Institute on the Prevention and Treatment of Drug Dependence, Vienna, Austria.

van de Wijngaart, G., Hoek, G., and Vernooy, R. 1983(a). Denemarken: een voorbeeld? Tijdschrift voor Alcohol, Drugs en andere Psychotrope stoffen 9:87-92.

van de Wijngaart, G. F. 1983(b). Heroin Addiction in the Netherlands. Paper presented at the Second International Congress on Drugs and Alcohol, Tel Aviv, Israel.

Vernooy, R. G. M. and van de Wijngaart, G. F. 1982. The City of Utrecht and the Heroin Problem, an Elaborated Example. Paper presented at the 33rd International Congress on Alcoholism and Drug Dependence, Tangier, Morocco.

Vernooy, R. G. M. and van de Wijngaart, G. F. 1984. Methadonverabreichung und die lage derheroinsuchtigen in den Niederlanden. Kriminologisches Journal 16:64-80.

Wooldrik, H. P. 1981. Drugs en de Wet. Bilthoven: FZA.

FURTHER READINGS (in English)

Bratter, T. E. and Kooyman, M. 1981. A structured environment for heroin addicts: The experiences of a community based American methadone clinic and a residential Dutch therapeutic community. International Journal of Social Psychiatry 27:189-203.

Dorn, N. and Northoft, B. 1982. Health Careers -- Teachers' Manual. London: ISDD.

Haes, W. de and Schuurman, J. 1985. Results of an evaluation study of three drug education methods. International Journal of Health Education 19(4) (supplement).

Ingleby, J. D. 1985. Professionals as socializers: The "Psy Complex." In A. Scull and S. Spitzer (eds.), Research in Law, Deviance and Social Control (Vol. 7). Greenwich, CT: Jai Press.

Janssen, O. and Swierstra, K. 1983. On Defining "Hard Core Addicts." Groningen: Institute of Criminology (RUG).

Kaplan, C. D. 1984. The uneasy consensus: Prohibitionist and experimentalist expectancies behind the International Narcotics Control System. Tijdschrift voor Criminologie 26:98-109.

Roorda, P. A. 1981. Methadone Treatment of Heroin Addicts in a House of Detention in Holland. Paper presented at the 11th International Institute on the Prevention and Treatment of Drug Dependence, Vienna, Austria.

Sylbing, G. 1984. The Use of Drugs and Alcohol by Dutch Youth. Paper presented at the 14th International Institute on the Prevention and Treatment of Drug Dependence, Amsterdam.

There are obvious reasons for us to look at substance use in an international perspective. The experience of other nations, as we have seen, is different from our own. Thus, we may be able to test our theories of substance use in other contexts. Moreover, researchers in other societies have different ideas than our own on how to approach these problems, and we profit from these as well. From this point of view, this section has been an important addition to our analysis of substance use.

Javetz and Shuval (Chapter 17) focus us on Israel for a view of adolescent attitudes towards drugs. This offers us an easy comparison to Forster's work (Chapter 4). Drug use is more prevalent in the U.S. In addition, there is not the attitudinal consensus in the U.S. which exists in Israel. By and large, Israeli youth view drug use as deviant. Those who do use drugs cite normative pressures to not use drugs. This leaves them in a dilemma: engaging in a behavior which is non-normative, while still basically ascribing to the norms.

Though the chapter by Teichman, Rahav, and Barnea (Chapter 18) also studies an Israeli population, its findings have more general impact. They agree with Clark, Salloway, and Daugherty (Chapter 6) that once substance abuse has "crystalized" as a behavior, treatment is difficult. They argue persuasively for a preventive approach. Though they see the initiation of substance use as a social process, they see substance abuse as an individual phenomenon which must be addressed on an individual level.

Teichman et al. note that at some point initiation behavior is supplanted by using behavior. What they mean to imply here is that the search for a new experience, for example, is replaced by the need to avoid psychological or physiological withdrawal. At this point, an individual's lifestyle assumes an addictive pattern. The authors' key concern is with prevention of this pattern. They see this as two-fold: 1) demand reduction and 2) supply reduction. The former is the role of educational programs; the latter is the role of government policies and law enforcement. Their focus is on demand reduction and they go on to specify the dimensions of a program to reduce demand through early education.

Toch's work (Chapter 19) also raises issues which we do not often address in the U.S. The Israelis are facing alcoholism as a relatively new problem. Like the U.S., Israel is a nation of immigrants. On the one hand, we have come to accept ethnic differences in drinking patterns. On the other hand, at a time when waves of new migrants are entering the U.S. from Southeast Asia, Russia, and Central America, we are paying less attention to the effects of acculturation on drinking behavior. From Toch's descriptions, the Israelis see this as an emerging problem. She goes on to question the role of acculturation in alcoholism and the role of genetic differences.

Sargent's work (Chapter 20) views substance-using behavior from a different point of view. Certainly, her analysis of alcohol and inequality in Australia is provocative. We are led by Sargent to consider the role of elites, the alcohol and drug industries, the therapeutic community, and the government in the perpetuation of substance abuse within our own society. As we have mentioned earlier, this is not a totally foreign notion (Prather, Chapter 12). However, it is not an issue which receives substantial attention in the U.S.

In the realm of heroin addiction, the Dutch have had an experience which also differs from the U.S. Van de Wijngaart (Chapter 21) puts the problem in historical, geographic, and cultural perspective for the Netherlands. This descriptive approach is not commonly seen in the U.S. Moreover, in the Netherlands, there is an organization known as the Dutch Junkie League, a kind of consumer's union for drug addicts. This organization, from van de Wijngaart's description, acts as a collective bargaining agent in helping to set policy toward drug addiction. Frankly, this rather enlightened social welfare orientation does not seem to lead to a solution to the problem for the Dutch. What we are led to wonder, however, is whether it tends to reduce the amount of criminal activity and violence which we have seen associated with drug abuse in this country (Goldstein, Chapter 13).

There are a number of conclusions to be reached. First, it is apparent that our experience in the U.S. is not universal. Australia, the Netherlands, and Israel have experiences different than our own. Second, their scholars see these problems somewhat differently than we do. Finally, though we pay lip service to enlightened social policy and demand such interventions as very early drug education, our compatriots in other countries seem to be ahead of us in implementing such policies.

SUMMARY AND CONCLUSIONS ABOUT PATTERNS AND FACTORS

Brenda Forster and Jeffrey Colman Salloway

SUBSTANTIVE FINDINGS

In this discussion, we will first summarize the data on patterns and factors that our authors have provided, then we will develop a socio-cultural model which can be used to classify and conceptualize these ideas.

The pattern of drug use by adolescents in the U.S. that emerges from these chapters is one of early use of three major drugs -- alcohol, marijuana, and cigarettes. Alcohol is clearly the most popular drug. It is used by over 90% of high school seniors (and adults). Of concern is the fact that age of first drink has been decreasing. In the studies reported here, between 1/10 and 1/3 of adolescents began use of alcohol by 10 years of age. Among the affluent (Forster, Chapter 4), 3/4 had experience with wine by the time they were 10. Most adolescents begin using alcohol in their later teens (15 to 18) in high school. About 1/3 of teenagers misuse alcohol regularly, 1/4 use alcohol weekly. Being drunk is a common experience (2/3 have been drunk by the time they graduate from high school at 18), and 2/3 take more than one drink at a time when they do drink. College students are currently using liquor rather than wine or beer as the drink of choice. In contrast, black college students do not center their social activities around alcohol, and only 5% (compared to 21% of whites) are heavy drinkers.

Recent trend studies by Johnson, Bachman, and O'Malley (1988; 1983) indicate that use of illicit drugs including marijuana is decreasing from the 2/3 indicated in Chapter 4 (alcohol and cocaine use is increasing, cigarette use is constant at about 1/3). Use of marijuana and other illegal drugs begins later than alcohol use, although 4% of the affluent 10-year-olds described in Chapter 4 were using marijuana. More serious still is the fact that 60% of drug users use more than one drug (Hoffman, Chapter 11). Johnson, Bachman, and O'Malley (1983) indicate that the decrease in marijuana use by high school seniors is associated with an increasing concern about health effects. This trend may indicate some positive effects of drug education attempts during the past 10 years. In Israel, where 50% of the population strongly opposed use of drugs (Javetz and Shuval, Chapter 17), less than 5% of older adolescents use illicit drugs.

In other sub-populations, alcohol and tranquilizers (instead of marijuana) are the main drugs being used. Females and the elderly are particularly implicated in using and dangerously combining these two drugs. Skid row alcoholics, which are the focus for stereotypes about alcoholics, comprise only about 1/4 of the alcoholic population. Of special concern is the finding (Winick, Chapter 14) that 10% of physicians and nurses are drug dependent. Finally, about 10% of the population in the U.S., 12% in the Netherlands, are involved in heroin use.

Summary of Factors

What light do these chapters shed on the factors associated with use of drugs? For the young, curiosity and sensation seeking are primary motives for trying a drug (Forster, Chapter 4; Javetz and Shuval, Chapter 17; Teichman et al., Chapter 18). This is also true for new heroin users (Wiebel, Chapter 15). Adult drug users, as well as adolescents, who continue using a drug after trying it say they do so because of its positive physical, emotional, and social effects. A drug (including alcohol and cigarettes) is used to bring pleasure; reduce tension, stress or nervousness; enhance feelings of power and self-worth; and to participate in social interactions. These reasons appear in the studies of adolescents (Forster, Chapter 4; Javetz and Shuval, Chapter 17; and Teichman et al., Chapter 18), death-row inmate families (Smykla, Chapter 9), Mexican-Americans (Markides and Krause, Chapter 10), the elderly and women (Butler et al., Chapter 7 and Prather, Chapter 12), heroin users (Wiebel, Chapter 15), and professionals (Clark et al., Chapter 6 and Winick, Chapter 14). In addition to these personal reasons, the studies all indicate the importance of the support (as role models and for encouragement) of significant others in the person's environment. Mexicans who are more acculturated to the Anglo social norms use more drugs; adolescents whose parents, siblings, and friends use drugs are more likely to use drugs themselves, use drugs earlier, and more heavily; women whose family, friends, and physician encourage use of drugs to help their personal situation are more likely to use and continue using tranquilizers; and new heroin users must have help in beginning their use of a drug that is part of a subculture. Along with social

557

support comes access to drugs either through family and friends, physicians, or work roles. Finally, the belief that the drug is okay and worth trying or can solve a felt problem is an important factor. In sum, curiosity, social support, access, positive attitude toward use, and good effects are the primary factors that emerge in these (and other studies).

Generally, males are more likely to use drugs than females (except tranquilizers, which more females use). Persons with less religious involvement have higher drug use than the religious. There is an indication that early and heavier drug users have less positive relations with their parents, have parents who are drug users and have poorer school and community relations. Several recent studies have indicated that these troubled children evidence symptoms of trouble before involvement with drugs (drugs don't cause the problems but may exacerbate them). Lerner and Vicary (1985) indicate that early drug users show symptoms of social withdrawal and emotional irritability and that they tend to have parents who are intolerant, disagree on child-rearing techniques and goals, and are inconsistent in disciplining (Kaplan, Martin, and Robbins, 1984; Blum and Richards, 1979; and Bearden and Woodside, 1978).

Finally, while the issue of the role of genes or biochemistry is raised by Toch in relation to alcoholism (Chapter 19, also see and Holden, 1985, for a review of this concern), research into the relationship of body chemistry to ease of addiction to other drugs is ongoing.

CONCLUSIONS

It is clear from these studies that individual substance use occurs in a social context and is highly influenced by that context. The action of governments, the media, general social acceptability of drug use, and role models significantly effect which substances will be used, in what amounts, and by whom. In addition, personal factors such as stress handling, sensation seeking, beliefs about drug use, and even body chemistry affect the likelihood of an individual's trying and continuing to use a particular drug. In the U.S., drug use is widespread and begins early, often before 10 years of age. However, early and heavy users tend to evidence emotional and social troubles even before beginning drug use. This troubled group comprises about 10% of the population and is most likely to experience abuse and addiction problems. However, most users of the popular drugs are not particularly disturbed and continue moderate drug use for social and personal reasons throughout their lives.

It is those who fall into patterns of abuse who represent the most serious problem for society at large. Once the pattern of habituated or addictive use is begun, treatment is very difficult and relapse is common. It is far more cost-effective to prevent such problems than to treat them.

We now turn to the development of a model which incorporates the theories and data on substance use which our authors have provided and which we have just summarized.

THEORIES OF SUBSTANCE USE AND ABUSE

The most immediate conclusion which confronts us as

we attempt to summarize what we have learned thus far is that there is not a single "cause" of substance use or abuse. Like any human activity, the patterns of use/abuse suggest a multi-causal matrix of forces which contribute to the behavior. One of our tasks, then, is to assess, as a theoretical exercise, the types of forces which we must consider in identifying "causes," so we will have a complete model with which to work.

A second task is to examine the methods by which we might evaluate the role of these "causes" and to critique the quality of the information we have assembled. Finally, we need to come to some substantive conclusions -- to ask what we know now about patterns that we did not know so many pages ago when we began our deliberations.

In the preceding chapters, the authors have set out, either explicitly or implicitly, two specific approaches to the understanding of substance abuse: 1) an epidemiological approach and 2) a social-psychological approach.

The epidemiological approach is macro-focused, emphasizing the environmental forces which surround substance use and abuse. It discusses this behavior in terms of a disease analogy. The clearest explication of an epidemiological approach is contained in Hoffman (Chapter 11). Hoffman considers the drug being used, the characteristics of the user, and the setting in which use occurs. This is exactly analogous to the epidemiologist's host-agent-environment system.

The second approach is social-psychological. This approach focuses on the particular forces which impinge on an individual in his/her substance-using behavior.

In contrast to the epidemiological approach, this model is micro-focused. It is exemplified in the theoretical statement seen in Teichman, Rahav, and Barnea (Chapter 18). This approach emphasizes interpersonal variables, personality variables, and attitudes in the decision to use drugs.

It must be understood that these two models, though they are differently focused, are by no means mutually exclusive. Some of these chapters emphasize one or the other model, but our authors have incorporated elements from each in discussions of specific substance-using problems. For example, (Wylie et al., Iutcovich and Vaughn, and Hanson and Engs, Chapters 1, 2, and 3) tend to be epidemiological in their discussion of alcohol use. However, (Butler et al., Smykla and Markides, and Krause, Chapters 7, 9, and 10) are far more social-psychological.

Forster's Chapter 4 on adolescent drug use looks at both types of theories and finds that both work. Hers is a two-part insight that should not be lost: 1) there is an ongoing level of normative cigarette, marijuana, and alcohol use but 2) for a small percentage of users, excessive and dangerous drug using is associated with personal pathology. For the former, "normal user" group, while ongoing moderate levels of cigarette, marijuana, and alcohol use may be seen as acceptable for social occasions, these users may present "social problems," such as driving under the influence of alcohol, or experiencing drug interaction effects (Coombs and Fawzy's Chapter 5 and Butler, Schuller-Friedman, and Shichor's Chapter 7). Problems of skid row lifestyles (Fagan, Chapter 8) or of drug-associated violence (Goldstein, Chapter 13) are more likely to occur for "pathological" users. The latter is a process of "hardening" or "crystallization" of drug use as part of a problem of personal pathology. For a subset of the drinking and drug-using population, this pattern becomes a permanent feature of behavior (Forster, Chapter 4, and Clark, Salloway, and Daugherty, Chapter 6). They lose control over this part of their lives and the substance abuse then begins to affect virtually every other part of their lives in the pattern which we have come to know as "addiction". Their substance-using pattern is likely to include multiple combinations of drugs with alcohol.

The pattern of personal pathology is not dichotomous. People may use drugs intermittently, on binges, or at low continuous levels. The discussion of drug use as individual pathology is material for many additional volumes. Our attention here, however, is directed at the growth of alcohol and drug use into a social problem.

The primary issue which we have addressed in the preceding pages is the inception of drug- and alcohol-using behavior. Implicit in our discussions have been theories of substance use or abuse. The majority of our authors have directed their attention toward the initiation of substance use/abuse. These theories discuss a range of variables which are described by the following socio-cultural categories:

THE SOCIO-CULTURAL MATRIX FOR SUBSTANCE USE
1. cultural influences .... (Societal)
2. social macro-structures ...... (Societal)
3. subcultural influences .... (Group)
4. social micro-structures ...... (Interpersonal)
5. social psychological factors . (Interpersonal)
6. characteristics of the
   substance .... (Substance)

In Table 4, page 564, we classify the factors identified in the previous research which are associated with alcohol and drug use. Our discussion of these factors follows.

Cultural Influences

As the initial premise of this volume suggests, there is a substantial cultural influence upon substance-using/abusing behavior. This is a theme which we presented in the Introduction and which virtually pervades the chapters. It is visible in Chapter 1 (Wylie, Gibbons, Echterling, and French) as the authors give us a vision of the standards of early drinking behavior which a community finds acceptable. In deciding what levels of drinking are acceptable, a community permits individuals to engage in a range of behaviors, from abstinence to abuse, which it sanctions. The premise, then, is that for most societies, there is a cultural acceptance of some levels of substance-using behavior. Much later, Javetz and Shuval (Chapter 17) and Toch (Chapter 19) remind us through the Israeli experience that not all cultures encourage drinking behavior. Nevertheless, in the case of the U.S. which we have discussed, a general cultural acceptance of some substance use is present.

This general acceptance in U.S. society of the place of substance for social and personal needs has been referred to in the literature under the drug-oriented society concept. We discussed this idea at length in our introduction to the book. Clearly this drug orientation has changed over time. Two examples of substances whose acceptability has changed in this

TABLE 4

SUMMARY OF FACTORS ASSOCIATED WITH
SUBSTANCE-USING BEHAVIORS CLASSIFIED
BY SOCIO-CULTURAL CATEGORIES

Cultural Influences

"Drug-oriented" societal values in U.S.
(Other countries such as Israel show less tolerance for use
of alcohol and other substances)
Media portrayals of alcohol and drug use

Social Macro-structures

Governmental regulations and control mechanisms which affect
supply
Illegal drug production and distribution structures
Alcohol and drug industry profit-making
Physician inclination to prescribe drugs
Therapist and counseling profits

Subcultural Influences

Groups at risk: adolescents, adult females, whites, elderly,
acculturating immigrants, individuals undergoing high
levels of stress (for example, families of death-row
inmates, medical personnel or other care-givers, army
personnel)
Participants in substance-using subcultures such as skid row,
S.R.O. hotels, prostitution, gangs

Social Micro-structures

Family and/or peer role models who accept and approve of
substance use
Availability of "initiators" and substance source persons for
information sharing and substance purchases

Social Psychological Factors

Personal belief that substance(s) are okay to use
Curiosity about experience
Sensation seeking
Perceived personal stress and anxiety
Experiencing depression or "moodiness"
"Macho" self-image

TABLE 4 (continued)

Isolation from supportive family network
Inability to resist peer pressure
Unaware of potentiating or problematic aspects
Don't consider as a drug*
Good effects of the substance**
Genetic make-up**
Addiction**

Substance Characteristics***

Availability
Legality
Source and cost of supply
Reputation and popularity
Substance effects including type (psychoactive, "upper,"
"downers," anesthesia), intensity, duration
Route and ease of administration
Purity of substance
Side effects
Potential for psychological and physiological addiction
Interaction effects
Withdrawal effects

----

* More likely for adults using legal over-the-counter or prescribed medications, alcohol, cigarettes, and caffeine.

** Associated with continued use/abuse.

*** Most of the information on this material is found in sources outside this volume.

century in the U.S. are alcohol consumption in general and cigarette smoking for women. Prohibition represented an unsuccessful attempt by a powerful minority to impose its value on the larger society. On the other hand, as women have become liberated in other areas of life, their use of cigarettes in public, as well as in private, has become acceptable. One cigarette company capitalizes on this cultural change by using a series of ads captioned "You've Come A Long Way, Baby" to tie cigarette usage to women's liberation. These ads also should remind us that the media has a strong influence on the drug-using orientation of U.S. society.

The conclusion to be derived here is that the larger culture of the society defines what is acceptable substance-using behavior. Further, it is apparent that the acceptable normative limits of substance-using behavior for U.S. culture as a whole are rather high. Table 5, page 567, presents the continuum of substance-use model that we developed in the Introduction. The continuum illustrates relationships among frequency of use, situation of use, and acceptability. As the current discussion indicates, where the abuse line is drawn varies for different substances and for different cultural contexts.

Social Macro-structures
Hand in glove with the culture of a society goes its macro-structure. Macro-structure is that set of relationships between major social institutions which characterize a society. These most typically include economic relations, political arrangements, and relations between the social classes.

TABLE 5

MODEL CONTINUUM OF SUBSTANCE USE BY BEHAVIOR CRITERIA

Frequency of Use	No Contact	Abstinence	Experimentation	Occasional Social Use	Moderate Social/ Personal Use	Frequent Social/ Personal Use or Binges	Daily Routine Use
Stimulus for Use	No Use		Recreational/Controlled Use		Dependent Use	Compulsive Use	Addictive Use
Evaluation of Use	Non-Use		Use			Abuse	

Macro-structural approaches to alcohol and drug use are less common in U.S. social science. However, four of our authors raise these issues for our consideration. The first is Hanson and Engs (Chapter 3) who point to the role of alcohol in black slavery. The second is Prather (Chapter 12) in her consideration of tranquilizer use among suburban women. She notes the structural relationships between the drug companies which manufacture the tranquilizers, the government regulatory agencies, and the physicians who prescribe them. Without these cooperative relationships, the system of drug distribution, which makes tranquilizer abuse possible, could not occur.

Sargent (Chapter 20) makes the matrix of relationships between social classes, government, and economic institutions a more explicit target of analysis. She terms this a power relations analysis. Her conclusions are especially interesting in terms of our previous discussion (Introduction) of the role of substance availability in use and abuse. Sargent points out that social class, political, and economic interests in Australia have developed a vested interest in the continuing availability and sale of alcohol. Moreover, she points out that those professions and agencies which treat alcoholism have a vested interest in the continuing abuse of the drug. This is not an indictment of those professions and agencies, but it is a cogent observation nonetheless.

There is a different macro-structural nexus at work in the case of heroin addiction in the Netherlands as described by van de Wijngaart (Chapter 21). What is different is not the association of treatment professionals and government regulators. Rather, van de Wijngaart points out the role of a voluntary association of heroin users, the Junkie League, in negotiating with government and professionals the circumstances of treatment and regulations.

The work of Hanson and Eng, Prather, Sargent, and van de Wijngaart is quite important for our purposes. They force us to consider the extent to which our normal processes of regulation of substance availability and use make abuse possible, probable, and even inevitable. Sargent goes so far as to suggest that the benefits to the social elite, the government, the manufacturers, and the treatment establishment are sufficient to justify the enormous personal and financial costs to families and individuals. This is a cost-benefit analysis which we rarely make explicit.

Subcultural Influence

Culture is the canvas, the background on which individual behavior takes place. It gives behavior shape, form, perspective, and meaning. However, culture is not uniform. Societies are made up of sub-cultures, and there can be substantial variance in behavioral shape, form, perspective, and meaning if a person identifies with a subculture apart from the larger, societal culture.

Subcultural acceptance is not static. Iutcovich and Vaughn (Chapter 2) show how the culture of drinking behavior among college students changes over time, altering drink preferences and, perhaps, also altering definitions of how much drinking is to be permitted. This change in view is reflected in the larger society as well. For example, the U.S. prohibited alcohol by a constitutional amendment then legalized it again.

The same theme emerges with regard to drug use/abuse. Forster (Chapter 4) demonstrates that drug-using behavior is sufficiently present in a well-to-do suburb that very young adolescents learn its acceptability. This finding emerges again in Prather's work (Chapter 12) where we see tranquilizer use as an accepted behavior among middle-class women.

The importance of subcultures in substance-use behavior becomes real when we consider the differences in drinking among black college students (Hanson and Engs, Chapter 3). Rates of drinking among black college students are lower than for a comparable white population. Moreover, the pattern of drinking is different than it is for whites. The differences between whites and blacks might be expected. These are rather different sub-groups and can be expected to have some cultural differences.

In another examination of the role of subcultures, Markides and Krause (Chapter 10) provide us an additional insight. As in the case of black college students, Markides and Krause find an ethnic difference of importance. In this case, it is cultural differences in drinking behavior as seen among Mexican-Americans. Here, however, Markides and Krause add two vital dimensions: 1) assimilation and 2) sex roles. They find that drinking behavior changes as people assimilate into the dominant culture. Their model for this change is twofold: 1) assimilation is a stressor, on the one hand, and 2) norms for drinking in the dominant culture differ from subcultural norms.

Of more importance for our purposes here, Markides and Krause point out that there is a marked difference in norms for drinking behavior between Mexican-American men and women. Thus, we note that subcultural norms may differ for men and for women. This is a lesson not to be taken lightly in a consideration of any culture. Sex-role differences must then become a consistent theme in our deliberations on all substance-using behavior.

We learn from Clark et al. (Chapter 6) and Winick (Chapter 14) that occupational subcultures also vary in their approaches to substance use. These chapters show that medical professionals learn a set of perceptions and values with regard to drugs that are at some variance from the culture generally. For this group, drugs have lost their awe. Their effects are seen as being functional. And more important still, these people see themselves as being stressed and fatigued to an extent that they feel justifies relaxation of societal norms against use.

What we learn is that subcultures vary markedly from the general culture. These subcultures may be a potent influence in promoting, preventing, or, perhaps, in treating substance abuse.

Social Micro-structures

Subcultures provide a normative context for substance use. As we consider social micro-structures, we find that they serve to modify behavior in two ways. First, they carry subcultures to the individual and reinforce the normative content of the sub-culture. Second, micro-structures provide access to substances, opportunities to use them, and the skills and techniques for their use.

Micro-structures include those persons in social situations which people come in contact with on a daily basis as part of their normal lives. Included in such a definition are family members, peers, and work colleagues in home-life interactions, school situations, work-place situations, and the like. The effect of micro-structures on substance use is a recurring theme in these chapters.

A common thread through these chapters is the role of peers in the initiation of drug and alcohol use. Forster (Chapter 4) and Javetz and Shuval (Chapter 17) both note the important role of peers in the formation of adolescent attitudes and behaviors toward drugs and alcohol. Adolescence is a period of life in which people loosen their bonds to family and the normative structure that families represent and begin to form a normative system of their own. At this time, peers are an important source of alternative definitions of what is appropriate behavior.

The role of family and peers is made evident in Coombs and Fawzy (Chapter 5) and then again in Wiebel's work (Chapter 15). Coombs and Fawzy note the effects of family role models and peers on adolescent drug use. This is repeated in the words of heroin users as Wiebel notes that most heroin users have been introduced to the drug by family members or by close friends.

These micro-structures serve several functions for the initiation of drug use. They provide access to the drug. They provide an alternative definition of the behavior, reassuring that it is "all right." They provide reinforcement of the motivation to try the new behavior. And, finally, they provide both the techniques for first use and a definitional system that helps the new user recognize the effects and identify them as pleasurable.

These are not necessarily "deviant" groups. On the contrary, for example, Clark, Salloway, and Daugherty (Chapter 6) and Winick (Chapter 14) describe the role of micro-structures in fostering substance use among one of our most valued occupational groups: health professionals. Medical students develop their own norms for drinking and drug use. Winick's doctors and nurses find that their work situations provide them easy access to drugs and a subculture which justifies their use.

Clark, Salloway, and Daugherty provide data which shows another effect of micro-structures which is notable. We have understood, thus far, that peers may provide a normative context and structural supports for the initiation of substance use. In their data, however, we find that much of the hard drinking that goes on occurs within one rather cohesive group of hard drinkers. This group may have evolved in one of several ways. These peers may have "learned" to drink heavily by reinforcing one another or they may have been hard drinkers before meeting and may have "found one another" and formed a cohesive sub-group around the behavior.

The micro-structure is an important influence in both the initiation of substance-using behavior and in its "hardening" into a chronic part of the life of the abuser. This implies that any method of prevention or treatment will have to pay attention to micro-structures to effect change.

The conclusion here is that the micro-structure is an important variable in creating and reinforcing behavior. There is a double message to be derived from this. Treating substance abuse and then returning a treated person to the same micro-structure is a sure

plan for a resumption of substance abuse. However, if
one can create a micro-structure which reinforces non-
abusing behavior, this may be an effective prevention
or treatment mode.

Social-psychological Factors

As we have suggested above, one of the major
approaches to substance use and abuse is couched in
terms of social-psychological theories. We have seen
these theories stated explicitly in Forster (Chapter 4)
and again in Teichman, Rahav, and Barnea (Chapter 18).
These chapters present effective summaries which need
not be restated here. Basically, they lay out a
picture of low-level use as an ongoing part of social
interaction. Substance use become problematic when any
number of events occur. An example might be the
transformation of a pre-existing personal or social
pathology, such as family problems or alienation, into
reliance on the drug or alcohol and eventual dependence
on it. Other relevant personal factors are summarized
in Table 4, page 564.

An alternative source of problematic usage might be
growing dependence as a result of role-modeling
behavior. When parents and older siblings use drugs or
alcohol, or when esteemed peers use them, this is a
powerful force toward entry into use.

Attitudes play a role in drug use. The exact place
of attitudes is problematic. Attitude change may be
crucial in loosening ties to cultural proscriptions
against substance use before such use actually begins.
At the same time, however, theories of cognitive
dissonance would suggest that attitudes shift as the
behavior begins to occur. Thus, one can conjecture
whether a change in attitudes is <u>causal</u> to use and

abuse or a secondary effect of a pre-existing change in behavior. On the one hand, we can see this change occurring (Javetz and Shuval, Chapter 17). On the other hand, however, without longitudinal data on attitudes, it is very difficult to tell if the attitudes cause the behavior change, the behavior change causes attitudes to shift, or if they occur simultaneously.

What is evident, however, is that the process of use becoming abuse sets in motion a number of other processes which have a dynamic and a force of their own. The most obvious is the growth of psychological and physical addiction itself. These aspects of substance abuse are not the subject of this volume. Nevertheless, the consequences of physical and psychological addiction is a part of society's concern in preventing and treating this behavior.

What is important for our concerns is that using drugs or alcohol subjects one to being labelled. the labels vary: drunk, junkie, addict, "alkie." The particular term is less relevant than the process by which non-abusers create a labelled category of social deviant. Once this label has been applied, it puts in motion a whole series of events over which the person labelled may have little control. This is best seen in Fagan's description of life on skid row (Chapter 8). A whole series of adjustments and identifications are made once the person has been labelled. Jobs may be lost along with friends and family.

Labels stigmatize. They make the motivations of the labelled person suspect: Is the asked-for loan a legitimate request or is it to buy alcohol or drugs? Is the absence from work a legitimate sick day or a hangover day? Is the poor work performance a function of circumstance or a failure because of drink or drugs? As the label is applied, as stigma attaches to the user, and as motivations become suspect, roles are lost, friends disappear and are replaced by fellow users, and the user finds him or herself bound to a deviant subculture. Escape from such a drug subculture and return to the mainstream of life is, as Fagan describes it, very, very difficult. While the data indicates that about 10% of a given population experience serious drug pathologies, that is a substantial number of people.

At some point, the self-perception of some users change. He or she identifies as a user. Those who are not users are, in turn, labelled as squares, up-tights, nerds. Friends are composed wholly of other users. At this point, the drug or alcohol has become the central feature of the user's life, the dimension about which he or she defines what is important and what is not. Being on the drug feels good. Being off the drug feels bad -- physically, psychologically, and socially. The amount and frequency of drug use increases substantially. Multiple combinations of drugs are used to achieve the desired effects. The user has become an abuser.

The Substance and Its Characteristics

In her conceptualization of drug-use behavior, Hoffman (Chapter 11) notes the importance of the nature of the substance itself. The pharmacological properties of specific drugs is not a topic which we can address in this volume on the socio-cultural matrix of chemical bonds. Yet, we would be remiss were we not to mention it as an issue and to encourage the reader toward other sources, some of which are mentioned in our Introduction.

In fact, the nature of the substance has been discussed in a number of our chapters and has assumed some importance. Coombs and Fawzy (Chapter 5) have alerted us to the problem of drug-interaction effects in adolescents. Butler, Schuller-Friedman, and Shichor (Chapter 7) have pointed out the same phenomenon of drug-interaction effects and their risks for the elderly.

Oftentimes, the nature of the substance has effects on its availability and use. The women in Prather's sample (Chapter 12) must get their drugs through legal or quasi-legal channels. Wiebel's (Chapter 15) heroin addicts are using a drug which requires not only that they have access to the drug but to the drug paraphernalia as well. For these two samples, the sources vary with the type of drug being used.

We can also question the effect of sex-roles on the type of drug used. Prather's women use tranquilizers, which seems to be principally a female drug. Heroin seems to be less sex-specific. In Chapter 13, Goldstein notes that drugs have different effects on behavior. He cites the role of barbiturates in perpetrating violence among its users.

We intend here to alert the reader to the need to consider, among all the other variables which we have discussed, that the drug itself is a variable of some potency. Its characteristics, effects, availability, mode of use, legality, even its physical form are important considerations in use and abuse.

METHODS AND THEIR MEANING

As we look back over these chapters, we find a wealth of information provided by researchers. Their methods of research vary and with each method comes limitations. There are, in particular, two important issues which we need to make explicit in an evaluation of the substantive findings which will form the conclusion to this chapter. These issues are: 1) definitions of use/abuse and 2) methods of data collection.

We find in these chapters a lack of easy distinctions between use, heavy use, and abuse of alcohol and drugs. If the ultimate goal is to prevent and treat substance abuse, how shall we distinguish between normative levels of use and potentially harmful abuse?

Clark, Salloway, and Daugherty (Chapter 6) begin their research with a normative base. They assess those norms internal to their medical-student respondents in order to judge how drinking behavior changes over time. This is all well and good, but is there some absolute level at which use begins to be problematic, perhaps, even before it is defined normatively as heavy use or abuse? This is an unanswered question in all of our chapters. It is a question which is not settled well in society as a whole either.

Are legal limits to be used as the standard of abuse? Toch (Chapter 19), Sargent (Chapter 20), and van de Wijngaart (Chapter 21) provide us with historical, cultural, and political perspectives which show that legal standards of drug use are a poor guide to what is likely to be harmful and what is not. Alcohol is freely available in most places. One can drink to damage with no penalty in the privacy of one's own home. Legal standards have done little to establish normative limits of alcohol use which will not be harmful. Nor has the research reported here set us standards which we can use as guidelines for prevention and treatment. When to intervene? We do not have a good standard by which to judge.

A second methodological critique lies in our researchers' reliance on self-report data. Overwhelmingly, these chapters are based on respondents's self-described drug and alcohol attitudes and behaviors. In Chapter 15, Wiebel's respondents tell of the ways in which they came to be heroin addicts. Winick (Chapter 14) relates the reasons that physicians and nurses give for their abuse of drugs and alcohol. Likewise, Prather (Chapter 12), Smykla (Chapter 9), and so on. This critique is not unique to these chapters. The most accessible source of data on people's behavior is the people themselves. However, when we rely on them, we assume that they are aware of the reasons for their behavior, that they are accurately reporting their awareness, and that they have not skewed their reports either to conform more closely to the normative standards of their culture or to their expectations of what the researcher wants to hear.

Occasionally, there are alternative methods which one can use to gather data on substance use and abuse. Observation is one. Use of arrest and treatment records is another. It should be obvious, however, that these methods have their own inadequacies built into them. The point is not that the findings which are presented are necessarily suspect; rather, one must exercise a measure of skepticism and caution in reaching conclusions.

However, with these cautions and our model in mind, the reader should have a reasonably good grasp of the patterns and factors associated with substance use.[1]

REFERENCES

Bearden, W. O. and Woodside, A. G. 1978. Normative and attitudinal control as moderating influences on marijuana use. Journal of Health and Social Behavior 19:199-204.

Blum, R. and Richards, L. 1979. Youthful drug use. In R. L. DuPont, A. Goldstein, and J. O'Donnell (eds.), Handbook on Drug Abuse. Washington, DC: Department of HEW.

Holden, C. 1985. Genes, personality and alcoholism. Psychology Today. January: 38-44.

Johnson, L. and Bachman, J. 1988. Patterns of drug use. ISR Newsletter. Winter: 3.

Johnson, L., Bachman, J. and O'Malley, P. 1983. Teenage drug use. ISR Newsletter. Autumn: 3.

Kaplan, H. B., Martin, S. S., and Robbins, C. 1984. Pathways to adolescent drug use: Self-derogation, peer influence, weakening of social controls, and early substance use. Journal of Health and Social Behavior 25:270-289.

Lerner, J. and Vicary, J. 1985. Reported in Science Digest. February: 69.

Stimmel, B. (ed.). 1984. Alcohol and drug abuse in the affluent. Advances in Alcohol and Substance Abuse 4: 1-103.

----

[1] Readers interested in the application of this model to materials on prevention and treatment of substance abuse are referred to Forster and Salloway (eds.), Preventions and Treatments of Alcohol and Drug Abuse: A Socio-epidemiological Sourcebook (forthcoming).

APPENDIX

TABLE 1

GENERAL MATRIX OF CHAPTERS BY SUBSTANCE CATEGORIES,
SUBJECT GROUP, DATA METHODS, AND THEORY FOCUS*

CHAPTER	SUBSTANCE CATEGORIES	SUBJECT GROUP**	DATA METHODS#	THEORY FOCUS##
1	Alcohol	Adolescents, Rural	Survey	1,4,5
2	Alcohol	College-Aged	Survey	2,4,5,6
3	Alcohol	College-Aged, Racial	Literature Review, Survey	3,4,6
4	Alcohol, Cannabis, Multi, Tobacco	Pre-Adolescents, Upper Middle Class	Survey	3,4,5
5	Alcohol, Cannabis, Depressants, Hallucinogens, Stimulants	Adolescents	Interview	4,5,6
6	Alcohol, Cannabis, Depressants, Narcotics, Stimulants, Tobacco	College-Aged	Survey-Longitudinal	3,4,5
7	Alcohol, Depressants, Hallucinogens, Narcotics, Stimulants	Aged	Survey	5,6
8	Alcohol	Addicts, Poor	Literature Review, Program Evaluation	3
9	Alcohol	Criminals	Interviews	5,6
10	Alcohol	Racial/Ethnic	Survey	3,4,5

* A chapter may be listed more than once if it discusses more than one aspect.
** The Multi-category is used for chapters which discuss subjects who use alcohol and other drugs but which either do not specify the particular substance used or focus on use of multiple substances.
# Observation-description is also sometimes called the Case-Study Method.
The code numbers for the Socio-Cultural Model are: 1 = Cultural; 2 = Macro-structures; 3 = Sub-cultural; 4 = Micro-structures; 5 = Social-psychological, and 6 = Substance Characteristics.

TABLE 1 (Continued)

CHAPTER	SUBSTANCE CATEGORIES	SUBJECT GROUP**	DATA METHODS#	THEORY FOCUS##
11	Alcohol, Cannabis, Depressants, Hallucinogens, Narcotics, Stimulants	Youths, Adults	Literature Review	1,3,4,5,6
12	Depressants	Females	Interview	2,4,5,6
13	Depressants, Narcotics	Females	Interview	3,4,5,6
14	Alcohol, Cannabis, Narcotics	Professionals	Interview	3,5
15	Narcotics	Adults	Interview	4,5,6
16	Alcohol, Cannabis, Depressants, Hallucinogens, Stimulants	Addicts, Poor	Phone Interview	3
17	Alcohol, Multi, Tobacco	Adolescents, Ethnic	Survey	1,3,4,5
18	Alcohol, Multi	Adolescents, Ethnic	Survey	4,5
19	Alcohol	Racial/Ethnic	Objective Indicators, Survey	1,3,5
20	Alcohol	Ethnic	Literature Review	2
21	Narcotics	Ethnic	Literature Review	1,2

_____

* A chapter may be listed more than once if it discusses more than one aspect.

** The Multi-category is used for chapters which discuss subjects who use alcohol and other drugs but which either do not specify the particular substance used or focus on use of multiple substances.

Observation-description is also sometimes called the Case-Study Method.

The code numbers for the Socio-Cultural Model are: 1 = Cultural; 2 = Macro-structures; 3 = Sub-cultural; 4 = Micro-structures; 5 = Social-psychological, and 6 = Substance characteristics.

TABLE 2

CHAPTERS CLASSIFIED BY SUBSTANCE CATEGORIES

SUBSTANCE CATEGORIES*	ADOLESCENTS PATTERNS AND FACTORS	ADULTS PATTERNS AND FACTORS
Alcohol	1,2,3,4,5 6,11,17,18	7,8,9,10, 11,14,16, 19,20
Cannabis	4,5,6,11	11,14,16
Depressants/ Sedative- Hypnotics	5,6,11	7,11,12,13, 16
Hallucinogens/ Psychedelics	5,11	7,11,16
Multi-Substance**	4,17,18	
Narcotics	6,11	7,11,13,14, 15,16,21
Stimulants	5,6,11	7,11,16
Tobacco	4,6,17	

----

* A chapter may be listed more than once if it discusses multi-drug use or more than one aspect.

** This category is used for chapters which discuss subjects who use alcohol and other drugs but which either do not specify the particular substances used or focus on use of multiple substance.

TABLE 3

CHAPTERS CLASSIFIED BY SUBJECT GROUP*

SUBJECT GROUP	PATTERNS AND FACTORS
Youths	
Pre-Adolescents	4,11
Adolescents	1,5,11,17,18
College-Aged	2,3,6,11
Adults	
Addicts	8,16
Aged	7
Families of Criminals	9
Females	12,13
General	11,15
Poor	8,16
Professionals	14
Racial/Ethnic Groups	3,10,19,20,21

----

* A chapter may be listed more than once if it addresses several categories.

TABLE 4

CHAPTERS CLASSIFIED BY DATA METHODS*

DATA METHODS	YOUTHS PATTERNS AND FACTORS	ADULTS PATTERNS AND FACTORS
Literature Review	3,11	8,11,20,21
Interview		
Face-to-Face	5	9,12,13,14, 15
Phone		16
Objective Indicators		19
Survey- Questionnaire		
Cross-Sectional	1,2,3,4,17, 18	7,10,19
Longitudinal	6	

---

* A chapter may appear more than once if it uses several methods.

TABLE 5

CHAPTERS CLASSIFIED BY THEORY FOCUS*

SOCIO-CULTURAL MODEL COMPONENTS	YOUTHS PATTERNS AND FACTORS	ADULTS PATTERNS AND FACTORS
Societal		
Cultural	1,11	11,17,19,21
Macro-structures	2	12,20,21
Group		
Sub-cultural	3,4,6,11	8,10,11,13, 14,16,17,19
Interpersonal		
Micro-structures	1,2,3,4,5, 6,11	10,11,12,13, 15,17,18
Social- psychological	1,2,4,5,6, 11	7,9,10,11,12, 13,14,15,17, 18,19
Substance		
Substance Characteristics	2,3,5,7,9, 11	11,12,13,15

---

* A chapter may be listed more than once if it addresses several
aspects of the model.

INTERDISCIPLINARY STUDIES IN ALCOHOL USE AND ABUSE

Fl